TAKING SIDES

Clashing Views on Controversial

Educational Issues

ELEVENTH EDITION

TAKING SIDES

Clashing Views on Controversial
Educational Issues
ELEVENTH EDITION

Selected, Edited, and with Introductions by

James Wm. Noll
University of Maryland

Dushkin/McGraw-Hill
A Division of The McGraw-Hill Companies

For Stephanie and Sonja

Photo Acknowledgment
Cover image: © 2001 by PhotoDisc, Inc.

Cover Art Acknowledgment
Charles Vitelli

Manufactured in the United States of America

Eleventh Edition

56789BAHBAH4321

Library of Congress Cataloging-in-Publication Data
Main entry under title:
Taking sides: clashing views on controversial educational issues/selected, edited, and with introductions by James Wm. Noll.—11th ed.
Includes bibliographical references and index.
1. Education—United States. I. Noll, James Wm., *comp.*
370.973
0-07-241033-7
ISSN: 1091-8817

Printed on Recycled Paper

Preface

$\mathbf{C}$ontroversy is the basis of change and often of improvement. Its lack signifies the presence of complacency, the authoritarian limitation of viewpoint expression, or the absence of realistic alternatives to the existing circumstances. An articulate presentation of a point of view on a controversial matter breathes new life into abiding human and social concerns. Controversy prompts reexamination and perhaps renewal.

Education is controversial. Arguments over the most appropriate aims, the most propitious means, and the most effective control have raged over the centuries. Particularly in the United States, where the systematic effort to provide education has been more democratically dispersed and more varied than elsewhere, educational issues have been contentiously debated. Philosophers, psychologists, sociologists, professional educators, lobbyists, government officials, school boards, local pressure groups, taxpayers, parents, and students have all voiced their views.

This book presents opposing or sharply varying viewpoints on educational issues of current concern. Part 1 offers for consideration five topics that have endured through history and are still debated today: the purposes of education, curriculum content and its imposition on the young, the motivational atmosphere in which learning takes place, the problem of church-state separation, and compulsory school attendance. Part 2 features issues that are fundamental to understanding the present circumstances that shape American education: the resurgence of moral education, the push toward a multicultural curriculum, the problem of desegregation and opportunity equalization, standards and testing, and the assessment of the effectiveness of public schooling. Part 3 examines more specific issues currently being debated: vouchers and choice plans, charter schools, religion in public schools, mainstreaming and inclusion policies, Afrocentric curricula, bilingual education, violence prevention, the plight of inner-city schools, computers in education, community service, and teachers' unions.

I have made every effort to select views from a wide range of thinkers—philosophers, psychologists, sociologists, professional educators, political leaders, historians, researchers, and gadflies.

Each issue is accompanied by an *introduction*, which sets the stage for the debate, and each issue concludes with a *postscript* that considers other views on the issue and suggests additional readings. I have also provided relevant Internet site addresses (URLs) on the *On the Internet* page that accompanies each part opener. By combining the material in this volume with the informational background provided by a good introductory textbook, the student should be prepared to address the problems confronting schools today.

My hope is that students will find challenges in the material presented here—provocations that will inspire them to better understand the roots of educational controversy, to attain a greater awareness of possible alternatives in dealing with the various issues, and to stretch their personal powers of creative thinking in the search for more promising resolutions of the problems.

Changes to this edition   This 11th edition offers three completely new issues: *Do High-Stakes Assessments Improve Learning?* (Issue 9); *Have Public Schools Adequately Accommodated Religion?* (Issue 13); and *Can Self-Governing Schools Rescue Urban Education?* (Issue 18). In addition, new selections have been placed in Issue 7 on multiculturalism, Issue 10 on public school failure, Issue 14 on inclusion, and Issue 16 on bilingual education. In all, there are 11 new selections.

A word to the instructor   An *Instructor's Manual With Test Questions* (multiple-choice and essay) is available through the publisher for the instructor using *Taking Sides* in the classroom. A general guidebook, called *Using Taking Sides in the Classroom,* which discusses methods and techniques for integrating the pro-con approach into any classroom setting, is also available. An online version of *Using Taking Sides in the Classroom* and a correspondence service for Taking Sides adopters can be found at http://www.dushkin.com/usingts/.

Taking Sides: Clashing Views on Controversial Educational Issues is only one title in the Taking Sides series. If you are interested in seeing the table of contents for any of the other titles, please visit the Taking Sides Web site at http://www.dushkin.com/takingsides/.

Acknowledgments   I am thankful for the kind and efficient assistance given to me by Theodore Knight, list manager for the Taking Sides series, and the staff at Dushkin/McGraw-Hill. I was also greatly assisted in my work by the suggestions from the many users of *Taking Sides.* Their comments have enhanced the quality of this edition of the book and are reflected in the new issues as well as the issues that have been retained. Special thanks go to:

Joseph K. Ball
Weber State University

Dan Kaczynski
University of West Florida

H. Jurgen Combs
Shenandoah University

Patricia A. Kroetch
South Dakota State University

Paul Crutchfield
Flagler College

Robert Leahy
Stetson University

Donna L. Ferrara
Southampton College/Long Island University

Eric F. Luce
University of Southern Mississippi

Elaine Haglund
California State University, Long Beach

Philip S. Morse
SUNY College at Fredonia

Guy Rose
Belmont University

William E. Salesses
University of St. Thomas

Isabelle L. Shannon
Virginia Wesleyan College

Tim J. Sharer
Wayne State College

Sherry Weeks
Piedmont College

James Wm. Noll
University of Maryland

Contents In Brief

Contents

Professor emeritus of education R. Freeman Butts warns that current efforts to redefine the relationship between religion and schooling are eroding the Constitution's intent. Professor of political science Robert L. Cord argues that none of the school practices currently being allowed violate the First Amendment's establishment clause.

Horace Mann, a leader of the common school movement in the nineteenth century, lays the groundwork for compulsory attendance laws. Barry McGhan, who heads the Center for Public School Renewal, argues that the time has come to switch to a voluntary attendance approach to schooling, which would benefit everyone involved.

Developmental psychologist Thomas Lickona, a leading exponent of the new character education, charts a course of action to deal with the moral decline of American youth. Writer-lecturer Alfie Kohn sees character education as mainly a collection of exhortations and extrinsic inducements that avoid more penetrating efforts at social and moral development.

Professor of language, literacy, and culture Sonia Nieto examines the realities of diversity in American society that underlie an effective approach to multicultural education. Former English instructor Thomas J. Famularo contends that the multiculturalism movement, rather than representing diversity, is centered on the themes of race and gender and the debunking of Western culture.

Teacher Kevin Walthers portrays the voucher movement as a means for strengthening professionalism and raising academic standards. Attorney John F. Lewis argues that vouchers and the school choice ideology do not deal with the problems facing the public schools.

Issue 12.   Can Charter Schools Revitalize Public Education?   212

Former assistant secretary of education Chester E. Finn, Jr., and his fellow researchers at the Hudson Institute argue that charter schools offer the benefits of both public and private schools and can revitalize urban education. Historian and journalist Phyllis Vine maintains that charter schools and similar entrepreneurial ventures inevitably sell children short.

Issue 13.   Have Public Schools Adequately Accommodated Religion?   228

Edd Doerr, executive director of Americans for Religious Liberty, asserts that a fair balance between free exercise rights and the obligation of neutrality has been achieved in the public schools. Warren A. Nord, a professor of the philosophy of religion, contends that the schools are still too secular and that a place in the curriculum must be found for religion.

Issue 14.   Is Full Inclusion of Disabled Students Desirable?   242

Attorney Jean B. Arnold and school superintendent Harold W. Dodge discuss the federal Individuals with Disabilities Education Act and argue that its implementation can benefit all students. Assistant professor of education Karen Agne argues that legislation to include students with all sorts of disabilities has had mostly negative effects.

Issue 15.   Do Black Students Need an Afrocentric Curriculum?   258

Black studies professor Molefi Kete Asante maintains that providing black students with an Afrocentric frame of reference will enhance their self-esteem and learning. Noted historian Arthur M. Schlesinger, Jr., documents his concerns about the recent spread of Afrocentric programs.

Rosalie Pedalino Porter, director of the Research in English Acquisition and Development Institute, contends that there is no consistent support for transitional bilingual education programs. Richard Rothstein, a research associate of the Economic Policy Institute, reviews the history of bilingual education and argues that, although many problems currently exist, there is no compelling reason to abandon these programs.

Albert Shanker, president of the American Federation of Teachers (AFT), advocates a "get tough" policy for dealing with violent and disruptive students. Professor of education Pedro A. Noguera maintains that the AFT's zero-tolerance stance and other "armed camp" attitudes fail to deal with the heart of the problem and do not build an atmosphere of trust.

Deborah Meier, a leading urban educator, contends that decaying public schools in large cities can be rejuvenated by the proliferation of self-governing exemplary schools. High school principal Emeral A. Crosby maintains that only a powerful political force and a massive infusion of funds can halt the downward spiral of urban school quality.

Issue 19. Should Technology Lead the Quest for Better Schools? 348

YES: **James H. Snider,** from "Education Wars: The Battle Over Information-Age Technology," *The Futurist* (May–June 1996) *350*

NO: **Neil Postman,** from "Virtual Students, Digital Classroom," *The Nation* (October 9, 1995) *357*

James H. Snider, a Northwestern University fellow, analyzes the politics of educational change and details the industrial-age barriers that he feels information-age technologies must overcome in order to implement a vastly improved educational system. Neil Postman, a professor of media ecology and author of numerous books on education and technology, voices serious concern about the dangers of mindless adherence to technological panaceas.

Issue 20. Is Mandatory Community Service Desirable and Legal? 366

YES: **Vito Perrone,** from "Learning for Life: When Do We Begin?" *Equity and Excellence in Education* (September 1993) *368*

NO: **Institute for Justice,** from " 'Compulsory Volunteering': Constitutional Challenges to Mandatory Community Service," *Litigation Backgrounder* (1994) *374*

Education professor Vito Perrone asserts that community service learning can revitalize the schools and build a service ethic in students. The Institute for Justice, a nonprofit, public-interest law center in Washington, D.C., argues that government-mandated service negates the spirit of voluntarism.

Issue 21. Do Teachers' Unions Have a Positive Influence on Reform? 382

YES: **Bob Chase,** from "Do Teachers Unions Have a Positive Influence on the Educational System? Yes," *Insight* (October 21, 1996) *384*

NO: **Myron Lieberman,** from "Do Teachers Unions Have a Positive Influence on the Educational System? No," *Insight* (October 21, 1996) *388*

Bob Chase, president of the National Education Association, fends off right-wing attacks on the public schools and teachers' unions by citing a record of positive reforms in recent years. Myron Lieberman, chairman of the Educational Policy Institute, assembles his own data to show that the unions are the major obstacle to school improvement in the United States.

Introduction

Ways of Thinking About Educational Issues

James Wm. Noll

Concern about the quality of education has been expressed by philosophers, politicians, and parents for centuries. There has been a perpetual and unresolved debate regarding the definition of education, the relationship between school and society, the distribution of decision-making power in educational matters, and the means for improving all aspects of the educational enterprise.

In recent decades the growing influence of thinking drawn from the humanities and the behavioral and social sciences has brought about the development of interpretive, normative, and critical perspectives, which have sharpened the focus on educational concerns. These perspectives have allowed scholars and researchers to closely examine the contextual variables, value orientations, and philosophical and political assumptions that shape both the status quo and reform efforts.

The study of education involves the application of many perspectives to the analysis of "what is and how it got that way" and "what can be and how we can get there." Central to such study are the prevailing philosophical assumptions, theories, and visions that find their way into real-life educational situations. The application situation, with its attendant political pressures, sociocultural differences, community expectations, parental influence, and professional problems, provides a testing ground for contending theories and ideals.

This "testing ground" image applies only insofar as the status quo is malleable enough to allow the examination and trial of alternative views. Historically, institutionalized education has been characteristically rigid. As a testing ground of ideas, it has often lacked an orientation encouraging innovation and futuristic thinking. Its political grounding has usually been conservative.

As social psychologist Allen Wheelis points out in *The Quest for Identity* (1958), social institutions by definition tend toward solidification and protectionism. His depiction of the dialectical development of civilizations centers on the tension between the security and authoritarianism of "institutional processes" and the dynamism and change-orientation of "instrumental processes."

The field of education seems to graphically illustrate this observation. Educational practices are primarily tradition bound. The twentieth-century reform movement, spurred by the ideas of John Dewey, A. S. Neill, and a host of critics who campaigned for change in the 1960s, challenged the structural rigidity of schooling. The current situation is one of contending forces: those who wish to continue the struggle for true reform, those who demand a return to a more traditional or basic model, and those who are shaping a new form of procedural conformity around the tenets of behaviorism and competency-based approaches.

We are left with the abiding questions: What is an "educated" person? What should be the primary purpose of organized education? Who should control the decisions influencing the educational process? Should the schools follow society or lead it toward change? Should schooling be compulsory?

Long-standing forces have molded a wide variety of responses to these fundamental questions. The religious impetus, nationalistic fervor, philosophical ideas, the march of science and technology, varied interpretations of "societal needs," and the desire to use the schools as a means for social reform have been historically influential. In recent times other factors have emerged to contribute to the complexity of the search for answers—social class differences, demographic shifts, increasing bureaucratization, the growth of the textbook industry, the changing financial base for schooling, teacher unionization, and strengthening of parental and community pressure groups.

The struggle to find the most appropriate answers to these questions now involves, as in the past, an interplay of societal aims, educational purposes, and individual intentions. Moral development, the quest for wisdom, citizenship training, socioeconomic improvement, mental discipline, the rational control of life, job preparation, liberation of the individual, freedom of inquiry—these and many others continue to be topics of discourse on education.

A detailed historical perspective on these questions and topics may be gained by reading the interpretations of noted scholars in the field. R. Freeman Butts has written a brief but effective summary portrayal in "Search for Freedom—The Story of American Education," *NEA Journal* (March 1960). A partial listing of other sources includes R. Freeman Butts and Lawrence Cremin, *A History of Education in American Culture*; S. E. Frost, Jr., *Historical and Philosophical Foundations of Western Education*; Harry Good and Edwin Teller, *A History of Education*; Adolphe Meyer, *An Educational History of the American People*; Robert L. Church and Michael W. Sedlak, *Education in the United States: An Interpretive History*; Merle Curti, *The Social Ideas of American Educators*; Henry J. Perkinson, *The Imperfect Panacea: American Faith in Education, 1865–1965*; Clarence Karier, *Man, Society, and Education*; V. T. Thayer, *Formative Ideas in American Education*; H. Warren Button and Eugene F. Provenzo, Jr., *History of Education and Culture in America*; David Tyack and Elisabeth Hansot, *Managers of Virtue: Public School Leadership in America, 1820–1980*; Joel Spring, *The American School, 1642–1990*; S. Alexander Rippa, *Education in a Free Society: An American History*; John D. Pulliam, *History of Education in America*; Edward Stevens and George H. Wood, *Justice, Ideology, and Education*; and Walter Feinberg and Jonas F. Soltis, *School and Society*.

These and other historical accounts of the development of schooling demonstrate the continuing need to address educational questions in terms of cultural and social dynamics. A careful analysis of contemporary education demands attention not only to the historical interpretation of developmental influences but also to the philosophical forces that define formal education and the social and cultural factors that form the basis of informal education.

EXAMINING VIEWPOINTS

In his book *A New Public Education* (1976), Seymour Itzkoff examines the interplay between informal and formal education, concluding that economic and technological expansion have pulled people away from the informal culture by placing a premium on success in formal education. This has brought about a reactive search for less artificial educational contexts within the informal cultural community, which recognizes the impact of individual personality in shaping educational experiences.

This search for a reconstructed philosophical base for education has produced a barrage of critical commentary. Those who seek radical change in education characterize the present schools as mindless, manipulative, factory-like, bureaucratic institutions that offer little sense of community, pay scant attention to personal meaning, fail to achieve curricular integration, and maintain a psychological atmosphere of competitiveness, tension, fear, and alienation. Others deplore the ideological movement away from the formal organization of education, fearing an abandonment of standards, a dilution of the curriculum, an erosion of intellectual and behavioral discipline, and a decline in adult and institutional authority.

Students of education (whether prospective teachers, practicing professionals, or interested laypeople) must examine closely the assumptions and values underlying alternative positions in order to clarify their own viewpoints. This tri-level task may best be organized around the basic themes of purpose, power, and reform. These themes offer access to the theoretical grounding of actions in the field of education, to the political grounding of such actions, and to the future orientation of action decisions.

A general model for the examination of positions on educational issues includes the following dimensions: identification of the viewpoint, recognition of the stated or implied assumptions underlying the viewpoint, analysis of the validity of the supporting argument, and evaluation of the conclusions and action-suggestions of the originator of the position. The stated or implied assumptions may be derived from a philosophical or religious orientation, from scientific theory, from social or personal values, or from accumulated experience. Acceptance by the reader of an author's assumptions opens the way for a receptive attitude regarding the specific viewpoint expressed and its implications for action. The argument offered in justification of the viewpoint may be based on logic, common experience, controlled experiments, information and data, legal precedents, emotional appeals, and/or a host of other persuasive devices.

Holding the basic model in mind, readers of the positions presented in this volume (or anywhere else, for that matter) can examine the constituent elements of arguments—basic assumptions, viewpoint statements, supporting evidence, conclusions, and suggestions for action. The careful reader will accept or reject the individual elements of the total position. One might see reasonableness in a viewpoint and its justification but be unable to accept the assumptions on which it is based. Or one might accept the flow of argument from assumptions to viewpoint to evidence but find illogic or impracticality in the stated conclusions and suggestions for action. In any event, the reader's personal view is tested and honed through the process of analyzing the views of others.

PHILOSOPHICAL CONSIDERATIONS

Historically, organized education has been initiated and instituted to serve many purposes—spiritual salvation, political socialization, moral uplift, societal stability, social mobility, mental discipline, vocational efficiency, and social reform, among others. The various purposes have usually reflected the dominant philosophical conception of human nature and the prevailing assumptions about the relationship between the individual and society. At any given time, competing conceptions may vie for dominance—social conceptions, economic conceptions, conceptions that emphasize spirituality, or conceptions that stress the uniqueness and dignity of the individual, for example.

These considerations of human nature and individual-society relationships are grounded in philosophical assumptions, and these assumptions find their way to such practical domains as schooling. In Western civilization there has been an identifiable (but far from consistent and clear-cut) historical trend in the basic assumptions about reality, knowledge, values, and the human condition. This trend, made manifest in the philosophical positions of idealism, realism, pragmatism, and existentialism, has involved a shift in emphasis from the spiritual world to nature to human behavior to the social individual to the free individual, and from eternal ideas to fixed natural laws to social interaction to the inner person.

The idealist tradition, which dominated much of philosophical and educational thought until the eighteenth and nineteenth centuries, separates the changing, imperfect, material world and the permanent, perfect, spiritual or mental world. As Plato saw it, for example, human beings and all other physical entities are particular manifestations of an ideal reality that in material existence humans can never fully know. The purpose of education is to bring us closer to the absolute ideals, pure forms, and universal standards that exist spiritually, by awakening and strengthening our rational powers. For Plato, a curriculum based on mathematics, logic, and music would serve this purpose, especially in the training of leaders whose rationality must exert control over emotionality and baser instincts.

Against this tradition, which shaped the liberal arts curriculum in schools for centuries, the realism of Aristotle, with its finding of the "forms" of things *within* the material world, brought an emphasis on scientific investigation and on environmental factors in the development of human potential. This fundamental view has influenced two philosophical movements in education: naturalism, based on following or gently assisting nature (as in the approaches of

John Amos Comenius, Jean-Jacques Rousseau, and Johann Heinrich Pestalozzi), and scientific realism, based on uncovering the natural laws of human behavior and shaping the educational environment to maximize their effectiveness (as in the approaches of John Locke, Johann Friedrich Herbart, and Edward Thorndike).

In the twentieth century, two philosophical forces (pragmatism and existentialism) have challenged these traditions. Each has moved primary attention away from fixed spiritual or natural influences and toward the individual as shaper of knowledge and values. The pragmatic position, articulated in America by Charles Sanders Peirce, William James, and John Dewey, turns from metaphysical abstractions toward concrete results of action. In a world of change and relativity, human beings must forge their own truths and values as they interact with their environments and each other. The European-based philosophy of existentialism, emerging from such thinkers as Gabriel Marcel, Martin Buber, Martin Heidegger, and Jean-Paul Sartre, has more recently influenced education here. Existentialism places the burdens of freedom, choice, and responsibility squarely on the individual, viewing the current encroachment of external forces and the tendency of people to "escape from freedom" as a serious diminishment of our human possibilities.

These many theoretical slants contend for recognition and acceptance as we continue the search for broad purposes in education and as we attempt to create curricula, methodologies, and learning environments that fulfill our stated purposes. This is carried out, of course, in the real world of the public schools in which social, political, and economic forces often predominate.

POWER AND CONTROL

Plato, in the fourth century B.C., found existing education manipulative and confining and, in the *Republic*, described a meritocratic approach designed to nurture intellectual powers so as to form and sustain a rational society. Reform-oriented as Plato's suggestions were, he nevertheless insisted on certain restrictions and controls so that his particular version of the ideal could be met.

The ways and means of education have been fertile grounds for power struggles throughout history. Many educational efforts have been initiated by religious bodies, often creating a conflict situation when secular authorities have moved into the field. Schools have usually been seen as repositories of culture and social values and, as such, have been overseen by the more conservative forces in society. To others, bent on social reform, the schools have been treated as a spawning ground for change. Given these basic political forces, conflict is inevitable.

When one speaks of the control of education, the range of influence is indeed wide. Political influences, governmental actions, court decisions, professional militancy, parental power, and student assertion all contribute to the phenomenon of control. And the domain of control is equally broad—school finances, curriculum, instructional means and objectives, teacher certification, accountability, student discipline, censorship of school materials, determination of access and opportunity, and determination of inclusion and exclusion.

The general topic of power and control leads to a multitude of questions: Who should make policy decisions? Must the schools be puppets of the government? Can the schools function in the vanguard of social change? Can cultural indoctrination be avoided? Can the schools lead the way to full social integration? Can the effects of social class be eradicated? Can and should the schools teach values? Dealing with such questions is complicated by the increasing power of the federal government in educational matters. Congressional legislation has broadened substantially from the early land grants and aid to agricultural and vocational programs to more recent laws covering aid to federally impacted areas, school construction aid, student loans and fellowships, support for several academic areas of the curriculum, work-study programs, compensatory education, employment opportunities for youth, adult education, aid to libraries, teacher preparation, educational research, career education, education of the handicapped, and equal opportunity for females. This proliferation of areas of influence has caused the federal administrative bureaucracy to blossom from its meager beginnings in 1867 into a cabinet-level Department of Education in 1979.

State legislatures and state departments of education have also grown in power, handling greater percentages of school appropriations and controlling basic curricular decisions, attendance laws, accreditation, research, and so on. Local school boards, once the sole authorities in policy making, now share the role with higher governmental echelons as the financial support sources shift away from the local scene. Simultaneously, strengthened teacher organizations and increasingly vocal pressure groups at the local, state, and national levels have forced a widening of the base for policy decisions.

SOME CONCLUDING REMARKS

The schools often seem to be either facing backward or to be completely absorbed in the tribulations of the present, lacking a vision of possible futures that might guide current decisions. The present is inescapable, obviously, and certainly the historical and philosophical underpinnings of the present situation must be understood, but true improvement often requires a break with conventionality—a surge toward a desired future.

The radical reform critique of government-sponsored compulsory schooling has depicted organized education as a form of cultural or political imprisonment that traps young people in an artificial and mainly irrelevant environment and rewards conformity and docility while inhibiting curiosity and creativity. Constructive reform ideas that have come from this critique include the creation of open classrooms, the de-emphasis of external motivators, the diversification of educational experience, and the building of a true sense of community within the instructional environment.

Starting with Francis Wayland Parker's schools in Quincy, Massachusetts, and John Dewey's laboratory school at the University of Chicago around the turn of the current century, the campaign to make schools into more productive and humane places has been relentless. The duplication of A. S. Neill's Summerhill model in the free school movement in the 1960s, the open classroom/

open space trends of recent years, the several curricular variations on applications of humanistic ideals, and the emergence of schools without walls, charter schools, privatization of management, and home schooling across the country testify to the desire to reform the present system or to build alternatives to it.

The progressive education movement, the development of "life adjustment" goals and curricula, and the "whole person" theories of educational psychology moved the schools toward an expanded concept of schooling that embraced new subject matters and new approaches to discipline during the first half of this century. Since the 1950s, however, pressure for a return to a narrower concept of schooling as intellectual training has sparked new waves of debate. Out of this situation have come attempts by educators and academicians to design new curricular approaches in the basic subject matter areas, efforts by private foundations to stimulate organizational innovations and to improve the training of teachers, and federal government support of the community school model and the career educational curriculum. Yet criticism of the schools abounds. The schools, according to many who use their services, remain too factorylike, too age-segregated, and too custodial. Alternative paths are still sought—paths that would allow action-learning, work-study, and a diversity of ways to achieve success.

H. G. Wells has told us that human history becomes more and more a race between education and catastrophe. What is needed in order to win this race is the generation of new ideas regarding cultural change, human relationships, ethical norms, the uses of technology, and the quality of life. These new ideas, of course, may be old ideas newly applied. One could do worse, in thinking through the problem of improving the quality of education, than to turn to the third-century philosopher Plotinus, who called for an education directed to "the outer, the inner, and the whole." For Plotinus, "the outer" represented the public person, or the socioeconomic dimension of the total human being; "the inner" reflected the subjective dimension, the uniquely experiencing individual, or the "I"; and "the whole" signified the universe of meaning and relatedness, or the realm of human, natural, and spiritual connectedness. It would seem that education must address all of these dimensions if it is to truly help people in the lifelong struggle to shape a meaningful existence. If educational experiences can be improved in these directions, the end result might be people who are not just filling space, filling time, or filling a social role, but who are capable of saying something worthwhile in their lives.

On the Internet . . .

The Center for Dewey Studies

The Center for Dewey Studies offers a wealth of source materials for the study of America's quintessential philosopher-educator, John Dewey.

http://www.siu.edu/~deweyctr/index2.html

Progressive Education

The Center for Contemporary Education offers material on progressive education.

http://www.parkcce.org/edres/prog.html

The National Paideia Center

The National Paideia Center promotes and supports the efforts of educators who are implementing the long-term systemic school reform known as the Paideia Program.

http://www.paideia.org

Coalition of Essential Schools

This site offers facts and ideas on this national curriculum movement.

http://www.essentialschools.org

Behaviorism in Current Context

According to this Web site, it is important that a reformation of behaviorism, as an empirical and objectively based science, takes place to meet the present challenges within the realm of human behavior.

http://www.oberlin.edu/~mjohnson/projectDescription.html

From Maslow to the 21st Century

This Association for Humanistic Psychology site features the theories of Carl Rogers, Abraham Maslow, Rollo May, and others.

http://ahpweb.org/aboutahp/whatis.html

Americans United for Separation of Church and State

Since 1947, Americans United for Separation of Church and State has worked to protect the constitutional principle of church-state separation.

http://www.au.org

PART 1

Enduring Issues

*W*hat *is the basic purpose of education? How should the curriculum be organized? What is the best way to teach and motivate students to learn? Does religion have any place in public education? Does the government have the right to compel school attendance? These questions have been discussed since the beginnings of organized schooling, and they continue to be debated today. In this section, the views of seven influential figures in American education—Horace Mann, John Dewey, Robert M. Hutchins, Mortimer J. Adler, John Holt, B. F. Skinner, and Carl R. Rogers—and three scholars in the field of education—R. Freeman Butts, Robert L. Cord, and Barry McGhan—are used to address these enduring questions.*

- Should Schooling Be Based on Social Experiences?

- Should the Curriculum Be Standardized for All?

- Should Behaviorism Shape Educational Practices?

- Should Church-State Separation Be Maintained?

- Should School Attendance Be Compelled?

ISSUE 1

Should Schooling Be Based on Social Experiences?

YES: John Dewey, from *Experience and Education* (Macmillan, 1938)

NO: Robert M. Hutchins, from *The Conflict in Education in a Democratic Society* (Harper & Row, 1953)

ISSUE SUMMARY

YES: Philosopher John Dewey suggests a reconsideration of traditional approaches to schooling, giving fuller attention to the social development of the learner and the quality of his or her total experience.

NO: Robert M. Hutchins, noted educator and one-time chancellor of the University of Chicago, argues for a liberal arts education geared to the development of intellectual powers.

Throughout history, organized education has served many purposes—the transmission of tradition, knowledge, and skills; the acculturation and socialization of the young; the building and preserving of political-economic systems; the provision of opportunity for social mobility; the enhancement of the quality of life; and the cultivation of individual potential, among others. At any given time, schools pursue a number of such goals, but the elucidation of a primary or overriding goal, which gives focus to all others, has been a source of continuous contention.

Schooling in America has been extended in the last 100 years to vast numbers of young people, and during this time the argument over aims has gained momentum. At the turn of the century, John Dewey was raising serious questions about the efficacy of the prevailing approach to schooling. He believed that schooling was often arid, pedantic, and detached from the real lives of children and youths. In establishing his laboratory school at the University of Chicago, Dewey hoped to demonstrate that experiences provided by schools could be meaningful extensions of the normal social activities of learners, having as their primary aim the full experiential growth of the individual.

In order to accomplish this, Dewey sought to bring the learner into an active and intimate relationship with the subject matter. The problem-solving or inquiry approach that he and his colleagues at Columbia University in New York City devised became the cornerstone of the "new education"—the progressive education movement.

In 1938 Dewey himself (as expressed in his selection that follows) sounded a note of caution to progressive educators who may have abandoned too completely the traditional disciplines in their attempt to link schooling with the needs and interests of the learners. Having spawned an educational revolution, Dewey, in his later years, emerges as more of a compromiser.

In that same year, William C. Bagley, in "An Essentialists' Platform for the Advancement of American Education," harshly criticized what he felt were anti-intellectual excesses promulgated by progressivism. In the 1950s and 1960s this theme was elaborated on by other academics, among them Robert M. Hutchins, Hyman Rickover, Arthur Bestor, and Max Rafferty, who demanded a return to intellectual discipline, higher standards, and moral guidance.

Hutchins's critique of Dewey's pragmatic philosophy was perhaps the best reasoned. He felt that the emphasis on immediate needs and desires of students and the focus on change and relativism detracted from the development of the intellectual skills needed for the realization of human potential.

A renewal of scholarly interest in the philosophical and educational ideas of both Dewey and Hutchins has resulted in a number of books, among which are *Hutchins' University: A Memoir of the University of Chicago* by William H. O'Neill (1991); *Robert M. Hutchins: Portrait of an Educator* by Mary Ann Dzuback (1991); *John Dewey and American Democracy* by Robert B. Westbrook (1991); *The End of Epistemology: Dewey and His Allies on the Spectator Theory of Knowledge* by Christopher B. Kulp (1992); and *The Promise of Pragmatism* by John Patrick Diggins (1994). Their continuing influence is charted by Rene Vincente Arcilla in "Metaphysics in Education after Hutchins and Dewey," *Teachers College Record* (Winter 1991).

More recent articles on the legacies of Dewey's progressivism and the traditionalism of Hutchins include "Rethinking Progressive School Reform," by Plank, Scotch, and Gamble, *American Journal of Education* (February 1996); "Education and the Pursuit of Happiness: John Dewey's Sympathetic Character," by Sam Stack, *Journal of Thought* (Summer 1996); "A Conversation Between John Dewey and Rudolph Steiner," by Jacques Ensign, *Educational Theory* (Spring 1996); "Toward a Theory of Progressive Education?" by Jurgen Herbst, *History of Education Quarterly* (Spring 1997); "Why Traditional Education Is More Progressive," by E. D. Hirsch, Jr., *The American Enterprise* (March 1997); and "The Plight of Children Is Our Plight," by William H. Schubert, *Educational Horizons* (Winter 1998).

In the following selections, Dewey charts what he considers a necessary shift from the abstractness and isolation of traditional schooling to the concreteness and vitality of the newer concept. Hutchins dissects the assumptions underlying Dewey's position and puts forth his own theory based on the premise that human nature is constant and functions the same in every society.

John Dewey

Experience and Education

$\mathbf{M}$ankind likes to think in terms of extreme opposites. It is given to formulating its beliefs in terms of *Either-Ors*, between which it recognizes no intermediate possibilities. When forced to recognize that the extremes cannot be acted upon, it is still inclined to hold that they are all right in theory but that when it comes to practical matters circumstances compel us to compromise. Educational philosophy is no exception. The history of educational theory is marked by opposition between the idea that education is development from within and that it is formation from without; that it is based upon natural endowments and that education is a process of overcoming natural inclination and substituting in its place habits acquired under external pressure.

At present, the opposition, so far as practical affairs of the school are concerned, tends to take the form of contrast between traditional and progressive education. If the underlying ideas of the former are formulated broadly, without the qualifications required for accurate statement, they are found to be about as follows: The subject-matter of education consists of bodies of information and of skills that have been worked out in the past; therefore, the chief business of the school is to transmit them to the new generation. In the past, there have also been developed standards and rules of conduct; moral training consists of forming habits of action in conformity with these rules and standards. Finally, the general pattern of school organization (by which I mean the relations of pupils to one another and to the teachers) constitutes the school as a kind of institution sharply marked off from other social institutions. Call up in imagination the ordinary schoolroom, its time schedules, schemes of classification, of examination and promotion, of rules of order, and I think you will grasp what is meant by "pattern of organization." If then you contrast this scene with what goes on in the family, for example, you will appreciate what is meant by the school being a kind of institution sharply marked off from any other form of social organization.

The three characteristics just mentioned fix the aims and methods of instruction and discipline. The main purpose or objective is to prepare the young for future responsibilities and for success in life, by means of acquisition of the organized bodies of information and prepared forms of skill which comprehend the material of instruction. Since the subject-matter as well as standards

From John Dewey, *Experience and Education* (Macmillan, 1938). Copyright © 1938 by Kappa Delta Pi, an International Honor Society in Education. Reprinted by permission.

4

of proper conduct are handed down from the past, the attitude of pupils must, upon the whole, be one of docility, receptivity, and obedience. Books, especially textbooks, are the chief representatives of the lore and wisdom of the past, while teachers are the organs through which pupils are brought into effective connection with the material. Teachers are the agents through which knowledge and skills are communicated and rules of conduct enforced.

I have not made this brief summary for the purpose of criticizing the underlying philosophy. The rise of what is called new education and progressive schools is of itself a product of discontent with traditional education. In effect it is a criticism of the latter. When the implied criticism is made explicit it reads somewhat as follows: The traditional scheme is, in essence, one of imposition from above and from outside. It imposes adult standards, subject-matter, and methods upon those who are only growing slowly toward maturity. The gap is so great that the required subject-matter, the methods of learning and of behaving are foreign to the existing capacities of the young. They are beyond the reach of the experience the young learners already possess. Consequently, they must be imposed; even though good teachers will use devices of art to cover up the imposition so as to relieve it of obviously brutal features.

But the gulf between the mature or adult products and the experience and abilities of the young is so wide that the very situation forbids much active participation by pupils in the development of what is taught. Theirs is to do—and learn, as it was the part of the six hundred to do and die. Learning here means acquisition of what already is incorporated in books and in the heads of the elders. Moreover, that which is taught is thought of as essentially static. It is taught as a finished product, with little regard either to the ways in which it was originally built up or to changes that will surely occur in the future. It is to a large extent the cultural product of societies that assumed the future would be much like the past, and yet it is used as educational food in a society where change is the rule, not the exception.

If one attempts to formulate the philosophy of education implicit in the practices of the new education, we may, I think, discover certain common principles amid the variety of progressive schools now existing. To imposition from above is opposed expression and cultivation of individuality; to external discipline is opposed free activity; to learning from texts and teachers, learning through experience; to acquisition of isolated skills and techniques by drill, is opposed acquisition of them as means of attaining ends which make direct vital appeal; to preparation for a more or less remote future is opposed making the most of the opportunities of present life; to static aims and materials is opposed acquaintance with a changing world.

Now, all principles by themselves are abstract. They become concrete only in the consequences which result from their application. Just because the principles set forth are so fundamental and far-reaching, everything depends upon the interpretation given them as they are put into practice in the school and the home. It is at this point that the reference made earlier to *Either-Or* philosophies becomes peculiarly pertinent. The general philosophy of the new education may be sound, and yet the difference in abstract principles will not decide the way in which the moral and intellectual preference involved shall be worked out in practice. There is always the danger in a new movement that in rejecting the aims and methods of that which it would supplant, it may develop its principles negatively rather than positively and constructively. Then it takes its clew in practice from that which is rejected instead of from the constructive development its own philosophy.

I take it that the fundamental unity of the newer philosophy is found in the idea that there is an intimate and necessary relation between the processes of actual experience and education. If this be true, then a positive and constructive development of its own basic idea depends upon having a correct idea of experience. Take, for example, the question of organized subject-matter.... The problem for progressive education is: What is the place and meaning of subject-matter and of organization *within* experience? How does subject-matter function? Is there anything inherent in experience which tends towards progressive organization of its contents? What results follow when the materials of experience are not progressively organized? A philosophy which proceeds on the basis of rejection, of sheer opposition, will neglect these questions. It will tend to suppose that because the old education was based on ready-made organization, therefore it suffices to reject the principle of organization *in toto*, instead of striving to discover what it means and how it is to be attained on the basis of experience. We might go through all the points of difference between the new and the old education and reach similar conclusions. When external control is rejected, the problem becomes that of finding the factors of control that are inherent within experience. When external authority is rejected, it does not follow that all authority should be rejected, but rather that there is need to search for a more effective source of authority. Because the older education imposed the knowledge, methods, and the rules of conduct of the mature person upon the young, it does not follow, except upon the basis of the extreme *Either-Or* philosophy, that the knowledge and skill of the mature person has no directive value for the experience of the immature. On the contrary, basing education upon personal experience may mean more multiplied and more intimate contacts between the mature and the immature than ever existed in the traditional school, and consequently more, rather than less, guidance by others. The problem, then, is: how these contacts can be established without violating the principle of learning through personal experience. The solution of this problem requires a well thought-out philosophy of the social factors that operate in the constitution of individual experience.

What is indicated in the foregoing remarks is that the general principles of the new education do not of themselves solve any of the problems of the actual or practical conduct and management of progressive schools. Rather, they set new problems which have to be worked out on the basis of a new philosophy of experience. The problems are not even recognized, to say nothing of being solved, when it is assumed that it suffices to reject the ideas and practices of the old education and then go to the opposite extreme. Yet I am sure that you will appreciate what is meant when I say that many of the newer schools tend to make little or nothing of organized subject-matter of study; to proceed as if any form of direction and guidance by adults were an invasion of individual freedom, and as if the idea that education should be concerned with the present and future meant that acquaintance with the past has little or no role to play in education. Without pressing these defects to the point of exaggeration, they at least illustrate what is meant by a theory and practice of education which proceeds negatively or by reaction against what has been current in education rather than by a positive and constructive development of purposes, methods, and subject-matter on the foundation of a theory of experience and its educational potentialities.

It is not too much to say that an educational philosophy which professes to be based on the idea of freedom may become as dogmatic as ever was the traditional education which is reacted against. For any theory and set of practices is dogmatic which is not based upon critical examination of its own underlying principles. Let us say that the new education emphasizes the freedom of the learner. Very well. A problem is now set. What does freedom mean and what are the conditions under which it is capable of realization? Let us say that the kind of external imposition which was so common in the traditional school limited rather than promoted the intellectual and moral development of the young. Again, very well. Recognition of this serious defect sets a problem. Just what is the role of the teacher and of books in promoting the educational development of the immature? Admit that traditional education employed as the subject-matter for study facts and ideas so bound up with the past as to give little help in dealing with the issues of the present and future. Very well. Now we have the problem of discovering the connection which actually exists *within* experience between the achievements of the past and the issues of the present. We have the problem of ascertaining how acquaintance with the past may be translated into a potent instrumentality for dealing effectively with the future. We may reject knowledge of the past as the *end* of education and thereby only emphasize its importance as a *means*. When we do that we have a problem that is new in the story of education: How shall the young become acquainted with the past in such a way that the acquaintance is a potent agent in appreciation of the living present? . . .

In short, the point I am making is that rejection of the philosophy and practice of traditional education sets a new type of difficult educational problem for those who believe in the new type of education. We shall operate blindly and in confusion until we recognize this fact; until we thoroughly appreciate that departure from the old solves no problems. What is said in the following pages is, accordingly, intended to indicate some of the main problems with which the newer education is confronted and to suggest the main lines along which their solution is to be sought. I assume that amid all uncertainties there is one permanent frame of reference: namely, the organic connection between education and personal experience; or, that the new philosophy of education is committed to some kind of empirical and experimental philosophy. But experience and experiment are not self-explanatory ideas. Rather, their meaning is part of the problem to be explored. To know the meaning of empiricism we need to understand what experience is.

The belief that all genuine education comes about through experience does not mean that all experiences are genuinely or equally educative. Experience and education cannot be directly equated to each other. For some experiences are miseducative. Any experience is miseducative that has the effect of arresting or distorting the growth of further experience. An experience may be such as to engender callousness; it may produce lack of sensitivity and of responsiveness. Then the possibilities of having richer experience in the future are restricted. Again, a given experience may increase a person's automatic skill in a particular direction and yet tend to land him in a groove or rut; the effect again is to narrow the field of further experience. An experience may be immediately enjoyable and yet promote the formation of a slack and careless attitude; this attitude then operates to modify the quality of subsequent experiences so as to prevent a person from getting out of them what they have to give. Again, experiences may be so disconnected from one another that, while each is agreeable or even exciting in itself, they are not linked cumulatively to one another. Energy is then dissipated and a person becomes scatter-brained. Each experience may be lively, vivid, and "interesting," and yet their disconnectedness may artificially generate dispersive, disintegrated, centrifugal habits. The consequence of formation of such habits is inability to control future experiences. They are then taken, either by way of enjoyment or of discontent and revolt, just as they come. Under such circumstances, it is idle to talk of self-control.

Traditional education offers a plethora of examples of experiences of the kinds just mentioned. It is a great mistake to suppose, even tacitly, that the traditional schoolroom was not a place in which pupils had experiences. Yet this is tacitly assumed when progressive education as a plan of learning by experience is placed in sharp opposition to the old. The proper line of attack is that the experiences which were had, by pupils and teachers alike, were largely of a wrong kind. How many students, for example, were rendered callous to ideas, and how many lost the impetus to learn because of the way in which learning was experienced by them? How many acquired special skills by means of automatic drill so that their power of judgment and capacity to act intelligently in new situations was limited? How many came to associate the learning process with ennui and boredom? How many found what they did learn so foreign to the situations of life outside the school as to give them no power of control over the latter? How many came to associate books with dull drudgery, so that they were "conditioned" to all but flashy reading matter?

If I ask these questions, it is not for the sake of wholesale condemnation of the old education. It is for quite another purpose. It is to emphasize the fact, first, that young people in traditional schools do have experiences; and, secondly, that the trouble is not the absence of experiences, but their defective and wrong character—wrong and defective from the standpoint of connection with further experience. The positive side of this point is even more important in connection with progressive education. It is not enough to insist upon the necessity of experience, nor even of activity in experience. Everything depends upon the *quality* of the experience which is had. The quality of an experience has two aspects. There is an immediate aspect of agreeableness or disagreeableness, and there is its influence upon later experiences. The first is obvious and easy to judge. The *effect* of an experience is not borne on its face. It sets a problem to the educator. It is his business to arrange for the kind of experiences which, while they do not repel the student, but rather engage his activities are, nevertheless, more than immediately enjoyable since they promote having desirable future experiences. Just as no man lives or dies to himself, so no experience lives or dies to itself. Wholly independent of desire or intent, every experience lives on in further experiences. Hence the central problem of an education based upon experience is to select the kind of present experiences that live fruitfully and creatively in subsequent experiences.

... Here I wish simply to emphasize the importance of this principle [of the continuity of experience] for the philosophy of educative experience. A philosophy of education, like my theory, has to be stated in words, in symbols. But so far as it is more than verbal it is a plan for conducting education. Like any plan, it must be framed with reference to what is to be done and how it is to be done. The more definitely and sincerely it is held that education is a development within, by, and for experience, the more important it is that there shall be clear conceptions of what experience is. Unless experience is so conceived that the result is a plan for deciding upon subject-matter, upon methods of instruction and discipline, and upon material equipment and social organization of the school, it is wholly in the air. It is reduced to a form of words which may be emotionally stirring but for which any other set of words might equally well be substituted unless they indicate operations to be initiated and executed. Just because traditional education was a matter of routine in which the plans and programs were handed down from the past, it does not follow that progressive education is a matter of planless improvisation.

The traditional school could get along without any consistently developed philosophy of education. About all it required in that line was a set of abstract words like culture, discipline, our great cultural heritage, etc., actual guidance being derived not from them but from custom and established routines. Just because progressive schools cannot rely upon established traditions and institutional habits, they must either proceed more or less haphazardly or be directed by ideas which, when they are made articulate and coherent, form a philosophy of education. Revolt against the kind of organization characteristic of the traditional school constitutes a demand for a kind of organization based upon ideas. I think that only slight acquaintance with the history of education is needed to prove that educational reformers and innovators alone have felt the need for a philosophy of education. Those who adhered to the established system needed merely a few fine-sounding words to justify existing practices. The real work was done by habits which were so fixed as to be institutional. The lesson for progressive education is that it requires in an urgent degree, a degree more pressing than was incumbent upon former innovators, a philosophy of education based upon a philosophy of experience.

I remarked incidentally that the philosophy in question is, to paraphrase the saying of Lincoln about democracy, one of education of, by, and for experience. No one of these words, *of, by,* or *for,* names anything which is self-evident. Each of them is a challenge to discover and put into operation a principle of order and organization which follows from understanding what education experience signifies.

It is, accordingly, a much more difficult task to work out the kinds of materials, of methods, and of social relationships that are appropriate to the new education than is the case with traditional education. I think many of the difficulties experienced in the conduct of progressive schools and many of the criticisms leveled against them arise from this source. The difficulties are aggravated and the criticisms are increased when it is supposed that the new education is somehow easier than the old. This belief is, I imagine, more or less current. Perhaps it illustrates again the *Either-Or* philosophy, springing from the idea that about all which is required is *not* to do what is done in traditional schools.

I admit gladly that the new education is *simpler* in principle than the old. It is in harmony with principles of growth, while there is very much which is artificial in the old selection and arrangement of subjects and methods, and artificiality always leads to unnecessary complexity. But the easy and the simple are not identical. To discover what is really simple and to act upon the discovery is an exceedingly difficult task. After the artificial and complex is once institutionally established and ingrained in custom and routine, it is easier to walk in the paths that have been beaten than it is, after taking a new point of view, to work out what is practically involved in the new point of view. The old Ptolemaic astronomical system was more complicated with its cycles and epicycles than the Copernican system. But until organization of actual astronomical phenomena on the ground of the latter principle had been effected the easiest course was to follow the line of least resistance provided by the old intellectual habit. So we come back to the idea that a coherent *theory* of experience, affording positive direction to selection and organization of appropriate educational methods and materials, is required by the attempt to give new direction to the work of the schools. The process is a slow and arduous one. It is a matter of growth, and there are many obstacles which tend to obstruct growth and to deflect it into wrong lines.

... [W]e must escape from the tendency to think of organization in terms of the *kind* of organization, whether of content (or subject-matter), or of methods and social relations, that mark traditional education. I think that a good deal of the current opposition to the idea of organization is due to the fact that it is so hard to get away from the picture of the studies of the old school. The moment "organization" is mentioned imagination goes almost automatically to the kind of organization that is familiar, and in revolting against that we are led to shrink from the very idea of any organization. On the other hand, educational reactionaries, who are now gathering force, use the absence of adequate intellectual and moral organization in the newer type of school as proof not only of the need of organization, but to identify any and every kind of organization with that instituted before the rise of experimental science. Failure to develop a conception of organization upon the empirical and experimental basis gives reactionaries a too easy victory. But the fact that the empirical sciences now offer the best type of intellectual organization which can be found in any field shows that there is no reason why we, who call ourselves empiricists, should be "pushovers" in the matter of order and organization.

Robert M. Hutchins

The Basis of Education

The obvious failures of the doctrines of adaptation, immediate needs, social reform, and of the doctrine that we need no doctrine at all may suggest to us that we require a better definition of education. Let us concede that every society must have some system that attempts to adapt the young to their social and political environment. If the society is bad, in the sense, for example, in which the Nazi state was bad, the system will aim at the same bad ends. To the extent that it makes men bad in order that they may be tractable subjects of a bad state, the system may help to achieve the social ideals of the society. It may be what the society wants; it may even be what the society needs, if it is to perpetuate its form and accomplish its aims. In pragmatic terms, in terms of success in the society, it may be a "good" system.

But it seems to me clearer to say that, though it may be a system of training, or instruction, or adaptation, or meeting immediate needs, it is not a system of education. It seems clearer to say that the purpose of education is to improve men. Any system that tries to make them bad is not education, but something else. If, for example, democracy is the best form of society, a system that adapts the young to it will be an educational system. If despotism is a bad form of society, a system that adapts the young to it will not be an educational system, and the better it succeeds in adapting them the less educational it will be.

Every man has a function as a man. The function of a citizen or a subject may vary from society to society, and the system of training, or adaptation, or instruction, or meeting immediate needs may vary with it. But the function of a man as man is the same in every age and in every society, since it results from his nature as a man. The aim of an educational system is the same in every age and in every society where such a system can exist: it is to improve man as man.

If we are going to talk about improving men and societies, we have to believe that there is some difference between good and bad. This difference must not be, as the positivists think it is, merely conventional. We cannot tell this difference by any examination of the effectiveness of a given program as the pragmatists propose; the time required to estimate these effects is usually too long and the complexity of society is always too great for us to say that the consequences of a given program are altogether clear. We cannot discover the difference between good and bad by going to the laboratory, for men and societies are not laboratory animals. If we believe that there is no truth, there is no knowledge, and there are no values except those which are validated by laboratory experiment, we cannot talk about the improvement of men and societies, for we can have no standard of judging anything that takes place among men or in societies.

Society is to be improved, not by forcing a program of social reform down its throat, through the schools, or otherwise, but by the improvement of the individuals who compose it. As Plato said, "Governments reflect human nature. States are not made out of stone or wood, but out of the characters of their citizens: these turn the scale and draw everything after them." The individual is the heart of society....

Man is by nature free, and he is by nature social. To use his freedom rightly he needs discipline. To live in society he needs the moral virtues. Good moral and intellectual habits are required for the fullest development of the nature of man.

To develop fully as a social, political animal man needs participation in his own government. A benevolent despotism will not do. You cannot expect the slave to show the virtues of the free man unless you first set him free. Only democracy, in which all men rule and are ruled in turn for the good life of the whole community, can be an absolutely good form of government....

Education deals with the development of the intellectual powers of men. Their moral and spiritual powers are the sphere of the family and the church. All three agencies must work in harmony; for, though a man has three aspects, he is still one man. But the schools cannot take over the role of the family and the church without promoting the atrophy of those institutions and failing in the task that is proper to the schools.

We cannot talk about the intellectual powers of men, though we can talk about training them, or amusing them, or adapting them, and meeting their immediate needs, unless our philosophy in general tells us that there is knowledge and that there is a difference between true and false. We must believe, too, that there are other means of obtaining knowledge than scientific experimentation. If knowledge can be sought only in the laboratory, many fields in which we thought we had knowledge will offer us nothing but opinion or superstition, and we shall be forced to conclude that we cannot know anything about the most important aspects of man and society. If we are to set about developing the intellectual powers of man through having them acquire knowledge of the most important subjects, we have to begin with the proposition that experimentation and empirical data will be of only limited use to us, contrary to the convictions of many American social scientists, and that philosophy, history, literature, and art give us knowledge, and significant knowledge, on the most significant issues.

If the object of education is the improvement of men, then any system of education that is without values is a contradiction in terms. A system that seeks bad values is bad. A system that denies the existence of values denies the possibility of education. Relativism, scientism, skepticism, and anti-intellectualism, the four horsemen of the philosophical apocalypse, have produced that chaos in education which will end in the disintegration of the West.

The prime object of education is to know what is good for man. It is to know the goods in their order. There is a hierarchy of values. The task of education is to help us understand it, establish it, and live by it. This Aristotle had in mind when he said: "It is not the possessions but the desires of men that must be equalized, and this is impossible unless they have a sufficient education according to the nature of things."

Such an education is far removed from the triviality of that produced by the doctrines of adaptation, of immediate needs, of social reform, or of the doctrine of no doctrine at all. Such an education will not adapt the young to a bad environment, but it will encourage them to make it good. It will not overlook immediate needs, but it will place these needs in their proper relationship to more distant, less tangible, and more important goods. It will be the only effective means of reforming society.

This is the education appropriate to free men. It is liberal education. If all men are to be free, all men must have this education. It makes no difference how they are to earn their living or what their special interests or aptitudes may be. They can learn to make a living, and they can develop their special interests and aptitudes, after they have laid the foundation of free and responsible manhood through liberal education. It will not do to say that they are incapable of such education. This claim is made by those who are too indolent or unconvinced to make the effort to give such education to the masses.

Nor will it do to say that there is not enough time to give everybody a liberal education before he becomes a specialist. In America, at least, the waste and frivolity of the educational system are so great that it would be possible through getting rid of them to give every citizen a liberal education and make him a qualified specialist, too, in less time than is now consumed in turning out uneducated specialists.

A liberal education aims to develop the powers of understanding and judgment. It is impossible that too many people can be educated in this sense, because there cannot be too many people with understanding and judgment. We hear a great deal today about the dangers that will come upon us through the frustration of educated people who have got educated in the expectation that education will get them a better job, and who then fail to get it. But surely this depends on the representations that are made to the young about what education is. If we allow them to believe that education will get them better jobs and encourage them to get educated with this end in view, they are entitled to a sense of frustration if, when they have got the education, they do not get the jobs. But, if we say that they should be educated in order to be men, and that everybody, whether he is ditch-digger or a bank president, should have this education because he is a man, then the ditch-digger may still feel frustrated, but not because of his education.

Nor is it possible for a person to have too much liberal education, because it is impossible to have too much understanding and judgment. But it is possible to undertake too much in the name of liberal education in youth. The object of liberal education in youth is not to teach the young all they will ever need to know. It is to give them the habits, ideas, and techniques that they need to continue to educate themselves. Thus the object of formal institutional liberal education in youth is to prepare the young to educate themselves throughout their lives.

I would remind you of the impossibility of learning to understand and judge many of the most important things in youth. The judgment and understanding of practical affairs can amount to little in the absence of experience with practical affairs. Subjects that cannot be understood without experience should not be taught to those who are without experience. Or, if these subjects are taught to those who are without experience, it should be clear that these subjects can be taught only by way of introduction and that their value to the student depends on his continuing to study them as he acquires experience. The tragedy in America is that economics, ethics, politics, history, and literature are studied in youth, and seldom studied again. Therefore the graduates of American universities seldom understand them.

This pedagogical principle, that subjects requiring experience can be learned only by the experienced, leads to the conclusion that the most important branch of education is the education of adults. We sometimes seem to think of education as something like the mumps, measles, whooping cough, or chicken pox. If a person has had education in childhood, he need not, in fact he cannot, have it again. But the pedagogical principle that the most important things can be learned only in mature life is supported by a sound philosophy in general. Men are rational animals. They achieve their terrestrial felicity by the use of reason. And this means that they have to use it for their entire lives. To say that they should learn only in childhood would mean that they were human only in childhood.

And it would mean that they were unfit to be citizens of a republic. A republic, a true *res publica*, can maintain justice, peace, freedom, and order only by the exercise of intelligence. When we speak of the consent of the governed, we mean, since men are not angels who seek the truth intuitively and do not have to learn it, that every act of assent on the part of the governed is a product of learning. A republic is really a common educational life in process. So Montesquieu said that, whereas the principle of a monarchy was honor, and the principle of a tyranny was fear, the principle of a republic was education.

Hence the ideal republic is the republic of learning. It is the utopia by which all actual political republics are measured. The goal toward which we started with the Athenians twenty-five centuries ago is an unlimited republic of learning and a worldwide political republic mutually supporting each other.

All men are capable of learning. Learning does not stop as long as a man lives, unless his learning power atrophies because he does not use it. Political freedom cannot endure unless it is accompanied by provision for the unlimited acquisition of knowledge. Truth is not long retained in human affairs without continual learning and relearning. Peace is unlikely unless there are continuous, unlimited opportunities for learning and unless men continuously avail themselves of them. The world of law and justice for which we yearn, the worldwide political republic, cannot be realized without the worldwide republic of learning. The civilization we seek will be achieved when all men are citizens of the world republic of law and justice and of the republic of learning all their lives long.

POSTSCRIPT

Should Schooling Be Based on Social Experiences?

Intellectual training versus social-emotional-mental growth—the argument between Dewey and Hutchins reflects a historical debate that flows from the ideas of Plato and Aristotle and that continues today. Psychologists, sociologists, curriculum and instruction specialists, and popular critics have joined philosophers in commenting on this central concern.

Followers of Dewey contend that training the mental powers cannot be isolated from other factors of development and, indeed, can be enhanced by attention to the concrete social situations in which learning occurs. Critics of Dewey worry that the expansion of effort into the social and emotional realm only detracts from the intellectual mission that is schooling's unique province.

Was the progressive education movement ruinous, or did it lay the foundation for the education of the future? A reasonably even-handed appraisal can be found in Lawrence Cremin's *The Transformation of the School* (1961). The free school movement of the 1960s, at least partly derived from progressivism, is analyzed in Allen Graubard's *Free the Children* (1973) and Jonathan Kozol's *Free Schools* (1972). Diane Ravitch's *Troubled Crusade* (1983) and Mary Eberstadt's "The Schools They Deserve," *Policy Review* (October/November 1999) offer effective critiques of progressivism.

Among the best general explorations of philosophical alternatives are Gerald L. Gutek's *Philosophical and Ideological Perspectives on Education* (1988); Edward J. Power's *Philosophy of Education: Studies in Philosophies, Schooling, and Educational Policies* (1990); and *Philosophical Foundations of Education* by Howard Ozmon and Samuel Craver (1990).

Also worth perusing are Philip W. Jackson's "Dewey's *Experience and Education* Revisited," *The Educational Forum* (Summer 1996); Jane Roland Martin's "A Philosophy of Education for the Year 2000," *Phi Delta Kappan* (January 1995); Jerome Bruner's 1996 book *The Culture of Education* (particularly chapter 3, "The Complexity of Educational Aims"); Robert Orrill's *Education and Democracy: Re-imaging Liberal Learning in America* (1997); and Christine McCarthy's "Dewey's Ethics: Philosophy or Science?" *Education Theory* (Summer 1999).

Questions that must be addressed include: Can the "either/or" polarities of this basic argument be overcome? Is the articulation of overarching general aims essential to the charting of a productive and worthwhile educational experience? And how can the classroom teacher relate to general philosophical aims?

ISSUE 2

Should the Curriculum Be Standardized for All?

YES: Mortimer J. Adler, from "The Paideia Proposal: Rediscovering the Essence of Education," *American School Board Journal* (July 1982)

NO: John Holt, from *Escape from Childhood* (E. P. Dutton, 1974)

ISSUE SUMMARY

YES: Philosopher Mortimer J. Adler contends that democracy is best served by a public school system that establishes uniform curricular objectives for all students.

NO: Educator John Holt argues that an imposed curriculum damages the individual and usurps a basic human right to select one's own path of development.

Controversy over the content of education has been particularly keen since the 1950s. The pendulum has swung from learner-centered progressive education to an emphasis on structured intellectual discipline to calls for radical reform in the direction of "openness" to the recent rally to go "back to basics."

The conservative viewpoint, articulated by such writers as Robert M. Hutchins, Clifton Fadiman, Jacques Barzun, Arthur Bestor, and Mortimer J. Adler, arises from concerns about the drift toward informalism and the decline in academic achievement in recent decades. Taking philosophical cues from Plato's contention that certain subject matters have universal qualities that prompt mental and characterological development, the "basics" advocates argue against incidental learning, student choice, and diminution of structure and standards. Barzun summarizes the viewpoint succinctly: "Nonsense is at the heart of those proposals that would replace definable subject matters with vague activities copied from 'life' or with courses organized around 'problems' or 'attitudes.'"

The reform viewpoint, represented by John Holt, Paul Goodman, Ivan Illich, Charles Silberman, Edgar Friedenberg, and others, portrays the typical traditional school as a mindless, indifferent, social institution dedicated to producing fear, docility, and conformity. In such an atmosphere, the viewpoint holds, learners either become alienated from the established curriculum or learn to play the school "game" and thus achieve a hollow success. Taking cues from the ideas of John Dewey and A. S. Neill, the "radical reformers" have given rise to a flurry of alternatives to regular schooling during recent decades. Among these are free schools, which follow the Summerhill model; urban storefront schools, which attempt to develop a true sense of "community"; "schools without walls," which follow the Philadelphia Parkway Program model; "commonwealth" schools, in which students, parents, and teachers share responsibility; and various "humanistic education" projects within regular school systems, which emphasize students' self-concept development and choice-making ability.

The utilitarian tradition that has descended from Benjamin Franklin, Horace Mann, and Herbert Spencer, Dewey's theory of active experiencing, and Neill's insistence on free and natural development support the reform position. The ideology rejects the factory model of schooling with its rigidly set curriculum, its neglect of individual differences, its social engineering function, and its pervasive formalism. "Basics" advocates, on the other hand, express deep concern over the erosion of authority and the watering down of demands upon students that result from the reform ideology.

Arguments for a more standardized curriculum have been embodied most recently in Theodore R. Sizer's Coalition of Essential Schools and the Core Knowledge Schools of E. D. Hirsch, Jr., whose 1996 book *The Schools We Need and Why We Don't Have Them* summarizes the basic points of this view. An interview with Hirsch by Mark F. Goldberg titled "Doing What Works" appeared in the September 1997 issue of *Phi Delta Kappan*. A thorough critique of Hirsch's position is presented by Kristen L. Buras in "Questioning Core Assumptions," *Harvard Educational Review* (Spring 1999). In 1998 Terry Roberts and the staff of the National Paideia Center at the University of North Carolina released *The Power of Paideia Schools: Defining Lives Through Learning.*

A broad spectrum of ideas on the curriculum may be found in John I. Goodlad's *A Place Called School* (1984), Maxine Green's *The Dialectic of Freedom* (1987), Theodore R. Sizer's *Horace* trilogy, and Ernest L. Boyer's *The Basic School* (1995).

In the following selections, Mortimer J. Adler outlines his "Paideia Proposal," which calls for a uniform and unified curriculum and methodological approach—a common schooling for the development of a truly democratic society. In opposition, John Holt goes beyond his earlier concerns about the oppressiveness of the school curriculum to propose complete freedom for the learner to determine all aspects of his or her educational development.

Mortimer J. Adler

 **YES**

The Paideia Proposal: Rediscovering the Essence of Education

In the first 80 years of this century, we have met the obligation imposed on us by the principle of equal educational opportunity, but only in a quantitative sense. Now as we approach the end of the century, we must achieve equality in qualitative terms.

This means a completely on-track system of schooling. It means, at the basic level, giving all the young the same kind of schooling, whether or not they are college bound.

We are aware that children, although equal in their common humanity and fundamental human rights, are unequal as individuals, differing in their capacity to learn. In addition, the homes and environments from which they come to school are unequal—either predisposing the child for schooling or doing the opposite.

Consequently, the Paideia Proposal, faithful to the principle of equal educational opportunity, includes the suggestion that inequalities due to environmental factors must be overcome by some form of preschool preparation—at least one year for all and two or even three for some. We know that to make such preschool tutelage compulsory at the public expense would be tantamount to increasing the duration of compulsory schooling from 12 years to 13, 14, or 15 years. Nevertheless, we think that this preschool adjunct to the 12 years of compulsory basic schooling is so important that some way must be found to make it available for all and to see that all use it to advantage.

The Essentials of Basic Schooling

The objectives of basic schooling should be the same for the whole school population. In our current two-track or multitrack system, the learning objectives are not the same for all. And even when the objectives aimed at those on the upper track are correct, the course of study now provided does not adequately realize these correct objectives. On all tracks in our current system, we fail to cultivate proficiency in the common tasks of learning, and we especially fail to develop sufficiently the indispensable skills of learning.

The uniform objectives of basic schooling should be threefold. They should correspond to three aspects of the common future to which all the children are destined: (1) Our society provides all children ample opportunity for personal development. Given such opportunity, each individual is under a moral obligation to make the most of himself and his life. Basic schooling must facilitate this accomplishment. (2) All the children will become, when of age, full-fledged citizens with suffrage and other political responsibilities. Basic schooling must do everything it can to make them good citizens, able to perform the duties of citizenship with all the trained intelligence that each is able to achieve. (3) When they are grown, all (or certainly most) of the children will engage in some form of work to earn a living. Basic schooling must prepare them for earning a living, but not by training them for this or that specific job while they are still in school.

To achieve these three objectives, the character of basic schooling must be general and liberal. It should have a single, required, 12-year course of study for all, with no electives except one—an elective choice with regard to a second language, to be selected from such modern languages as French, German, Italian, Spanish, Russian, and Chinese. The elimination of all electives, with this one exception, excludes what *should* be excluded—all forms of specialization, including particularized job training.

In its final form, the Paideia Proposal will detail this required course of study, but I will summarize the curriculum here in its bare outline. It consists of three main columns of teaching and learning, running through the 12 years and progressing, of course, from the simple to the more complex, from the less difficult to the more difficult, as the students grow older. Understand: The three columns (see Table 1) represent three distinct modes of teaching and learning. They do not represent a series of courses. A specific course or class may employ more than one mode of teaching and learning, but all three modes are essential to the overall course of study.

The first column is devoted to acquiring knowledge in three subject areas: (A) language, literature, and the fine arts; (B) mathematics and natural science; (C) history, geography, and social studies.

The second column is devoted to developing the intellectual skills of learning. These include all the language skills necessary for thought and communication—the skills of reading, writing, speaking, listening. They also include mathematical and scientific skills; the skills of observing, measuring, estimating, and calculating; and skills in the use of the computer and of other scientific instruments. Together, these skills make it possible to think clearly and critically. They once were called the liberal arts—the intellectual skills indispensable to being competent as a learner.

The third column is devoted to enlarging the understanding of ideas and values. The materials of the third column are books (*not* textbooks), and other products of human artistry. These materials include books of every variety—historical, scientific, and philosophical as well as poems, stories, and essays—and also individual pieces of music, visual art, dramatic productions, dance productions, film or television productions. Music and works of visual art can be used in seminars in which ideas are discussed; but as with poetry and fiction,

Table 1

The Paideia Curriculum

	Column One	Column Two	Column Three
Goals	Acquisition of Organized Knowledge	Development of Intellectual Skills and Skills of Learning	Improved Understanding of Ideas and Values
	by means of	*by means of*	*by means of*
Means	Didactic Instruction, Lecturing, and Textbooks	Coaching, Exercises, Supervised Practice	Maieutic or Socratic Questioning and Active Participation
	in these three subject areas	*in these operations*	*in these activities*
Subject Areas, Operations, and Activities	Language, Literature, and Fine Arts; Mathematics and Natural Science; History, Geography, and Social Studies	Reading, Writing, Speaking, Listening, Calculating, Problem Solving, Observing, Measuring, Estimating, Exercising Critical Judgment	Discussion of Books (Not Textbooks) and Other Works of Art; Involvement in Music, Drama, and Visual Arts

The three columns do not correspond to separate courses, nor is one kind of teaching and learning necessarily confined to any one class.

they also are to be experienced aesthetically, to be enjoyed and admired for their excellence. In this connection, exercises in the composition of poetry, music, and visual works and in the production of dramatic works should be used to develop the appreciation of excellence.

The three columns represent three different kinds of learning on the part of the student and three different kinds of instruction on the part of teachers.

In the first column, the students are engaged in acquiring information and organized knowledge about nature, man, and human society. The method of instruction here, using textbooks and manuals, is didactic. The teacher lectures, invites responses from the students, monitors the acquisition of knowledge, and tests that acquisition in various ways.

In the second column, the students are engaged in developing habits of performance, which is all that is involved in the development of an art or skill. Art, skill, or technique is nothing more than a cultivated, habitual ability to do a certain kind of thing well, whether that is swimming and dancing, or reading and writing. Here, students are acquiring linguistic, mathematical, scientific, and historical *know-how* in contrast to what they acquire in the first column, which is *know-that* with respect to language, literature, and the fine arts, mathematics and science, history, geography, and social studies. Here, the method of instruction cannot be didactic or monitorial; it cannot be dependent on textbooks. It must be coaching, the same kind used in the gym to develop bodily skills; only here it is used by a different kind of coach in the classroom to develop intellectual skills.

In the third column, students are engaged in a process of enlightenment, the process whereby they develop their understanding of the basic and controlling ideas in all fields of subject matter and come to appreciate better all the human values embodied in works of art. Here, students move progressively from understanding less to understanding more—understanding better what they already know and appreciating more what they already have experienced. Here, the method of instruction cannot be either didactic or coaching. It must be the Socratic, or maieutic, method of questioning and discussing. It should not occur in any ordinary classroom with the students sitting in rows and the teacher in front of the class, but in a seminar room, with the students sitting around a table and the teacher sitting with them as an equal, even though a little older and wiser.

Of these three main elements in the required curriculum, the third column is completely innovative. Nothing like this is done in our schools, and because it is completely absent from the ordinary curriculum of basic schooling, the students never have the experience of having their minds addressed in a challenging way or of being asked to think about the important ideas, to express their thoughts, to defend their opinions in a reasonable fashion.

The only thing that is innovative about the second column is the insistence that the method of instruction here must be coaching carried on either with one student at a time or with very small groups of students. Nothing else can be effective in the development of a skill, be it bodily or intellectual. The absence of such individualized coaching in our schools explains why most of the students cannot read well, write well, speak well, listen well, or perform well any of the other basic intellectual operations.

The three columns are closely interconnected and integrated, but the middle column—the one concerned with linguistic, mathematical, and scientific skills—is central. It both supports and is supported by the other two columns. All the intellectual skills with which it is concerned must be exercised in the study of the three basic subject-matters and in acquiring knowledge about them, and these intellectual skills must be exercised in the seminars devoted to the discussion of books and other things.

In addition to the three main columns in the curriculum, ascending through the 12 years of basic schooling, there are three adjuncts: One is 12 years of physical training, accompanied by instruction in bodily care and hygiene. The second, running through something less than 12 years, is the development of basic manual skills, such as cooking, sewing, carpentry, and the operation of all kinds of machines. The third, reserved for the last year or two, is an introduction to the whole world of work—the range of occupations in which human beings earn their livings. This is not particularized job training. It is the very opposite. It aims at a broad understanding of what is involved in working for a living and of the various ways in which that can be done. If, at the end of 12 years, students wish training for specific jobs, they should get that in two-year community or junior colleges, or on the job itself, or in technical institutes of one sort or another.

Everything that has not been specifically mentioned as occupying the time of the school day should be reserved for after-hours and have the status of extra-curricular activities.

Please, note: The required course of study just described is as important for what it *displaces* as for what it introduces. It displaces a multitude of elective courses, especially those offered in our secondary schools, most of which make little or no contribution to general, liberal education. It eliminates all narrowly specialized job training, which now abounds in our schools. It throws out of the curriculum and into the category of optional extracurricular activities a variety of things that have little or no educational value.

If it did not call for all these displacements, there would not be enough time in the school day or year to accomplish everything that is essential to the general, liberal learning that must be the content of basic schooling.

The Quintessential Element

So far, I have set forth the bare essentials of the Paideia Proposal with regard to basic schooling. I have not yet mentioned the quintessential element—the *sine qua non*—without which nothing else can possibly come to fruition, no matter how sound it might be in principle. The heart of the matter is the quality of learning and the quality of teaching that occupies the school day, not to mention the quality of the homework after school.

First, the learning must be active. It must use the whole mind, not just the memory. It must be learning by discovery, in which the student, never the teacher, is the primary agent. Learning by discovery, which is the only genuine learning, may be either unaided or aided. It is unaided only for geniuses. For most students, discovery must be aided.

Here is where teachers come in—as aids in the process of learning by discovery not as knowers who attempt to put the knowledge they have into the minds of their students. The quality of the teaching, in short, depends crucially upon how the teacher conceives his role in the process of learning, and that must be as an aid to the student's process of discovery.

I am prepared for the questions that must be agitating you by now: How and where will we get the teachers who can perform as teachers should? How will we be able to staff the program with teachers so trained that they will be competent to provide the quality of instruction required for the quality of learning desired?

The first part of our answer to these questions is negative: We *cannot* get the teachers we need for the Paideia program from schools of education as *they are now constituted*. As teachers are now trained for teaching, they simply will not do. The ideal—an impracticable ideal—would be to ask for teachers who are, themselves, truly educated human beings. But truly educated human beings are too rare. Even if we could draft all who are now alive, there still would be far too few to staff our schools.

Well, then, what can we look for? Look for teachers who are actively engaged in the process of *becoming* educated human beings, who are themselves deeply motivated to develop their own minds. Assuming this is not too much to ask for the present, how should teachers be schooled and trained in the future? First, they should have the same kind of basic schooling that is recommended in the Paideia Proposal. Second, they should have additional schooling, at the college and even the university level, in which the same kind of general, liberal learning is carried on at advanced levels—more deeply, broadly, and intensively than it can be done in the first 12 years of schooling. Third, they must be given something analogous to the clinical experience in the training of physicians. They must engage in practice-teaching under supervision, which is another way of saying that they must be *coached* in the arts of teaching, not just given didactic instruction in educational psychology and in pedagogy. Finally, and most important of all, they must learn how to teach well by being exposed to the performances of those who are masters of the arts involved in teaching.

It is by watching a good teacher at work that they will be able to perceive what is involved in the process of assisting others to learn by discovery. Perceiving it, they must then try to emulate what they observe, and through this process, they slowly will become good teachers themselves.

The Paideia Proposal recognizes the need for three different kinds of institutions at the collegiate level: The two-year community or junior college should offer a wide choice of electives that give students some training in one or another specialized field, mainly those fields of study that have something to do with earning a living. The four-year college also should offer a wide variety of electives, to be chosen by students who aim at the various professional or technical occupations that require advanced study. Those elective majors chosen by students should be accompanied, for all students, by one required minor, in which the kind of general and liberal learning that was begun at the level of basic schooling is continued at a higher level in the four years of college. And we should have still a third type of collegiate institution—a four-year college in which general, liberal learning at a higher level constitutes a required course of study that is to be taken by all students. *It is this third type of college, by the way, that should be attended by all who plan to become teachers in our basic schools.*

At the university level, there should be a continuation of general, liberal learning at a still higher level to accompany intensive specialization in this or that field of science or scholarship, this or that learned profession. Our insistence on the continuation of general, liberal learning at all the higher levels of schooling stems from our concern with the worst cultural disease that is rampant in our society—*the barbarism of specialization.*

There is no question that our technologically advanced industrial society needs specialists of all sorts. There is no question that the advancement of knowledge in all fields of science and scholarship, and in all the learned professions, needs intense specialization. But for the sake of preserving and enhancing our cultural traditions, as well as for the health of science and scholarship, we need specialists who also are generalists—generally cultivated human beings, not just good plumbers. We need truly educated human beings who can perform their special tasks better precisely because they have general cultivation as well as intensely specialized training.

Changes indeed are needed in higher education, but those improvements cannot reasonably be expected unless improvement in basic schooling makes that possible.

The Future of Our Free Institutions

I already have declared as emphatically as I know how that the quality of human life in our society depends on the quality of the schooling we give our young people, both basic and advanced. But a marked elevation in the quality of human life is not the only reason improving the quality of schooling is so necessary—not the only reason we must move heaven and earth to stop the deterioration of our schools and turn them in the opposite direction. The other reason is to safeguard the future of our free institutions.

They cannot prosper, they may not even survive, unless we do something to rescue our schools from their current deplorable deterioration. Democracy, in the full sense of that term, came into existence only in this century and only in a few countries on earth, among which the United States is an outstanding example. But democracy came into existence in this century, only in its initial conditions, all of which hold out promises for the future that remain to be fulfilled. Unless we do something about improving the quality of basic schooling for all and the quality of advanced schooling for some, there is little chance that those promises ever will be fulfilled. And if they are not, our free institutions are doomed to decay and wither away.

We face many insistently urgent problems. Our prosperity and even our survival depend on the solution of those problems—the threat of nuclear war, the exhaustion of essential resources and of supplies of energy, the pollution or spoilage of the environment, the spiraling of inflation accompanied by the spread of unemployment.

To solve these problems, we need resourceful and innovative leadership. For that to arise and be effective, an educated populace is needed. Trained intelligence—not only on the part of leaders, but also on the part of followers—holds the key to the solution of the problems our society faces. Achieving peace, prosperity and plenty could put us on the threshold of an early paradise. But a much better educational system than now exists also is needed, for that alone can carry us across the threshold. Without it, a poorly schooled population will not be able to put to good use the opportunities afforded by the achievement of the general welfare. Those who are not schooled to enjoy society can only despoil its institutions and corrupt themselves.

NO

John Holt

Escape from Childhood

Young people should have the right to control and direct their own learning, that is, to decide what they want to learn, and when, where, how, how much, how fast, and with what help they want to learn it. To be still more specific, I want them to have the right to decide if, when, how much, and by whom they want to be *taught* and the right to decide whether they want to learn in a school and if so which one and for how much of the time.

No human right, except the right to life itself, is more fundamental than this. A person's freedom of learning is part of his freedom of thought, even more basic than his freedom of speech. If we take from someone his right to decide what he will be curious about, we destroy his freedom of thought. We say, in effect, you must think not about what interests and concerns *you*, but about what interests and concerns *us*.

We might call this the right of curiosity, the right to ask whatever questions are most important to us. As adults, we assume that we have the right to decide what does or does not interest us, what we will look into and what we will leave alone. We take this right for granted, cannot imagine that it might be taken away from us. Indeed, as far as I know, it has never been written into any body of law. Even the writers of our Constitution did not mention it. They thought it was enough to guarantee citizens the freedom of speech and the freedom to spread their ideas as widely as they wished and could. It did not occur to them that even the most tyrannical government would try to control people's minds, what they thought and knew. That idea was to come later, under the benevolent guise of compulsory universal education.

This right to each of us to control our own learning is now in danger. When we put into our laws the highly authoritarian notion that someone should and could decide what all young people were to learn and, beyond that, could do whatever might seem necessary (which now includes dosing them with drugs) to compel them to learn it, we took a long step down a very steep and dangerous path. The requirement that a child go to school, for about six hours a day, 180 days a year, for about ten years, whether or not he learns anything there, whether or not he already knows it or could learn it faster or better somewhere else, is such gross violation of civil liberties that few adults would stand for it. But the child who resists is treated as a criminal. With this requirement we created an industry, an army of people whose whole work was to tell young people what they had to learn and to try to make them learn it. Some of these people, wanting to exercise even more power over others, to be even more "helpful," or simply because the industry is not growing fast enough to hold all the people who want to get into it, are now beginning to say, "If it is good for children for us to decide what they shall learn and to make them learn it, why wouldn't it be good for everyone? If compulsory education is a good thing, how can there be too much of it? Why should we allow anyone, of any age, to decide that he has had enough of it? Why should we allow older people, any more than young, not to know what we know when their ignorance may have bad consequences for all of us? Why should we not *make* them know what they *ought* to know?"

They are beginning to talk, as one man did on a nationwide TV show, about "womb-to-tomb" schooling. If hours of homework every night are good for the young, why wouldn't they be good for us all—they would keep us away from the TV set and other frivolous pursuits. Some group of experts, somewhere, would be glad to decide what we all ought to know and then every so often check up on us to make sure we knew it—with, of course, appropriate penalties if we did not.

I am very serious in saying that I think this is coming unless we prepare against it and take steps to prevent it. The right I ask for the young is a right that I want to preserve for the rest of us, the right *to decide what goes into our minds.* This is much more than the right to decide whether or when or how much to go to school or what school you want to go to. That right is important, but it is only part of a much larger and more fundamental right, which I might call the right to Learn, as opposed to being Educated, *i.e.*, made to learn what someone else thinks would be good for you. It is not just compulsory schooling but compulsory Education that I oppose and want to do away with.

That children might have the control of their own learning, including the right to decide if, when, how much, and where they wanted to go to school, frightens and angers many people. They ask me, "Are you saying that if the parents wanted the child to go to school, and the child didn't want to go, that he wouldn't have to go? Are you saying that if the parents wanted the child to go to one school, and the child wanted to go to another, that the child would have the right to decide?" Yes, that is what I say. Some people ask, "If school wasn't compulsory, wouldn't many parents take their children out of school to exploit their labors in one way or another?" Such questions are often both snobbish and hypocritical. The questioner assumes and implies (though rarely says) that these bad parents are people poorer and less schooled than he. Also, though he appears to be defending the right of children to go to school, what he really is defending is the right of the state to compel them to go whether they want to or not. What he wants, in short, is that children should be in school, not that they should have any choice about going.

But saying that children should have the right to choose to go or not to go to school does not mean that the ideas and wishes of the parents would have no weight. Unless he is estranged from his parents and rebelling against them, a child cares very much about what they think and want. Most of the time, he doesn't want to anger or worry or disappoint them. Right now, in families where the parents feel that they have some choice about their children's schooling, there is much bargaining about schools. Such parents, when their children are little, often ask them whether they want to go to nursery school or kindergarten. Or they may take them to school for a while to try it out. Or, if they have a choice of schools, they may take them to several to see which they think they will like the best. Later, they care whether the child likes his school. If he does not, they try to do something about it, get him out of it, find a school he will like.

I know some parents who for years had a running bargain with their children. "If on a given day you just can't stand the thought of school, you don't feel well, you are afraid of something that may happen, you have something of your own that you very much want to do—well, you can stay home." Needless to say, the schools, with their supporting experts, fight it with all their might— Don't Give in to Your Child, Make Him Go to School, He's Got to Learn. Some parents, when their own plans make it possible for them to take an interesting trip, take their children with them. They don't ask the schools' permission, they just go. If the child doesn't want to make the trip and would rather stay in school, they work out a way for him to do that. Some parents, when their child is frightened, unhappy, and suffering in school, as many children are, just take him out. Hal Bennett, in his excellent book *No More Public School*, talks about ways to do this.

A friend of mine told me that when her boy was in third grade, he had a bad teacher, bullying, contemptuous, sarcastic, cruel. Many of the class switched to another section, but this eight-year-old, being tough, defiant, and stubborn, hung on. One day—his parents did not learn this until about two years later—having had enough of the teacher's meanness, he just got up from his desk and without saying a word, walked out of the room and went home. But for all his toughness and resiliency of spirit, the experience was hard on him. He grew more timid and quarrelsome, less outgoing and confident. He lost his ordinary good humor. Even his handwriting began to go to pieces—it was much worse in the spring of the school year than in the previous fall. One spring day he sat at breakfast, eating his cereal. After a while he stopped eating and sat silently thinking about the day ahead. His eyes filled up with tears, and two big ones slowly rolled down his cheeks. His mother, who ordinarily stays out of the school life of her children, saw this and knew what it was about. "Listen," she said to him, "we don't have to go on with this. If you've had enough of that teacher, if she's making school so bad for you that you don't want to go any more, I'll be perfectly happy just to pull you right out. We can manage it. Just say the word." He was horrified and indignant. "No!" he said, "I couldn't do that." "Okay," she said, "whatever you want is fine. Just let me know." And so they left it. He had decided that he was going to tough it out, and he did. But I am sure knowing that he had the support of his mother and the chance to give it up if it got too much for him gave him the strength he needed to go on.

To say that children should have the right to control and direct their own learning, to go to school or not as they choose, does not mean that the law would forbid the parents to express an opinion or wish or strong desire on the matter. It only means that if their natural authority is not strong enough the parents can't call in the cops to make the child do what they are not able to persuade him to do. And the law may say that there is no limit to the amount of pressure or coercion the parents can apply to the child to deny him a choice that he has a legal right to make.

When I urge that children should control their learning, there is one argument that people bring up so often that I feel I must anticipate and meet it here. It says that schools are a place where children can for a while be protected against the bad influences of the world outside, particularly from its greed, dishonesty, and commercialism. It says that in school children may have a glimpse of a higher way of life, of people acting from other and better motives than greed and fear. People say, "We know that society is bad enough as it is and that if children go out into the larger world as soon as they wanted, they would be tempted and corrupted just that much sooner."

They seem to believe that schools are better, more honorable places than the world outside—what a friend of mine at Harvard once called "museums of virtue." Or that people in school, both children and adults, act from higher and better motives than people outside. In this they are mistaken. There are, of course, some good schools. But on the whole, far from being the opposite of, or an antidote to, the world outside, with all its envy, fear, greed, and obsessive competitiveness, the schools are very much like it. If anything, they are worse, a terrible, abstract, simplified caricature of it. In the world outside the school, some work, at least, is done honestly and well, for its own sake, not just to get ahead of others; people are not everywhere and always being set in competition against each other; people are not (or not yet) in every minute of their lives subject to the arbitrary, irrevocable orders and judgement of others. But in most schools, a student is every minute doing what others tell him, subject to their judgement, in situations in which he can only win at the expense of other students.

This is a harsh judgement. Let me say again, as I have before, that schools are worse than most of the people in them and that many of these people do many harmful things they would rather not do, and a great many other harmful things that they do not even see as harmful. The whole of school is much worse than the sum of its parts. There are very few people in the U.S. today (or perhaps anywhere, any time) in *any* occupation, who could be trusted with the kind of power that schools give most teachers over their students. Schools seem to me among the most anti-democratic, most authoritarian, most destructive, and most dangerous institutions of modern society. No other institution does more harm or more lasting harm to more people or destroys so much of their curiosity, independence, trust, dignity, and sense of identity and worth. Even quite kindly schools are inhibited and corrupted by the knowledge of children and teachers alike that they are *performing* for the judgement and approval of others—the children for the teachers; the teachers for the parents, supervisors, school board, or the state. No one is ever free from feeling that he is being judged all the time, or soon may be. Even after the best class experiences teachers must ask themselves, "Were we right to do that? Can we prove we were right? Will it get us in trouble?"

What corrupts the school, and makes it so much worse than most of the people in it, or than they would like it to be, is its power—just as their powerlessness corrupts the students. The school is corrupted by the endless anxious demand of the parents to know how their child is doing—meaning is he ahead of the other kids—and their demand that he be kept ahead. Schools do not protect children from the badness of the world outside. They are at least as bad as the world outside, and the harm they do to the children in their power creates much of the badness of the world outside. The sickness of the modern world is in many ways a school-induced sickness. It is in school that most people learn to expect and accept that some expert can always place them in some sort of rank or hierarchy. It is in school that we meet, become used to, and learn to believe in the totally controlled society. We do not learn much science, but we learn to worship "scientists" and to believe that anything we might conceivably need or want can only come, and someday will come, from them. The school is the closest we have yet been able to come to Huxley's *Brave New World*, with its alphas and betas, deltas and epsilons—and now it even has its soma. Everyone, including children, should have the right to say "No!" to it.

POSTSCRIPT

Should the Curriculum Be Standardized for All?

The free/open school movement values small, personalized educational settings in which students engage in activities that have personal meaning. One of the movement's ideological assumptions, emanating from the philosophy of Jean-Jacques Rousseau, is that given a reasonably unrestrictive atmosphere, the learner will pursue avenues of creative and intellectual self-development. This confidence in self-motivation is the cornerstone of Holt's advocacy of freedom for the learner, a position he elaborates upon in his books *Instead of Education* (1988) and *Teach Your Own* (1982). The argument has gained some potency with recent developments in home-based computer-assisted instruction.

Adler's proposal for a unified curricular and methodological approach, released in 1982 by the Institute for Philosophical Research, was fashioned by a group of distinguished scholars and practitioners and has its roots in such earlier works as Arthur Bestor's *Educational Wastelands* (1953), Mortimer Smith's *The Diminished Mind* (1954), and Paul Copperman's *The Literacy Hoax* (1978). The proposal has been widely discussed since its release, and it has been implemented in a number of school systems. See, for example, "Launching Paideia in Chattanooga," by Cynthia M. Gettys and Anne Wheelock, *Educational Leadership* (September 1994). The essentialist position articulated by Adler is echoed in a number of recent calls for a more standardized and challenging curriculum by such thinkers as E. D. Hirsch, Jr., Allen Bloom, William Bennett, Diane Ravitch, and Lynne Cheney.

Holt's plea for freedom from an imposed curriculum has a new champion in John Taylor Gatto, New York City and New York State Teacher of the Year. Gatto has produced two provocative books, *Dumbing Us Down: The Hidden Curriculum of Compulsory Schooling* (1992) and *Confederacy of Dunces: The Tyranny of Compulsory Schooling* (1992), an excerpt from which appears in the Spring 1994 issue of *The Educational Forum*. Two other thought-stirring works that build upon Holt's basic views are Lewis J. Perelman's *School's Out: The New Technology and the End of Education* (1992) and George Leonard's "Notes: The End of School," *The Atlantic Monthly* (May 1992). A less ideological appraisal can be found in Paul Gagnon's "What Should Children Learn?" *The Atlantic Monthly* (December 1995). Theodore R. Sizer offers a plea for individualized instruction in "No Two Are Quite Alike," *Educational Leadership* (September 1999).

ISSUE 3

Should Behaviorism Shape Educational Practices?

YES: B. F. Skinner, from *Beyond Freedom and Dignity* (Alfred A. Knopf, 1971)

NO: Carl R. Rogers, from *Freedom to Learn for the Eighties* (Merrill, 1983)

ISSUE SUMMARY

YES: B. F. Skinner, an influential proponent of behaviorism and professor of psychology, critiques the concept of "inner freedom" and links learning and motivation to the influence of external forces.

NO: Professor of psychology and psychiatry Carl R. Rogers offers the "humanistic" alternative to behaviorism, insisting on the reality of subjective forces in human motivation.

Intimately enmeshed with considerations of aims and purposes and determination of curricular elements are the psychological base that affects the total setting in which learning takes place and the basic means of motivating learners. Historically, the atmosphere of schooling has often been characterized by harsh discipline, regimentation, and restriction. The prison metaphor often used by critics in describing school conditions rings true all too often.

Although calls to make schools pleasant have been sounded frequently, they have seldomly been heeded. Roman rhetorician Marcus Fabius Quintilian (ca. A.D. 35–ca. 100) advocated a constructive and enjoyable learning atmosphere. John Amos Comenius in the seventeenth century suggested a gardening metaphor in which learners were given kindly nurturance. Johann Heinrich Pestalozzi established a model school in the nineteenth century that replaced authoritarianism with love and respect.

Yet school as an institution retains the stigma of authoritarian control —attendance is compelled, social and psychological punishment is meted out, and the decision-making freedom of students is limited and often curtailed. These practices lead to rather obvious conclusions: the prevailing belief is either that young people are naturally evil and wild and therefore must be tamed in a restricting environment or that schooling as such is so unpalatable that people must be forced and cajoled to reap its benefits—or both.

Certainly, philosopher John Dewey (1895–1952) was concerned about this circumstance, citing at one time the superintendent of his native Burlington, Vermont, school district as admitting that the schools were a source of "grief and mortification" and were "unworthy of patronage." Dewey rejected both the need for "taming" and the defeatist attitude that the school environment must remain unappealing. He hoped to create a motivational atmosphere that would engage learners in real problem-solving activities, thereby sustaining curiosity, creativity, and attachment. The rewards were to flow from the sense of accomplishment and freedom, which was to be achieved through the disciplined actions necessary to solve the problem at hand.

More recent treatment of the allied issues of freedom, control, and motivation has come from the two major camps in the field of educational psychology: the behaviorists (rooted in the early-twentieth-century theories of Ivan Pavlov, Edward L. Thorndike, and John B. Watson) and the humanists (emanating from the Gestalt and field theory psychologies developed in Europe and America earlier in the twentieth century).

B. F. Skinner has been the dominant force in translating behaviorism into recommendations for school practices. He and his disciples, often referred to as "neobehaviorists," have contributed to widely used innovations such as behavioral objectives in instruction and testing, competency-based education, mastery learning, assertive discipline, and outcome-based education. The humanistic viewpoint has been championed by Carl R. Rogers, Abraham Maslow, Fritz Perls, Rollo May, and Erich Fromm, most of whom ground their psychological theories in the philosophical assumptions of existentialism and phenomenology.

Skinner believes that "inner" states are merely convenient myths, that motives and behaviors are shaped by environmental factors. These shaping forces, however, need not be negative, nor must they operate in an uncontrolled manner. Our present understanding of human behavior allows us the freedom to shape the environmental forces, which in turn shape us. With this power, Skinner contends, we can replace aversive controls in schooling with positive reinforcements that heighten the students' motivation level and make learning more efficient.

Recent manifestations of the continuing interest in Skinner's behaviorism and the humanistic psychology of Rogers include Virginia Richardson's "From Behaviorism to Constructivism in Teacher Education," *Teacher Education and Special Education* (Summer 1996) and Tobin Hart's "From Category to Contact: Epistemology and the Enlivening and Deadening of Spirit in Education," *Journal of Humanistic Education and Development* (September 1997).

Skinner deals with the problem of freedom and control in the selection that follows. In the second selection, Carl R. Rogers critiques Skinner's behaviorist approach and sets forth his argument supporting the reality of freedom as an inner human state that is the wellspring of responsibility, will, and commitment.

B. F. Skinner

 **YES**

Beyond Freedom and Dignity

Almost all living things act to free themselves from harmful contacts. A kind of freedom is achieved by the relatively simple forms of behavior called reflexes. A person sneezes and frees his respiratory passages from irritating substances. He vomits and frees his stomach from indigestible or poisonous food. He pulls back his hand and frees it from a sharp or hot object. More elaborate forms of behavior have similar effects. When confined, people struggle ("in rage") and break free. When in danger they flee from or attack its source. Behavior of this kind presumably evolved because of its survival value; it is as much a part of what we call the human genetic endowment as breathing, sweating, or digesting food. And through conditioning similar behavior may be acquired with respect to novel objects which could have played no role in evolution. These are no doubt minor instances of the struggle to be free, but they are significant. We do not attribute them to any love of freedom; they are simply forms of behavior which have proved useful in reducing various threats to the individual and hence to the species in the course of evolution.

A much more important role is played by behavior which weakens harmful stimuli in another way. It is not acquired in the form of conditioned reflexes, but as the product of a different process called operant conditioning. When a bit of behavior is followed by a certain kind of consequence, it is more likely to occur again, and a consequence having this effect is called a reinforcer. Food, for example, is a reinforcer to a hungry organism; anything the organism does that is followed by the receipt of food is more likely to be done again whenever the organism is hungry. Some stimuli are called negative reinforcers; any response which reduces the intensity of such a stimulus—or ends it—is more likely to be emitted when the stimulus recurs. Thus, if a person escapes from a hot sun when he moves under cover, he is more likely to move under cover when the sun is again hot. The reduction in temperature reinforces the behavior it is "contingent upon"—that is, the behavior it follows. Operant conditioning also occurs when a person simply avoids a hot sun—when, roughly speaking, he escapes from the *threat* of a hot sun.

Negative reinforcers are called aversive in the sense that they are the things organisms "turn away from." The term suggests a spatial separation—moving or running away from something—but the essential relation is temporal. In a standard apparatus used to study the process in the laboratory, an arbitrary response simply weakens an aversive stimulus or brings it to an end. A great deal of physical technology is the result of this kind of struggle for freedom. Over the centuries, in erratic ways, men have constructed a world in which they are relatively free of many kinds of threatening or harmful stimuli—extremes of temperature, sources of infection, hard labor, danger, and even those minor aversive stimuli called discomfort.

Escape and avoidance play a much more important role in the struggle for freedom when the aversive conditions are generated by other people. Other people can be aversive without, so to speak, trying; they can be rude, dangerous, contagious, or annoying, and one escapes from them or avoids them accordingly. They may also be "intentionally" aversive—that is, they may treat other people aversively because of what follows. Thus, a slave driver induces a slave to work by whipping him when he stops; by resuming work the slave escapes from the whipping (and incidentally reinforces the slave driver's behavior in using the whip). A parent nags a child until the child performs a task; by performing the task the child escapes nagging (and reinforces the parent's behavior). The blackmailer threatens exposure unless the victim pays; by paying, the victim escapes from the threat (and reinforces the practice). A teacher threatens corporal punishment or failure until his students pay attention; by paying attention the students escape from the threat of punishment (and reinforce the teacher for threatening it). In one form or another intentional aversive control is the pattern of most social coordination—in ethics, religion, government, economics, education, psychotherapy, and family life.

A person escapes from or avoids aversive treatment by behaving in ways which reinforce those who treated him aversively until he did so, but he may escape in other ways. For example, he may simply move out of range. A person may escape from slavery, emigrate or defect from a government, desert from an army, become an apostate from a religion, play truant, leave home, or drop out of a culture as a hobo, hermit, or hippie. Such behavior is as much a product of the aversive conditions as the behavior the conditions were designed to evoke. The latter can be guaranteed only by sharpening the contingencies or by using stronger aversive stimuli.

Another anomalous mode of escape is to attack those who arrange aversive conditions and weaken or destroy their power. We may attack those who crowd us or annoy us, as we attack the weeds in our garden, but again the struggle for freedom is mainly directed toward intentional controllers—toward those who treat others aversively in order to induce them to behave in particular ways. Thus, a child may stand up to his parents, a citizen may overthrow a government, a communicant may reform a religion, a student may attack a teacher or vandalize a school, and a dropout may work to destroy a culture.

It is possible that man's genetic endowment supports this kind of struggle for freedom: when treated aversively people tend to act aggressively or to be reinforced by signs of having worked aggressive damage. Both tendencies should have had evolutionary advantages, and they can easily be demonstrated. If two organisms which have been coexisting peacefully receive painful shocks, they immediately exhibit characteristic patterns of aggression toward each other.

The aggressive behavior is not necessarily directed toward the actual source of stimulation; it may be "displaced" toward any convenient person or object. Vandalism and riots are often forms of undirected or misdirected aggression. An organism which has received a painful shock will also, if possible, act to gain access to another organism toward which it can act aggressively. The extent to which human aggression exemplifies innate tendencies is not clear, and many of the ways in which people attack and thus weaken or destroy the power of intentional controllers are quite obviously learned.

What we may call the "literature of freedom" has been designed to induce people to escape from or attack those who act to control them aversively. The content of the literature is the philosophy of freedom, but philosophies are among those inner causes which need to be scrutinized. We say that a person behaves in a given way because he possesses a philosophy, but we infer the philosophy from the behavior and therefore cannot use it in any satisfactory way as an explanation, at least until it is in turn explained. The literature of freedom, on the other hand, has a simple objective status. It consists of books, pamphlets, manifestoes, speeches, and other verbal products, designed to induce people to act to free themselves from various kinds of intentional control. It does not impart a philosophy of freedom; it induces people to act.

The literature often emphasizes the aversive conditions under which people live, perhaps by contrasting them with conditions in a freer world. It thus makes the conditions more aversive, "increasing the misery" of those it is trying to rescue. It also identifies those from whom one is to escape or those whose power is to be weakened through attack. Characteristic villains of the literature are tyrants, priests, generals, capitalists, martinet teachers, and domineering parents.

The literature also prescribes modes of action. It has not been much concerned with escape, possibly because advice has not been needed; instead, it has emphasized how controlling power may be weakened or destroyed. Tyrants are to be overthrown, ostracized, or assassinated. The legitimacy of a government is to be questioned. The ability of a religious agency to mediate supernatural sanctions is to be challenged. Strikes and boycotts are to be organized to weaken the economic power which supports aversive practices. The argument is strengthened by exhorting people to act, describing likely results, reviewing successful instances on the model of the advertising testimonial, and so on.

The would-be controllers do not, of course, remain inactive. Governments make escape impossible by banning travel or severely punishing or incarcerating defectors. They keep weapons and other sources of power out of the hands of revolutionaries. They destroy the written literature of freedom and imprison or kill those who carry it orally. If the struggle for freedom is to succeed, it must then be intensified.

The importance of the literature of freedom can scarcely be questioned. Without help or guidance people submit to aversive conditions in the most surprising way. This is true even when the aversive conditions are part of the natural environment. Darwin observed, for example, that the Fuegians seemed to make no effort to protect themselves from the cold; they wore only scant clothing and made little use of it against the weather. And one of the most striking things about the struggle for freedom from intentional control is how often it has been lacking. Many people have submitted to the most obvious religious, governmental, and economic controls for centuries, striking for freedom only sporadically, if at all. The literature of freedom has made an essential contribution to the elimination of many aversive practices in government, religion, education, family life, and the production of goods.

The contributions of the literature of freedom, however, are not usually described in these terms. Some traditional theories could conceivably be said to define freedom as the absence of aversive control, but the emphasis has been on how the condition *feels*. Other traditional theories could conceivably be said to define freedom as a person's condition when he is behaving under nonaversive control, but the emphasis has been upon a state of mind associated with doing what one wants. According to John Stuart Mill, "Liberty consists in doing what one desires." The literature of freedom has been important in changing practice (it has changed practices whenever it has had any effect whatsoever), but it has nevertheless defined its task as the changing of states of mind and feelings. Freedom is a "possession." A person escapes from or destroys the power of a controller in order to feel free, and once he feels free and can do what he desires, no further action is recommended and none is prescribed by the literature of freedom, except perhaps eternal vigilance lest control be resumed.

The feeling of freedom becomes an unreliable guide to action as soon as would-be controllers turn to nonaversive measures, as they are likely to do to avoid the problems raised when the controllee escapes or attacks. Nonaversive measures are not as conspicuous as aversive and are likely to be acquired more slowly, but they have obvious advantages which promote their use. Productive labor, for example, was once the result of punishment: the slave worked to avoid the consequences of not working. Wages exemplify a different principle; a person is paid when he behaves in a given way so that he will continue to behave in that way. Although it has long been recognized that rewards have useful effects, wage systems have evolved slowly. In the nineteenth century it was believed that an industrial society required a hungry labor force; wages would be effective only if the hungry worker could exchange them for food. By making labor less aversive—for instance, by shortening hours and improving conditions—it has been possible to get men to work for lesser rewards. Until recently teaching was almost entirely aversive: the student studies to escape the consequences of not studying, but nonaversive techniques are gradually being discovered and used. The skillful parent learns to reward a child for good behavior rather than punish him for bad. Religious agencies move from the threat of hellfire to an emphasis on God's love, and governments turn from aversive sanctions to various kinds of inducements. . . . What the layman calls a reward is a "positive reinforcer," the effects of which have been exhaustively studied in the experimental analysis of operant behavior. The effects are not as easily recognized as those of aversive contingencies because they tend to be deferred, and applications have therefore been delayed, but techniques as powerful as the older aversive techniques are now available. . . .

The literature of freedom has never come to grips with techniques of control which do not generate escape or counterattack because it has dealt with the problem in terms of states of mind and feelings. In his book *Sovereignty,* Bertrand de Jouvenel quotes two important figures in that literature. According to Leibnitz, "Liberty consists in the power to do what one wants to do," and according to Voltaire, "When I can do what I want to do, there is my liberty for me." But both writers add a concluding phrase: Leibnitz, "... or in the power to want what can be got," and Voltaire, more candidly, "... but I can't help wanting what I do want." Jouvenel relegates these comments to a footnote, saying that the power to want is a matter of "interior liberty" (the freedom of the inner man!) which falls outside the "gambit of freedom."

A person wants something if he acts to get it when the occasion arises. A person who says "I want something to eat" will presumably eat when something becomes available. If he says "I want to get warm," he will presumably move into a warm place when he can. These acts have been reinforced in the past by whatever was wanted. What a person *feels* when he feels himself wanting something depends upon the circumstances. Food is reinforcing only in a state of deprivation, and a person who wants something to eat may feel parts of that state—for example, hunger pangs. A person who wants to get warm presumably feels cold. Conditions associated with a high probability of responding may also be felt, together with aspects of the present occasion which are similar to those of past occasions upon which behavior has been reinforced. Wanting is not, however, a feeling, nor is a feeling the reason a person acts to get what he wants. Certain contingencies have raised the probability of behavior and at the same time have created conditions which may be felt. Freedom is a matter of contingencies of reinforcement, not of the feelings the contingencies generate. The distinction is particularly important when the contingencies do not generate escape or counterattack....

The literature of freedom has encouraged escape from or attack upon all controllers. It has done so by making any indication of control aversive. Those who manipulate human behavior are said to be evil men, necessarily bent on exploitation. Control is clearly the opposite of freedom, and if freedom is good, control must be bad. What is overlooked is control which does not have aversive consequences at any time. Many social practices essential to the welfare of the species involve the control of one person by another, and no one can suppress them who has any concern for human achievements.... [I]n order to maintain the position that all control is wrong, it has been necessary to disguise or conceal the nature of useful practices, to prefer weak practices just because they can be disguised or concealed, and—a most extraordinary result indeed!—to perpetuate punitive measures.

The problem is to be free men, not from control, but from certain kinds of control, and it can be solved only if our analysis takes all consequences into account. How people feel about control, before or after the literature of freedom has worked on their feelings, does not lead to useful distinctions.

Were it not for the unwarranted generalization that all control is wrong, we should deal with the social environment as simply as we deal with the nonsocial. Although technology has freed men from certain aversive features of the environment, it has not freed them from the environment. We accept the fact that we depend upon the world around us, and we simply change the nature of the dependency. In the same way, to make the social environment as free as possible of aversive stimuli, we do not need to destroy that environment or escape from it; we need to redesign it.

Man's struggle for freedom is not due to a will to be free, but to certain behavioral processes characteristic of the human organism, the chief effect of which is the avoidance of or escape from so-called "aversive" features of the environment. Physical and biological technologies have been mainly concerned with natural aversive stimuli; the struggle for freedom is concerned with stimuli intentionally arranged by other people. The literature of freedom has identified the other people and has proposed ways of escaping from them or weakening or destroying their power. It has been successful in reducing the aversive stimuli used in intentional control, but it has made the mistake of defining freedom in terms of states of mind or feelings, and it has therefore not been able to deal effectively with techniques of control which do not breed escape or revolt but nevertheless have aversive consequences. It has been forced to brand all control as wrong and to misrepresent many of the advantages to be gained from a social environment. It is unprepared for the next step, which is not to free men from control but to analyze and change the kinds of control to which they are exposed.

Carl R. Rogers  **NO**

Freedom to Learn

One of the deepest issues in modern life, in modern man, is the question as to whether the concept of personal freedom has any meaning whatsoever in our present-day scientific world. The growing ability of the behavioral scientist to predict and to control behavior has brought the issue sharply to the fore. If we accept the logical positivism and strictly behavioristic emphases which are predominant in the American psychological scene, there is not even room for discussion....

But if we step outside the narrowness of the behavioral sciences, this question is not only *an* issue, it is one of the primary issues which define modern man. Friedman in his book (1963, p. 251) makes his topic "the problematic of modern man—the alienation, the divided nature, the unresolved tension between personal freedom and psychological compulsion which follows on 'the death of God'." The issues of personal freedom and personal commitment have become very sharp indeed in a world in which man feels unsupported by a supernatural religion, and experiences keenly the division between his awareness and those elements of his dynamic functioning of which he is unaware. If he is to wrest any meaning from a universe which for all he knows may be indifferent, he must arrive at some stance which he can hold in regard to these timeless uncertainties.

So, writing as both a behavioral scientist and as one profoundly concerned with the human, the personal, the phenomenological and the intangible, I should like to contribute what I can to this continuing dialogue regarding the meaning of and the possibility of freedom.

Man Is Unfree

... In the minds of most behavioral scientists, man is not free, nor can he as a free man commit himself to some purpose, since he is controlled by factors outside of himself. Therefore, neither freedom nor commitment is even a possible concept to modern behavioral science as it is usually understood.

To show that I am not exaggerating, let me quote a statement from Dr. B. F. Skinner of Harvard, who is one of the most consistent advocates of a strictly behavioristic psychology. He says,

> The hypothesis that man is not free is essential to the application of scientific method to the study of human behavior. The free inner man who is held responsible for his behavior is only a prescientific substitute for the kinds of causes which are discovered in the course of scientific analysis. All these alternative causes lie *outside* the individual (1953, p. 477).

This view is shared by many psychologists and others who feel, as does Dr. Skinner, that all the effective causes of behavior lie outside of the individual and that it is only through the external stimulus that behavior takes place. The scientific description of behavior avoids anything that partakes in any way of freedom. For example, Dr. Skinner (1964, pp. 90–91) describes an experiment in which a pigeon was conditioned to turn in a clockwise direction. The behavior of the pigeon was "shaped up" by rewarding any movement that approximated a clockwise turn until, increasingly, the bird was turning round and round in a steady movement. This is what is known as operant conditioning. Students who had watched the demonstration were asked to write an account of what they had seen. Their responses included the following ideas: that the pigeon was conditioned to *expect* reinforcement for the right kind of behavior; that the pigeon *hoped* that something would bring the food back again; that the pigeon *observed* that a certain behavior seemed to produce a particular result; that the pigeon *felt* that food would be given it because of its action; that the bird came to *associate* his action with the clock of the food dispenser. Skinner ridicules these statements because they all go beyond the observed behavior in using such words as *expect, hope, observe, felt,* and *associate.* The whole explanation from his point of view is that the bird was reinforced when it emitted a given kind of behavior; the pigeon walked around until the food container again appeared; a certain behavior produced a given result; food was given to the pigeon when it acted in a given way; the click of the food dispenser was related in time to the bird's action. These statements describe the pigeon's behavior from a scientific point of view.

Skinner goes on to point out that the students were undoubtedly reporting what they would have expected, felt and hoped under similar circumstances. But he then makes the case that there is no more reality to such ideas in the human being than there is in the pigeon, that it is only because such words have been reinforced by the verbal community in which the individual has developed, that such terms are used. He discusses the fact that the verbal community which conditioned them to use such terms saw no more of their behavior than they had seen of the pigeon's. In other words the internal events, if they indeed exist, have no scientific significance.

As to the methods used for changing the behavior of the pigeon, many people besides Dr. Skinner feel that through such positive reinforcement human behavior as well as animal behavior can be "shaped up" and controlled. In his book *Walden Two*, Skinner says,

> Now that we know how positive reinforcement works and how negative doesn't, we can be more deliberate and hence more successful in our cultural design. We can achieve a sort of control under which the controlled, though they are following a code much more scrupulously than was ever the case under the old system, nevertheless *feel free*. They are doing what they want to do, not what they are forced to do. That's the source of the tremendous power of positive reinforcement—there is no restraint and no revolt. By a careful cultural design we control not the final behavior but the *inclination* to behave—the motives, the desires, the wishes. The curious thing is that in that case *the question of freedom never arises* (1948, p. 218).

... I think it is clear from all of this that man is a machine—a complex machine, to be sure, but one which is increasingly subject to scientific control. Whether behavior will be managed through operant conditioning as in *Walden Two* or whether we will be "shaped up" by the unplanned forms of conditioning implied in social pressure, or whether we will be controlled by electrodes in the brain, it seems quite clear that science is making out of man an object and that the purpose of such science is not only understanding and prediction but control. Thus it would seem to be quite clear that there could be no concept so foreign to the facts as that man is free. Man is a machine, man is unfree, man cannot commit himself in any meaningful sense; he is simply controlled by planned or unplanned forces outside of himself.

Man Is Free

I am impressed by the scientific advances illustrated in the examples I have given. I regard them as a great tribute to the ingenuity, insight, and persistence of the individuals making the investigations. They have added enormously to our knowledge. Yet for me they leave something very important unsaid. Let me try to illustrate this, first from my experience in therapy.

I think of a young man classed as schizophrenic with whom I had been working for a long time in a state hospital. He was a very inarticulate man, and during one hour he made a few remarks about individuals who had recently left the hospital; then he remained silent for almost forty minutes. When he got up to go, he mumbled almost under his breath, "If some of *them* can do it, maybe I can too." That was all—not a dramatic statement, not uttered with force and vigor, yet a statement of choice by this young man to work toward his own improvement and eventual release from the hospital. It is not too surprising that about eight months after that statement he was out of the hospital. I believe this experience of responsible choice is one of the deepest aspects of psychotherapy and one of the elements which most solidly underlies personality change.

I think of another young person, this time a young woman graduate student, who was deeply disturbed and on the borderline of a psychotic break. Yet after a number of interviews in which she talked very critically about all of the people who had failed to give her what she needed, she finally concluded: "Well, with that sort of a foundation, it's really up to *me*. I mean it seems to be really apparent to me that I can't depend on someone else to *give* me an education." And then she added very softly: "I'll really have to get it myself." She goes on to explore this experience of important and responsible choice. She finds it a frightening experience, and yet one which gives her a feeling of strength. A force seems to surge up within her which is big and strong, and yet she also feels very much alone and sort of cut off from support. She adds: "I am going to begin to do more things that I know I should do." And she did.

I could add many other examples. One young fellow talking about the way in which his whole life had been distorted and spoiled by his parents finally comes to the conclusion that, "Maybe now that I *see* that, it's up to *me*." . . .

For those of you [who] have seen the film *David and Lisa*—and I hope that you have had that rich experience—I can illustrate exactly what I have been discussing. David, the adolescent schizophrenic, goes into a panic if he is touched by anyone. He feels that "touching kills," and he is deathly afraid of it, and afraid of the closeness in human relationships which touching implies. Yet toward the close of the film he makes a bold and positive choice of the kind I have been describing. He has been trying to be of help to Lisa, the girl who is out of touch with reality. He tries to help at first in an intellectually contemptuous way, then increasingly in a warmer and more personal way. Finally, in a highly dramatic movement, he says to her, "Lisa, take my hand." He *chooses*, with obvious conflict and fear, to leave behind the safety of his untouchableness, and to venture into the world of real human relationships where he is literally and figuratively in *touch* with another. You are an unusual person if the film does not grow a bit misty at this point.

Perhaps a behaviorist could try to account for the reaching out of his hand by saying that it was the result of intermittent reinforcement of partial movements. I find such an explanation both inaccurate and inadequate. It is the *meaning* of the *decision* which is essential to understanding the act.

What I am trying to suggest in all of this is that I would be at a loss to explain the positive change which can occur in psychotherapy if I had to omit the importance of the sense of free and responsible choice on the part of my clients. I believe that this experience of freedom to choose is one of the deepest elements underlying change.

The Meaning of Freedom

Considering the scientific advances which I have mentioned, how can we even speak of freedom? In what sense is a client free? In what sense are any of us free? What possible definition of freedom can there be in the modern world? Let me attempt such a definition.

In the first place, the freedom that I am talking about is essentially an inner thing, something which exists in the living person quite aside from any of the outward choices of alternatives which we so often think of as constituting freedom. I am speaking of the kind of freedom which Viktor Frankl vividly describes in his experience of the concentration camp, when everything—possessions, status, identity—was taken from the prisoners. But even months and years in such an environment showed only "that everything can be taken from a man but one thing: the last of the human freedoms—to choose one's own attitude in any given set of circumstances, to choose one's own way" (1959, p. 65). It is this inner, subjective, existential freedom which I have observed. It is the realization that "I can live myself, here and now, by my own choice." It is the quality of courage which enables a person to step into the uncertainty of the unknown as he chooses himself. It is the discovery of meaning from within oneself, meaning which comes from listening, sensitively and openly to the complexities of what one is experiencing. It is the burden of being responsible for the self one chooses to be. It is the recognition of a person that he is an emerging process, not a static end product. The individual who is thus deeply and courageously thinking his own thoughts, becoming his own uniqueness, responsibly choosing himself, may be fortunate in having hundreds of objective outer alternatives from which to choose, or he may be unfortunate in having none. But his freedom exists regardless. So we are first of all speaking of something which exists within the individual, something phenomenological rather than external, but nonetheless to be prized.

The second point in defining this experience of freedom is that it exists not as a contradiction of the picture of the psychological universe as a sequence of cause and effect, but as a complement to such a universe. Freedom rightly understood is a fulfillment by the person of the ordered sequence of his life. The free man moves out voluntarily, freely, responsibly, to play his significant part in a world whose determined events move through him and through his spontaneous choice and will.

I see this freedom of which I am speaking, then, as existing in a different *dimension* than the determined sequence of cause and effect. I regard it as a freedom which exists in the subjective person, a freedom which he courageously uses to live his potentialities. The fact that this type of freedom seems completely irreconcilable with the behaviorist's picture of man is something which I will discuss a bit later. . . .

The Emergence of Commitment

I have spoken thus far primarily about freedom. What about commitment? Certainly the disease of our age is lack of purpose, lack of meaning, lack of commitment on the part of individuals. Is there anything which I can say in regard to this?

It is clear to me that in therapy, as indicated in the examples that I have given, commitment to purpose and to meaning in life is one of the significant elements of change. It is only when the person decides, "I am someone; I am someone worth being: I am committed to being myself," that change becomes possible.

At a very interesting symposium at Rice University recently, Dr. Sigmund Koch sketched the revolution which is taking place in science, literature and the arts, in which a sense of commitment is again becoming evident after a long period in which that emphasis has been absent.

Part of what he meant by that may be illustrated by talking about Dr. Michael Polanyi, the philosopher of science, formerly a physicist, who has been presenting his notions about what science basically is. In his book, *Personal Knowledge*, Polanyi makes it clear that even scientific knowledge is personal knowledge, committed knowledge. We cannot rest comfortably on the belief that scientific knowledge is impersonal and "out there," that it has nothing to do with the individual who has discovered it. Instead, every aspect of science is pervaded by disciplined personal commitment, and Polanyi makes the case very persuasively that the whole attempt to divorce science from the person is a completely unrealistic one. I think I am stating his belief correctly when I say that in his judgment logical positivism and all the current structure of science cannot save us from the fact that all knowing is uncertain, involves risk, and is grasped and comprehended only through the deep, personal commitment of a disciplined search.

Perhaps a brief quotation will give something of the flavor of his thinking. Speaking of great scientists, he says:

> So we see that both Kepler and Einstein approached nature with intellectual passions and with beliefs inherent in these passions, which led them to their triumphs and misguided them to their errors. These passions and beliefs were theirs, personally, even universally. I believe that they were competent to follow these impulses, even though they risked being misled by them. And again, what I accept of their work today, I accept personally, guided by passions and beliefs similar to theirs, holding in my turn that my impulses are valid, universally, even though I must admit the possibility that they may be mistaken (1959, p. 145).

Thus we see that a modern philosopher of science believes that deep personal commitment is the only possible basis on which science can firmly stand. This is a far cry indeed from the logical positivism of twenty or thirty years ago, which placed knowledge far out in impersonal space.

Let me say a bit more about what I mean by commitment in the psychological sense. I think it is easy to give this word a much too shallow meaning, indicating that the individual has, simply by conscious choice, committed himself to one course of action or another. I think the meaning goes far deeper than that. Commitment is a total organismic direction involving not only the conscious mind but the whole direction of the organism as well.

In my judgment, commitment is something that one *discovers* within oneself. It is a trust of one's total reaction rather than of one's mind only. It has much to do with creativity. Einstein's explanation of how he moved toward his formulation of relativity without any clear knowledge of his goal is an excellent example of what I mean by the sense of commitment based on a total organismic reaction. He says:

> "During all those years there was a feeling of direction, of going straight toward something concrete. It is, of course, very hard to express that feeling in words but it was decidedly the case and clearly to be distinguished from later considerations about the rational form of the solution" (quoted in Wertheimer, 1945, p. 183–184).

Thus commitment is more than a decision. It is the functioning of an individual who is searching for the directions which are emerging within himself. Kierkegaard has said, "The truth exists only in the process of becoming, in the process of appropriation" (1941, p. 72). It is this individual creation of a tentative personal truth through action which is the essence of commitment.

Man is most successful in such a commitment when he is functioning as an integrated, whole, unified individual. The more that he is functioning in this total manner the more confidence he has in the directions which he unconsciously chooses. He feels a trust in his experiencing, of which, even if he is fortunate, he has only partial glimpses in his awareness.

Thought of in the sense in which I am describing it, it is clear that commitment is an achievement. It is the kind of purposeful and meaningful direction which is only gradually achieved by the individual who has come increasingly to live closely in relationship with his own experiencing—a relationship in which his unconscious tendencies are as much respected as are his conscious choices. This is the kind of commitment toward which I believe individuals can move. It is an important aspect of living in a fully functioning way.

The Irreconcilable Contradiction

I trust it will be very clear that I have given two sharply divergent and irreconcilably contradictory points of view. On the one hand, modern psychological science and many other forces in modern life as well, hold the view that man is unfree, that he is controlled, that words such as purpose, choice, commitment have no significant meaning, that man is nothing but an object which we can more fully understand and more fully control. Enormous strides have been and are being made in implementing this perspective. It would seem heretical indeed to question this view.

Yet, as Polanyi has pointed out in another of his writings (1957), the dogmas of science can be in error. He says:

> In the days when an idea could be silenced by showing that it was contrary to religion, theology was the greatest single source of fallacies. Today, when any human thought can be discredited by branding it as unscientific, the power previously exercised by theology has passed over to science; hence science has become in its turn the greatest single source of error.

So I am emboldened to say that over against this view of man as unfree, as an object, is the evidence from therapy, from subjective living, and from objective research as well, that personal freedom and responsibility have a crucial significance, that one cannot live a complete life without such personal freedom and responsibility, and that self-understanding and responsible choice make a sharp and measurable difference in the behavior of the individual. In this context, commitment does have meaning. Commitment is the emerging and changing total direction of the individual, based on a close and acceptant relationship between the person and all of the trends in his life, conscious and unconscious. Unless, as individuals and as a society, we can make constructive use of this capacity for freedom and commitment, mankind, it seems to me, is set on a collision course with fate. . . .

A part of modern living is to face the paradox that, viewed from one perspective, man is a complex machine. We are every day moving toward a more precise understanding and a more precise control of this objective mechanism which we call man. On the other hand, in another significant dimension of his existence, man is subjectively free; his personal choice and responsibility account for the shape of his life; he is in fact the architect of himself. A truly crucial part of his existence is the discovery of his own meaningful commitment to life with all of his being.

POSTSCRIPT

Should Behaviorism Shape Educational Practices?

The freedom-determinism or freedom-control argument has raged in philosophical, political, and psychological circles down through the ages. Is freedom of choice and action a central, perhaps *the* central, characteristic of being human? Or is freedom only an illusion, a refusal to acknowledge the external shaping of all human actions?

Moving the debate into the field of education, John Dewey depicted a developmental freedom that is acquired through improving one's ability to cope with problems. A. S. Neill (*Summerhill: A Radical Approach to Child Rearing,* 1984), who advanced the ideas of early-twentieth-century progressive educators and the establishment of free schools, sees a more natural inborn freedom in human beings, which must be protected and allowed to flourish. Skinner refuses to recognize this "inner autonomous man" but sees freedom resulting from the scientific reshaping of the environment that influences us.

Just as Skinner has struggled to remove the stigma from the word *control,* arguing that it is the true gateway to freedom, John Holt, in *Freedom and Beyond* (1972), contends that freedom and free activities are not "unstructured" —indeed, that the structure of an open classroom is vastly more complicated than the structure of a traditional classroom.

If both of these views have validity, then we are in a position, as Dewey counselled, to go beyond either-or polemics on these matters and build a more constructive educational atmosphere. Jerome S. Bruner has consistently suggested ways in which free inquiry and subject matter structure can be effectively blended. Arthur W. Combs, in a report titled *Humanistic Education: Objectives and Assessment* (1978), helped to bridge the ideological gap between humanists and behaviorists by demonstrating that subjective outcomes can be assessed by direct or modified behavioral techniques.

Skinner's death in 1990 prompted a number of evaluations, among them "Skinner's Stimulus: The Legacy of Behaviorism's Grand Designer," by Jeff Meade, *Teacher* (November/December 1990) and "The Life and Contributions of Burrhus Frederic Skinner," by Robert P. Hawkins, *Education and Treatment of Children* (August 1990).

Other perspectives on the learning atmosphere in schools may be found in *In Search of Understanding: The Case for Constructivist Classrooms* by Jacqueline G. Brooks and Martin G. Brooks (1993); Dave Perkins, "The Many Faces of Constructivism," *Educational Leadership* (November 1999); and Robert J. Sternberg, "Ability and Expertise," *American Educator* (Spring 1999).

ISSUE 4

Should Church-State Separation
Be Maintained?

YES: R. Freeman Butts, from "A History and Civics Lesson for All of Us," *Educational Leadership* (May 1987)

NO: Robert L. Cord, from "Church-State Separation and the Public Schools: A Re-evaluation," *Educational Leadership* (May 1987)

ISSUE SUMMARY

YES: Professor emeritus of education R. Freeman Butts warns that current efforts to redefine the relationship between religion and schooling are eroding the Constitution's intent.

NO: Professor of political science Robert L. Cord offers a more accommodating interpretation of this intent, one that allows for the school practices that Butts condemns as unconstitutional.

T he religious grounding of early schooling in America certainly cannot be denied. Nor can the history of religious influences on the conduct of America's governmental functions and school practices. In the nineteenth century, however, protests against the prevailing Protestant influence in the public schools were lodged by Catholics, Jews, nonbelievers, and other groups, giving rise to a number of issues that revolve around interpretations of the "establishment of religion" and the "free exercise of religion" clauses of the Constitution.

Twentieth-century U.S. Supreme Court cases such as *Cochran* (1930), *Everson* (1947), *McCollum* (1948), *Zorach* (1952), *Engel* (1962), and *Murray* (1963) attempted to clarify the relationship between religion and schooling. Most of these decisions bolstered the separation of church and state position. Only recently has a countermovement, led in some quarters by the Christian Coalition organization of Pat Robertson, sought to sway public and legal opinion toward an emphasis on the "free exercise" clause and toward viewing the influence of secular humanism in the schools as "an establishment of religion."

At both the legislative and judicial levels, attempts were made in the 1980s to secure an official place in public education for voluntary prayer, moments of silent meditation, and creationism in the science curriculum. Censorship of textbooks and other school materials, access to facilities by religious groups, and the right of parents to withdraw their children from instruction deemed to be morally offensive and damaging have also been promoted. Humanists (who may be either religious or nonreligious) find a good deal of distortion in these recent attacks on the "secularization" of schooling, and they argue that the materials used in the schools are consistent with the historical goals of character development while also being in tune with the realities of the present times.

John Buchanan of People for the American Way argues that public schools are places where young people of differing backgrounds and beliefs can come together and learn tolerance. He and others worry that parental veto power will undermine decision making and impair school effectiveness. Bill Keith of the Creation Science Legal Defense Fund contends that a parent's liberty with regard to a child's education is a fundamental right, an enduring American tradition.

In the 1990s congressional attempts to pass a constitutional amendment allowing voluntary prayer in public schools were stymied, and two U.S. Supreme Court rulings came down on the side of church-state separation, although not without ambiguity. In the 1992 graduation prayer case *Lee v. Weisman,* which originated in Rhode Island, the 5–4 decision held that clergy-led devotionals at commencement exercises violated the establishment clause because of the coercive effect of the practice. In 1996, reviewing *Moore v. Ingrebretsen,* the Court rejected an appeal by Mississippi officials who sought to allow student-led prayer in public schools. State lawmakers had stipulated that "invocations, benedictions, or nonsectarian, non-proselytizing student-initiated voluntary prayer shall be permitted." The appellate court had upheld the suspension of enforcement of that law (except in cases of voluntary, student-led prayer at graduation ceremonies). A detailed examination of this aspect of the church-state separation issue can be found in Martha M. McCarthy's "Public School Prayer Continues to Spark Controversy and Possibly a Constitutional Amendment," *Educational Horizons* (Winter 1996).

Resolution of the philosophical questions regarding the content and conduct of public education has become increasingly politicized. Who should control the school curriculum and its materials—school boards, professional educators, community groups, the federal or state governments, parents, or students? Should censorship boards operate at the local, state, or national level —or none of the above? Where does the line get drawn between benevolent intervention and thought control? Can schools be value-neutral?

In the following selections, R. Freeman Butts makes the case that legal and historical scholarship points to the broader, separatist, and secular meaning of the First Amendment, which controls the answers to many of these questions. Robert L. Cord bases his argument for a more accommodating interpretation on his findings in primary historical sources and on the actions of the framers of the Constitution.

R. Freeman Butts

 **YES**

A History and Civics Lesson for All of Us

As chairman of the Commission on the Bicentennial of the U.S. Constitution, former Chief Justice Warren E. Burger urges that the occasion provide "a history and civics lesson for all of us." I heartily agree, but the lesson will depend on which version of history you read—and believe.

From May 1982, when President Reagan advocated adoption of a constitutional amendment to permit organized prayer in public schools, Congress has been bitterly divided during the repeated efforts to pass legislation aimed either at amending the Constitution or stripping the Supreme Court and other federal courts of jurisdiction to decide cases about prayers in the public schools. Similar controversies have arisen over efforts of the Reagan administration to promote vouchers and tuition tax credits to give financial aid to parents choosing to send their children to private religious schools.

School/Religion Controversies

I would like to remind educators that the present controversies have a long history, and the way we understand that history makes a difference in our policy judgments. A watershed debate occurred, for example, in 1947 when the Supreme Court spelled out the meaning of the part of the First Amendment which reads, "Congress shall make no law respecting an establishment of religion." The occasion was a challenge to a New Jersey law giving tax money to Catholic parents to send their children by bus to parochial schools. The Court split 5-4 in that case, *Everson* v. *Board of Education*, on whether this practice was, in effect, "an establishment of religion" and thus unconstitutional, but there was no disagreement on the principle. Justice Hugo Black wrote for the majority.

> The "establishment of religion" clause of the First Amendment means at least this: Neither a state nor the Federal Government can pass laws which aid one religion, aid all religions, or prefer one religion over another.... No tax in any amount, large or small, can be levied to support any religious activities or institutions, whatever they may be called, or whatever form they may adopt to teach or practice religion.... In the words of Jefferson,

From R. Freeman Butts, "A History and Civics Lesson for All of Us," *Educational Leadership,* vol. 44, no. 8 (May 1987), pp. 21–25. Copyright © 1987 by The Association for Supervision and Curriculum Development. Reprinted by permission. All rights reserved.

the clause against establishment of religion by law was intended to erect "a wall of separation between Church and State."[1]

The *Everson* majority accepted this broad principle, but decided, nevertheless, that bus fares were merely welfare aid to parents and children and not aid to the religious schools themselves. The 1948 *McCollum* case prohibited released time for religious instruction in the public schools of Champaign, Illinois, because it violated the *Everson* principle.

These two cases set off a thunderous denunciation of the Supreme Court and calls for impeachment of the justices. They also sent historians of education scurrying to original sources to see how valid this broad and liberal interpretation was.

Establishment Principle

The two books at that time that gave most attention to the establishment principle as it related to education were James M. O'Neill's *Religion and Education Under the Constitution*[2] and my own, *The American Tradition in Religion and Education.*[3] O'Neill found the Court's interpretation appalling; I found it basically true to Madison and the majority of the framers of the First Amendment. My book was cited in 1971 in the concurring opinions of Justices Brennan, Douglas, and Black in *Lemon* v. *Kurtzman.*[4] Chief Justice Burger summarized for a unanimous court the accumulated precedents since *Everson* and listed three tests of constitutional state action in education: a secular purpose; neither advancement nor inhibition of religion; and no excessive government entanglement with religion.

With that decision, I concluded that my views of the framers' intentions had been pretty well accepted: namely, that "an establishment of religion" in the 1780s was "a multiple establishment" whereby public aid could go to several churches, and that this is what the majority of framers, particularly Madison, intended to prohibit in the First Amendment.

Indeed, single religious establishments had existed in nine of the early colonies, but by 1789 when the First Congress drafted the First Amendment, religious diversity had become such a powerful political force that seven states, which included the vast majority of Americans, had either disestablished their churches or had never established any. Only six state constitutions still permitted "an establishment of religion," and all six provided tax funds for several churches, not just one.[5] Naturally, some representatives and senators from those states did not want their multiple establishment threatened by a Bill of Rights in the new federal government. But Madison did.

Madison had prevented just such a multiple establishment in Virginia in 1785 and 1786 and managed instead the passage of Jefferson's powerful Statute for Religious Freedom. In his speech of 8 June 1789, when he introduced his Bill of Rights proposals in the House, he made a double-barreled approach to religious freedom. He proposed (1) to prohibit Congress from establishing religion on a national basis, and (2) to prohibit the states from infringing "equal rights of conscience."

After considerable discussion and some changes of language, the House of Representatives approved both of Madison's proposals and sent them to the Senate. The Senate, however, did not approve the prohibition on the states. Furthermore, a minority in the Senate made three attempts to narrow the wording of the First Amendment to prohibit Congress from establishing a single church or giving preference to one religious sect or denomination. The majority, however, rejected all such attempts to narrow Madison's proposal, and the Senate finally accepted the wording of Madison's conference committee. This was then finally adopted by both houses. Madison's broad and liberal interpretation of the establishment clause as applied to Congress had won.[6]

Neither Madison nor the majority of framers intended for government to disdain religion. They intended that republican government guarantee equal rights of conscience to all persons, but it took some 150 years before Madison's views were applied specifically to the states through the Fourteenth Amendment. That is what the Supreme Court did in *Everson.*

Framers' Intentions Redefined

But today, "a jurisprudence of original intention" has revived the debates of the 1940s and 1950s, expounding much the same views as those of O'Neill namely that "the framers" intended only to prohibit Congress from establishing a single national church, but would permit aid to all religions on a nonpreferential basis and would even permit the states to establish a single church if they wished. These arguments are now being resurrected or reincarnated (to use the secular meaning of those terms) with even more sophisticated scholarship by such authors as Walter Berns of Georgetown University, Michael Malbin of the American Enterprise Institute, and Robert L. Cord of Northeastern University.[7]

Their works have been cited in legal briefs in several state actions and in at least one federal district court decision, while an increasingly vigorous campaign has been launched by conservative members of Congress and the Reagan administration to appeal to the history of "original intention."

These efforts reached a crescendo of confrontation in summer and fall of 1985, following two Supreme Court decisions. In *Wallace* v. *Jaffree* on 4 June 1985, the Court reversed Federal Judge W. Brevard Hand's decision that Alabama's laws providing for prayer in the public schools were, indeed, permissible and did not violate the First Amendment's prohibition against "an establishment of religion." Relying in part on Cord's version of history, Judge Hand argued that the Supreme Court had long erred in its reading of the original intention of the framers of the First Amendment. He said that they intended solely to prevent the federal government from establishing a single national church such as the Church of England; therefore, the Congress could aid all churches if it did not give preference to any one; that a state was free to establish a state religion if it chose to do so and, thus, could require or permit prayers in its public schools.

The Supreme Court reversed this decision (6-3), and Justice John Paul Stevens, writing for the Court, rebuked Judge Hand by referring to his "newly discovered historical evidence" as a "remarkable conclusion" wholly at odds with the firmly established constitutional provision that "the several States have no greater power to restrain the individual freedoms protected by the First Amendment than does the Congress of the United States." Justice Stevens emphasized that the Court had confirmed and endorsed time and time again the principle of incorporation, by which the Fourteenth Amendment imposes the same limitations on the states that it imposes on Congress regarding protection of civil liberties guaranteed by the First Amendment and the original Bill of Rights.[8]

However, the confrontations between these views of history were not over. In his long dissenting opinion in *Jaffree*, Associate Justice William H. Rehnquist, now Chief Justice, reasserted an "accommodationist" view of church and state relations. Relying on O'Neill's and Cord's version of history, he argued that the "wall of separation between church and state" is a metaphor based on bad history and that the *Everson* principle "should be frankly and explicitly abandoned." Justice Byron R. White's dissent also supported such "a basic reconsideration of our precedents."

Soon after, on 1 July 1985, the Supreme Court ruled in *Aguilar* v. *Fenton* (5-4) that the practices of New York City and Grand Rapids, Michigan, in sending public school teachers to private religious schools to teach remedial and enhancement programs for disadvantaged children, were also unconstitutional. Justice William J. Brennan, delivering the Court's opinion, cited the *Everson* principle that the state should remain neutral and not become entangled with churches in administering schools. Dissents were written by the Chief Justice and Justices Sandra Day O'Connor, White, and Rehnquist.[9]

These Supreme Court decisions were greeted with some surprise and considerable elation by liberals and with dismay by conservatives. Attorney General Edwin Meese III quickly and forcefully responded on 10 July 1985 in a speech before the American Bar Association. He explicitly criticized the Court's decisions on religion and education as a misreading of history and commended Justice Rehnquist's call for overruling *Everson*. Secretary of Education William Bennett echoed the complaint that the Supreme Court was misreading history. And, then, in October 1985 Justices Brennan and Stevens both gave speeches sharply criticizing the Attorney General's campaign for a "jurisprudence of original intention."

In addition, the White House, the Attorney General, the Justice Department, the Secretary of Education, the former Republican majority of the Senate Judiciary Committee, the new Chief Justice, and the conservative justices of the Supreme Court, by public statements are now ranged against the liberal and centrist members of the Supreme Court and such notable constitutional scholars as Laurence Tribe of Harvard, Herman Schwartz of American University, A. E. Dick Howard of the University of Virginia, and Leonard W. Levy of the Claremont Graduate School. They all appeal to history, but whose version of history do you read—and believe?

All in all, I think it fair to say that the predominant stream of constitutional, legal, and historical scholarship points to the broader, separatist, and secular meaning of the First Amendment against the narrower, cooperationist, or accommodationist meaning. A nonspecialist cannot encompass the vast literature on this subject, but a valuable and readily available source of evidence is the recently published book by Leonard Levy, professor of humanities and chairman of the Claremont University Graduate Faculty of History. He is editor of the *Encyclopedia of the American Constitution* and the author of a dozen books devoted mostly to the Bill of Rights.

In his book on the First Amendment's establishment clause Levy concludes, and I fully agree, that the meaning of "an establishment of religion" is as follows:

> After the American Revolution seven of the fourteen states that comprised the Union in 1791 authorized establishments of religion by law. Not one state maintained a single or preferential establishment of religion. An establishment of religion meant to those who framed and ratified the First Amendment what it meant in those seven states, and in all seven it meant public support of religion on a nonpreferential basis. It was specifically this support on a nonpreferential basis that the establishment clause of the First Amendment sought to forbid.[10]

Acceptance of a narrow, accommodationist view of the history of the establishment clause must not be allowed to be turned into public policies that serve to increase public support for religious schools in any form: vouchers, tax credits, or aid for extremes of "parental choice." They must not be allowed to increase the role of religion in public schools by organized prayer, teaching of Creationism, censorship of textbooks on the basis of their "secular humanism," or "opting out" of required studies in citizenship on the grounds that they offend any sincerely held religious belief, as ruled by Federal District Judge Thomas Hull in Greeneville, Tennessee, in October 1986.[11]

These practices not only violate good public policy, but they also vitiate the thrust toward separation of church and state which, with minor exceptions, marked the entire careers of Madison and Jefferson. William Lee Miller, professor of religious studies at the University of Virginia, wrote the following succinct summary of their views:

> Did "religious freedom" for Jefferson and Madison extend to atheists? Yes. To agnostics, unbelievers, and pagans? Yes. To heretics and blasphemers and the sacrilegious? Yes. To the Jew and the Gentile, the Christian and Mohametan, the Hindoo, and infidel of every denomination? Yes. To people who want freedom *from* religion? Yes. To people who want freedom *against* religion? Yes....
>
> Did this liberty of belief for Jefferson and Madison entail separation of church and state? Yes. A ban on tax aid to religion? Yes. On state help to religion? Yes. Even religion-in-general? Yes. Even if it were extended without any favoritism among religious groups? Yes. The completely voluntary way in religion? Yes.
>
> Did all the founders agree with Jefferson and Madison? Certainly not. Otherwise there wouldn't have been a fight.[12]

The fight not only continues, but seems to be intensifying on many fronts. So, it behooves educators to study these issues in depth, to consider the best historical scholarship available, and to judge present issues of religion and education accordingly.

Notes

1. *Everson* v. *Board of Education,* 330 U.S. 1 (1947). Black was joined by Chief Justice Vinson and Justices Douglas, Murphy, and Reed.

2. James M. O'Neill, *Religion and Education Under the Constitution* (New York: Harper, 1949). O'Neill was chairman of the department of speech at Queens College, New York. See also Wilfrid Parsons, S.J., *The First Freedom: Considerations on Church and State in the United States* (New York: Declan X. McMullen, 1948).

3. R. Freeman Butts, *The American Tradition in Religion and Education* (Boston: Beacon Press, 1950). I was professor of education at Teachers College, Columbia University, teaching courses in the history of education. See O'Neill's review of my book in *America,* 9 September 1950, pp. 579–583. See also Leo Pfeffer, *Church, State, and Freedom* (Boston: Beacon Press, 1953) for views similar to mine.

4. *Lemon* v. *Kurtzman,* 403 U.S. 602 (1971). The law struck down in Pennsylvania would have paid part of the salaries of private school teachers of nonreligious subjects.

5. Those six states were Massachusetts, Connecticut, New Hampshire, Maryland, South Carolina, and Georgia.

6. R. Freeman Butts, *Religion, Education, and the First Amendment: The Appeal to History* (Washington, D.C.: People for the American Way, 1985), 35. R. Freeman Butts, "James Madison, the Bill of Rights, and Education," *Teachers College Record* 60, 3 (December 1958): 123–128.

7. Walter Berns, *The First Amendment and the Future of American Democracy* (New York: Basic Books, 1976). Michael J. Malbin, *Religion and Politics: The Intentions of the Authors of the First Amendment* (Washington, D.C.: American Enterprise Institute, 1978). Robert L. Cord, *Separation of Church and State: Historical Fact and Current Fiction* (New York: Lambeth Press, 1982) with a Foreword by William F. Buckley, Jr.

8. *Wallace* v. *Jaffree,* 105 S.Ct. 2479 (1985).

9. *Aguilar* v. *Felton,* 105 S.Ct. 3232 (1985).

10. Leonard W. Levy, *The Establishment Clause: Religion and the First Amendment* (New York: Macmillan, 1986), p. xvi.

11. *Mozert* v. *Hawkins,* U.S. District Court for Eastern District of Tennessee, 24 October 1986.

12. *The Washington Post National Weekly Edition,* 13 October 1986, pp. 23–24.

Robert L. Cord

 **NO**

Church-State Separation and the Public Schools: A Re-evaluation

For four decades—since the *Everson* v. *Board of Education*[1] decision in 1947 —a volatile national debate has raged about the meaning and scope of the First Amendment's establishment clause that mandates separation of church and state. Many of the U.S. Supreme Court's decisions about this matter involve education; therefore, their importance is great to school administrators and teachers who establish and execute policy.

Because of the vagueness of Supreme Court decision making in this important area of constitutional law, public school educators have been accused of violating the First Amendment by allowing or disallowing, for example, the posting of the Ten Commandments, a meeting on school property of a student religious club, or a moment of silent meditation and/or prayer. Today even the very textbooks that students read have become a subject of litigation by parents against a school system, a controversy most likely to end before the Supreme Court.

As this national debate rages, most scholars generally agree that the Founding Fathers' intentions regarding church-state separation are still extremely relevant and important. While the framers of the Constitution and the First Amendment could not foresee many twentieth century problems—especially those growing from advanced technology—many church-state concerns that they addressed in 1787 and 1789 are similar to those we face today.

Constitution's Words Not Trivial

Further, if a nation, such as the United States, proclaims that its written Constitution protects individual liberties and truly provides legal restrictions on the actions of government, the words of that organic law—and the principles derived from them—cannot be treated as irrelevant trivia by those who temporarily govern. That is the surest single way to undo constitutional government, for constitutional government requires that the general power of government be defined and limited by law *in fact* as well as in theory.[2]

From Robert L. Cord, "Church-State Separation and the Public Schools: A Re-evaluation," *Educational Leadership,* vol. 44, no. 8 (May 1987), pp 26–32. Copyright © 1987 by The Association for Supervision and Curriculum Development. Reprinted by permission. All rights reserved.

Published in 1979 to the praise of many respected constitutional scholars, the encyclopedic *Congressional Quarterly's Guide to the U.S. Supreme Court*
provided the following meaning of the establishment clause.

> The two men most responsible for its inclusion in the Bill of Rights con-
> strued the clause *absolutely.* Thomas Jefferson and James Madison thought
> that the prohibition of establishment meant that a presidential proclamation
> of Thanksgiving Day was just as improper as a tax exemption for churches.[3]

Despite this authoritative statement, the historical facts are that, as President, James Madison issued at least four Thanksgiving Day proclamations—
9 July 1812, 23 July 1813, 16 November 1814, and 4 March 1815.[4] If Madison
interpreted the establishment clause absolutely, he violated both his oath of office and the very instruments of government that he helped write and labored
to have ratified.[5]

Similarly, if President Thomas Jefferson construed the establishment
clause absolutely, he also violated his oath of office, his principles, and the
Constitution when, in 1802, he signed into federal law tax exemption for the
churches in Alexandria County, Virginia.[6]

Since Jefferson and Madison held the concept of separation of church and
state most dear, in my judgment, neither man—as president or in any other
public office under the federal Constitution—was an absolutist and neither violated his understanding of the First Amendment's establishment clause. For
me, it therefore logically follows that President Madison did not think issuing Thanksgiving Day Proclamations violated the constitutional doctrine of
church-state separation, and that President Jefferson held the same view about
tax exemption for churches.

Whoever wrote the paragraph quoted from the prestigious *Guide to the
U.S. Supreme Court,* I assume, did not intend to deceive, but evidently did not
check primary historical sources, was ignorant of Madison's and Jefferson's actions when each was president, and mistakenly relied on inadequate secondary
historical writings considered authoritative, as no doubt the paragraph from
the *Guide* is, too. This indicates that much misunderstanding and/or misinformation exists about the meaning of the constitutional concept of separation of
church and state.

In that context, I examine ideas critical of my writing published in a
monograph—*Religion, Education, and the First Amendment: The Appeal to History*
—by the eminent scholar, R. Freeman Butts. There he characterized my book,
Separation of Church and State: Historical Fact and Current Fiction, as a manifestation of some "conservative counterreformation," the purpose of which is "to
attack once again the [U.S. Supreme] Court's adherence to the principle of separation between church and state" by characterizing that principle as a "myth"
or a "fiction" or merely "rhetoric."[7] The very first paragraph of my book refutes
this erroneous characterization.

> Separation of Church and State is probably the most distinctive concept that
> the American constitutional system has contributed to the body of politi-
> cal ideas. In 1791, when the First Amendment's prohibition that "Congress
> shall make no law respecting an establishment of religion" was added to

the United States Constitution, no other country had provided so carefully   .
to prevent the combination of the power of religion with the power of the
national government.[8]

While primary historical sources exist that substantiate the Founding Fathers' commitment to church-state separation, other primary sources convince me that much of what the United States Supreme Court and noted scholars have written about it is historically untenable and, in many instances, sheer fiction at odds with the words and actions of the statesmen who placed that very principle in our Constitution.

Absolute Separation v. "No Preference" Doctrine

In the 40-year-old *Everson* case the Supreme Court justices, while splitting 5-4 over the immediate issue, were unanimous in proclaiming that the purpose of the establishment clause—and the intention of its framers in the First Congress —was to create a "high and impregnable" wall of separation between church and state.[9]

Unlike the *Everson* Court, Professor Butts, and all "absolute separationist" scholars, I think the full weight of historical evidence—especially the documented public words and deeds of the First Amendment's framers, including James Madison and our early presidents and Congresses—indicates that they embraced a far narrower concept of church-state separation. In my judgment, they interpreted the First Amendment as prohibiting Congress from (1) creating a national religion or establishment, and (2) placing any one religion, religious sect, or religious tradition in a legally preferred position.[10]

Simply put, the framers of the establishment clause sought to preclude discriminatory government religious partisanship, not nondiscriminatory government accommodation or, in some instances, government collaboration with religion. When this "no religious preference" interpretation of the establishment clause is substituted for the Supreme Court's "high and impregnable wall" interpretation, it is easier to understand many historical documents at odds with the absolutists' position. They substantiate that all our early Congresses, including the one that proposed to the states what subsequently became the First Amendment, and all our early presidents, including Jefferson and Madison, in one way or another used sectarian means to achieve constitutional secular ends.

Everson Case

In the *Everson* case, writing the Court's opinion, Justice Black sought to bolster his "high and impregnable wall" dictum with appeals to some carefully chosen actions of Madison, Jefferson, the Virginia Legislature of 1786, and the framers of the First Amendment. Omitted from all of the *Everson* opinions are any historical facts that run counter to that theory. In his writings, I think Professor Butts employs a similar technique of "history by omission." By this I mean that he fails to address indisputable historical facts that are irreconcilable with his absolute separationist views. A few examples will substantiate this extremely important point.

Mentioning Madison's successful Virginia battle against the "Bill Establishing a Provision for Teachers of the Christian Religion" and "Jefferson's historic statute for religious freedom in 1786,"[11] Professor Butts does not explain away Jefferson's Virginia "Bill for Punishing Disturbers of Religious Worship and Sabbath Breakers," which was introduced by Madison in the Virginia Assembly in 1785 and became law in 1786.[12] Further, while he emphasizes Madison's role in introducing and guiding the Bill of Rights through the First Congress,[13] Professor Butts does not explain why the "absolutist" Madison served as one of six members of a Congressional Committee which, without recorded dissent, recommended the establishment of a Congressional Chaplain System. Adopting the Committee's recommendation, the First Congress voted a $500 annual salary from public funds for a Senate chaplain and a like amount for a House chaplain, both of whom were to offer public prayers in Congress.[14]

Nor does Professor Butts explain why, as an absolute separationist, James Madison would, as president, issue discretionary proclamations of Thanksgiving, calling for a day "to be set apart for the devout purposes of rendering the Sovereign of the Universe and the Benefactor of Man [identified earlier in the proclamation by Madison as "Almighty God"] the public homage due to His holy attributes...."[15]

Unexplained also is why Professor Butts' absolute separationist version of Thomas Jefferson would, as president, conclude a treaty with Kaskaskia Indians which, in part, called for the United States to build them a Roman Catholic Church and pay their priest, and subsequently would urge Congress to appropriate public funds to carry out the terms of the treaty.[16] An understanding of what the framers of our Constitution thought about church-state separation would also be furthered if we had explanations of why Presidents Washington, John Adams, and Jefferson apparently did not think they were breaching the "high and impregnable" wall when they signed into law Congressional bills that, in effect, purchased with enormous grants of federal land, in controlling trusts, the services of the "Society of the United Brethren for propagating the Gospel among the Heathen" to minister to the needs of Christian and other Indians in the Ohio Territory.[17] Like the majority of the Supreme Court, Professor Butts does not comment on these historical documents and events.

When all the historical evidence is considered, I think it relatively clear that the establishment clause was designed to prevent Congress from either establishing a national religion or from putting any one religion, religious sect, or religious tradition into a legally preferred position. In *Everson*, the Supreme Court interpreted the Fourteenth Amendment as prohibiting state legislatures, or their instrumentalities such as school boards, from doing likewise. As a result, the interpretation of the establishment clause by Supreme Court decisions governs the permissible range of both state and federal legislative authority.

Professor Butts thinks my definition of an "establishment of religion" too narrow, and the prohibition which I think the framers intended "plausible but false."[18] Plausible because in the sixteenth and seventeenth centuries, establishments in Europe and in the early American colonies usually meant the establishment of a single church. False because Professor Butts contends that, by the end of the eighteenth century, in America the term "establishment of religion" had taken on a different meaning.

His argument is that "the idea of a single church as constituting 'an establishment of religion' was no longer embedded in the legal framework of any American state when the First Amendment was being debated in Congress in the summer of 1789." Adding that in all of the states that still retained establishments, "multiple establishments were the rule," Professor Butts concludes that "the founders and the framers could not have been ignorant of this fact; they knew very well that this is what the majority in the First Congress intended to prohibit at the federal level."[19]

Butts' Argument Untenable

This argument is simply untenable when considered with the primary historical record. Professor Butts virtually ignored the documents most crucial to an understanding of what the religion clauses were designed to prohibit at the federal level—the suggested constitutional amendments from the various State Ratifying Conventions. Those documents show that they feared, among other things, that important individual rights might be infringed by the powerful new national legislature authorized by the adoption of the federal Constitution.

Their amendments indicate that the states feared interference with the individual's right of conscience and an exclusive religious establishment, *not a multiple national establishment,* as Professor Butts wants us to believe. Typical was the Maryland Ratifying Convention's proposed amendment stating "that there will be no national religion established by law; but that all persons be equally entitled to protection in their religious liberty."[20]

The Virginia Ratifying Convention proposed a "Declaration of Bill of Rights" as amendments to the Constitution that was echoed by North Carolina, Rhode Island, and New York Conventions. Virginia's Article Twenty, adopted 27 June 1788, stated:

> That religion, or the duty which we owe to our Creator, and the manner of discharging it, can be directed only by reason and conviction, not by force or violence; and therefore all men have an equal, natural, and unalienable right to the free exercise of religion, according to the dictates of conscience, and that no particular religious sect or society ought to be favored or established, by law, in preference to others.[21]

States Wanted Nonpreference

In short, when it came to religious establishments, the State Ratifying Conventions proposed "nonpreference" amendments.

With these proposals in mind, it is easier to understand the wording of Madison's original religion amendment: "The Civil rights of none shall be abridged on account of religious belief or worship, nor shall any national religion be established, nor shall the full and equal rights of Conscience be in any manner, or on any pretext, infringed."[22] Madison wanted the Constitution to forbid the federal government from interfering with the rights of conscience or establish an exclusive national religion—not religions—and the record said so.

The "nonpreference" interpretation is further bolstered by Madison's original wording of his own establishment clause and his later interpretation on the floor of the House of Representatives of the intended prohibitions of the amendment. On 15 August 1789, using virtually the same words employed by the petitioning State Ratifying Conventions,

> Mr. Madison said, he apprehended the meaning of the words to be, that Congress should not establish a religion, and enforce the legal observation of it by law, nor compel men to worship God in any manner contrary to their conscience. Whether the words are necessary or not, he did not mean to say, but... he thought it as well expressed as the nature of the language would admit.[23]

Further, the House record indicates that Madison said that "he believed that the people feared one sect might obtain a preeminence, or two combine together, and establish a religion to which they would compel others to conform."[24] Certainly Madison's statements from the record of the First Congress and the other primary documents mentioned here run contrary to the "multiple establishment" thesis.

Implications for the Public Schools

Professionals in education may wonder appropriately what the impact would be on public education should the U.S. Supreme Court now choose to reverse some of its major rulings and adopt the narrower interpretation of church-state separation which I believe was intended and embraced by the First Amendment's framers.

First, the establishment clause would continue to prohibit Congress and individual states from creating, in Madison's words, "a national religion."

Second, in keeping with the framers' intent, the establishment clause's "no preference" doctrine, applied directly to the federal government and to the states by the Fourteenth Amendment, would constitutionally preclude all governmental entities from placing any one religion, religious sect, or religious tradition into a preferred legal status. As a consequence, in public schools, the recitation of the Lord's Prayer or readings taken solely from the New Testament would continue to be unconstitutional because they place the Christian religion in a preferred position.

Similarly, the posting of the Ten Commandments only or reading only from the Old Testament would place the Judeo-Christian tradition in an unconstitutionally favored religious status. However, unendorsed readings or postings from many writings considered sacred by various religions, such as the Book of Mormon, the interpretative writings of Mary Baker Eddy, the Bible, the Koran, the Analects of Confucius, would be constitutional. A decision to teach only "creationism" or Genesis would be unconstitutional, while a course in cosmology, exploring a full range of beliefs about the origin of life or the nature of the universe—religious, areligious, or nonreligious—would not violate the First Amendment any more than would a course on comparative religions without teacher endorsement.

In all circumstances where the state is pursuing a valid educational goal, and is religiously nonpartisan in doing so, the professional leadership of the educational unit would decide, as in any other policy, whether such an activity was educationally appropriate or desirable. This would be the case whether the educational unit was a school, a school district, or an entire state educational system. Consequently, adherence to the "no preference" doctrine would return many policy decisions to the appropriate educational authorities, elected or appointed, and reduce the all too frequent present pattern of government by judiciary.

Third, although the First Amendment's free exercise of religion clause would not be contracted by the "no preference" principle, that interpretation would, in some instances, expand the individual's free exercise of religion and other First Amendment rights. This would happen where "equal access" is currently denied public school students.

Equal Access Act

The Equal Access Act of 1984 (Public Law 98-377) prohibits public high schools receiving federal aid from preventing voluntary student groups, including religious ones, from meeting in school facilities before and after class hours or during a club period, if other extracurricular groups have access.[25] The constitutionality of refusing "equal access" to voluntary student religious organizations was litigated in the lower courts[26] before reaching the U.S. Supreme Court in *Bender* v. *Williamsport* in March 1986.[27]

In deciding equal access cases, the lower federal courts applied the Supreme Court's "three part *Lemon*" test to determine whether the establishment clause had been violated. Under this test, first described in *Lemon* v. *Kurtzman,* the Supreme Court held that in order to pass constitutional muster under the establishment clause, the challenged governmental policy or activity must (1) have a secular purpose, (2) be one that has a principal or primary effect which neither advances nor inhibits religion, and (3) not foster an excessive government entanglement with religion.[28]

The "no preference" doctrine, on the other hand, would provide a relatively clearer and easier-to-apply test. Alleged violations would be measured by two simple questions: (1) Is the governmental action within the constitutional power of the acting public body? and (2) Does the governmental action elevate any one religion, religious sect, or religious tradition into a preferred legal status? Either a "no" to the first question or a "yes" to the second would make the policy unconstitutional.

Unlike the *Lemon* interpretation, the "no preference" interpretation poses less danger to a student's individual First and Fourteenth Amendment liberty. The Third U.S. Circuit Court's decision in *Bender* v. *Williamsport* illustrates this point. There the court held that it was constitutional for a school board to refuse to permit a student-initiated nondenominational prayer club to meet during the regularly scheduled activity period in a public school room.[29] As I see it, that decision subordinated three First Amendment freedoms—free exercise of religion, freedom of speech, and voluntary assembly—to one misinterpreted First Amendment guarantee. Under the "no preference" doctrine, equal access would be guaranteed to *all* religious or, for that matter, irreligious student groups under the same conditions that apply to any other voluntary student group.

Application of the "no preference" interpretation also avoids enormous dangers to an "open society" possible under the *Lemon* test. Can we not see that a court which can hold today that a classroom could not be used by a voluntary religious student group because that use may have as its primary effect the advancement of religion, can tomorrow, by the same logic, bar meeting rooms to students who want to discuss atheism or a book negative about religion, such as Bertrand Russell's *Why I Am Not a Christian,* because the primary effect there might be said to inhibit religion? By the use of *Lemon's* "primary effect" test, books about religion or those said to be irreligious can be removed from public school libraries. Is C. S. Lewis' *The Screwtape Letters* safe? And what about *Inherit the Wind,* or Darwin's *Origin of the Species?* Are we so frightened of ourselves that we are willing to disallow, in our institutions of learning, scrutinization of ultimate issues and values because of fear about where an open marketplace of ideas may eventually take the nation?

Finally, while some actions such as an uncoerced moment of silence for meditation and/or prayer in a public schoolroom[30] or the teaching of educationally deprived students from low-income families for several hours each week in a parochial school by public school teachers, recently held unconstitutional,[31] would be constitutional under the "no preference" interpretation, that does not mean they would automatically become educational policy. In all public educational entities, large or small, what would become policy would be up to the legally empowered decision makers in each of those entities.

Notes

1. 330 U.S. 1 (1947).
2. Charles H. McIlwain, *Constitutionalism: Ancient and Modern,* rev. ed. (Ithaca, N.Y.: Great Seal Books, 1958), 19-22.
3. *Congressional Quarterly's Guide to the United States Supreme Court* (Washington, D.C.: Congressional Quarterly, Inc., 1979), 461. Emphasis added. The First Amendment has two religion clauses, the "establishment" clause and the "free exercise" clause. U.S. Constitution Amendment I: "Congress shall make no law respecting an establishment of religion, or prohibiting the free exercise thereof...."
4. These proclamations, in their entirety, are published in James D. Richardson, *A Contemplation of the Messages and Papers of the Presidents, 1789-1897,* vol. I (Washington, D.C.: Bureau of National Literature and Art, 1901), 34-35; and Robert L. Cord, *Separation of Church and State: Historical Fact and Current Fiction* (Grand Rapids, Michigan: Baker Book House, 1988), 257-260.
5. After he had left the presidency, and toward the end of his life, Madison wrote a document commonly known as the "Detached Memoranda," which was first published as recently as 1946 in *William and Mary Quarterly* 3 (1946): 534. In it Madison *does* say that Thanksgiving Day proclamations are unconstitutional,

as are chaplains in Congress. In light of his actions in public office, these were obviously not his views as a congressman and president. For a fuller discussion of Madison's "Detached Memoranda," see Cord, *Separation*, 29-36.

6. *2 Statutes at Large* 194, Seventh Congress, Sess. 1, Chap. 52. Jefferson *did* believe Thanksgiving Proclamation violated the First Amendment and, unlike Washington, John Adams, and James Madison, declined to issue them.

7. R. Freeman Butts, *Religion, Education, and the First Amendment: The Appeal to History* (Washington, D.C.: People for the American Way, 1986), 9. Butts, an educational historian, is William F. Russell Professor Emeritus, Teachers College, Columbia University; Senior Fellow of the Kettering Foundation; and Visiting Scholar at the Hoover Institution, Stanford University.

8. Cord, *Separation*, XIII.

9. For an extensive critique of the *Everson* case and its interpretation of the establishment clause, see Cord, *Separation*, 103-133.

10. For in-depth study of the "no preference" principle, see Robert L. Cord, "Church-State Separation: Restoring the 'No Preference' Doctrine of the First Amendment," *Harvard Journal of Law & Public Policy* 9 (1986): 129.

11. Butts, *Religion*, 18.

12. Cord, *Separation*, 215-218.

13. Butts, *Religion*, 18-21.

14. Cord, *Separation*, 22-26.

15. Quoted from President Madison's "Proclamation" of "the 9th day of July A.D. 1812." This proclamation is republished in its entirety in Cord, *Separation*, 257.

16. For the entire text of the treaty, see Ibid., 261-263.

17. The full texts of these laws are republished in Cord, 263-270.

18. Butts, *Religion*, 16.

19. Ibid., 18.

20. Jonathan Elliott, *Debates on the Federal Constitution*, vol. II (Philadelphia: J.B. Lippincott Co., 1901), 553.

21. Ibid., vol. III, 659.

22. *Annals of the Congress of the United States, The Debates and Proceedings in the Congress of the United States*, vol. I, Compiled from Authentic Materials, by Joseph Gales, Senior (Washington, D.C.: Gales and Seaton, 1834), 434.

23. Ibid., 730.

24. Ibid., 731.

25. *Congressional Quarterly Weekly Report*, vols. 42, p. 1545, 1854; 43, p. 1807.

26. *Brandon* v. *Board of Education*, 635 F. 2d 971 (2d Cir. 1980); *cert. denied*, 454 U.S. 1123 (1981); *Lubbock Civil Liberties Union* v. *Lubbock Independent School District*, 669 F. 2d 1038 (5th Cir. 1982), *cert. denied*, 459 U.S. 1155 (1983).

27. *Bender* v. *Williamsport*, 475 U.S. 534, 89 L.Ed. 2d 501 (1986). While the Third Circuit Court dealt with the "equal access" question, the Supreme Court did not reach that constitutional issue because one of the parties to the suit in the Circuit Court lacked standing and, therefore, that Court should have dismissed the case for want of jurisdiction. Ibid., 516.

28. *Lemon* v. *Kurtzman,* 403 U.S. 602, 612, 613 (1971).

29. *Bender* v. *Williamsport,* 741 F. 2d 538, 541 (3rd Cir. 1984).

30. In *Wallace* v. *Jaffree,* 105 S. Ct. 2479 (1985), the U.S. Supreme Court held such a law unconstitutional.

31. In *Grand Rapids* v. *Ball,* 473 U.S. 373, 87 L.Ed. 2d 267 (1985) and *Aguilar* v. *Felton,* 473 U.S. 402, 87 L.Ed. 2d 290 (1985), the Supreme Court held similar programs unconstitutional.

POSTSCRIPT

Should Church-State Separation Be Maintained?

If the Constitution indeed attempts to guarantee the protection of minority opinions from a possibly oppressive majority, can it be applied equally to all parties in any value-laden dispute such as those involving the relationship of church and state? An exhaustive review of historical cases dealing with manifestations of this basic problem may be found in Martha McCarthy's article "Religion and Public Schools," in the August 1985 issue of the *Harvard Educational Review*.

A wide variety of articles is available on this volatile area of concern, including "Textbook Censorship and Secular Humanism in Perspective," by Franklin Parker, *Religion and Public Education* (Summer 1988); Rod Farmer's "Toward a Definition of Secular Humanism," *Contemporary Education* (Spring 1987); Mel and Norma Gabler's "Moral Relativism on the Ropes," *Communication Education* (October 1987); and Donald Vandenberg's "Education and the Religious," *Teachers College Record* (Fall 1987).

Three other provocative sources of insights are Thomas W. Goodhue's "What Should Public Schools Say About Religion?" *Education Week* (April 23, 1986); "How Prayer and Public Schooling Can Coexist," Eugene W. Kelly, Jr., *Education Week* (November 12, 1986); and Edward A. Wynne's "The Case for Censorship to Protect the Young," *Issues in Education* (Winter 1985).

Other excellent sources are Warren A. Nord, "The Place of Religion in the World of Public School Textbooks," and Mark G. Yudof, "Religion, Textbooks, and the Public Schools," both in *The Educational Forum* (Spring 1990); James Davison Hunter's "Modern Pluralism and the First Amendment," *The Brookings Review* (Spring 1990); "Taking a Few Bricks Off the Wall: The Effect of Three Recent Cases on the Separation of Church and State," *Journal of Law and Education* (Spring 1995); Elliott A. Wright, "Religion in American Education: A Historical View," *Phi Delta Kappan* (September 1999); and Michael H. Romanowski and Keith M. Talbert, "Addressing the Influence of Religion and Faith in American History," *The Clearing House* (January/February 2000).

Books that explore aspects of the issue include *The Rights of Religious Persons in Public Education* by John W. Whitehead (1991); *Religious Fundamentalism and American Education: The Battle for the Public Schools* by Eugene F. Provenzo, Jr. (1990); *A Standard for Repair: The Establishment of Religion Clause of the U.S. Constitution* by Jeremy Gunn (1992); and *Why We Still Need Public Schools: Church/State Relations and Visions of Democracy* edited by Art Must, Jr. (1992).

In the end, the main problem is one of finding an appropriate balance between the two First Amendment clauses within the context of public schooling and making that balance palatable and realizable at the local school level.

ISSUE 5

Should School Attendance
Be Compelled?

YES: Horace Mann, from *Tenth Annual Report* and *Twelfth Annual Report* (1846 and 1848)

NO: Barry McGhan, from "Compulsory School Attendance: An Idea Past Its Prime?" *The Educational Forum* (Winter 1997)

ISSUE SUMMARY

YES: Horace Mann, a leader of the common school movement in the nineteenth century, presents the basic arguments for publicly funded education in which all citizens could participate and lays the groundwork for compulsory attendance laws.

NO: Barry McGhan, who heads the Center for Public School Renewal, argues that the time has come to switch to a voluntary attendance approach to schooling, which would benefit everyone involved.

T he common school crusade, led by Massachusetts education leader Horace Mann (1796–1859) and other activists, built on the growing sentiment among citizens and business leaders that public schools were needed to deal with the increase in immigration, urbanization, and industrialism, as well as to bind together the American population and to prepare everyone for participatory democracy.

As the free public school movement got underway, however, it became clear that quite a few parents were reluctant to send their children to school because many of them contributed to the economic well-being of the family. Mann, who had observed first-hand the effectiveness of compulsory school attendance in Prussia, pushed for such legislation in Massachusetts. In 1852 an Act Concerning the Attendance of Children at School was passed, compelling all children from age 8 to 14 to attend school (public or private) for at least 12 weeks each year. Between that time and 1918 all of the states passed similar laws with expanded periods of attendance and stiff penalties for noncompliance.

For the most part, the right of the government to compel school attendance went unchallenged. In the 1920s there were even efforts to eliminate all alternatives to public schooling as a means of compliance. Such an effort in Oregon was challenged in court, and the U.S. Supreme Court ultimately ruled, in *Pierce v. Society of Sisters* (1925), that such legislation unreasonably interferes with parental rights. While this ruling preserved the private school option, it did not alter the governmental prerogative to compel school attendance.

Beginning in the 1950s an increasing number of activists and scholars produced sharp criticisms of this governmental authority, and this barrage has continued to the present day. Among the more widely discussed of these works are Paul Goodman's *Compulsory Mis-education* (1964), Ivan Illich's *Deschooling Society* (1971), Carl Bereiter's *Must We Educate?* (1973), John Holt's *Instead of Education* (1976), Roger White's *Absent With Cause* (1980), and John Taylor Gatto's *Dumbing Us Down: The Hidden Curriculum of Compulsory Schooling* (1992).

Goodman felt that attendance should only be compelled during the elementary school years and that adolescents need more freedom and support to fashion their own education and training. Illich campaigned for the abolition of all compulsory education, contending that only in a "deschooled" society could meaningful education occur. He argued that the present laws led to an artificial system of sifting and rewarding that is unfair and unproductive. More recently, Gatto has attacked the historical basis of compulsory schooling. For him, Mann's admiration of the Prussian approach guaranteed the evolution of a system that emphasizes obedience and subordination rather than the unleashing of the intellectual and creative powers of the individual.

Jackson Toby, in "Obsessive Compulsion," *National Review* (June 28, 1999), condemns the folly of mandatory high school attendance. Toby cites three myths undergirding present policies: (1) adolescents can be educated whether they like it or not; (2) the students who will leave school as soon as they can will generate a crime wave; and (3) those who do not complete high school are doomed to live an economically and culturally impoverished life.

The home schooling movement, which has expanded during the past three decades, is another manifestation of parental concern over the manipulativeness of a governmentally mandated system. Almost all states have accommodated parents who select this alternative while still maintaining varying degrees of control over the process. According to Howard Klepper, in "Mandatory Rights and Compulsory Education," *Law and Philosophy* (May 1996), the public has a right to an educated citizenry in order to ensure the collective good. "The best way we know to protect this public right," he states, "is to compel schooling." The justification of compulsory education involves not individual benefit but societal benefit.

In the following selections, Mann's original argument for a system of common schools to bind together the diverse people of the new nation is opposed by Barry McGhan's present-day position that compelled attendance is no longer appropriate.

Horace Mann

 **YES**

The Education of Free Men

I believe in the existence of a great, immutable principle of natural law, or natural ethics,—a principle antecedent to all human institutions and incapable of being abrogated by any ordinances of man,—a principle of divine origin, clearly legible in the ways of Providence as those ways are manifested in the order of nature and in the history of the race,—which proves the *absolute right* of every human being that comes into the world to an education; and which, of course, proves the correlative duty of every government to see that the means of that education are provided for all.

In regard to the application of this principle of natural law,—that is, in regard to the extent of the education to be provided for all, at the public expense, —some differences of opinion may fairly exist, under different political organizations; but under a republican government, it seems clear that the minimum of this education can never be less than such as is sufficient to qualify each citizen for the civil and social duties he will be called to discharge;—such an education as teaches the individual the great laws of bodily health; as qualifies for the fulfilment of parental duties; as is indispensable for the civil functions of a witness or a juror; as is necessary for the voter in municipal affairs; and finally, for the faithful and conscientious discharge of all those duties which devolve upon the inheritor of a portion of the sovereignty of this great republic. . . .

In obedience to the laws of God and to the laws of all civilized communities, society is bound to protect the natural life; and the natural life cannot be protected without the appropriation and use of a portion of the property which society possesses. We prohibit infanticide under penalty of death. We practise a refinement in this particular. The life of an infant is inviolable even before he is born; and he who feloniously takes it, even before birth, is as subject to the extreme penalty of the law, as though he had struck down manhood in its vigor, or taken away a mother by violence from the sanctuary of home, where she blesses her offspring. But why preserve the natural life of a child, why preserve unborn embryos of life, if we do not intend to watch over and to protect them, and to expand their subsequent existence into usefulness and happiness? As individuals, or as an organized community, we have no natural right; we can derive no authority or countenance from reason; we can cite no attribute or purpose of the divine nature, for giving birth to any human being,

From Horace Mann, *Tenth Annual Report* and *Twelfth Annual Report* (1846, 1848).

and then inflicting upon that being the curse of ignorance, of poverty and of vice, with all their attendant calamities. We are brought then to this startling but inevitable alternative. The natural life of an infant should be extinguished as soon as it is born, or the means should be provided to save that life from being a curse to its possessor; and therefore every State is bound to enact a code of laws legalizing and enforcing Infanticide, or a code of laws establishing Free Schools! ...

⋅⟨⊙⟩⋅

Under the Providence of God, our means of education are the grand machinery by which the "raw material" of human nature can be worked up into inventors and discoverers, into skilled artisans and scientific farmers, into scholars and jurists, into the founders of benevolent institutions, and the great expounders of ethical and theological science. By means of early education, those embryos of talent may be quickened, which will solve the difficult problems of political and economical law; and by them, too, the genius may be kindled which will blaze forth in the Poets of Humanity. Our schools, far more than they have done, may supply the Presidents and Professors of Colleges, and Superintendents of Public Instruction, all over the land; and send, not only into our sister states, but across the Atlantic, the men of practical science, to superintend the construction of the great works of art. Here, too, may those judicial powers be developed and invigorated, which will make legal principles so clear and convincing as to prevent appeals to force; and, should the clouds of war ever lower over our country, some hero may be found,—the nursling of our schools, and ready to become the leader of our armies,—that best of all heroes, who will secure the glories of a peace, unstained by the magnificient murders of the battle-field. ...

Without undervaluing any other human agency, it may be safely affirmed that the Common School, improved and energized, as it can easily be, may become the most effective and benignant of all the forces of civilization. Two reasons sustain this position. In the first place, there is a universality in its operation, which can be affirmed of no other institution whatever. If administered in the spirit of justice and conciliation, all the rising generation may be brought within the circle of its reformatory and elevating influences. And, in the second place, the materials upon which it operates are so pliant and ductile as to be susceptible of assuming a greater variety of forms than any other earthly work of the Creator. The inflexibility and ruggedness of the oak, when compared with the lithe sapling or the tender germ, are but feeble emblems to typify the docility of childhood, when contrasted with the obduracy and intractableness of man. It is these inherent advantages of the Common School, which, in our own State, have produced results so striking, from a system so imperfect, and an administration so feeble. In teaching the blind, and the deaf and dumb, in kindling the latent spark of intelligence that lurks in an idiot's mind, and in the more holy work of reforming abandoned and outcast children, education has proved what it can do, by glorious experiments. These wonders, it has done in its infancy, and with the lights of a limited experience; but, when its faculties shall be fully developed, when it shall be trained to wield its mighty energies for the protection of society against the giant vices which now invade and torment it;—against intemperance, avarice, war, slavery, bigotry, the woes of want and the wickedness of waste,—then, there will not be a height to which these enemies of the race can escape, which it will not scale, nor a Titan among them all, whom it will not slay. . . .

Now, surely, nothing but Universal Education can counter-work this tendency to the domination of capital and the servility of labor. If one class possesses all the wealth and the education, while the residue of society is ignorant and poor, it matters not by what name the relation between them may be called; the latter, in fact and in truth, will be the servile dependants and subjects of the former. But if education be equably diffused, it will draw property after it, by the strongest of all attractions; for such a thing never did happen, and never can happen, as that an intelligent and practical body of men should be permanently poor. Property and labor, in different classes, are essentially antagonistic; but property and labor, in the same class, are essentially fraternal. The people of Massachusetts have, in some degree, appreciated the truth, that the unexampled prosperity of the State,—its comfort, its competence, its general intelligence and virtue,—is attributable to the education, more or less perfect, which all its people have received; but are they sensible of a fact equally important?—namely, that it is to this same education that two thirds of the people are indebted for not being, to-day, the vassals of as severe a tyranny, in the form of capital, as the lower classes of Europe are bound to in the form of brute force.

Education, then, beyond all other devices of human origin, is the great equalizer of the conditions of men—the balance-wheel of the social machinery. I do not here mean that it so elevates the moral nature as to make men disdain and abhor the oppression of their fellow-men. This idea pertains to another of its attributes. But I mean that it gives each man the independence and the means, by which he can resist the selfishness of other men. It does better than to disarm the poor of their hostility towards the rich; it prevents being poor. Agrarianism is the revenge of poverty against wealth. The wanton destruction of the property of others,—the burning of hay-ricks and corn-ricks, the demolition of machinery, because it supersedes hand-labor, the sprinkling of vitriol on rich dresses,—is only agrarianism run mad. Education prevents both the revenge and the madness. On the other hand, a fellow-feeling for one's class or caste is the common instinct of hearts not wholly sunk in selfish regards for person, or for family. The spread of education, by enlarging the cultivated class or caste, will open a wider area over which the social feelings will expand; and, if this education should be universal and complete, it would do more than all things else to obliterate factitious distinctions in society. . . .

But to all doubters, disbelievers, or despairers, in human progress, it may still be said, there is one experiment which has never yet been tried. It is an experiment which, even before its inception, offers the highest authority for its ultimate success. Its formula is intelligible to all; and it is as legible as though written in starry letters on an azure sky. It is expressed in these few and simple words:—*"Train up a child in the way he should go, and when he is old he will not depart from it."* This declaration is positive. If the conditions are complied with, it makes no provision for a failure. Though pertaining to morals, yet, if the terms of the direction are observed, there is no more reason to doubt the result, than there would be in an optical or a chemical experiment.

But this experiment has never yet been tried. Education has never yet been brought to bear with one hundredth part of its potential force, upon the natures of children, and, through them, upon the character of men, and of the race. In all the attempts to reform mankind which have hitherto been made, whether by changing the frame of government, by aggravating or softening the severity of the penal code, or by substituting a government-created, for a God-created religion;—in all these attempts, the infantile and youthful mind, its amenability to influences, and the enduring and self-operating character of the influences it receives, have been almost wholly unrecognized. Here, then, is a new agency, whose powers are but just beginning to be understood, and whose mighty energies, hitherto, have been but feebly invoked; and yet, from our experience, limited and imperfect as it is, we do know that, far beyond any other earthly instrumentality, it is comprehensive and decisive. . . .

If, then, a government would recognize and protect the rights of religious freedom, it must abstain from subjugating the capacities of its children to any legal standard of religious faith, with as great fidelity as it abstains from controlling the opinions of men. It must meet the unquestionable fact, that the old spirit of religious domination is adopting new measures to accomplish its work, —measures, which, if successful, will be as fatal to the liberties of mankind, as those which were practised in by-gone days of violence and terror. These new measures are aimed at children instead of men. They propose to supersede the necessity of subduing free thought, *in the mind of the adult,* by forestalling the development of any capacity of free thought, *in the mind of the child.* They expect to find it easier to subdue the free agency of children, by binding them in fetters of bigotry, than to subdue the free agency of men, by binding them in fetters of iron. For this purpose, some are attempting to deprive children of their right to labor, and, of course, of their daily bread, unless they will attend a government school, and receive its sectarian instruction. Some are attempting to withhold all means, even of secular education, from the poor, and thus punish them with ignorance, unless, with the secular knowledge which they desire, they will accept theological knowledge which they condemn. Others, still, are striving to break down all free Public School systems, where they exist, and to prevent their establishment, where they do not exist, in the hope, that on the downfall of these, their system will succeed. The sovereign antidote against these machinations, is, Free Schools for all, and the right of every parent to determine the religious education of his children.

Barry McGhan

Compulsory School Attendance: An Idea Past Its Prime?

The growing clamor for school choice has raised much debate about the quality of education in the United States. However, such debate obscures an important, though subtle, message—that the era of U.S. compulsory education is perhaps coming to an end. Because the premise of most school-choice options is to provide alternatives to traditional education deemed appropriate for targeted audiences, a principal effect of the choice movement will be to challenge the idea that every child between the ages of 6 and 16 has to be in class every school day.

Interest in school choice is not another educational fad, but instead is rooted in real and perceived social changes that are becoming incongruent with regulations for compulsory attendance. Hopefully, in our efforts to meet educational challenges stimulated by changing societal expectations, we will not allow public education itself to be dismantled. However, if compulsory attendance is removed as a requirement of public education, perhaps much of the current complaining about schools would diminish.

Compulsory education has not yet been openly challenged by school-choice proposals, in part, because it is so deeply ingrained in our thinking. "Compulsory education" is virtually synonymous with "public education"—we fail to see it as a separate element of schooling. There are, however, signs that this situation may be starting to change. In recent months, news stories have addressed:

- the American Federation of Teachers' "zero tolerance" discipline policy (Portner 1995);
- the Colorado legislature's reconsideration of compulsory-attendance regulations (Miller 1995); and
- the governor of New York's support for a rule that gives teachers the right to suspend students for up to 10 days (Lindsay 1996).

To get a sharper image of the connection between choice and compulsion we must clarify what "school choice" means. For most, it generally means that parents will be able to choose schools in ways other than moving to a specific neighborhood or paying for private-school tuition. Typical choice proposals include:

- cross-district enrollment laws that allow students to attend schools outside of the district in which they live;
- public charter-school legislation (recently passed in various states); and
- public vouchers for private schools.

Interest in school choice appears to come from a belief that introducing a market system into education will create competition for students and cause schools to improve. Although there is little hard evidence for or against this idea, it has a certain appeal to some people. Indeed, competition may improve education, but only if schools have the freedom to choose with whom they will work.

The idea that schools also need freedom to choose is the other—largely unexamined—side of the school-choice coin. As we shall see, the *institution's* choice is the most important of the two sides, because it provides the context in which parental choice becomes desirable. Moreover, institutional school choice is the essential ingredient in parental school choice. Without it, the idea that a market system can improve education will be largely a false promise.

Walsh (1994) indicated that the public values safety, order, and basic skills above all else. Ponessa (1996) revealed that the public believes that private schools outperform public schools. Yet research comparing public and private schools is inconclusive—some studies suggest that private schools do better; others show that public schools do better (Cibulka 1989).

Why does the public have a higher opinion of private than public schools, when even the experts disagree on their comparative performances? Clearly, the public believes that private schools provide a more controlled learning environment.

Private schools have two organizational advantages that—people believe—lead to instructional benefits. Private schools do not have to put up with every out-of-control student or parent that comes into their schools; thus, they appear to provide greater assurance that they can deliver basic skills. All of the forms of school choice now being discussed will be unsatisfactory to parents *unless* the schools their children attend have the choice not to work with uncooperative students. With compulsory attendance, students are compelled to go, and public schools must take them!

The public also believes that private schools more easily remove incompetent teachers and administrators. Ineffective public-school evaluation policies allow poor teachers to gain tenure. Once tenure is gained, laws and union contracts are so protective of employee rights that incompetents often continue to work for years after they are first challenged.

Of these two differences between private and public schools, the idea of easing employment regulations to facilitate dealing with incompetence is well known and often discussed. For that reason, and because it is probably a small problem in most schools, I will not cover it here. The idea of changing compulsory attendance, however, is much less frequently mentioned and has not been part of recent discussions of school-choice proposals.

Voluntary Public Education

Compulsory school attendance is a 19th-century idea that has apparently outlived its usefulness. During the years when the nation was experiencing rapid industrialization and urbanization, keeping children out of the streets and workplaces was as important to the growing union movement's interest in employment as it was to the social reformers of the time (Gumbert and Spring 1974). Having children in school fit the country's view of itself as a modern nation ready to take its place with other world powers.

The time has come to make K–12 public-school attendance voluntary again. Why? The short answer is that schools are *especially* susceptible to the increasing disorder in our society. Parents are worried about gangs, drugs, violence, and discipline, and these societal problems are appearing among ever younger children (Montgomery 1996). Parents want schools that are in control of their internal environment—and they would love it if those schools were in their own neighborhoods. Teachers want to work in schools where they spend their time teaching rather than dealing with disruptive behavior. Although there are no absolute guarantees of a safe and orderly environment, eliminating compulsory attendance will give schools an important measure of control they now lack.

States must provide voluntary public-education systems. In such systems, people could be offered the equivalent of 13 years of free public instruction any time during their lives, but *only* if they want it.

Personal Experience

For seven years I taught in a public alternative high school for dropouts and other at-risk students. Two out of three students at this school became winners. The key element in the school's success was its option to drop those students with whom it could not work, which created a purposeful climate that allowed troubled students, finally, to succeed. In short, the staff had the luxury to choose a set of reasonable operational rules and enforce them strongly.

At enrollment, students agreed to abide by a small set of behavioral rules. Breaking some rules, like "no fighting," created an immediate vacancy for someone on the waiting list. Breaking others, like "making progress toward graduation," took longer to create a vacancy because the staff wanted to give as many opportunities as possible before exiting someone from the program. The power to control its environment—even with a clientele composed almost entirely of at-risk students—made the school the success it was.

Most public-school magnet programs probably function like this alternative school. They draw students from throughout districts that are also divided into attendance areas served by regular public schools. Thus, magnet/alternative schools can act very much like private schools. They can send the uncooperative student back to his or her home school. This power, combined with the fact that the instruction is free, is likely to account for the waiting lists at many magnet schools.

Organizational Theory

Etzioni (1961) developed a system of classifying organizations by the methods they use to require individuals to comply with their rules. The three principal types of compliance are coercive, remunerative, and normative. Thus, for example, prisons force compliance; factories purchase it; and churches ask for and inspire it. Like churches, schools are best characterized as normative organizations.

Clearly, adults are usually successful in socializing children to adopt the behaviors of a particular family and culture. Most often, however, effective *school* learning occurs only when students choose to cooperate, because schools deal with children in groups for only a few hours a day. Under these conditions, schools can do little more than persuade students to learn. If lack of cooperation threatens the school's control of the learning process, then disassociation is the only route left. The growing interest in parental school choice shows a fundamental understanding of this concept.

Some will argue that schools just need tougher rules; but forced cooperation generally does not work. Students become disruptive, and older students skip school. Even outwardly submissive children can be miles away from the business of school in their thoughts. Others will say that teachers must merely teach in a more engaging manner, yet such measures only go so far. Some students, at certain times in their lives, are simply unmanageable in a group setting. Ultimately, schools cannot *effectively* coerce or purchase cooperation; voluntary cooperation of students is critical.

Possible Drawbacks

Are there reasons for opposing a shift to voluntary education? Would making public-school attendance voluntary mean that a significant proportion of the population will go uneducated? Would we become a nation of home-schoolers or throw legions out onto the streets? Probably not.

At the beginning of this century, when most states enacted compulsory-attendance laws, the economic benefit of schooling was not clear to the farmers and factory workers of the day. Getting kids into school required the force of law. In our technological world, as we stand on the brink of a new century, the importance of a good education is much clearer. Voluntary public school will have plenty of clients.

We ought not to forget the custodial function that schools serve. Most parents want and need help with child care, even if some are not all that keenly focused on the education that goes with it. Home schooling is an enormous commitment that most families are not prepared to make. Making attendance in public schools voluntary would give schools an opportunity to encourage parental behavior that promotes good education practice along with safe custody.

We can control the improper kicking out of "undesirables" by tightening the system that allocates money to schools based on their enrollment. Often, school-suspension policies are loosely administered and have few negative consequences for administrators and teachers. The practice of dropping students becomes a simplistic solution when a school loses many students over the course of a year with no reduction in staff. In Michigan, the allocation for a single student is worth about 10 percent of a teacher's salary. Thus, the elimination of 10 students should also eliminate one staff salary. Tightened enrollment accounting means that educators would only eliminate students when it is necessary to protect the learning environment of the school. Otherwise, they would be putting themselves at risk.

Some research on schools' expulsion, suspension, and dropping practices shows that minorities and students with disabilities more likely get kicked out of school than nondisabled European-American students (Harris and Bennet 1982). If this indicates discrimination, then developing a close connection between enrollment counts and staffing will reduce it. Educators would have to pay to discriminate. Schools that develop a reputation for dropping students would suffer declining enrollments and loss of work for teachers.

Some Implications of Voluntary Public Schooling

There are numerous implications to voluntary public schooling. Permit me to list just a few:

- No students should be barred from any appropriate public school that has room for them, whether within or outside their home district.
- Exclusion should only *follow* enrollment and always be performance-based.
- All staff should have a voice in deciding which students get dropped, because one or more of them may be at risk for continued employment.
- Students could be given multiple chances to succeed at a given school. Learning contracts that specify expected behavior for returnees will work well.
- A review/appeals committee composed of parents and teachers could be created for each school.
- Special programs can be created for difficult students. Such programs would receive grants above normal per-pupil allotments and could pay higher wages to the teachers who staff them.
- Voluntary enrollment may increase the variation in student ages for a given level of the curriculum. Thus, we must develop non-graded K–12 education programs that students can access at any time in their lives, regardless of age.

- Parents need access to information about the quality of education that competing schools offer. We must devise some system of data collection and distribution so that parents can be knowledgeable consumers of education for their children.
- Children and parents will learn, from their earliest school experience, that there are real limits to inappropriate, uncooperative behavior.
- Current ideas about the rights and responsibilities of parents, children, and educators would change. Rights would be more closely connected to responsibilities.
- An increased level of civility among all participants will be promoted, providing opportunities for negotiation rather than threats and intimidation.

Creating Voluntary Education

Perhaps the worst aspect of compulsory attendance is that it creates an unwholesome situation by excusing people from being responsible for their behavior. Students and parents feel excused from behavior that recognizes the rights of others because the school "owes" them a place. Educators feel excused from taking steps to control inappropriate behavior because they have to accept and keep everyone who comes through the door. Compulsory attendance creates a climate of tolerance for intolerable behavior that even permeates the upper levels of high school, where students *can* be legally dropped.

Compulsory attendance also detracts from instructional time. An often-heard truism is that teachers spend 95 percent of their time dealing with 5 percent of their students. Although this estimate may be an exaggeration, significant instructional time is lost while teachers handle repeatedly disruptive students. Eliminating a few students who are not ready to learn will help educators use their time more effectively with the majority who are there to learn.

We must not treat the proposal to eliminate compulsory attendance as a simple solution to a complex set of problems. Changing this one aspect of public education without making other changes will not work. A better system of financial allocations based on enrollment is critical. We must protect students' right of access to public education, providing dropouts with options to return when they are demonstrably ready, restructure curriculum content and delivery, and develop a convenient system of assessing the quality of schools' performance that enables parents to make informed choices.

Public schools play an essential role in the political, economic, and social lives of people in the United States, providing students the educational foundation for the preservation and development of constitutional government and democracy, and opportunities to gain the knowledge and skills needed to become self-sufficient contributors to society. Finally, public schools provide an opportunity for children from many walks of life to interact with each other and thus learn something about people outside of their own family and social circle. Such common school experiences provide the basis for people to interact as citizens and find ways to strengthen their communities. Eliminating compulsory attendance will help preserve public education for future generations and eliminate the need for the most divisive proposal for school choice—public vouchers for private schools—because safety and order will be available in every public school, which would essentially become a magnet or charter school.

Creating voluntary public-school systems will not satisfy all interested parties. Parents who want their offspring to have a particular religious education or the connections that come with certain private schools will not be satisfied, but taxpayers interested in developing a well-educated and productive populace have no obligation to meet these special needs.

Finally, an education system in which individuals are responsible to get whatever part of a basic education *they* decide they need and want is more in keeping with U.S. traditions of freedom, democracy, independence, and opportunity than the current system. Making K–12 public-school attendance voluntary will truly make education a matter of choice.

References

Cibulka, J. G. 1989. Searching for clarity in public and private school comparisons. *Educational Researcher* 18(4): 52–55.

Etzioni, A. 1961. *A comparative analysis of complex organizations.* New York: The Free Press.

Gumbert, E. B., and J. H. Spring. 1974. *The superschool and the superstate: American education in the twentieth century, 1918–1979.* New York: John Wiley and Sons.

Harris, J. J., and C. Bennet, eds. 1982. *Student discipline: Legal, empirical, and educational perspectives.* Bloomington: Indiana University Press.

Lindsay, D. 1996. N.Y. bills give teachers power to oust pupils. *Education Week* 15(25): 1, 24.

Miller, L. 1995. Colo. bill would kill compulsory age for school. *Education Week* 15(11): 1, 22.

Montgomery, L. 1996. Youngest offenders are a growing threat. *The Detroit Free Press,* 10 April.

Ponessa, J. 1996. Teachers agree stress needed on "the basics." *Education Week* 15(22): 1, 17.

Portner, J. 1995. Districts turn to expulsions to keep order. *Education Week* 14(30): 1, 10–11.

Walsh, M. 1994. School "experts" found out of sync with public. *Education Week* 14(6): 6.

POSTSCRIPT

Should School Attendance Be Compelled?

One of the most recent serious critiques of compulsory attendance laws was provided by Len Botstein, the long-time president of Bard College, in his book *Jefferson's Children: Education and the Promise of American Culture* (1997). Botstein argues that it is time to abolish compulsoriness at the secondary school level in recognition of the biological, sociological, and psychological changes in modern adolescents. "The American high school is obsolete," he contends, "and no amount of testing or mere imposition of national standards will make the difference." Syndicated columnist George F. Will concurs that age 18 is too old for the intellectual regimentation and social confinement of today's high school. This attack on holding adolescents in school, along with the success of home schooling at the elementary level, adds pressure for further change and accommodation.

Some other sources of opinion on the issue of compulsory schooling are "Are Mandatory School Attendance Laws Inherently Unjust?" by Judith A. Boss and Katherine D. Wurtz, *The Educational Forum* (Spring 1994); "Mandatory Schooling: A Teacher's Eye View," *Reason* (January 1997); "End Compulsory Schooling," by Sheldon Richman and David B. Kopel, Independence Issue Paper (January 10, 1996); Matt Hern, ed., *Deschooling Our Lives* (1995); "Education Reform and the Justification of Compulsory Schooling," by Clark Robenstine, *Journal of Thought* (Fall 1993); "School's Out for Absentees," by Valerie Richardson, *Insight on the News* (January 1996); "Compulsory Schooling in Europe," by Bryan T. Peck, *Phi Delta Kappan* (January 1995); Barry McGhan, "Choice and Compulsion: The End of an Era," *Phi Delta Kappan* (April 1998); *The Parents' Guide to Alternatives in Education* by Ronald E. Koetzsch (1997); and *The Teenage Liberation Handbook*, rev. ed., by Grace Llewellyn (1998).

One of the arguments against compulsoriness is that the law forces young people who do not want to be in school to be there, thereby setting the scene for disruption of the learning of those who do want to be there. This is probably the central factor in current calls for reconsideration of compulsory attendance laws. But would alteration of the present laws merely shift the problem from the school to the street?

Compulsory education is often justified in terms of the individual's right to education. But does it make sense to compel someone to exercise a right? On the other hand, would the demolition of attendance laws set young people adrift without appropriate guidance and resources in the most crucial years of their lives and condemn many of them to low levels of employment and personal development?

On the Internet ...

Character Education Resources

This site promotes character and citizenship by disseminating materials and funding training conferences for educators.

http://www.charactereducationinfo.org

Multicultural Education and Ethnic Groups: Selected Internet Sources

This site provides a wide variety of materials on ethnic diversity.

http://www.library.csustan.edu/lboyer/multicultural/main.htm

Eighth Floor: Multicultural Education

This New Horizons for Learning site features articles, reading lists, and Internet links on multiculturalism.

http://www.newhorizons.org/multicultural.html

Welcome to African American History

This site treats the topic of school integration in the United States in the full context of African American history.

http://www.watson.org/~lisa/blackhistory/

Yahoo! Standards and Testing

This site offers an index to sources on standardized exams.

http://dir.yahoo.com/education/standards_and_testing/

Standards, Testing and Accountability

This Thomas B. Fordham Foundation site is dedicated to examining reform issues.

http://www.edexcellence.net/topics/standards.html

Educational Philosophy: What's Wrong With Public Schools?

This site advocates home schooling and is highly critical of public schools.

http://www.hometaught.com/public_schools.htm

PART 2

Current Fundamental Issues

*T*he issues discussed in this section cover basic social, cultural, and political problems currently under consideration by education experts, social scientists, and politicians, as well as by parents and the media. Positions on these issues are expressed by Thomas Lickona, Alfie Kohn, Sonia Nieto, Thomas J. Famularo, Doris Y. Wilkinson, Ray C. Rist, Nina Hurwitz, Sol Hurwitz, Martin G. Brooks, Jacqueline Grennon Brooks, William J. Bennett and his colleagues, and Forrest J. Troy.

- Can "Character Education" Reverse Moral Decline?

- Should Multiculturalism Permeate the Curriculum?

- Are School Integration Efforts Doomed to Failure?

- Do High-Stakes Assessments Improve Learning?

- Have Public Schools Failed Society?

ISSUE 6

Can "Character Education" Reverse Moral Decline?

YES: Thomas Lickona, from "The Return of Character Education," *Educational Leadership* (November 1993)

NO: Alfie Kohn, from "How Not to Teach Values: A Critical Look at Character Education," *Phi Delta Kappan* (February 1997)

ISSUE SUMMARY

YES: Developmental psychologist Thomas Lickona, a leading exponent of the new character education, details the rationale behind the movement and charts a course of action to deal with the moral decline of American youth.

NO: Writer-lecturer Alfie Kohn sees current attempts at character education as mainly a collection of exhortations and extrinsic inducements that avoid more penetrating efforts at social and moral development.

D o schools have a moral purpose? Can virtue be taught? Should the shaping of character be as important as the training of the intellect? Should value-charged issues be discussed in the classroom?

Much of the history of education chronicles the ways in which philosophers, theorists, educators, politicians, and the general public have responded to these and similar questions. In almost all countries (and certainly in early America), the didactic teaching of moral values, often those of a particular religious interpretation, was central to the process of schooling. Although the direct connection between religion and public education in the United States has faded, the image of the teacher as a value model persists, and the ethical dimension of everyday activities and human relations insinuates itself into the school atmosphere. Normative discourse inundates the educational environment; school is often a world of "rights" and "wrongs" and "oughts" and "don'ts."

Problems emerge when the attempt is made to delineate the school's proper role in setting value guidelines: Can school efforts supplement the efforts of home and church? Can the schools avoid representing a "middle-class morality" that disregards the cultural base of minority group values? Should the schools do battle against the value-manipulating forces of the mass media and the popular culture?

During the 1960s and 1970s a number of psychology-based approaches supplanted the traditional didacticism. Psychologist Lawrence Kohlberg fashioned strategies that link ethical growth to levels of cognitive maturity, moving the student through a range of stages that demand increasingly sophisticated types of moral reasoning. Another approach popularized during this period was "values clarification," developed and refined by Louis Raths, Merrill Harmin, Sidney Simon, and Howard Kirschenbaum. This moral education program attempted to assist learners in understanding their own attitudes, preferences, and values, as well as those of others, and placed central emphasis on feelings, emotions, sensitivity, and shared perceptions.

The current concern that many people have about the moral condition of American society and its young people in particular is prompting a reevaluation of the school's role in teaching values. "The schools are failing to provide the moral education they once did; they have abandoned moral teaching," says William Kilpatrick, author of *Why Johnny Can't Tell Right from Wrong* (1992). "If we want our children to possess the traits of character we most admire, we need to teach them what those traits are and why they deserve both admiration and allegiance," says William J. Bennett in the introduction to his best-selling book *The Book of Virtues* (1993). Both of these thinkers reject the moral relativism associated with values clarification and with similar approaches, and they call for a character-development strategy based upon time-tested materials that contribute to "moral literacy."

Evidence that character education continues to be a hot topic can be seen in books such as Gertrude Himmelfarb's *The De-Moralization of Society: From Victorian Virtues to Modern Values* (1995), *The Moral Intelligence of Children* by Robert Coles (1997), Ivor A. Pritchard's *Good Education: The Virtues of Learning* (1998), *The Students Are Watching: Schools and the Moral Contract* by Theodore R. Sizer and Nancy Faust Sizer (1999), and *Building Character in Schools* by Kevin A. Ryan and Karen E. Bohlin (1999).

The following articles are also recommended: "The Missing Ingredient in Character Education," by Thomas J. Lasley II, *Phi Delta Kappan* (April 1997); "Should Morals Be Taught in the Classroom?" (a debate), *NEA Today* (May 1997); "Education and Character: A Conservative View," by Denis P. Doyle, *Phi Delta Kappan* (February 1997); "The Death of Character Education," by Timothy Rusnak and Frank Ribich, *Educational Horizons* (Fall 1997); and "Character Education: Reclaiming the Social," by Barbara J. Duncan, *Educational Theory* (Winter 1997).

In the selections that follow, Thomas Lickona makes the case for a new character education movement and charts the course that this effort must take in order to have a pronounced effect on the moral life of students. Alfie Kohn contends that character educators such as Lickona should scrutinize their programs in terms of their ultimate goals, their view of human nature, and the meaning of the values that they attempt to instill.

Thomas Lickona

The Return of Character Education

To educate a person in mind and not in morals is to educate a menace to society.

— Theodore Roosevelt

Increasing numbers of people across the ideological spectrum believe that our society is in deep moral trouble. The disheartening signs are everywhere: the breakdown of the family; the deterioration of civility in everyday life; rampant greed at a time when one in five children is poor; an omnipresent sexual culture that fills our television and movie screens with sleaze, beckoning the young toward sexual activity at ever earlier ages; the enormous betrayal of children through sexual abuse; and the 1992 report of the National Research Council that says the United States is now *the* most violent of all industrialized nations.

As we become more aware of this societal crisis, the feeling grows that schools cannot be ethical bystanders. As a result, character education is making a comeback in American schools.

Early Character Education

Character education is as old as education itself. Down through history, education has had two great goals: to help people become smart and to help them become good.

Acting on that belief, schools in the earliest days of our republic tackled character education head on—through discipline, the teacher's example, and the daily school curriculum. The Bible was the public school's sourcebook for both moral and religious instruction. When struggles eventually arose over whose Bible to use and which doctrines to teach, William McGuffey stepped onto the stage in 1836 to offer his McGuffey Readers, ultimately to sell more than 100 million copies.

McGuffey retained many favorite Biblical stories but added poems, exhortations, and heroic tales. While children practiced their reading or arithmetic,

From Thomas Lickona, "The Return of Character Education," *Educational Leadership,* vol. 51, no. 3 (November 1993), pp. 6–11. Copyright © 1993 by The Association for Supervision and Curriculum Development. Reprinted by permission. All rights reserved.

they also learned lessons about honesty, love of neighbor, kindness to animals, hard work, thriftiness, patriotism, and courage.

Why Character Education Declined

In the 20th century, the consensus supporting character education began to crumble under the blows of several powerful forces.

Darwinism introduced a new metaphor—evolution—that led people to see all things, including morality, as being in flux.

The philosophy of logical positivism, arriving at American universities from Europe, asserted a radical distinction between *facts* (which could be scientifically proven) and *values* (which positivism held were mere expressions of feeling, not objective truth). As a result of positivism, morality was relativized and privatized—made to seem a matter of personal "value judgment," not a subject for public debate and transmission through the schools.

In the 1960s, a worldwide rise in personalism celebrated the worth, autonomy, and subjectivity of the person, emphasizing individual rights and freedom over responsibility. Personalism rightly protested societal oppression and injustice, but it also delegitimized moral authority, eroded belief in objective moral norms, turned people inward toward self-fulfillment, weakened social commitments (for example, to marriage and parenting), and fueled the socially destabilizing sexual revolution.

Finally, the rapidly intensifying pluralism of American society (Whose values should we teach?) and the increasing secularization of the public arena (Won't moral education violate the separation of church and state?), became two more barriers to achieving the moral consensus indispensable for character education in the public schools. Public schools retreated from their once central role as moral and character educators.

The 1970s saw a return of values education, but in new forms: values clarification and Kohlberg's moral dilemma discussions. In different ways, both expressed the individualist spirit of the age. Values clarification said, don't impose values; help students choose their values freely. Kohlberg said, develop students' powers of moral reasoning so they can judge which values are better than others.

Each approach made contributions, but each had problems. Values clarification, though rich in methodology, failed to distinguish between personal preferences (truly a matter of free choice) and moral values (a matter of obligation). Kohlberg focused on moral reasoning, which is necessary but not sufficient for good character, and underestimated the school's role as a moral socializer.

The New Character Education

In the 1990s we are seeing the beginnings of a new character education movement, one which restores "good character" to its historical place as the central desirable outcome of the school's moral enterprise. No one knows yet how broad or deep this movement is; we have no studies to tell us what percentage of schools are making what kind of effort. But something significant is afoot.

In July 1992, the Josephson Institute of Ethics called together more than 30 educational leaders representing state school boards, teachers' unions, universities, ethics centers, youth organizations, and religious groups. This diverse assemblage drafted the Aspen Declaration on Character Education, setting forth eight principles of character education.[1]

The Character Education Partnership was launched in March 1993, as a national coalition committed to putting character development at the top of the nation's educational agenda. Members include representatives from business, labor, government, youth, parents, faith communities, and the media.

The last two years have seen the publication of a spate of books—such as *Moral, Character, and Civic Education in the Elementary School, Why Johnny Can't Tell Right From Wrong,* and *Reclaiming Our Schools: A Handbook on Teaching Character, Academics, and Discipline*—that make the case for character education and describe promising programs around the country. A new periodical, the *Journal of Character Education,* is devoted entirely to covering the field.[2]

Why Character Education Now?

Why this groundswell of interest in character education? There are at least three causes:

1. The decline of the family.   The family, traditionally a child's primary moral teacher, is for vast numbers of children today failing to perform that role, thus creating a moral vacuum. In her recent book *When the Bough Breaks: The Cost of Neglecting Our Children,* economist Sylvia Hewlett documents that American children, rich and poor, suffer a level of neglect unique among developed nations (1991). Overall, child well-being has declined despite a decrease in the number of children per family, an increase in the educational level of parents, and historically high levels of public spending in education.

In "Dan Quayle Was Right," (April 1993) Barbara Dafoe Whitehead synthesizes the social science research on the decline of the two biological-parent family in America:

> If current trends continue, less than half of children born today will live continuously with their own mother and father throughout childhood....
> An increasing number of children will experience family break-up two or even three times during childhood.

Children of marriages that end in divorce and children of single mothers are more likely to be poor, have emotional and behavioral problems, fail to achieve academically, get pregnant, abuse drugs and alcohol, get in trouble with the law, and be sexually and physically abused. Children in stepfamilies are generally worse off (more likely to be sexually abused, for example) than children in single-parent homes.

No one has felt the impact of family disruption more than schools. White-head writes:

> Across the nation, principals report a dramatic rise in the aggressive, acting-out behavior characteristic of children, especially boys, who are living in single-parent families. Moreover, teachers find that many children are so upset and preoccupied by the explosive drama of their own family lives that they are unable to concentrate on such mundane matters as multiplication tables.

Family disintegration, then, drives the character education movement in two ways: schools have to teach the values kids aren't learning at home; and schools, in order to conduct teaching and learning, must become caring moral communities that help children from unhappy homes focus on their work, control their anger, feel cared about, and become responsible students.

2. Troubling trends in youth character. A second impetus for renewed character education is the sense that young people in general, not just those from frac-tured families, have been adversely affected by poor parenting (in intact as well as broken families); the wrong kind of adult role models; the sex, violence, and materialism portrayed in the mass media; and the pressures of the peer group. Evidence that this hostile moral environment is taking a toll on youth character can be found in 10 troubling trends: rising youth violence; increasing dis-honesty (lying, cheating, and stealing); growing disrespect for authority; peer cruelty; a resurgence of bigotry on school campuses, from preschool through higher education; a decline in the work ethic; sexual precocity; a growing self-centeredness and declining civil responsibility; an increase in self-destructive behavior; and ethical illiteracy.

The statistics supporting these trends are overwhelming.[3] For example, the U.S. homicide rate for 15- to 24-year-old males is 7 times higher than Canada's and 40 times higher than Japan's. The U.S. has one of the highest teenage preg-nancy rates, the highest teen abortion rate, and the highest level of drug use among young people in the developed world. Youth suicide has tripled in the past 25 years, and a survey of more than 2,000 Rhode Island students, grades six through nine, found that two out of three boys and one of two girls thought it "acceptable for a man to force sex on a woman" if they had been dating for six months or more (Kikuchi 1988).

3. A recovery of shared, objectively important ethical values. Moral decline in society has gotten bad enough to jolt us out of the privatism and relativism dominant in recent decades. We are recovering the wisdom that we do share a basic morality, essential for our survival; that adults must promote this morality by teaching the young, directly and indirectly, such values as respect, respon-sibility, trustworthiness, fairness, caring, and civil virtue; and that these values are not merely subjective preferences but that they have objective worth and a claim on our collective conscience.

Such values affirm our human dignity, promote the good of the indi-vidual and the common good, and protect our human rights. They meet the classic ethical tests of reversibility (Would you want to be treated this way?) and universalizability (Would you want all persons to act this way in a similar situation?). They define our responsibilities in a democracy, and they are recognized by all civilized people and taught by all enlightened creeds. *Not* to teach children these core ethical values is grave moral failure.

What Character Education Must Do

In the face of a deteriorating social fabric, what must character education do to develop good character in the young?

First, it must have an adequate theory of what good character is, one which gives schools a clear idea of their goals. Character must be broadly conceived to encompass the cognitive, affective, and behavioral aspects of morality. Good character consists of knowing the good, desiring the good, and doing the good. Schools must help children *understand* the core values, *adopt* or commit to them, and then *act upon* them in their own lives.

The cognitive side of character includes at least six specific moral qualities: awareness of the moral dimensions of the situation at hand, knowing moral values and what they require of us in concrete cases, perspective-taking, moral reasoning, thoughtful decision making, and moral self-knowledge. All these powers of rational moral thought are required for full moral maturity and citizenship in a democratic society.

People can be very smart about matters of right and wrong, however, and still choose the wrong. Moral education that is merely intellectual misses the crucial emotional side of character, which serves as the bridge between judgment and action. The emotional side includes at least the following qualities: conscience (the felt obligation to do what one judges to be right), self-respect, empathy, loving the good, self-control, and humility (a willingness to both recognize and correct our moral failings).

At times, we know what we should do, feel strongly that we should do it, yet still fail to translate moral judgment and feeling into effective moral behavior. Moral action, the third part of character, draws upon three additional moral qualities: competence (skills such as listening, communicating, and cooperating), will (which mobilizes our judgment and energy), and moral habit (a reliable inner disposition to respond to situations in a morally good way).

Developing Character

Once we have a comprehensive concept of character, we need a comprehensive approach to developing it. This approach tells schools to look at themselves through a moral lens and consider how virtually everything that goes on there affects the values and character of students. Then, plan how to use all phases of classroom and school life as deliberate tools of character development.

If schools wish to maximize their moral clout, make a lasting difference in students' character, and engage and develop all three parts of character (knowing, feeling, and behavior), they need a comprehensive, holistic approach. Having a comprehensive approach includes asking, Do present school practices support, neglect, or contradict the school's professed values and character education aims?

In classroom practice, a comprehensive approach to character education calls upon the individual teacher to:

- *Act as caregiver, model, and mentor,* treating students with love and respect, setting a good example, supporting positive social behavior, and correcting hurtful actions through one-on-one guidance and whole-class discussion;
- *Create a moral community,* helping students know one another as persons, respect and care about one another, and feel valued membership in, and responsibility to, the group;
- *Practice moral discipline,* using the creation and enforcement of rules as opportunities to foster moral reasoning, voluntary compliance with rules, and a respect for others;
- *Create a democratic classroom environment,* involving students in decision making and the responsibility for making the classroom a good place to be and learn;
- *Teach values through the curriculum,* using the ethically rich content of academic subjects (such as literature, history, and science), as well as outstanding programs (such as *Facing History and Ourselves*[4] and *The Heartwood Ethics Curriculum for Children*[5]), as vehicles for teaching values and examining moral questions;
- *Use cooperative learning* to develop students' appreciation of others, perspective taking, and ability to work with others toward common goals;
- *Develop the "conscience of craft"* by fostering students' appreciation of learning, capacity for hard work, commitment to excellence, and sense of work as affecting the lives of others;
- *Encourage moral reflection* through reading, research, essay writing, journal keeping, discussion, and debate;
- *Teach conflict resolution,* so that students acquire the essential moral skills of solving conflicts fairly and without force.

Besides making full use of the moral life of classrooms, a comprehensive approach calls upon the school *as a whole* to:

- *Foster caring beyond the classroom,* using positive role models to inspire altruistic behavior and providing opportunities at every grade level to perform school and community service;
- *Create a positive moral culture in the school,* developing a schoolwide ethos (through the leadership of the principal, discipline, a schoolwide sense of community, meaningful student government, a moral community among adults, and making time for moral concerns) that supports and amplifies the values taught in classrooms;

- *Recruit parents and the community as partners in character education,* letting parents know that the school considers them their child's first and most important moral teacher, giving parents specific ways they can reinforce the values the school is trying to teach, and seeking the help of the community, churches, businesses, local government, and the media in promoting the core ethical values.

The Challenges Ahead

Whether character education will take hold in American schools remains to be seen. Among the factors that will determine the movement's long-range success are:

- *Support for schools.* Can schools recruit the help they need from the other key formative institutions that shape the values of the young —including families, faith communities, and the media? Will public policy act to strengthen and support families, and will parents make the stability of their families and the needs of their children their highest priority?
- *The role of religion.* Both liberal and conservative groups are asking, How can students be sensitively engaged in considering the role of religion in the origins and moral development of our nation? How can students be encouraged to use their intellectual and moral resources, including their faith traditions, when confronting social issues (For example, what is my obligation to the poor?) and making personal moral decisions (For example, should I have sex before marriage?)?
- *Moral leadership.* Many schools lack a positive, cohesive moral culture. Especially at the building level, it is absolutely essential to have moral leadership that sets, models, and consistently enforces high standards of respect and responsibility. Without a positive schoolwide ethos, teachers will feel demoralized in their individual efforts to teach good values.
- *Teacher education.* Character education is far more complex than teaching math or reading; it requires personal growth as well as skills development. Yet teachers typically receive almost no preservice or inservice training in the moral aspects of their craft. Many teachers do not feel comfortable or competent in the values domain. How will teacher education colleges and school staff development programs meet this need?

"Character is destiny," wrote the ancient Greek philosopher Heraclitus. As we confront the causes of our deepest societal problems, whether in our intimate relationships or public institutions, questions of character loom large. As we close out a turbulent century and ready our schools for the next, educating for character is a moral imperative if we care about the future of our society and our children.

Notes

1. For a copy of the Aspen Declaration and the issue of *Ethics* magazine reporting on the conference, write the Josephson Institute of Ethics, 310 Washington Blvd., Suite 104, Marina del Rey, CA 90292.

2. For information write Mark Kann, Editor, *The Journal of Character Education,* Jefferson Center for Character Education, 202 S. Lake Ave., Suite 240, Pasadena, CA 91101.

3. For documentation of these youth trends, see T. Lickona, (1991), *Educating for Character: How Our Schools Can Teach Respect and Responsibility* (New York: Bantam Books).

4. *Facing History and Ourselves* is an 8-week Holocaust curriculum for 8th graders. Write Facing History and Ourselves National Foundation, 25 Kennard Rd., Brookline, MA 02146.

5. *The Heartwood Ethics Curriculum for Children* uses multicultural children's literature to teach universal values. Write The Heartwood Institute, 12300 Perry Highway, Wexford, PA 15090.

References

Benninga, J. S., ed. (1991). *Moral, Character, and Civic Education in the Elementary School.* New York: Teachers College Press.

Hewlett, S. (1991). *When the Bough Breaks: The Cost of Neglecting Our Children.* New York: Basic Books.

Kikuchi, J. (Fall 1988). "Rhode Island Develops Successful Intervention Program for Adolescents." *National Coalition Against Sexual Assault Newsletter.*

National Research Council. (1992). *Understanding and Preventing Violence.* Washington, D.C.: National Research Council.

Whitehead, B. D. (April 1993) "Dan Quayle Was Right." *The Atlantic* 271: 47–84.

Wynne, E. A., and K. Ryan. (1992). *Reclaiming Our Schools: A Handbook on Teaching Character, Academics, and Discipline.* New York: Merrill.

Alfie Kohn

 **NO**

How Not to Teach Values

Were you to stand somewhere in the continental United States and announce, "I'm going to Hawaii," it would be understood that you were heading for those islands in the Pacific that collectively constitute the 50th state. Were you to stand in Honolulu and make the same statement, however, you would probably be talking about one specific island in the chain—namely, the big one to your southeast. The word *Hawaii* would seem to have two meanings, a broad one and a narrow one; we depend on context to tell them apart.

The phrase *character education* also has two meanings. In the broad sense, it refers to almost anything that schools might try to provide outside of academics, especially when the purpose is to help children grow into good people. In the narrow sense, it denotes a particular style of moral training, one that reflects particular values as well as particular assumptions about the nature of children and how they learn.

Unfortunately, the two meanings of the term have become blurred, with the narrow version of character education dominating the field to the point that it is frequently mistaken for the broader concept. Thus educators who are keen to support children's social and moral development may turn, by default, to a program with a certain set of methods and a specific agenda that, on reflection, they might very well find objectionable.

My purpose in this article is to subject these programs to careful scrutiny and, in so doing, to highlight the possibility that there are other ways to achieve our broader objectives. I address myself not so much to those readers who are avid proponents of character education (in the narrow sense) but to those who simply want to help children become decent human beings and may not have thought carefully about what they are being offered.

Let me get straight to the point. What goes by the name of character education nowadays is, for the most part, a collection of exhortations and extrinsic inducements designed to make children work harder and do what they're told. Even when other values are also promoted—caring or fairness, say—the preferred method of instruction is tantamount to indoctrination. The point is to drill students in specific behaviors rather than to engage them in deep, critical reflection about certain ways of being. This is the impression one gets from reading articles and books by contemporary proponents of character education as well as the curriculum materials sold by the leading national programs. The impression is only strengthened by visiting schools that have been singled out for their commitment to character education. To wit:

> A huge, multiethnic elementary school in Southern California uses a framework created by the Jefferson Center for Character Education. Classes that the principal declares "well behaved" are awarded Bonus Bucks, which can eventually be redeemed for an ice cream party. On an enormous wall near the cafeteria, professionally painted Peanuts characters instruct children: "Never talk in line." A visitor is led to a fifth-grade classroom to observe an exemplary lesson on the current character education topic. The teacher is telling students to write down the name of the person they regard as the "toughest worker" in school. The teacher then asks them, "How many of you are going to be tough workers?" (Hands go up.) "Can you be a tough worker at home, too?" (Yes.)

> A small, almost entirely African American School in Chicago uses a framework created by the Character Education Institute. Periodic motivational assemblies are used to "give children a good pep talk," as the principal puts it, and to reinforce the values that determine who will be picked as Student of the Month. Rule number one posted on the wall of a kindergarten room is "We will obey the teachers." Today, students in this class are listening to the story of "Lazy Lion," who orders each of the other animals to build him a house, only to find each effort unacceptable. At the end, the teacher drives home the lesson: "Did you ever hear Lion say thank you?" (No.) "Did you ever hear Lion say please?" (No.) "It's good to always say... what?" (Please.) The reason for using these words, she points out, is that by doing so we are more likely to get what we want.

> A charter school near Boston has been established specifically to offer an intensive, homegrown character education curriculum to its overwhelmingly white, middle-class student body. At weekly public ceremonies, certain children receive a leaf that will then be hung in the Forest of Virtue. The virtues themselves are "not open to debate," the headmaster insists, since moral precepts in his view enjoy the same status as mathematical truths. In a first-grade classroom, a teacher is observing that "it's very hard to be obedient when you want something. I want you to ask yourself, 'Can I have it—and why not?'" She proceeds to ask the students, "What kinds of things show obedience?" and, after collecting a few suggestions, announces that she's "not going to call on anyone else now. We could go on forever, but we have to have a moment of silence and then a spelling test."

Some of the most popular schoolwide strategies for improving students' character seem dubious on their face. When President Clinton mentioned the importance of character education in his 1996 State of the Union address, the only specific practice he recommended was requiring students to wear uniforms. The premises here are first, that children's character can be improved by forcing them to dress alike, and second, that if adults object to students' clothing, the best solution is not to invite them to reflect together about how this problem might be solved, but instead to compel them all to wear the same thing.

A second strategy, also consistent with the dominant philosophy of character education, is an exercise that might be called "If It's Tuesday, This Must Be Honesty." Here, one value after another is targeted, with each assigned its own day, week, or month. This seriatim approach is unlikely to result in a lasting commitment to any of these values, much less a feeling for how they may be related. Nevertheless, such programs are taken very seriously by some of the same people who are quick to dismiss other educational programs, such as those intended to promote self-esteem, as silly and ineffective.

Then there is the strategy of offering students rewards when they are "caught" being good, an approach favored by right-wing religious groups[1] and orthodox behaviorists but also by leaders of—and curriculum suppliers for—the character education movement.[2] Because of its popularity and because a sizable body of psychological evidence germane to the topic is available, it is worth lingering on this particular practice for a moment.

In general terms, what the evidence suggests is this: the more we reward people for doing something, the more likely they are to lose interest in whatever they had to do to get the reward. Extrinsic motivation, in other words, is not only quite different from intrinsic motivation but actually tends to erode it.[3] This effect has been demonstrated under many different circumstances and with respect to many different attitudes and behaviors. Most relevant to character education is a series of studies showing that individuals who have been rewarded for doing something nice become less likely to think of themselves as caring or helpful people and more likely to attribute their behavior to the reward.

"Extrinsic incentives can, by undermining self-perceived altruism, decrease intrinsic motivation to help others," one group of researchers concluded on the basis of several studies. "A person's kindness, it seems, cannot be bought."[4] The same applies to a person's sense of responsibility, fairness, perseverance, and so on. The lesson a child learns from Skinnerian tactics is that the point of being good is to get rewards. No wonder researchers have found that children who are frequently rewarded—or, in another study, children who receive positive reinforcement for caring, sharing, and helping—are less likely than other children to keep doing those things.[5]

In short, it makes no sense to dangle goodies in front of children for being virtuous. But even worse than rewards are awards—certificates, plaques, trophies, and other tokens of recognition whose numbers have been artificially limited so only a few can get them. When some children are singled out as "winners," the central message that every child learns is this: "Other people are potential obstacles to my success."[6] Thus the likely result of making students beat out their peers for the distinction of being the most virtuous is not only less intrinsic commitment to virtue but also a disruption of relationships and, ironically, of the experience of community that is so vital to the development of children's character.

Unhappily, the problems with character education (in the narrow sense, which is how I'll be using the term unless otherwise indicated) are not restricted to such strategies as enforcing sartorial uniformity, scheduling a value of the week, or offering students a "doggie biscuit" for being good. More deeply troubling are the fundamental assumptions, both explicit and implicit, that inform character education programs. Let us consider five basic questions that might be asked of any such program: At what level are problems addressed? What is the underlying theory of human nature? What is the ultimate goal? Which values are promoted? And finally, How is learning thought to take place?

At What Level Are Problems Addressed?

One of the major purveyors of materials in this field, the Jefferson Center for Character Education in Pasadena, California, has produced a video that begins with some arresting images—quite literally. Young people are shown being led away in handcuffs, the point being that crime can be explained on the basis of an "erosion of American core values," as the narrator intones ominously. The idea that social problems can be explained by the fact that traditional virtues are no longer taken seriously is offered by many proponents of character education as though it were just plain common sense.

But if people steal or rape or kill solely because they possess bad values— that is, because of their personal characteristics—the implication is that political and economic realities are irrelevant and need not be addressed. Never mind staggering levels of unemployment in the inner cities or a system in which more and more of the nation's wealth is concentrated in fewer and fewer hands; just place the blame on individuals whose characters are deficient. A key tenet of the "Character Counts!" Coalition, which bills itself as a nonpartisan umbrella group devoid of any political agenda, is the highly debatable proposition that "negative social influences can [be] and usually are overcome by the exercise of free will and character."[7] What is presented as common sense is, in fact, conservative ideology.

Let's put politics aside, though. If a program proceeds by trying to "fix the kids"—as do almost all brands of character education—it ignores the accumulated evidence from the field of social psychology demonstrating that much of how we act and who we are reflects the situations in which we find ourselves. Virtually all the landmark studies in this discipline have been variations on this theme. Set up children in an extended team competition at summer camp and you will elicit unprecedented levels of aggression. Assign adults to the roles of prisoners or guards in a mock jail, and they will start to become their roles. Move people to a small town, and they will be more likely to rescue a stranger in need. In fact, so common is the tendency to attribute to an individual's personality or character what is actually a function of the social environment that social psychologists have dubbed this the "fundamental attribution error."

A similar lesson comes to us from the movement concerned with Total Quality Management associated with the ideas of the late W. Edwards Deming. At the heart of Deming's teaching is the notion that the "system" of an organization largely determines the results. The problems experienced in a corporation, therefore, are almost always due to systemic flaws rather than to a lack of effort or ability on the part of individuals in that organization. Thus, if we are troubled by the way students are acting, Deming, along with most social psychologists, would presumably have us transform the structure of the classroom rather than try to remake the students themselves—precisely the opposite of the character education approach.

What Is the View of Human Nature?

Character education's "fix-the-kids" orientation follows logically from the belief that kids need fixing. Indeed, the movement seems to be driven by a stunningly dark view of children—and, for that matter, of people in general. A "comprehensive approach [to character education] is based on a somewhat dim view of human nature," acknowledges William Kilpatrick, whose book *Why Johnny Can't Tell Right from Wrong* contains such assertions as: "Most behavior problems are the result of sheer 'willfulness' on the part of children."[8]

Despite—or more likely because of—statements like that, Kilpatrick has frequently been invited to speak at character education conferences.[9] But that shouldn't be surprising in light of how many prominent proponents of character education share his views. Edward Wynne says his own work is grounded in a tradition of thought that takes a "somewhat pessimistic view of human nature."[10] The idea of character development "sees children as self-centered," in the opinion of Kevin Ryan, who directs the Center for the Advancement of Ethics and Character at Boston University as well as heading up the character education network of the Association for Supervision and Curriculum Development. Yet another writer approvingly traces the whole field back to the bleak world view of Thomas Hobbes: it is "an obvious assumption of character education," writes Louis Goldman, that people lack the instinct to work together. Without laws to compel us to get along, "our natural egoism would lead us into 'a condition of warre one against another.' "[12] This sentiment is echoed by F. Washington Jarvis, headmaster of the Roxbury Latin School in Boston, one of Ryan's favorite examples of what character education should look like in practice. Jarvis sees human nature as "mean, nasty, brutish, selfish, and capable of great cruelty and meanness. We have to hold a mirror up to the students and say, 'This is who you are. Stop it.' "[13]

Even when proponents of character education don't express such sentiments explicitly, they give themselves away by framing their mission as a campaign for self-control. Amitai Etzioni, for example, does not merely include this attribute on a list of good character traits; he *defines* character principally in terms of the capacity "to control impulses and defer gratification."[14] This is noteworthy because the virtue of self-restraint—or at least the decision to give special emphasis to it—has historically been preached by those, from St. Augustine to the present, who see people as basically sinful.

In fact, at least three assumptions seem to be at work when the need for self-control is stressed: first, that we are all at war not only with others but with ourselves, torn between our desires and our reason (or social norms); second, that these desires are fundamentally selfish, aggressive, or otherwise unpleasant; and third, that these desires are very strong, constantly threatening to overpower us if we don't rein them in. Collectively, these statements describe religious dogma, not scientific fact. Indeed, the evidence from several disciplines converges to cast doubt on this sour view of human beings and, instead, supports the idea that it is as "natural" for children to help as to hurt. I will not rehearse that evidence here, partly because I have done so elsewhere at some length.[15] Suffice it to say that even the most hard-headed empiricist might well conclude that the promotion of prosocial values consists to some extent of supporting (rather than restraining or controlling) many facets of the self. Any educator who adopts this more balanced position might think twice before joining an educational movement that is finally inseparable from the doctrine of original sin.

What Is the Ultimate Goal?

It may seem odd even to inquire about someone's reasons for trying to improve children's character. But it is worth mentioning that the whole enterprise —not merely the particular values that are favored—is often animated by a profoundly conservative, if not reactionary, agenda. Character education based on "acculturating students to conventional norms of 'good' behavior... resonates with neoconservative concerns for social stability," observed David Purpel.[16] The movement has been described by another critic as a "yearning for some halcyon days of moral niceties and social tranquillity."[17] But it is not merely a *social* order that some are anxious to preserve (or recover): character education is vital, according to one vocal proponent, because "the development of character is the backbone of the economic system" now in place.[18]

Character education, or any kind of education, would look very different if we began with other objectives—if, for example, we were principally concerned with helping children become active participants in a democratic society (or agents for transforming a society *into* one that is authentically democratic). It would look different if our top priority were to help students develop into principled and caring members of a community or advocates for social justice. To be sure, these objectives are not inconsistent with the desire to preserve certain traditions, but the point would then be to help children decide which traditions are worth preserving and why, based on these other considerations. That is not at all the same as endorsing anything that is traditional or making the preservation of tradition our primary concern. In short, we want to ask character education proponents what goals they emphasize—and ponder whether their broad vision is compatible with our own.

Which Values?

Should we allow values to be taught in school? The question is about as sensible as asking whether our bodies should be allowed to contain bacteria. Just as humans are teeming with microorganisms, so schools are teeming with values. We can't see the former because they're too small; we don't notice the latter because they're too similar to the values of the culture at large. Whether or not we deliberately adopt a character or moral education program, we are always teaching values. Even people who insist that they are opposed to values in school usually mean that they are opposed to values other than their own.[19]

And that raises the inevitable question: Which values, or whose, should we teach? It has already become a cliché to reply that this question should not trouble us because, while there may be disagreement on certain issues, such as abortion, all of us can agree on a list of basic values that children ought to have. Therefore, schools can vigorously and unapologetically set about teaching all of those values.

But not so fast. Look at the way character education programs have been designed and you will discover, alongside such unobjectionable items as "fairness" or "honesty," an emphasis on values that are, again, distinctly conservative—and, to that extent, potentially controversial. To begin with, the famous Protestant work ethic is prominent: children should learn to "work hard and complete their tasks well and promptly, even when they do not want to," says Ryan.[20] Here the Latin question *Cui bono?* comes to mind. Who benefits when people are trained not to question the value of what they have been told to do but simply to toil away at it—and to regard this as virtuous?[21] Similarly, when Wynne defines the moral individual as someone who is not only honest but also "diligent, obedient, and patriotic,"[22] readers may find themselves wondering whether these traits really qualify as *moral*—as well as reflecting on the virtues that are missing from this list.

Character education curricula also stress the importance of things like "respect," "responsibility," and "citizenship." But these are slippery terms, frequently used as euphemisms for uncritical deference to authority. Under the headline "The Return of the 'Fourth R' "—referring to "respect, responsibility, or rules"—a news magazine recently described the growing popularity of such practices as requiring uniforms, paddling disobedient students, rewarding those who are compliant, and "throwing disruptive kids out of the classroom."[23] Indeed, William Glasser observed some time ago that many educators "teach thoughtless conformity to school rules and call the conforming child 'responsible.' "[24] I once taught at a high school where the principal frequently exhorted students to "take responsibility." By this he meant specifically that they should turn in their friends who used drugs.

Exhorting students to be "respectful" or rewarding them if they are caught being "good" may likewise mean nothing more than getting them to do whatever the adults demand. Following a lengthy article about character education in the *New York Times Magazine,* a reader mused, "Do you suppose that if Germany had had character education at the time, it would have encouraged children to fight Nazism or to support it?"[25] The more time I spend in schools that are enthusiastically implementing character education programs, the more I am haunted by that question.

In place of the traditional attributes associated with character education, Deborah Meier and Paul Schwarz of the Central Park East Secondary School in New York nominated two core values that a school might try to promote: "empathy and skepticism: the ability to see a situation from the eyes of another and the tendency to wonder about the validity of what we encountered."[26] Anyone who brushes away the question "Which values should be taught?" might speculate on the concrete differences between a school dedicated to turning out students who are empathic and skeptical and a school dedicated to turning out students who are loyal, patriotic, obedient, and so on.

Meanwhile, in place of such personal qualities as punctuality or perseverance, we might emphasize the cultivation of autonomy so that children come to experience themselves as "origins" rather than "pawns," as one researcher put it.[27] We might, in other words, stress self-determination at least as much as self-control. With such an agenda, it would be crucial to give students the chance to participate in making decisions about their learning and about how they want their classroom to be.[28] This stands in sharp contrast to a philosophy of character education like Wynne's, which decrees that "it is specious to talk about student choices" and offers students no real power except for when we give "some students authority over other students (for example, hall guard, class monitor)."[29]

Even with values that are widely shared, a superficial consensus may dissolve when we take a closer look. Educators across the spectrum are concerned about excessive attention to self-interest and are committed to helping students transcend a preoccupation with their own needs. But how does this concern play out in practice? For some of us, it takes the form of an emphasis on *compassion*; for the dominant character education approach, the alternative value to be stressed is *loyalty*, which is, of course, altogether different.[30] Moreover, as John Dewey remarked at the turn of the century, anyone seriously troubled about rampant individualism among children would promptly target for extinction the "drill-and-skill" approach to instruction: "The mere absorbing of facts and truths is so exclusively individual an affair that it tends very naturally to pass into selfishness."[31] Yet conservative champions of character education are often among the most outspoken supporters of a model of teaching that emphasizes rote memorization and the sequential acquisition of decontextualized skills.

Or take another example: all of us may say we endorse the idea of "cooperation," but what do we make of the practice of setting groups against one another in a quest for triumph, such that cooperation becomes the means and victory is the end? On the one hand, we might find this even more objectionable than individual competition. (Indeed, we might regard a "We're Number One!" ethic as a reason for schools to undertake something like character education in the first place.) On the other hand, "school-to-school, class-to-class, or row-to-row academic competitions" actually have been endorsed as part of a character education program,[32] along with contests that lead to awards for things like good citizenship.

The point, once again, is that it is entirely appropriate to ask which values a character education program is attempting to foster, notwithstanding the ostensible lack of controversy about a list of core values. It is equally appropriate to put such a discussion in context—specifically, in the context of which values are *currently* promoted in schools. The fact is that schools are already powerful socializers of traditional values—although, as noted above, we may fail to appreciate the extent to which this is true because we have come to take these values for granted. In most schools, for example, students are taught—indeed, compelled—to follow the rules regardless of whether the rules are reasonable and to respect authority regardless of whether that respect has been earned. (This process isn't always successful, of course, but that is a different matter.) Students are led to accept competition as natural and desirable, and to see themselves more as discrete individuals than as members of a community. Children in American schools are even expected to begin each day by reciting a loyalty oath to the Fatherland, although we call it by a different name. In short, the question is not whether to adopt the conservative values offered by most character education programs, but whether we want to consolidate the conservative values that are already in place.

What Is the Theory of Learning?

We come now to what may be the most significant, and yet the least remarked on, feature of character education: the way values are taught and the way learning is thought to take place.

> The character education coordinator for the small Chicago elementary school also teaches second grade. In her classroom, where one boy has been forced to sit by himself for the last two weeks ("He's kind of pesty"), she is asking the children to define tolerance. When the teacher gets the specific answers she is fishing for, she exclaims, "Say that again," and writes down only those responses. Later comes the moral: "If somebody doesn't think the way you think, should you turn them off?" (No.)
>
> Down the hall, the first-grade teacher is fishing for answers on a different subject. "When we play games, we try to understand the—what?" (Rules.) A moment later, the children scramble to get into place so she will pick them to tell a visitor their carefully rehearsed stories about conflict resolution. Almost every child's account, narrated with considerable prompting by the teacher, concerns name-calling or some other unpleasant incident that was "correctly" resolved by finding an adult. The teacher never asks the children how they felt about what happened or invites them to reflect on what else might have been done. She wraps up the activity by telling the children, "What we need to do all the time is clarify—make it clear—to the adult what you did."

The schools with character education programs that I have visited are engaged largely in exhortation and directed recitation. At first one might assume this is due to poor implementation of the programs on the part of individual educators. But the programs themselves—and the theorists who promote them —really do seem to regard teaching as a matter of telling and compelling. For example, the broad-based "Character Counts!" Coalition offers a framework of six core character traits and then asserts that "young people should be specifically and repeatedly told what is expected of them." The leading providers of curriculum materials walk teachers through highly structured lessons in which character-related concepts are described and then students are drilled until they can produce the right answers.

Teachers are encouraged to praise children who respond correctly, and some programs actually include multiple-choice tests to ensure that students have learned their values. For example, here are two sample test questions prepared for teachers by the Character Education Institute, based in San Antonio, Texas: "Having to obey rules and regulations (a) gives everyone the same right to be an individual, (b) forces everyone to do the same thing at all times, (c) prevents persons from expressing their individually [sic]"; and "One reason why parents might not allow their children freedom of choice is (a) children are always happier when they are told what to do and when to do it, (b) parents aren't given a freedom of choice; therefore, children should not be given a choice either, (c) children do not always demonstrate that they are responsible enough to be given a choice." The correct answers, according to the answer key, are (a) and (c) respectively.

The Character Education Institute recommends "engaging the students in discussions," but only discussions of a particular sort: "Since the lessons have been designed to logically guide the students to the right answers, the teacher should allow the students to draw their own conclusions. However, if the students draw the wrong conclusion, the teacher is instructed to tell them why their conclusion is *wrong*."[33]

Students are told what to think and do, not only by their teachers but by highly didactic stories, such as those in the Character Education Institute's "Happy Life" series, which end with characters saying things like "I am glad that I did not cheat," or "Next time I will be helpful," or "I will never be selfish again." Most character education programs also deliver homilies by way of posters and banners and murals displayed throughout the school. Children who do as they are told are presented with all manner of rewards, typically in front of their peers.

Does all of this amount to indoctrination? Absolutely, says Wynne, who declares that "school is and should and must be inherently indoctrinative."[34] Even when character education proponents tiptoe around that word, their model of instruction is clear: good character and values are *instilled in* or *transmitted to* students. We are "planting the ideas of virtue, of good traits in the young," says William Bennett.[35] The virtues or values in question are fully formed, and, in the minds of many character education proponents, divinely ordained. The children are—pick your favorite metaphor—so many passive receptacles to be filled, lumps of clay to be molded, pets to be trained, or computers to be programmed.

Thus, when we see Citizen-of-the-Month certificates and "Be a good sport!" posters, when we find teachers assigning preachy stories and principals telling students what to wear, it is important that we understand what is going on. These techniques may appear merely innocuous or gimmicky; they may strike us as evidence of a scattershot, let's-try-anything approach. But the truth is that these are elements of a systematic pedagogical philosophy. They are manifestations of a model that sees children as objects to be manipulated rather than as learners to be engaged.

Ironically, some people who accept character education without a second thought are quite articulate about the bankruptcy of this model when it comes to teaching academic subjects. Plenty of teachers have abandoned the use of worksheets, textbooks, and lectures that fill children full of disconnected facts and skills. Plenty of administrators are working to create schools where students can actively construct meaning around scientific and historical and literary concepts. Plenty of educators, in short, realize that memorizing right answers and algorithms doesn't help anyone to arrive at a deep understanding of ideas.

And so we are left scratching our heads. Why would all these people, who know that the "transmission" model fails to facilitate intellectual development, uncritically accept the very same model to promote ethical development? How could they understand that mathematical truths cannot be shoved down students' throats but then participate in a program that essentially tries to shove moral truths down the same throats? In the case of individual educators, the simple answer may be that they missed the connection. Perhaps they just failed to recognize that "a classroom cannot foster the development of autonomy in the intellectual realm while suppressing it in the social and moral realms," as Constance Kamii and her colleagues put it not long ago.[36]

In the case of the proponents of character education, I believe the answer to this riddle is quite different. The reason they are promoting techniques that seem strikingly ineffective at fostering autonomy or ethical development is that, as a rule, they are not *trying* to foster autonomy or ethical development. The goal is not to support or facilitate children's social and moral growth, but simply to "demand good behavior from students," in Ryan's words.[37] The idea is to get compliance, to *make* children act the way we want them to.

Indeed, if these are the goals, then the methods make perfect sense—the lectures and pseudo-discussions, the slogans and the stories that conk students on the head with their morals. David Brooks, who heads the Jefferson Center for Character Education, frankly states, "We're in the advertising business." The way you get people to do something, whether it's buying Rice Krispies or becoming trustworthy, is to "encourage conformity through repeated messages."[38] The idea of selling virtues like cereal nearly reaches the point of self-parody in the Jefferson Center's curriculum, which includes the following activity: "There's a new product on the market! It's Considerate Cereal. Eating it can make a person more considerate. Design a label for the box. Tell why someone should buy and eat this cereal. Then list the ingredients."[39]

If "repeated messages" don't work, then you simply force students to conform: "Sometimes compulsion is what is needed to get a habit started," says William Kilpatrick.[40] We may recoil from the word "compulsion," but it is the premise of that sentence that really ought to give us pause. When education is construed as the process of inculcating *habits*—which is to say, unreflective actions—then it scarcely deserves to be called education at all. It is really, as Alan

Lockwood saw, an attempt to get "mindless conformity to externally imposed standards of conduct."[41]

Notice how naturally this goal follows from a dark view of human nature. If you begin with the premise that "good conduct is not our natural first choice," then the best you can hope for is "the development of good habits"[42] —that is, a system that gets people to act unthinkingly in the manner that someone else has deemed appropriate. This connection recently became clear to Ann Medlock, whose Giraffe Project was designed to evoke "students' own courage and compassion" in thinking about altruism, but which, in some schools, was being turned into a traditional, authoritarian program in which students were simply told how to act and what to believe. Medlock recalls suddenly realizing what was going on with these educators: "Oh, *I* see where you're coming from. You believe kids are no damn good!"[43]

The character education movement's emphasis on habit, then, is consistent with its view of children. Likewise, its process matches its product. The transmission model, along with the use of rewards and punishments to secure compliance, seems entirely appropriate if the values you are trying to transmit are things like obedience and loyalty and respect for authority. But this approach overlooks an important distinction between product and process. When we argue about which traits to emphasize—compassion or loyalty, cooperation or competition, skepticism or obedience—we are trafficking in value judgments. When we talk about how best to teach these things, however, we are being descriptive rather than just prescriptive. Even if you like the sort of virtues that appear in character education programs, and even if you regard the need to implement those virtues as urgent, the attempt to transmit or instill them dooms the project because that is just not consistent with the best theory and research on how people learn. (Of course, if you have reservations about many of the values that the character educators wish to instill, you may be *relieved* that their favored method is unlikely to be successful.)

I don't wish to be misunderstood. The techniques of character education may succeed in temporarily buying a particular behavior. But they are unlikely to leave children with a *commitment* to that behavior, a reason to continue acting that way in the future. You can turn out automatons who utter the desired words or maybe even "emit" (to use the curious verb favored by behaviorists) the desired actions. But the words and actions are unlikely to continue—much less transfer to new situations—because the child has not been invited to integrate them into his or her value structure. As Dewey observed, "The required beliefs cannot be hammered in; the needed attitudes cannot be plastered on."[44] Yet watch a character education lesson in any part of the country and you will almost surely be observing a strenuous exercise in hammering and plastering.

For traditional moralists, the constructivist approach is a waste of time. If values and traditions and the stories that embody them already exist, then surely "we don't have to reinvent the wheel," remarks Bennett.[45] Likewise an exasperated Wynne: "Must each generation try to completely reinvent society?"[46] The answer is no—and yes. It is not as though everything that now exists must be discarded and entirely new values fashioned from scratch. But the process of learning does indeed require that meaning, ethical or otherwise, be actively invented and reinvented, from the inside out. It requires that children be given the opportunity to make sense of such concepts as fairness or courage, regardless of how long the concepts themselves have been around. Children must be invited to reflect on complex issues, to recast them in light of their own experiences and questions, to figure out for themselves—and with one another—what kind of person one ought to be, which traditions are worth keeping, and how to proceed when two basic values seem to be in conflict.[47]

In this sense, reinvention is necessary if we want to help children become moral people, as opposed to people who merely do what they are told—or reflexively rebel against what they are told.

Notes

1. See, for example, Linda Page, "A Conservative Christian View on Values," *School Administrator,* September 1995, p. 22.

2. See, for example, Kevin Ryan, "The Ten Commandments of Character Education," *School Administrator,* September 1995, p. 19; and program materials from the Character Education Institute and the Jefferson Center for Character Education.

3. See Alfie Kohn, *Punished by Rewards: The Trouble with Gold Stars, Incentive Plans, A's, Praise, and Other Bribes* (Boston: Houghton Mifflin, 1993); and Edward L. Deci and Richard M. Ryan, *Intrinsic Motivation and Self-Determination in Human Behavior* (New York: Plenum, 1985).

4. See C. Daniel Batson et al., "Buying Kindness: Effect on an Extrinsic Incentive for Helping on Perceived Altruism," *Personality and Social Psychology Bulletin,* vol 4, 1978, p. 90; Cathleen L. Smith et al., "Children's Causal Attributions Regarding Help Giving," *Child Development,* vol. 59, 1979, pp. 203–10; and William Edward Upton III, "Altruism, Attribution, and Intrinsic Motivation in the Recruitment of Blood Donors," *Dissertation Abstracts International* 34B, vol 12, 1974, p. 6260.

5. Richard A. Fabes et al., "Effects of Rewards on Children's Prosocial Motivation: A Socialization Study," *Developmental Psychology,* vol. 25, 1989, pp. 509–15; and Joan Grusec, "Socializing Concern for Others in the Home," *Develomental Psychology,* vol. 27, 1991, pp. 338–42.

6. See Alfie Kohn, *No Contest: The Case Against Competition,* rev. ed. (Boston: Houghton Mifflin, 1992).

7. This statement is taken from an eight-page brochure produced by the "Character Counts!" Coalition, a project of the Josephson Institute of Ethics. Members of the coalition include the American Federation of Teachers, the National Association of Secondary School Principals, the American Red Cross, the YMCA, and many other organizations.

8. William Kilpatrick, *Why Johnny Can't Tell Right from Wrong* (New York: Simon & Schuster, 1992), pp. 96, 249.

9. For example, Kilpatrick was selected in 1995 to keynote the first in a series of summer institutes on character education sponsored by Thomas Lickona.

10. Edward Wynne, "Transmitting Traditional Values in Contemporary Schools," in Larry P. Nucci, ed., *Moral Development and Character Education: A Dialogue* (Berkeley, Calif.: McCutchan, 1989), p. 25.

11. Kevin Ryan, "In Defense of Character Education," in Nucci, p. 16.

12. Louis Goldman, "Mind, Character, and the Deferral of Gratification," *Educational Forum*, vol. 60, 1996, p. 136. As part of "educational reconstruction," he goes on to say, we must "connect the lower social classes to the middle classes who may provide role models for self-discipline" (p. 139).

13. Jarvis is quoted in Wray Herbert, "The Moral Child," *U.S. News & World Report*, 3 June 1996, p. 58.

14. Amitai Etzioni, *The Spirit of Community: The Reinvention of American Society* (New York: Simon & Schuster, 1993), p. 91.

15. See Alfie Kohn, *The Brighter Side of Human Nature: Altruism and Empathy in Everyday Life* (New York: Basic Books, 1990); and "Caring Kids: The Role of the Schools," *Phi Delta Kappan*, March 1991, pp. 496–506.

16. David E. Purpel, "Moral Education: An Idea Whose Time Has Gone," *The Clearing House*, vol. 64, 1991, p. 311.

17. This description of the character education movement is offered by Alan L. Lockwood in "Character Education: The Ten Percent Solution," *Social Education*, April/May 1991, p. 246. It is a particularly apt characterization of a book like *Why Johnny Can't Tell Right from Wrong*, which invokes an age of "chivalry" and sexual abstinence, a time when moral truths were uncomplicated and unchallenged. The author's tone, however, is not so much wistful about the past as angry about the present: he denounces everything from rock music (which occupies an entire chapter in a book about morality) and feminism to the "multiculturalists" who dare to remove "homosexuality from the universe of moral judgment" (p. 126).

18. Kevin Walsh of the University of Alabama is quoted in Eric N. Berg, "Argument Grows That Teaching of Values Should Rank with Lessons," *New York Times*, 1 January 1992, p. 32.

19. I am reminded of a woman in a Houston audience who heatedly informed me that she doesn't send her child to school "to learn to be nice." That, she declared, would be "social engineering." But a moment later this woman added that her child ought to be "taught to respect authority." Since this would seem to be at least as apposite an example of social engineering, one is led to conclude that the woman's real objection was to the teaching of *particular* topics or values.

20. Kevin Ryan, "Mining the Values in the Curriculum," *Educational Leadership*, November 1993, p. 16.

21. Telling students to "try hard" and "do their best" begs the important questions. *How*, exactly, do they do their best? Surely it is not just a matter of blind effort. And *why* should they do so, particularly if the task is not engaging or meaningful to them, or if it has simply been imposed on them? Research has found that the attitudes students take toward learning are heavily influenced by whether they have been led to attribute their success (or failure) to innate ability, to effort, or to other factors—and that traditional classroom practices such as grading and competition lead them to explain the results in terms of ability (or its absence) and to minimize effort whenever possible. What looks like "laziness" or insufficient perseverance, in other words, often turns out to be a rational decision to avoid challenge; it is rational because this route proves most expedient for performing well or maintaining an image of oneself as smart. These systemic factors, of course, are complex and often threatening for educators to address; it is much easier just to impress on children the importance of doing their best and then blame them for lacking perseverance if they seem not to do so.

22. Edward A. Wynne, "The Great Tradition in Education: Transmitting Moral Values," *Educational Leadership*, December 1985/January 1986, p. 6.

23. Mary Lord, "The Return of the 'Fourth R,' " *U.S. News & World Report*, 11 September 1995, p. 58.

24. William Glasser, *Schools Without Failure* (New York: Harper & Row, 1969), p. 22.

25. Mare Desmond's letter appeared in the *New York Times Magazine*, 21 May 1995, p. 14. The same point was made by Robert Primack, "No Substitute for Critical Thinking: A Response to Wynne," *Educational Leadership*, December 1985/January 1986, p. 12.

26. Deborah Meier and Paul Schwarz, "Central Park East Secondary School," in Michael W. Apple and James A. Beane, eds., *Democratic Schools* (Alexandria, Va.: Association for Supervision and Curriculum Development, 1995), pp. 29–30.

27. See Richard de Charms, *Personal Causation: The Internal Affective Determinants of Behavior* (Hillsdale, N.J.: Erlbaum, 1983). See also the many publications of Edward Deci and Richard Ryan.

28. See, for example, Alfie Kohn, "Choices for Children: Why and How to Let Students Decide," *Phi Delta Kappan*, September 1993, pp. 8–20; and Child Development Project, *Ways We Want Our Class to Be: Class Meetings That Build Commitment to Kindness and Learning* (Oakland, Calif.: Developmental Studies Center, 1996).

29. The quotations are from Wynne, "The Great Tradition," p. 9; and Edward A. Wynne and Herbert J. Walberg, "The Complementary Goals of Character Development and Academic Excellence," *Educational Leadership*, December 1985/January 1986, p. 17. William Kilpatrick is equally averse to including students in decision making; he speaks longingly of the days when "schools were unapologetically authoritarian," declaring that "schools can learn a lot from the Army," which is a "hierarchial [sic], authoritarian, and undemocratic institution" (see *Why Johnny Can't*, p. 228).

30. The sort of compassion I have in mind is akin to what the psychologist Ervin Staub described as a "prosocial orientation" (see his *Positive Social Behavior and Morality*, vols. 1 and 2 [New York: Academic Press, 1978 and 1979])—a generalized inclination to care, share, and help across different situations and with different people, including those we don't know, don't like, and don't look like. Loyally lending a hand to a close friend is one thing; going out of one's way for a stranger is something else.

31. John Dewey, *The School and Society* (Chicago: University of Chicago Press, 1900; reprint, 1990), p. 15.

32. Wynne and Walberg, p. 17. For another endorsement of competition among students, see Kevin Ryan, "In Defense," p. 15.

33. This passage is taken from page 21 of an undated 28-page "Character Education Curriculum" produced by the Character Education Institute. Emphasis in original.

34. Wynne, "Great Tradition," p. 9. Wynne and other figures in the character education movement acknowledge their debt to the French social scientist Emile Durkheim, who believed that "all education is a continuous effort to impose on the child ways of seeing, feeling, and acting which he could not have arrived at spontaneously. . . . We exert pressure upon him in order that he may learn proper consideration for others, respect for customs and conventions, the need for work, etc." (See Durkheim, *The Rules of Sociological Method* [New York: Free Press, 1938], p. 6.)

35. This is from Bennett's introduction to *The Book of Virtues* (New York: Simon & Schuster, 1993), pp. 12–13.

36. Constance Kamii, Faye B. Clark, and Ann Dominick, "The Six National Goals: A Road to Disappointment," *Phi Delta Kappan*, May 1994, p. 677.

37. Kevin Ryan, "Character and Coffee Mugs," *Education Week*, 17 May 1995, p. 48.

38. The second quotation is a reporter's paraphrase of Brooks. Both it and the direct quotation preceding it appear in Philip Cohen, "The Content of Their Character: Educators Find New Ways to Tackle Values and Morality," *ASCD Curriculum Update*, Spring 1995, p. 4.

39. See B. David Brooks, *Young People's Lessons in Character: Student Activity Workbook* (San Diego: Young People's Press, 1996), p. 12.

40. Kilpatrick, p. 231.

41. To advocate this sort of enterprise, he adds, is to "caricature the moral life." See Alan L. Lockwood, "Keeping Them in the Courtyard: A Response to Wynne," *Educational Leadership,* December 1985/January 1986, p. 10.

42. Kilpatrick, p. 97.

43. Personal communication with Ann Medlock, May 1996.

44. John Dewey, *Democracy and Education* (New York: Free Press, 1916; reprint, 1966), p. 11.

45. Bennett, p. 11.

46. Wynne, "Character and Academics," p. 142.

47. For a discussion of how traditional character education fails to offer guidance when values come into conflict, see Lockwood, "Character Education."

POSTSCRIPT

Can "Character Education" Reverse Moral Decline?

Former secretary of education William J. Bennett has stated that we must not permit disputes over political and theological matters to suffocate the obligation we have to instruct our young in the importance of good character (see "Moral Literacy and the Formation of Character," *NASSP Bulletin,* December 1988). Yet in the public domain, questions of whose values should be presented and whether or not religion-based values can be proffered take on a political cast that is hard to dismiss. Two books that address specific aspects of this dilemma are *The Moral Life of Schools* by Philip W. Jackson, Robert E. Boostrom, and David T. Hansen (1993) and *Reclaiming Our Schools* by Edward A. Wynne and Kevin Ryan (1993).

For a full perspective on the issue of values and moral education, review John Dewey, *Moral Principles in Education* (1911); Abraham Maslow, *New Knowledge in Human Values* (1959); Milton Rokeach, *The Nature of Human Values* (1973); and Robert Coles, *The Moral Life of Children* (1986).

Alternative approaches to moral education can be explored in "Correct Habits and Moral Character: John Dewey and Traditional Education," by Patrick K. Dooley, *Journal of Thought* (Fall 1991); Howard Kirschenbaum, "A Comprehensive Model of Values Education and Moral Education," *Phi Delta Kappan* (June 1992); *The Moral Self: Building a Better Paradigm* edited by Gil Noam and Thomas Wren (1993); "The Three Rs of Moral Education," by M. Jean Bouas, and "Education and Family Values," by John Martin Rich, *The Educational Forum* (Winter 1993); and "Restoring Our Moral Voice," by Amitai Etzioni, *The Public Interest* (Summer 1994).

A number of journals have produced issues around the theme of character education that can be valuable sources of information. Among them are *The Clearing House* (May–June 1991), featuring articles by Maxine Greene, Nel Noddings, John Martin Rich, Kevin Ryan, and Henry A. Giroux; *The Journal of Education* (Spring 1993), particularly an article by Edwin J. Delattre and William E. Russell titled "Schooling, Moral Principles, and the Formation of Character"; and *Educational Leadership* (November 1993), which contains over 20 articles on the subject of character education. For an elaboration of Lickona's theories and opinions, see his 1991 book *Education for Character: How Our Schools Can Teach Respect and Responsibility.* Multiple articles on the issue can be found in *The Educational Forum* (Winter 1996), *Journal of Education* (nos. 2 and 3, 1997), *Phi Delta Kappan* (February 1998), *The School Administrator* (May 1998), and *NASSP Bulletin* (October 1999).

ISSUE 7

Should Multiculturalism Permeate the Curriculum?

YES: Sonia Nieto, from "What Does It Mean to Affirm Diversity?" *The School Administrator* (May 1999)

NO: Thomas J. Famularo, from "The Intellectual Bankruptcy of Multiculturalism," *USA Today Magazine*, a publication of the Society for the Advancement of Education (May 1996)

ISSUE SUMMARY

YES: Professor of language, literacy, and culture Sonia Nieto examines the realities of diversity in American society that underlie an effective approach to multicultural education.

NO: Former English instructor Thomas J. Famularo contends that the multiculturalism movement, rather than representing diversity, is centered on the themes of race and gender and the debunking of Western culture.

During the past 20 years or so, American public schools have been encouraged to embrace multiculturalism as a curricular focus. The "No One American" statement, issued by the American Association of Colleges of Teacher Education in 1972, set the tone for the movement by calling for an effort to support cultural diversity and global understanding. In the 1980s a number of influential writers, such as Allan Bloom, E. D. Hirsch, Jr., Arthur M. Schlesinger, Jr., William J. Bennett, and Nathan Glazer, warned of the divisive nature of multiculturalism and called for a renewed curricular focus on cultural commonalities shaped by the Western tradition.

Thus was launched the so-called culture wars, which have persisted on an educational battlefield that extends from kindergarten to graduate school. Several books, including Bennett's *To Reclaim a Legacy* (1984), Lynne Cheney's *American Memory: A Report on the Humanities in the Nation's Public Schools* (1988), and Dinesh D'Souza's *Illiberal Education: The Politics of Race and Sex on Campus* (1991), stirred much of the public's concern over what many felt was an encroachment by the multiculturalists upon the traditional canon and

the subsequent diminishment of cultural literacy. In defense of multiculturalism, Ira Shor, in his book *Culture Wars: School and Society in the Conservative
Restoration* (1987), argues that the underlying motivation of the cultural literacy
"backlash" was to restore conservative themes and "right words" that establish
"raw authority at the top" while discrediting the liberalism of the 1960s. Also
supportive of a multicultural curriculum is Asa G. Hilliard III, who contends
that the traditional Eurocentric curriculum is warped and restrictive; that the
primary goal of multiculturalism is to present a truthful and meaningful ren-
dition of the whole of human experience; and that a pluralistic curriculum is
not a matter of ethnic quotas for "balance," as some conservatives contend.

A number of prominent scholars have joined the fray. Harold Bloom, in
The Western Canon (1994), deplores multiculturalism and other "isms" that
politicize choice. Thomas Sowell devotes chapters of *Inside American Education:
The Decline, the Deception, the Dogmas* (1993) to what he considers misconcep-
tions put forth by multiculturalists and bilingual education advocates. Richard
Bernstein, in *Dictatorship of Virtue: Multiculturalism and the Battle for America's Future* (1994), expresses fear that there is a pulling away from certain
cultural norms, adherence to which has traditionally enabled Americans "to
board the great engine of upward social mobility." Also noteworthy are the
many books and articles of James A. Banks, a leader in the multicultural education movement, and Nathan Glazer's *We Are All Multiculturalists Now* (1997).
Recent articles of note include "Multiculturalism Is Driving Us Apart," by Linda
Chavez, *USA Today Magazine* (May 1996); "Multicultural Education as a Moral
Responsibility," by Michael R. Hillis, *The Educational Forum* (Winter 1996);
"Multiculturalism, Diversity, and Cultural Pluralism," by Vanessa J. Lawrence,
Journal of Black Studies (January 1997); and Dennis Wrong's "Adversarial Iden-
tities and Multiculturalism," *Society* (January/February 2000).

Two social realities undergird the multiculturalist effort to reform the
curriculum at all levels: the traditional curriculum has neglected the contributions made by minority groups to the American culture, and the economy
is becoming more and more globalized. Given these conditions, the multicultural approach may be seen as serving to give a new and expanded definition
to the "American experience." What effect a multicultural curriculum will
have on American traditions and social institutions remains to be seen. Serious questions continue to be debated—questions involving the future path of
cultural development in American society, and sociological questions about
the relationships between the institutionally dominant majority culture and
the minority cultures, the populations of which are increasing.

In the following opposing selections, Sonia Nieto, author of *Affirming
Diversity*, 3rd ed. (2000) and *The Light in Their Eyes* (1999), pleads for greater
attention to and respect for ethnic minorities and poor children in their quest
for social justice. Thomas J. Famularo argues that multiculturalism, which began as an attempt to increase awareness of ethnic and minority contributions
to history and culture, has evolved into an approach that makes diversity and
difference the prime movers of the curriculum.

Sonia Nieto

 **YES**

What Does It Mean to Affirm Diversity?

About 15 years ago, I was interviewing a young woman for admission to our multicultural teacher education program and I asked her why she had chosen to apply for this particular program. (At the time, we had a number of undergraduate teacher preparation programs from which students to choose.)

The young woman, let's call her Nancy, mentioned that she was doing a prepracticum at Marks Meadow School, the laboratory school of our School of Education at the University of Massachusetts. Marks Meadow is an extraordinarily diverse place with children from every corner of the globe representing multiple languages and various social and economic backgrounds.

When the children in her 1st-grade classroom were doing self-portraits, one of them asked Nancy for a brown crayon. She was momentarily confounded by his request, thinking *Why brown?* It never before had occurred to her that children would make their faces anything other than the color of the white paper they used. "I decided then and there that I needed this program," she confessed.

As naive as her reaction was, it was the beginning of Nancy's awakening to diversity. It was also a courageous disclosure of her own ignorance.

Ill-Prepared for Diversity

It is by now a truism that our country's public schools are undergoing a dramatic shift that reflects the growing diversity of our population. Yet many educators and the schools in which they work seem no better prepared for this change than was Nancy a decade and a half ago. Most educators nationwide are very much like Nancy: white, middle-class, monolingual English-speaking women and men who have had little direct experience with cultural, ethnic, linguistic or other kinds of diversity, but they are teaching students who are phenomenally diverse in every way.

Given this scenario, what do educators—teachers, aides, curriculum developers, principals, superintendents and school board members—need to know to create effective schools for students of all backgrounds, and how can they learn it? Let me suggest five realities that educators need to appreciate and understand if this is to happen:

Affirming diversity is above all about social justice.

Contrary to what the pundits who oppose multicultural education might say, multicultural education is *not* about political correctness, sensitivity training or ethnic cheerleading. It is primarily about social justice. Given the vastly unequal educational outcomes among students of different backgrounds, equalizing conditions for student learning needs to be at the core of a concern for diversity.

If this is the case, "celebrating diversity" through special assembly programs, multicultural dinners or ethnic celebrations are hollow activities if they do not also confront the structural inequalities that exist in schools.

A concern for social justice means looking critically at why and how our schools are unjust for some students. It means that we need to analyze school policies and practices that devalue the identities of some students while overvaluing others: the curriculum, testing, textbooks and materials, instructional strategies, tracking, the recruitment and hiring of staff and parent involvement strategies. All of these need to be viewed with an eye toward making them more equitable for all students, not just those students who happen to be white, middle class and English speaking.

Students of color and poor students bear the brunt of structural inequality.

Schools inevitably reflect society, and the evidence that our society is becoming more unequal is growing every day. We have all read the headlines: The United States has one of the highest income disparities in the world, and the combined wealth of the top 1 percent of U.S. families is about the same as the entire bottom 80 percent.

Growing societal inequities are mirrored in numerous ways in schools, from highly disparate financing of schools in rich and poor communities, to academic tracking that favors white above black and brown students, to SAT scores that correlate perfectly with income rather than with intelligence or ability. Although it is a worthy goal, equality is far from a reality in most of our schools, and those who bear the burden of inequality are our children, particularly poor children of all backgrounds and many children of Latino, Native American, Asian American and African American backgrounds. The result is schools that are racist and classist, if not by intention, at least by result.

Inequality is a fact of life, but many educators refuse to believe or accept it, and they persist in blaming children, their families, their cultural and linguistic backgrounds, laziness or genetic inferiority as the culprits. Once educators accept the fact that inequality is alive and thriving in our schools, they can proceed to do something about it. Until they do, little will change.

Positive Acculturation

Diversity is a valuable resource.

I went to elementary school in Brooklyn, N.Y., during the 1950s. My classmates were enormously diverse in ethnicity, race, language, social class and family structure.

But even then, we were taught as if we were all cut from the same cloth. Our mothers were urged to speak to us in English at home (fortunately, my mother never paid attention, and it is because of this that I am fluent in Spanish today), and we were given the clear message that anything having to do with our home cultures was not welcome in school. To succeed in school, we needed to learn English, forget our native language and behave like the kids we read about in our basal readers.

Of course, learning English and learning it well is absolutely essential for academic and future life success, but the assumption that one must discard one's identity along the way needs to be challenged. There is nothing shameful in knowing a language other than English. In fact, becoming bilingual can benefit individuals and our country in general.

As educators, we no longer can afford to behave as if diversity were a dirty word. Every day, more research underscores the positive influence that cultural and linguistic diversity has on student learning. Immigrant students who maintain a positive ethnic identity as they acculturate and who become fluent bilinguals are more likely to have better mental health, do well academically and graduate from high school than those who completely assimilate. Yet we insist on erasing cultural and linguistic differences as if they were a burden rather than an asset.

Effectively teaching students of all backgrounds means respecting and affirming who they are.

To become effective teachers of all students, educators must undergo a profound shift in their beliefs, attitudes and values about difference.

In many U.S. classrooms, cultural, linguistic and other differences are commonly viewed as temporary, if troublesome, barriers to learning. Consequently, students of diverse backgrounds are treated as walking sets of deficiencies, as if they had nothing to bring to the educational enterprise.

Anybody who has walked into a classroom knows that teaching and learning are above all about relationships, and these relationships can have a profound impact on students' futures. But significant relationships with students are difficult to develop when teachers have little understanding of the students' families and communities. The identities of nonmainstream students frequently are dismissed by schools and teachers as immaterial to academic achievement.

When this is the case, it is unlikely that students will form positive relationships with their teachers or, as a result, with learning. It is only when educators and schools accept and respect who their students are and what they know that they can begin to build positive connections with them.

Affirming diversity means becoming a multicultural person.

Over the years, I have found that educators believe they are affirming diversity simply because they say they are. But mouthing the words is not enough. Children sense instantly when support for diversity is superficial.

Because most educators in the United States have not had the benefit of firsthand experiences with diversity, it is a frightening concept for many of them. If we think of teaching as a life-long journey of personal transformation, becoming a multicultural person is part of the journey. It is different for each person.

For Nancy, it began with recognition of her own ignorance. For others, it means learning a second language or working collaboratively with colleagues to design more effective strategies of reaching all students. However we begin the journey, until we take those tentative first steps, what we say about diversity is severely limited by our actions.

Comfort With Differences

Taking these realities to heart means we no longer can think of some students as void of any dignity and worth simply because they do not confirm to our conventional image. All students of all backgrounds bring talents and strengths to their learning and as educators we need to find ways to build on these.

Acknowledging and affirming diversity is to everyone's interest, including middle-class white students. Understanding people of other backgrounds, speaking languages other than English and learning to respect and appreciate differences are skills that benefit all students and our nation as a whole. We do all our students a disservice when we prepare them to live in a society that no longer exists.

Given the tremendous diversity in our society, it makes eminent good sense to educate all our students to be comfortable with differences.

Thomas J. Famularo

 **NO**

The Intellectual Bankruptcy
of Multiculturalism

It is along ideological lines that the debate over multiculturalism has assumed its current form and substance. Thomas Sowell, in *Inside American Education*, states that the "ideological components of multiculturalism can be summarized as a cultural relativism which finds the prominence of Western civilization in the world or in the schools intolerable." Recently, this anti-West aspect of multiculturalism was evidenced at Yale University, where a $20,000,000 grant by Texas billionaire Lee M. Bass, exclusively for the development of programs and courses in Western culture, met highly politicized faculty opposition, with the result that Yale returned the money.

John O'Sullivan, editor of *National Review*, decries the multiculturalist assertion that America is an "idea rather than a nation [possessing] a distinctive but encompassing American identity." Peter W. Cookson, Jr., author of *School Choice: The Struggle for the Soul of American Education*, offers the insight that multiculturalism's hostility to the West and repudiation of an identifiable American culture is augmented by a radically new definition of community, one that swerves from the traditional emphasis on "family, neighborhood, church, lodge, and school to race, gender, occupation, and sexual preference."

These ideological divisions within U.S. society threaten to rend the nation into hostile factions. For example, Richard Bernstein, in *Dictatorship of Virtue: Multiculturalism and the Battle for America's Future*, brands ideological multiculturalists as "radical-left inhabitants of a political dreamland." Its critics maintain that multiculturalism is not—and never can be—a viable educational principle.

A few points of clarification regarding multiculturalism's recent evolution might be helpful. What began during the early part of this century as a shift towards increased awareness of ethnic and minority contributions to American history has evolved into a pedagogy that makes diversity and difference the prime movers of the curriculum.

In response to the New York State Department of Education's *A Curriculum of Inclusion* (1989), Diane Ravitch, writing in *The American Scholar* (Summer 1990), argued that current manifestations of multiculturalism extend far

From Thomas J. Famularo, "The Intellectual Bankruptcy of Multiculturalism," *USA Today Magazine* (May 1996). Copyright © 1996 by Thomas J. Famularo. Reprinted by permission of The Society for the Advancement of Education.

beyond the kind of pluralism that "seeks a richer common culture" to "multicultural particularism," which denies that a "common culture is possible or desirable."

According to the authors of *A Curriculum of Inclusion*, including controversial City University of New York (CUNY) former Black Studies chairman Leonard Jeffries, multiculturalism no longer should be construed to mean "adding marginal examples of 'other' cultures to an assumed dominant culture." On the contrary, multiculturalists adamantly gainsay the idea of an identifiable and definable American culture that might form the basis of a core curriculum. "The old curriculum is essentially based on the premise that America has one cultural heritage augmented by minor contributions from other peoples who by and large have presented 'problems' to the primary culture. To combat teaching and learning based on this premise, a radical, new approach to building a curriculum is needed," *A Curriculum of Inclusion* claims. Multicultural particularism, counters Ravitch, "is a bad idea whose time has come. It is also a fashion spreading like wildfire through the education system."

As multiculturalism is infused into mainstream American public education, I am reminded of a question asked by a former Brooklyn College colleague which captures the ultimate unfeasibility of multicultural education: "What comes out?" Although learning should be lifelong, schooling is a finite process. Inevitably, additions to the curriculum made in the name of diversity and inclusion render the necessity of displacement. A curriculum can contain just so much, and because education succeeds only when it includes prolonged and in-depth consideration of specific books, authors, ideas, and historical events, more in education often is less.

As far back as 1984, the Committee of Correspondence, a St. Louis-based international network of educational reformers, offered both a definition and defense of multicultural education: Knowledge of "diverse intellectual and cultural traditions," they wrote, should be a primary objective of a democratic curriculum, and this knowledge must include "not only the familiar academic disciplines and traditions of high culture, but the great multiplicity of cultures, perspectives and ways of knowing of the western and non-western world."

The committee faltered, however, in regard to the possible implementation of multicultural education by allowing that "There are difficult dilemmas in how to realize [this] in everyday schools and curriculum practice." These dilemmas must be "negotiated out of the conflicting values and interests of the students, teachers, and members of the local community." The key question, which the committee did not entertain, is whether or not this process of negotiation can result in anything other than what one educator has described as "dens of babble."

Multicultural education is undermined by two fatal flaws. The first is that the more the curriculum represents a multicultural test based upon "exposure to diversity," the more shallow and superficial learning becomes. By disavowing the "difficult dilemma" of choosing what comes out, multiculturalism ultimately reduces education to its shallowest possibilities—the mere glossing over of diverse subject matter—and renders the kind of understanding that comes from intensive, prolonged study of selected material impossible to attain.

Multiculturalism's second fatal flaw is that it necessarily precludes the single most important requirement for successful education—coherent means to a discernible end. By denying the existence of desirability of a distinctive American culture, thereby repudiating the need for public education to assist in the process of assimilation, multicultural education is both aimless and rudderless. Multicultural curricula career to and fro, touching fleetingly upon cultural tidbits of theoretically limitlessly diverse groups.

The culture wars that have ravaged American society for more than 30 years have forced America's public schools to capitulate to the relativism inherent in multiculturalism and to abandon education based upon desired ends for the cafeteria-style taste-test type of learning which does not work. Ravitch reasons that the final results of this "fractionation" are high school graduates who can "no longer be said to share a common body of knowledge, not to mention a common culture."

In an attempt to validate multiculturalism's emphasis on particularism and its concomitant subversion of cultural commonality, knowledge and facts in multicultural education consistently are subordinated to so-called "critical thinking skills." I say "so-called" because my experience with hundreds of college freshmen invariably revealed young adults who were as oblivious to real critical thinking concepts such as induction, deduction, syllogism, appeal to authority, point-counterpoint, comparison, and contrast as they were to rudimentary historical facts and dates. The dismal truth is that, more often than not, critical thinking in the classroom means little more than subjective questioning and unsubstantiated, unreasoned, personal opinion. Attempts to structure student opinion according to classical logical models often are met by multiculturalist accusations of Eurocentricity and pro-Western prejudices.

As an instructor of English at Brooklyn and Lehman Colleges of CUNY during the 1980s, I never had to look far for the results of education that substitutes critical thinking skills for the teaching of selected factual knowledge. The defining characteristic of my freshman students transcended race, sex, and ethnic heritage. Although predominantly intelligent, they essentially were empty vessels devoid of quantifiable academic information.

Contrary to the assertions of proponents of multiculturalism that limitless pluralism enriches education, the de-emphasizing of specific core material and factual knowledge in high school resulted in what it inevitably must have —a plague of ignorance. Multiculturalism's subordination of facts and knowledge to critical thinking skills demonstrates its educational bankruptcy, for any critical opinion worthy of a passing grade must evolve out of knowledge and be grounded in objective facts.

Anyone familiar with the nation's campus culture clashes knows what the call for diversity in education too often really is—a red herring for a radical agenda. When Stanford University, for instance, recommends only three subjects of study in the music segment of its required Culture, Ideas, Values course —Reggae lyrics, Rastafarian poetry, and Andean music—it answers the question "What comes out?" with a list that includes Bach, Mozart, and Beethoven. It constructs, as well, a curriculum which, far from being representatively diverse, is unified around a theme of race and sex and the debunking of Western culture.

Ironically, many multiculturalists, either consciously or instinctively, recognize the intellectual bankruptcy of the cultural particularism they ostensibly espouse. Multicultural curricula, overtly committed to diversity and difference, almost invariably are focused on underlying, latent, and often dogmatic themes.

In what direction is multiculturalism headed? Although educators such as Thomas Sowell have written of "the multiple evidences of declining educational quality during the period when multiculturalism and other non-academic preoccupations have taken up more and more of the curriculum," educational leaders attempted to plunge ahead into the multicultural morass with the ill-conceived National Standards for United States History, a part of the Clinton Administration's Goals 2000 Act.

As is inevitable with a multicultural curriculum, in order to make room for diverse additions, the National Education Standards and Improvement Council needed to make equivalent quantitative subtractions. Omitted from this proposed curriculum—in the name of respect for diversity—were, among other touchstones of traditional American history, the First Continental Congress, Robert E. Lee, Alexander Graham Bell, Thomas Edison, Albert Einstein, Jonas Salk, and the Wright brothers. Ultimately, students educated within the vague parameters of this multicultural curriculum will learn the hard truth —that any "critical" opinion of the birth of our nation without knowledge of the First Continental Congress or of the Civil War without considering Robert E. Lee is not based on sufficient factual knowledge and, therefore, has little or no value in the marketplace of ideas.

Goals 2000 risks continued educational decline. Its emphasis on multicultural diversity within the curriculum is not America's only choice. Educators should continue to explore other possibilities such as more diversity *of* schools and less diversity *within* schools.

A Success Story

One example worthy of study is Mortimer J. Adler's Chattanooga, Tenn.-based Paideia schools, founded on his prescription of "one required course of study for all." Syndicated columnist William Raspberry visited the Paideia schools in 1994 and was impressed with the high quality of teaching and learning that goes on there. "Parents of rich children and poor, black and white, camp out as long as a week in advance of registration to secure a place in these new schools," he wrote. He described a district that once was an "academic basket case," but where students now regularly achieve at the honor student level and for which the college acceptance rate approaches 98%.

In the same article, Raspberry juxtaposed the Paideia success story with the "disservice" of the old Georgia Tech "multicultural education" that urged minority students to take light course loads, shun the more difficult subjects such as science, and sign up for the "special multi-cultural tutoring program." The Paideia program, Raspberry indicated, proves that all students, regardless of race or cultural heritage, are capable of rising to the highest of expectations and that to think otherwise is "borderline racist."

In contradistinction to Goals 2000, Adler warns against a national curriculum that would be "unpardonably presumptuous in a country, such as ours, which is radically pluralistic." Within each individual school, he argues, a "single track" of connected courses should lead to a definable end. Unlike the multiculturalists who seek limitless curricular inclusion, Adler advocates the elimination of all material that might dilute, confuse, or clutter up the curriculum.

In the final book of his Paideia trilogy, *The Paideia Program: An Educational Syllabus,* Adler addresses the assumption that a focused curriculum breeds provincialism and narrowness of mind—"that learning about the United States only, or even about Western civilization, is not enough":

"What is meant by Oriental? Is it Chinese, and if so, Northern or Southern or Mandarin? Is it Japanese or Korean? Is it Javanese or Cambodian? Is it Indian (Hindu) or Pakistani (Moslem)? One could go on asking and each new name would point to a notably different culture. In short, what we face is several lifetimes of work to master diverse histories, each remote from that of New England or Texas, between which we ourselves see enough differences to require special effort in the teaching of a unified American history.

"What may we conclude? Are American school children to remain 'provincial' in the sense of knowing only the history of the West? Two answers suggest themselves. First, 'world history' is a term that can apply to information that varies in depth—deeper 'at home' (wherever home may be) than elsewhere. It is still a kind of knowledge of the world to know that something exists or took place, and even something of what it amounted to, without presuming to say how it was and is regarded by those in whose country it occurred. Every educated mind shows this variation in depth and range: natural limitations make encyclopedic knowledge an impossibility."

Adler's Paideia proposal is realistic and grounded in sound pedagogy. It evolves out of a distinction that the multiculturalists either fail to grasp or refuse to make. While the Paideia schools are *select* schools, they are neither exclusionary nor elitist. Their emphasis is on Western culture. Their selectivity is justifiable because it is not grounded in irrational bigotry, but in cultural choice (which is what multiculturalism is supposed to be, but never is, about).

This rationale for school choice has begun to trickle into mainstream public opinion. E. R. Shipp, a New York-based journalist, has demanded a public school curriculum that "places ancient Africa at the center of education for our 20th century African-American children." In doing so, she eloquently makes the case for another Paideia school.

Multiculturalism, writes *National Review's* O'Sullivan, is "liberalism deconstructing itself." He very well may be right. It will not be until the educational bankruptcy of multiculturalism is exposed fully that the deconstruction of American public education will be halted successfully.

POSTSCRIPT

Should Multiculturalism Permeate the Curriculum?

T he issue of multicultural education is complex and difficult to resolve because it reverberates to the core of the American democratic experience. Is the nation strengthened and its minority populations empowered by the process of assimilation into a culture with primarily Western European origins? Or is the United States—which is an immigrant nation—constantly redefined by the cultural influences that come to its shores?

Further research will reveal a wealth of theories and opinions that illuminate the basic problem and its many aspects. Recommended sources include "Dimensions of Multicultural Education," by Carlos F. Diaz, *National Forum* (Winter 1994); "Self-Esteem and Multiculturalism in the Public Schools," by Kay S. Hymowitz, *Dissent* (Winter 1992); "Multicultural Education: Five Views," by Christine E. Sleeter, *Kappa Delta Pi Record* (Fall 1992); Valerie Ooka Pang, John Rivera, and Jill Kerper Mora, "The Ethic of Caring," *Eductional Forum* (Fall 1999); and Peter Skerry, "Do We Really Want Immigrants to Assimilate?" *Society* (March/Arpil 2000).

The political perspective on this topic is examined in Henry A. Giroux, "Curriculum, Multiculturalism, and the Politics of Identity," *NASSP Bulletin* (December 1992); Christine Canning, "Preparing for Diversity: A Social Technology for Multicultural Community Building," *The Educational Forum* (Summer 1993); and Francis J. Ryan, "Will Multiculturalism Undercut Student Individuality?" *Educational Horizons* (Spring 1993).

Some theme issues of journals to explore are "Polarizing American Culture," *Society* (July/August 1993); "Multicultural Education," *Phi Delta Kappan* (September 1993); "Critical Perspectives on Diversity," *The Educational Forum* (Summer 1993); and two issues of *National Forum* that focus on "Immigration and the Changing Face of America" (Summer 1994) and "Multiculturalism and Diversity" (Winter 1994).

Some articles of note include a provocative defense of Western culture by Bernard Lewis, "Eurocentrism Revisited," *Commentary* (December 1994) and Carl A. Grant, "Challenging the Myths About Multicultural Education," *Multicultural Education* (Winter 1994). Further ideas can be found in Todd Gitlin's *The Twilight of Common Dreams* (1995), David A. Hollinger's *Postethnic America* (1995), Michael Lind's *The Next American Nation* (1995), and Lawrence W. Levine's *The Opening of the American Mind* (1996).

ISSUE 8

Are School Integration Efforts Doomed to Failure?

YES: Doris Y. Wilkinson, from "Integration Dilemmas in a Racist Culture," *Society* (March/April 1996)

NO: Ray C. Rist, from "Color, Class, and the Realities of Inequality," *Society* (March/April 1996)

ISSUE SUMMARY

YES: Sociology professor Doris Y. Wilkinson argues that school integration has been an abysmal failure because of sustained opposition by Euro-Americans at all levels of the economic hierarchy.

NO: Ray C. Rist, a professor of education and of sociology, asserts that, although American society is still overwhelmingly separated by race in schools and elsewhere, a fundamental restructuring of the educational system can reverse the present course.

T he 40th anniversary of the U.S. Supreme Court decision in *Brown v. Board of Education of Topeka, Kansas* (1954), was marked by a number of appraisals of the progress that has been made in the long and arduous process of racial desegregation in public education and in U.S. society as a whole. For example, "The Growth of Segregation in American Schools: Changing Patterns of Separation and Poverty Since 1968," by Gary Orfield et al., *Equity and Excellence in Education* (April 1994) analyzes research by the Harvard Project on School Desegregation. This report's dismal conclusions regarding the level of segregation that exists in American schools today lend support to Jonathan Kozol's portrayal of schools in poverty-stricken areas in *Savage Inequalities: Children in America's Schools* (1991). In his book, Kozol argues that prevailing school funding practices have ensured that schools in poor, mostly minority districts would remain of the lowest quality, both physically and socially. Similarly, an editorial in the May 23, 1994, issue of *The Nation* titled *"Brown at 40"* describes a Topeka that is still segregated, a situation shaped by racism, classism, local politics, and a lack of political activism.

Has educator and politician Horace Mann's optimistic nineteenth-century promise that the public schools would be "a great equalizer" and a "balance wheel of the social machinery" been realized? Or has the flight of whites and middle-class blacks from U.S. urban centers doomed social integration? Civil rights legislation, the use of federal power to force local jurisdictions to use busing to achieve desegregation, affirmative action campaigns, controlled choice plans, and the establishment of magnet schools (those with a focused theme) to promote integration have certainly produced some positive results. But population shifts and the immigration waves of recent decades—along with some failures within the strategies listed above—have brought about resegregation in and around many major urban centers. In Kansas City, for example, a great sum of money has been spent under federal court pressure to revitalize the public school system by establishing an elaborate magnet school approach. Although some students have benefited, particularly at the elementary school level, the results have been disappointing in terms of desegregation, white retention in the system, and test score improvement for minority students.

In "Rethinking 'Brown,'" *The Executive Educator* (June 1992), David A. Splitt analyzes the U.S. Supreme Court ruling in *Freeman v. Pitts* (1992), a Georgia case that allows lower courts to consider the quality of education that minority students are receiving when deciding whether to modify or dismiss desegregation orders. He notes that this alteration of high court opinion—which, based on the *Brown* decision, previously held that "separate educational facilities are inherently unequal"—seems to be rooted in the contention that "minority students, given the same quality of teaching, staff, and facilities, can achieve the same educational success as white students" whether or not the school is racially integrated. Splitt adds, however, that this new nonintegration approach to equality does not address such social problems as "the racial mistrust and ignorance that arise when children grow up having minimal contact with other races and cultures."

Eric Foner and Randall Kennedy, in "Reclaiming Integration," *The Nation* (December 14, 1998), contend that "integration, the ideal that once inspired an interracial mass movement to dream of a better America, has lately fallen into disuse or disfavor.... Those who still claim to favor the idea of integration often reduce it to a matter of 'color-blind' laws and social practices." Other provocative notions are expressed by Richard D. Kahlenberg in "Integrate, But Not By Race," *The Washington Post* (November 14, 1999) and by Steve Farcas and Jean Johnson in "Does School Integration Work?" *USA Today Magazine* (January 2000).

In the following selections, Doris Y. Wilkinson offers an analysis of the cultural and social psychological effects of forced school integration on African American children and indicates that the benefits of racial association in the elementary, middle, and secondary school grades are a myth. Ray C. Rist expresses his view that the promise of overcoming racial inequalities in the United States has indeed not been fulfilled because the emphasis has been on creating artificially integrated schools through busing, redistricting, quotas, and magnets. Nevertheless, he holds out hope that the present levels of racial isolation and inequality can be lessened through a fundamental reassessment of the educational system.

129

Doris Y. Wilkinson  **YES**

Integration Dilemmas in a Racist Culture

Since the demise of the institution of slavery in the United States, the last leading industrialized country to relinquish this inhumane system, economic and social integration of Americans of African descent has been exceedingly problematic. As various forms of racial interaction have unfolded throughout history, principally "black versus white" (e.g., slavery, Jim Crowism, desegregation), a language to accompany them has been cultivated. The vocabulary of resistance to the inherently contradictory structural phenomenon of school integration has included an array of political concepts such as "states' rights," "desegregation," "reverse discrimination," "quotas," "affirmative action," "preferential treatment," and, more recently, the seductive language of "diversity" and "multiculturalism." During its evolution, racial integration has been fraught with complexities and has been the target of sustained opposition by Americans of European ancestry at all levels of the economic class hierarchy.

With the waning of the twentieth century, among the central questions that remain in the United States are those involving interracial relations. Specifically: (1) Was the dismantling of the black segregated school a "necessary and sufficient" condition for structural integration? (2) What have been the behavioral, psychological, academic, and cultural consequences of a judicial decree targeted at the constitutionality of racially disparate public schools on a heretofore ecologically isolated and economically powerless yet close-knit and communal population? (3) How does a governing stratum in a democracy incorporate descendants of slaves in its educational institutions in relatively equal ways without erasing the traditions, values, and customs of the marginalized group? Rather than addressing the last question, which has not been resolved since the Emancipation Proclamation or the overturning of Jim Crow laws, I will briefly explore the consequences of a "facilities" emphasis on children.

To illustrate the theme of this exploration into the cultural and social psychological effects of forced public school integration on African American children, my personal observations and experiences under segregation and the voices of two teachers of African descent will be introduced. This supporting information renders a profile of the contemporary integration crisis and the myth of the benefits of racial association in the elementary, middle, and secondary grades.

The paradoxical character of racially based structural integration in the public school context is evident. This integration dilemma emanates from a race-conscious society and a judicial declaration regarding the constitutionality of dual systems and the presumed negative impact of the all-black school. With respect to this, it is the thesis of this discussion that public school integration and the associated demolition of the black school has had a devastating impact on African American children—their self-esteem, motivation to succeed, conceptions of heroes or role models, respect for adults, and academic performance. Racial animosities have also intensified. Unless rational alternatives are devised that take into account the uniqueness of the African American heritage, busing and compulsory school integration will become even more destructive to their health and ultimately to the nation as a whole.

Rethinking *Brown I* and *Brown II*

Whatever one's ideological orientation, it is not unreasonable to accept the notion that the constitutionality of segregation could have been questioned on grounds other than its psychological effects. For in constitutionally framing the racially entrenched fiction that "any school that is black is inferior and that blacks cannot succeed without the benefit of the company of whites," the Supreme Court reflected the potency of racialistic thinking. It is demonstrably true that in the South and in the Northern urban communities, the African American public school was inferior in the quality of its buildings, facilities, and textbooks.

Nevertheless, this did not apply to the dedication and capabilities of teachers, the unbiased learning environment, or the opportunities for developing healthy self-attitudes. What was unanticipated by the Court in the two *Brown v. Board of Education of Topeka* cases was the pervasive and irreversible damage that might be inflicted on poor black children reared in stable yet ecologically constructed social worlds.

Before the Supreme Court's *Brown* decision, racial discrimination and structural segregation in public and private schools, in colleges and universities, and in all facets of daily life in the southern United States were normative and legal. Arguing the substance of the desegregation case, the Court asserted that "racial discrimination in public education is unconstitutional and all provisions of federal, state or local law requiring or permitting such discrimination must yield to this principle." Separate educational facilities were declared to be "inherently unequal." The revolutionary nature of this decision resonated in its profound influence on centuries-old social customs, on class arrangements, on the rigid racial hierarchy, and on fundamental dimensions of African-American life that had solidified under segregation. In rearguing the question of community relief, the Supreme Court affirmed that District Courts were to act in accordance with the opinion and "to admit the parties to these cases to public schools on a racially nondiscriminatory basis with all deliberate speed." The Court's insistence was anchored in constitutional precepts and in a demarcated set of beliefs about the interconnections between social structure and collective psychology. This resulted in the assumption that segregation was harmful to children of African ancestry principally because "it had the sanction of law."

Taking into account community circumstances, the need for "practical flexibility in shaping remedies" was specified in *Brown II*. The follow-up pronouncement stipulated replacing the dual system within a sensible time frame. The Court reasoned that what was "at stake is the personal interest of the plaintiffs in admission to public schools as soon as practicable on a non-discriminatory basis." Since spatially distinct educational systems had been entrenched for centuries, the Court alluded to potential organizational difficulties. Nonetheless, it failed to grasp or predict the profound cultural significance of what was evolving. The pronouncement was an amalgam of structural psychology mirroring the political ethos of the times. Thus, in the historic 1954 decision, the cardinal principle was that segregated schools were not only unconstitutional but that the black school was fundamentally deficient. Racial isolation from whites was construed as permanently harmful to the self-feelings of African American children. The possibility of socially disruptive outcomes from unwarranted racial contact and the demolition of the black school was neither incorporated in any arguments nor anticipated.

Coming of Age in a Segregated Town

In the city of Lexington, Kentucky, a relatively quiet family-oriented town, where residential segregation and employment and social discrimination still exist, I attended all-black elementary and secondary neighborhood schools. At that time, in the late 1940s and 1950s, there was no awareness of the prospect of integration nor of alternatives to racial separation. My family could not shop in the department stores, sit at the lunch counters, use rest rooms in a service station, live in any neighborhood that they chose, drink at any water fountain, vote without fear, eat in downtown restaurants, enter the front door of hospitals or theaters, attend the local university, or even sit in the front of buses used for local and interstate transportation. I am a product of this form of inflexible and degrading structural, social, and economic discrimination. However, I grew up at a time when African American children had two parents in the home, the extended family was prominent, neighborhoods were safe, teachers taught basic literacy skills, drugs and violence were virtually unknown, and families were secure in their communities.

In contradistinction to the aftermath of imposed public school integration, within the structurally and culturally unique African American school, motivation was high and the quality of the learning environment was constructive. The positive communal features emerging out of ecological apartheid counteracted myths of "racial inferiority." African American children could become champions in speech contests, valedictorians, artists, captains of the football and basketball teams, class president, editor of the student newspaper, or homecoming queen; and black boys dated black girls. Taught by African American teachers, mostly women, who were often their neighbors and Sunday school teachers, children learned to read, to write, and to do arithmetic in the first grade. Those born in the post-Depression and World War II years also grew up with healthy self-images and high achievement aspirations.

Out of racist segregation and discrimination, the African American neighborhood molded a set of cohesive values, beliefs, legends, customs, and family lifestyles. Across the country, the schools for Americans of African descent were named after creative warriors in the struggle for freedom—Paul Lawrence Dunbar, Booker T. Washington, Frederick Douglass, and George Washington Carver. These names symbolized a rich heritage and provided models for historical continuity. Racial integration of public schools drastically transformed all of this. Dr. Robert Douglas, Professor of Pan-African Studies at the University of Louisville, has stated that integration "tore the underlying fabric of black communities apart."

With the implementation of the 1954 decision in the South, many schools designed for African American children were closed. The names that once embraced the halls of these virtually "natural institutions" were erased or reassigned to predominantly white schools, depriving them of their historical and cultural relevance. Teachers were either transferred or lost their jobs. And the African American principal—often a male hero and community leader—became obsolete. The loss of this black role model and parental figure has had far-reaching ramifications.

Because residential separation has remained as the most virulent social indicator of racist attitudes and practices, busing was invented as the tool to enforce the Court's judgment. At the time of its introduction, there were no apparent options. Transporting children thus became the technique for dismantling the historically segregated school. As the process of racial integration unraveled across the country, new types of organizational and adjustment problems surfaced. Beginning with removing children from their neighborhoods, busing constituted an expensive remedy that affected mostly poor children and families. Those transported remain primarily African Americans who must leave home in the early-morning hours for long bus trips to attend schools with strangers—other children who are not members of their neighborhood, racial group, or social class. Not only were poor and working-class children used as the agents of change, but the African American school was gradually disassembled across the country. What could be more harmful than taking children away from familiar environments for the purposes of implementing a dominant-sector philosophy?

Segregation Within Integration: An Ironic Outcome

To address the challenge of documenting and critically evaluating the impact of forced school integration on African American children, I interviewed two of my first cousins who have taught in public schools for more than twenty-five years. Products of rigid discrimination and a segregated school system, both women are competent and effective teachers. They have also experienced profound transformations in the social organization of elementary and secondary schools. Their voices are representative of others across the country. The first, who has taught for over thirty years, offers critical insights into the integration quandary. When asked to describe how school desegregation has affected African American children, she stated:

> The black child has gotten cheated through integration with lots of whites. [The] black child has to prove himself [or herself]. With integration, [we] got more money, better facilities, better textbooks. [But] what is missing is nurturing and the caring. This has had negative effects. Kids who could have been leaders are pretty much ignored. [You] can't ignore somebody and expect them to behave, to fit in.

She expressed deep concern about one practice that harms the learning potential of African American students: frequently and disproportionately issuing them hall passes. Such permissions are excuses to "get in the hall" and out of the classroom. Unfortunately, there is a tendency for teachers to approve hall passes "just to get rid of them." On the other hand, "to say 'no' indicates caring." She noted that since African American students often do not receive positive feedback in the classroom, those who congregate in the halls tend to be loud because "they're seeking negative attention." In the middle-class white environment, this attention-seeking behavior ultimately crystallizes animosity and racist stereotypes.

Another cousin, who has also taught for over twenty-five years in different grades as well as in special education, was asked: "What has integration done for or to African American children?" With wisdom and understanding of elementary and secondary school cultures, she observed irony in the fact that integration has actually "separated our black kids. It has divided them." Racial stratification and separation permeate the integrated school.

> The ones they bus to schools are from the projects. Integration prevents these kids from participating in extracurricular activities. They have to ride the bus and can't participate in clubs, organizations. As far as the parents are concerned, they are from the projects and don't have access to transportation.

> You get a few of these kids in one school; they group together. They want to be seen; they become behavior problems. Then, they're put in special education classes; [or] they're put in behavior disorder classes. They congregate. They don't do their work, [thus] they're labeled as slow. Then they're tracked. What happens as a result of that? Low self-esteem. "I'm slow anyway, so why try?"

> It's interesting that black kids are a minority in the [white] school but a majority in the special education and behavior disorder classes.

> [At meal time,] they go by classes to the cafeteria. They go in and look for each other. They get together and become noisy. Then, they are put on school suspension.

I then asked if she thought this peculiar form of integration could work. Her immediate response was no. She stated that what has evolved is not interracial desegregation but racial exclusion.

> I don't think it's integration. I think it's separation. The kids live in the projects across from each other. [However], in the morning, they're separated by busing. That's why when they get to school, they look for people like themselves.

Additionally, the social life of African American teenage girls has been affected severely by the breakup of the communal black high school. "They don't have any black guys to date. [But] black guys will date white girls." Thus, few African American youth participate in student activities. From this alienating social world, it is highly probable that the cycle of alienation experienced in the middle and high school years may be a prime factor in dropout rates, interracial tension, teenage pregnancy, and the number of female-headed households.

My final question to these women centered on what could be a resolution to the integration dilemma. Both feel that the only answer is "neighborhood schools."

> I don't think the solution is integration of schools. The solution is integration of neighborhoods. When they started integration, black kids were bused out of the inner city into white schools.

> The neighborhood school is a fallacy. Let there be only magnet schools. They [local and state governments] integrated by closing black schools. Black teachers were sent to white schools. ... Black students were bused out of the neighborhood and bused out of similar economic conditions. [They] were used for numbers—to meet quotas.

Integration as "Reverse Discrimination"

The views of two talented teachers—who experienced segregation and the changing character of public schools—reveal the multiple human costs associated with displacing the black school and forcing children to integrate. Presently, children and adolescents in the United States, who live in familiar enclaves, are the victims of structurally based philosophies that have not taken into account the intergenerational fragmentation and psychological impairment of African American children's identities and hopes. Integration in elementary, middle, and high schools across the country is simply not working. Racial animosities are at an all-time high. African American children are not developing in constructive and unbiased environments. As many middle-class teachers enter the classroom with negative attitudes toward them and their parents, their feelings of self-worth and academic potential are damaged.

Where busing has been used to propel integration, when there are few black students in a classroom, they experience prolonged isolation in a predominantly white setting. Excluded from learning opportunities, they are also disengaged from student social circles that result in the cultivation of leadership skills and lasting friendships. Furthermore, minimal communication transpires between white teachers and African American parents. One disturbing result is that too often the Parent Teacher Association tends not to represent a cohesive and meaningful bond between the family and the neighborhood. Because parents lack an understanding of what occurs in the classroom, they feel a loss of control.

Essentially, in a historically race-conscious country founded on the ideology of white supremacy, separate facilities, amenities, and services in all institutional spheres will always be unequal. Even in a "desegregated" or partially integrated society, the economically deprived and politically disenfranchised will never be treated fairly. The destruction of the healthy aspects of African American family life that flowed from the sense of community under segregation will have a permanent influence on African Americans and the larger society. Although segregated schools were "separate and unequal," within their boundaries African American children were not exposed to denigrating racial imagery from the teachers, tracking, low expectations, or race hatred. Hence, the constitutional and structural benefits gained from obligatory school integration do not outweigh the immeasurable cultural and psychological losses. As Chicago attorney Thomas Hood stated at a meeting of the Kentucky African American Heritage Commission, "the same people in charge of desegregation had been in charge of segregation. Instead of integrating, they disintegrated." Such an occurrence epitomizes genuine "reverse discrimination." Therein rests a principal contradiction associated with the mandatory transformation of the public school.

At this political moment, integration of the schools has been an abysmal failure. Although this mandated change was a necessary prerequisite for granting access to public accommodations and all other institutions in the United States, in the school setting, it is malfunctioning. One is thus compelled to ask what the rationale is for maintaining the philosophy and practice of compulsory school integration. The data are sparse and inconsistent on the benefits of busing and school "integration." It is known, however, that African American children are failing, dropping out at alarming rates, and graduating without basic literacy skills. In addition, their developmental and cultural needs are not being met. Suppressed motivation, low achievement, poor test performance, and attrition rates for these children are major signals of the failure of school integration. Also, in the desegregated school, racial hostility and "hate speech" have reached an all-time high. Similarly, violence is a frequent mode of conflict resolution.

While the guiding supposition of the 1954 Supreme Court ruling—that racially separate educational facilities are inherently unequal—was accurate, the assumption of a direct link between structural inequality, in the case of the black school, and intellectual and psychological deficiencies is questionable. What has been neglected in integration history over the past forty to forty-five years has been a rational assessment of the emotional, motivational, learning, and community impact of abolishing the black school on poor and working-class African American children. Few performance and behavioral outcomes were of concern or envisioned in the Court's edict to desegregate "with all deliberate speed" and to concomitantly dismantle schools set aside for Americans of African descent. Especially ignored was the cultural chaos that would ensue for a disenfranchised and disempowered population accustomed to surviving under absolute ecological and institutional segregation. This extraordinary dilemma permeates the entire social and political fabric of the United States at the culmination of the twentieth century.

Color, Class, and the Realities of Inequality

The *Brown v. Board of Education of Topeka* decision got it right in 1954 and still has it right today—segregated school environments are not good learning environments for either black or white kids. The reasons for dismantling the segregated school systems of the early 1950s are as valid today as they were then. A democratic society simply cannot isolate and set apart by the force of law a large number of its citizens simply on the basis of their race or any other ascribed characteristic. This is discriminatory and fundamentally immoral. That the systematically segregated systems of the 1950s needed to be abolished is not a debatable point.

But while the legal justification for segregation has been eliminated and the formal structure of dual school systems has been dismantled, the present reality is still that U.S. society is separated overwhelmingly by race—in schools as elsewhere. What we find in schools is an accurate reflection of what we find across the national landscape.

Schools do not misrepresent our present state of affairs. The extreme levels of racial isolation that were de jure in the 1950s are de facto in the 1990s. And if we briefly pause to consider again the words from the Kerner Commission Report of 1967, "Our Nation is moving toward two societies, one black, one white—separate and unequal," we ought not now to be surprised that we are where we are.

Across the United States, more than two-thirds of all black children go to elementary and secondary schools that are predominantly minority. In the urban school districts of the country, more than half of all black children are in schools where their classmates are nearly all black as well. Indeed, in many urban neighborhoods, school upon school enrolls not a single white child. The data, incidentally, are no less compelling for Hispanic students. Their isolation is now greater than that of black youth.

The realities of the 1990s undercut the remedies developed in response to *Brown* in the 1950s. Racial separation still is the norm for black children in the United States. Thus, the current arguments by Supreme Court Justice Clarence Thomas and others—that so long as there is no legal separation of the

From Ray C. Rist, "Color, Class, and the Realities of Inequality," *Society* (March/April 1996). Copyright © 1996 by Transaction Publishers. Reprinted by permission.

races, blacks should be self-reliant and go their own way in their own schools
—do not hold. The reasons for the existence of "majority minority" schools
are now largely outside the control of the nation's public schools themselves.
Schools reflect the neighborhoods and communities in which they are situated.
Racial isolation, reinforced by socioeconomic isolation, defines the political
geography of the contemporary United States. And in a series of recent decisions
involving Atlanta, Oklahoma City, and Kansas City, the U.S. Supreme Court has
given its stamp of approval to this present configuration.

At one time, we thought we could overcome economic inequalities and
housing segregation essentially by creating artificially integrated schools. These
schools were to reflect not the reality of the United States but the hope for the
United States. We used busing, we used redistricting, we used magnet schools,
and we used quotas to try both to lure and to coerce the suburbs into sending their white children to city schools, which were and still are overwhelming
minority. The interpretation of *Brown* and many subsequent desegregation efforts that mixing kids of different races made things better for the black kids
in particular—regardless of economic class differences—was and is a tenuous
proposition.

The Supreme Court decision of June 1995 *(Missouri v. Jenkins)* has essentially confirmed a trend in its rulings: that the Court will end court-ordered
desegregation plans, even when that leaves the black and Hispanic students
in racially isolated schools. The message is clear to urban schools in particular: Deal with your own problems. Do not look to suburban busing plans,
do not look to arguments on achievement gaps between predominantly black
and predominantly white schools, do not look to mandated integration, do not
look to massive infusions of state money, and most directly, do not look to a
sympathetic judiciary to intervene.

Stated bluntly, the Court's 5 to 4 ruling in *Missouri v. Jenkins* has made it
clear that it and the U.S. judicial system are now out of the business of protecting black and Hispanic students from any lingering consequences or damages
from legal segregation.

While the Kansas City case is something of an exception, it does make a
point and make it forcefully. The Kansas City desegregation effort is the nation's
largest and most costly. On the orders of a federal judge, officials poured more
than 1.3 billion state dollars into the district—building seventeen new schools,
raising teachers' salaries, upgrading facilities, adding teacher's aides, and the
like—all to lure white students from the suburbs back into the city schools.
Furthermore, and this is also critical, the judge stipulated that the achievement
scores of the black students must meet national standards on scholastic tests as
evidence that they were no longer receiving an inferior education.

The Supreme Court has said enough is enough. The efforts of the judge
in the Kansas City case, the Supreme Court ruled, should have been limited to
ensuring that the history of racial segregation in the schools has been brought
to an end. It was not the judge's responsibility nor the burden of the schools
to try to undo what was happening with the movement to the suburbs, the
emergence of private schools, and declining public confidence in the public
schools. If black students remain isolated in public schools in Kansas City, so

be it. It was the responsibility neither of the State of Missouri nor of the suburbs surrounding Kansas City to address what was going on in the city schools. In the view of the Court, racial isolation does not now merit or require the remedies that were used to end racial segregation.

Are Black Schools Disaster Zones?

Here we come to the heart of the current discussion. Now that both the political realities and the judicial realities say that what we see is what we get, racial separation of black and white (and, indeed, Hispanic) students will be the norm into the twenty-first century. Given this, the fundamental question is: Can black children in racially isolated schools receive a quality education? Theoretically, there is no reason they cannot, but in reality, few do.

Many educators and civil rights supporters have sought to bring the remedies for the lack of quality and performance in our schools under the umbrella of the *Brown* decision. Few dispute the current dismal state of the school systems responsible for the education of millions of minority children and youth. And few dispute that the engines of opportunity that good schools represent for Americans have never more than sputtered along for minority youth in our schools. What to do? The strategy heretofore has been to claim that the conditions are the result of segregation and push for desegregation remedies.

This argument no longer holds, says the Supreme Court.

What the country can choose to confront—or not—is the reality that when racial isolation occurs, all students suffer, but for minority students the suffering is often particularly acute. This has been so in the past and it is so now. Minority youngsters have fewer resources in their schools and communities and less political support to redress the imbalance. The situation grows even graver because effective policy tools to redress this educational inequality are now fewer: There is an absence of sufficient federal funds, there is a retreat in judicial oversight, and there is the fifteen-year trend of economic decline in real wages for millions of U.S. families, minority and nonminority. Racial isolation fosters political and economic neglect.

Compounding and reinforcing this educational inequality is the startling socioeconomic inequality and residential segregation in the United States. Large numbers of minority children come from economically marginal if not outright poor families. In 1993, almost 40 percent of all welfare recipients were black, and another 19 percent were Hispanic—close to 60 percent of all those on welfare. Perhaps even more critical, more than one-third of all black children are presently on welfare, as are more than 20 percent of all Hispanic children. This is in contrast to the 6 percent of white children on welfare. Overall, the poverty rate for U.S. children is three times that of the average for all other Organization for Economic Cooperation and Development countries. Today, children are six times more likely to be poor than are the elderly. And each year in the United States, ten thousand children die as a direct result of living in poverty.

Wealth Concentrated

On the other end of the scale, the top 1 percent of the population in the United States, with an average worth of $2.35 million each, hold 46.2 percent of all stocks and 54.2 percent of all bonds. The next 9 percent hold most of the rest. The bottom 90 percent of the U.S. population hold just 10 percent of that wealth. And as a footnote illustrating how the disparities are growing, the value of the New York Stock Exchange has grown more than 400 percent in the last 150 months, while the average real wage during this same period has declined about 15 percent.

Reflecting on the present state of economic affairs in the United States, Harold Howe has recently written:

> America is already deep in an economic rut that promotes the enhancement of the rich, the erosion of the middle class, and an increase in the number of the poor. The current congressional leadership is busy cementing these trends, which arise in part from a belief that most of America's poor are in that condition because of their own shortcomings—a concept that flourishes among the idealogues of the Right and is flatly denied by all balanced research on the subject.

In this context, the debate regarding the opportunities for a quality education in a predominantly black school needs to be reframed. The issue, I submit, is not one of race. There is no inherent reason that black children's performance in school would not equal white children's—were black children's life circumstances such that they had no higher rates of poverty, no higher rates of violence facing themselves and their communities, and no higher rates of teenage pregnancy and out-of-wedlock births and such that they had housing, nutrition, stability in their families, employment among their parents, equal wages with whites (whites now earn on average 60 percent more than blacks), and medical care comparable to that of whites.

But the reality is that the majority of black children do not enjoy such comparable circumstances, and their academic performance in schools is not equal. All things are seldom equal. In U.S. society, socioeconomic class distinctions and consequences cannot be avoided. The result is a dual class system of education.

This is why Justice Thomas, writing with the majority on the Kansas City case, missed the mark when he noted:

> It never ceases to amaze me that the courts are so willing to assume that anything black is inferior.... (T)he point of the Equal Protection Clause is not to enforce strict race mixing but to insure that blacks and white[s] are treated equally by the state and without regard to skin color.

The issue is not that minority schools are not getting their share of funding or are laboring under a stigma of inferiority, as was the premise of *Brown*. The issue now is inequality—inequality operating in a self-perpetuating mode outside the purview of the Equal Protection Clause.

Given that the causes of racial isolation are now different from those documented in the *Brown* case, then so, too, must be the remedies. The various approaches mentioned earlier are no longer in the tool kit. Continuing to mandate integration is no longer politically an option.

The question remains of what to do. How are we to create quality educational environments for black and Hispanic youth across this nation? Can we create schools that give these young people the opportunity to achieve at high levels of academic performance and come as adults to sit at the American feast? To answer bluntly, we are not sure. A variety of approaches are being discussed, and a few are being tried, but none are sufficiently robust to be "scaled up" to a national strategy. The educational community, sometimes alone, sometimes with the business community and others, have developed countless "weak thrust, weak effect" strategies that are well intentioned but very short on sustained results.

What all children need, and what poor children in particular need, is what James Coleman called "social capital"—the shared experiences of youth and adults across areas of responsibility, recreation, and social contacts. These experiences constitute the web of positive life events that bind all of us in community. In the best of all circumstances, they would transcend generational, racial, and class differences. But even if they cannot, they are the thread that weaves us into a sense of belonging. But Coleman saw these relationships as steadily eroding:

> What I mean by social capital is the raising of children in the norms, the social networks, and the relationships between adults and children that are of value for the child's growing up.... Altogether, the social capital in family and neighborhood available for raising children has declined precipitously. The cost will, of course, be borne by the next generation, and borne disproportionally by the disadvantaged of the next generation.

What Really Does Come Next?

In the short term, what we see is what we get. Projecting to the next five or ten years, the current configurations of inequality in schooling as elsewhere are already set in place. Without, for example, a national urban Marshall Plan, a national investment trust fund that directs resources to the poorest U.S. children and families, or a targeted children's allowance that dramatically reduces the number of children living in poverty, there is no reason to assume any change in the status quo. We presently lack the political will to initiate such change.

Indeed, we lack the political will because we collectively do not even see the condition of black and Hispanic youth in schools as a problem. In an October 8, 1995, poll jointly released by the *Washington Post*, the Kaiser Family Foundation, and Harvard University, 56 percent of whites surveyed thought that the "average African-American is as well or better off than the average white" with respect to education. By comparison, 40 percent of Hispanics agreed with this proposition, as did 38 percent of Asians and 29 percent of blacks. With respect to jobs, housing, and income, again, the percentage of whites who said

African-Americans were as well or better off than whites were 58 percent, 45 percent, and 41 percent, respectively. With attitudes among whites thus relatively complacent, when a black member of the Supreme Court argues for the rights of predominantly black schools to go their own way, and when nearly a third of the blacks surveyed think their education is as good as or better than that of whites, the pressure for change rapidly fizzles.

But beyond the matter of political will is the issue of institutional capacity. There is no evidence to suggest that our schools as currently configured have the institutional capacity to successfully teach (or even reach) black and Hispanic children and create positive learning environments on a broad and sustained basis. There are individual exceptions, but by their exceptionality, they further strengthen the central premise. Even if we as a society were to come to the unlikely agreement that we must systematically address the conditions of the millions of minority youth in our schools, we come up against the brick wall of institutional incapacity. Students who come through such systems do so in spite of the institutional configuration, not because of it. And because we do not remotely grasp the impacts of poorly designed and executed educational systems, we seek out scapegoats in the teachers, students, and parents.

The incapacity is not limited to the inner-city schools of our nation. Relatively affluent school systems do not stand as models to less-wealthy urban districts of how to serve all students. Providing a passport to college may well be the prime responsibility of the nation's wealthier suburban schools, but that is not the same as nurturing creativity and curiosity, instilling the discipline to undertake serious study, or experiencing the demand for high performance.

The challenge for the educational system in general, and for those parts of the system that are (mis)educating minority children in particular, is to begin to do the hard thinking and careful assessment of what alternative structures might reverse the present course. In the cities in particular, we need to fundamentally reexamine the nineteenth-century agrarian model (only vaguely restructured in the 1930s) of education that still holds the U.S. system in its grasp. It is said that it takes a battle fleet a thousand square miles of ocean and three hours to turn around. That is a hair-pin curve compared to what it will take to turn around U.S. schooling.

This call for a fundamental reassessment of the U.S. educational system is not to be confused with current calls for more homework, changes to the curriculum, higher standards, tighter graduation requirements, opening schools year round to do in shifts what is now done in a nine-month block, new measures of accountability, vouchers, privatization, or more funding. Furthermore, such an assessment should not be left solely in the hands of educators. Those locked into and rewarded by a dysfunctional system should not be the only ones to contribute to the design of its replacement.

It would be well to begin to ask some fundamental questions about why U.S. schooling appears to be flawed and how the inadequacies are to be addressed. It would also be well to question what we know about contemporary adolescence, about work in the twenty-first century, and about institutional redesign.

Looking beyond the immediate term, we can ask what would mobilize the country to undertake the necessary changes to our educational system. Only one possibility presents itself—self-interest.

Consider these recent words from Stephen Graubard:

> In the absence of a declared enemy—the Soviet Union—and in the absence of what are presumed to be more efficient democracies, whose educational programs have appeal, the threat of foreign competition is unlikely to have great immediate resonance for the American public. In these circumstances, it will not be fear of foreigners that will stimulate change, nor even shame, but something substantially more powerful: social and economic necessity. The country cannot continue with the present educational inequality. It is too divisive, too destructive of human potential, too unjust. If those facts are properly perceived, and are placed in a context that looks not only at what the country's present economic condition is, but what it is likely to be if the present practices prevail into the first decades of the twenty-first century, it is just possible that the country will begin to find its way out of the social and political labyrinth that presently imprisons it. The American public must be made aware of the precariousness of its inattention to the danger signals that are so evident to those who see the country from abroad.

For the short term, those interested in the well-being of poor and minority children will have to aim their efforts directly at the schools attended by these children and forget looking to the courts for help. They also cannot look to the existing social and economic structures to support their concerns. Under the pressure of the twin wedges of race and class, the distance between those with means and those without is ever more rapidly widening. Beyond that, those interested in the future of the United States and its well-being will have to replace rhetoric with serious dialogue, substitute courage for convention, and end the conspiracy of silence about how race-bound and social class-bound we are as a nation.

POSTSCRIPT

Are School Integration Efforts Doomed to Failure?

On the interrelated issues of school segregation, racism, poverty, and urban decline, a number of classic studies can provide valuable information and analysis. Among them are *The Other America* by Michael Harrington (1962), *Equality of Educational Opportunity* by James S. Coleman et al. (1966), *Schooling in Capitalist America* by Samuel Bowles and Herbert Gintis (1976), and *Old and New Ideas About School Desegregation* by Charles V. Willie (1984).

Books addressing the issue include *Making Schools Work for Underachieving Minority Students* edited by Josie G. Bain and Joan L. Herman (1990); *The Education of African-Americans* edited by Charles V. Willie, Antoine M. Garibaldi, and Wornie L. Reed (1991); and *The Homeless* by Christopher Jencks (1994). Pungent descriptions of desegregation and inner-city schools can be found in *The World We Created at Hamilton High* by Gerald Grant (1988), *Warriors Don't Cry: A Searing Memoir of the Battle to Integrate Little Rock's Central High* by Melba Pattillo Beals (1994), and *The Uptown Kids: Struggle and Hope in the Projects* by Terry Williams and William Kornblum (1994).

Among the many articles that have been published on racial discrimination in the United States, the following are especially recommended: "Reverse Racism, or How the Pot Got to Call the Kettle Black," by Stanley Fish, *The Atlantic Monthly* (November 1993); "Twenty-Five Years After the Coleman Report: What Should We Have Learned?" by James M. Towers, *The Clearing House* (January–February 1992); Jonathan Kozol, "Inequality and the Will to Change," *Equity and Choice* (Spring 1992); Sharon D. Michalove, "The Educational Crusade of Jonathan Kozol," *The Educational Forum* (Spring 1993); Paul T. Hill, "Reinventing Urban Public Education," *Phi Delta Kappan* (January 1994); and Forrest R. White, "*Brown* Revisited," *Phi Delta Kappan* (September 1994).

The March/April 1996 issue of *Society* contains excellent articles on racial integration, as does the December 1997 issue of *Equity and Excellence in Education*. Gary Orfield's research was released in book form in 1996 as *Dismantling Desegregation: The Quiet Reversal of Brown v. Board of Education*. Recommended articles include "Education and Race," by Arthur Hu, *National Review* (September 15, 1997); "Is School Desegregation Still a Viable Policy Option?" by Jennifer Hochschild, *PS: Political Science and Politics* (September 1997); "Can Education Reduce Social Inequity?" by Robert E. Slavin, *Educational Leadership* (December 1997); "Poverty's Children," by Jonathan Kozol, *The Progressive* (October 1995); and "Altered Destinies," by Gene I. Maeroff, *Phi Delta Kappan* (February 1998).

ISSUE 9

Do High-Stakes Assessments
Improve Learning?

YES: Nina Hurwitz and Sol Hurwitz, from "Tests That Count," *American School Board Journal* (January 2000)

NO: Martin G. Brooks and Jacqueline Grennon Brooks, from "The Courage to Be Constructivist," *Educational Leadership* (November 1999)

ISSUE SUMMARY

YES: High school teacher Nina Hurwitz and education consultant Sol Hurwitz assemble evidence from states that are leading the movement to set high standards of educational performance and cautiously conclude that it could stimulate long-overdue renewal.

NO: High school superintendent Martin G. Brooks and associate professor of education Jacqueline Grennon Brooks contend that the push for standardized state assessments constricts student learning and prevents implementation of constructivism.

In the 1980s a number of national reports found America's public schools to be seriously lacking in the production of students who were qualified to compete successfully in the emerging global economy. Among these reports were the National Commission on Excellence in Education's *A Nation at Risk*, the Education Commission of the States' *Action for Excellence*, the Twentieth Century Fund's *Making the Grade*, and the National Science Foundation's *Educating Americans for the Twenty-First Century*. In response to these calls for higher standards, the Bush administration adopted the following national goals in its "America 2000" plan: all children starting school prepared to learn, at least 90 percent of students graduating from high school, all students being able to cope with challenging subject matter (particularly math and science), all adults being literate and responsible citizens, and all graduates being able to compete in a global economy.

To move toward these goals the Republican administration emphasized more choice and competition, more influence from business leaders, and the development of nationwide curriculum standards and testing programs. The Clinton administration adopted the goals, renaming them "Goals 2000: Educate America," but downplayed the role of the private sector and placed responsibility for assessing student progress on the individual states.

To date, many states have risen to the challenge, imposing statewide standardized tests of subject matter and mental skills. In some cases, states have set up procedures for taking over the administration of chronically underperforming local schools. In others, schools that dramatically increase student performance are rewarded in some tangible way.

Peter Sacks, in *Standardized Minds: The High Price of America's Testing Culture and What We Can Do to Change It* (1999), contends that "the case against standardized testing is as intellectually and ethically rigorous as any argument about social policy . . . and yet such testing continues to dominate the education system, carving further inroads into the employment arena as well." He further warns that "when thinking becomes standardized people are easily objectified, their skills and talents translated into the language and mechanisms of commercial enterprise." This sentiment is shared by Alfie Kohn who, in "Unlearning How We Learn," *Principal* (March 2000), says that "raising standards has come to mean little more than higher scores on poorly-designed standardized tests," leading to abandonment of the best kind of teaching and learning.

This central concern about the direct impact of test mania on the nature of the learning process has been widely voiced by educators who advocate instructional approaches based on the theory of constructivism. Drawn from the thinking of John Dewey, Jean Piaget, Lev Vygotsky, Howard Gardner, and others, constructivism views learning as an active, group-oriented process in which students "construct" an understanding of knowledge utilized in problem-solving situations. Such sense-making activities can be time-consuming and therefore can get in the way of teachers and schools whose primary focus is on test performance. Applications of the theory are explained in Mark Windschitl's "The Challenges of Sustaining a Constructivist Classroom Culture," *Phi Delta Kappan* (June 1999) and "The Many Faces of Constructivism," by David Perkins, *Educational Leadership* (November 1999).

Those who see the standards and testing movement as the clearest path to school improvement include Joan L. Herman, "The State of Performance Assessments," *The School Administrator* (December 1998); Jerry Jesness, "Why Johnny Can't Fail: How the 'Floating Standard' Has Destroyed Public Education," *Reason* (July 1999); and Mike Schmoker, "The Results We Want," *Educational Leadership* (February 2000). These and other advocates feel that a standardized testing program ensures acquisition of basic skills, holds schools accountable for results, and identifies problem areas.

In the following selections, Nina Hurwitz and Sol Hurwitz examine experiences with high-stakes testing in Texas, Chicago, and New York in order to identify crucial elements of successful implementation, while Martin G. Brooks and Jacqueline Grennon Brooks argue that the central aim of improving student learning on a long-term basis is not well served by high-stakes accountability pressures.

Nina Hurwitz and Sol Hurwitz    **YES**

Tests That Count

T hey are tests that count, high-stakes tests that can deny promotion or graduation to students with failing scores. Schools with too many low-performing students can be exposed to the glare of publicity, placed on probation, or closed. A widening coalition of governors, business leaders, parents, and teachers—appalled that youngsters can advance through school, receive a diploma, and seek further education or a job without mastering basic skills—is promoting the use of these tests as a means of boosting standards and improving accountability in public education.

The movement is gaining national momentum. Forty-nine states have adopted performance standards for elementary and secondary education; 26 have high school exit exams in place or in process; 19 publicly identify failing schools. President Clinton is in the vanguard, calling for higher standards and a crackdown on social promotion. Last fall he urged the nation's governors, "Look dead in the eye some child who has been held back [and say], 'We'll be hurting you worse if we tell you you're learning something when you're not.'"

High Standards, High Stakes

High-stakes testing is forcing the debate over a fundamental question in American education—whether it is possible to achieve both excellence and equity. On one side are those who claim that tests with consequences are the only sure route to higher standards and stricter accountability. On the other are those who contend that high-stakes tests are a command-and-control instrument for "standardizing" education and punishing disadvantaged and minority children. But a more pragmatic middle position is evolving based on the experience of front-line practitioners: High-stakes testing can work with clear but limited goals, flexibility in meeting those goals, and the will to address head-on the problems of students at risk of failure.

Texas, Chicago, and New York City and state, discussed below, are being carefully watched by educators and decision makers nationwide for both positive and negative lessons. The states are driving the high-stakes movement: Kentucky, Maryland, Massachusetts, North Carolina, and Virginia are running noteworthy programs as well.

Even as states and school districts attempt to raise standards and impose high-stakes tests, they are confronted with excessive numbers of their urban, minority, and disadvantaged students who are failing these tests. In urban districts, large-scale failure is inevitable, says *Education Week*'s Ron Wolk, given the shoddy education these students are receiving. "For tens of thousands of urban youngsters, it's a kind of double jeopardy," Wolk declares. "The system failed to educate them adequately, and now it punishes them for not being educated." Schools and school districts might face punishment as well: Low scores could result in the reorganization of schools or a shift of resources to charter schools or private-school vouchers.

Parent advocacy and civil rights groups are challenging the tests on racial and equity grounds. The penalties, they claim, fall disproportionately on minority and at-risk students, who have been shortchanged in their education. Meanwhile, teachers and researchers are beginning to question the tests' educational validity: Do they, in fact, improve learning?

Educators are unanimous that high-stakes tests should be aligned with curriculum and instruction—they should measure what students have been taught and are expected to know—and that teachers should be involved in the process. But only gradually are states and school districts committing sufficient resources and time to achieve proper alignment with full teacher participation. The time lag, educators argue, makes it risky to impose consequences prematurely.

Disagreement between states and urban school districts over which test to use means students in the same grade might have to take two tests—in the same subject. Learning suffers, educators say, when teachers spend time preparing students for too many tests. "The first thing to go in a school or district where these tests matter," says education expert Alfie Kohn, "is a more vibrant, integrated, active, and effective kind of instruction." [See "Raising the Scores, Ruining the Schools," *ASBJ*, October 1999.] A fifth-grade teacher in Virginia concurs: "Sometimes, when I wish I could stay longer on a subject, I have to move on to prepare my kids for the tests."

A 1999 study titled *High Stakes* by the prestigious National Research Council sharply criticized the practice of relying solely on tests to determine promotion or graduation. Such decisions, the council argued, "should be buttressed by other relevant information about the student's knowledge and skills, such as grades, teacher recommendations, and extenuating circumstances." Many educators question the value of holding kids back *period*—but certainly not without a highly structured, and often costly, intervention and remediation strategy.

The growing public demand for standards with accountability has made high-stakes testing a tempting political issue. The public is fed up with low standards and courses that lack content—they want American students to be able to compete favorably with kids in other countries. Test scores provide an aura of businesslike accountability for superintendents, principals, and teachers and a stimulus for students. Initially, at least, testing seems easy and inexpensive compared with more deep-seated reforms such as hiring and training competent teachers, reducing class size, or repairing crumbling school buildings. But achieving accountability is neither simple nor cheap.

The states and school districts that have had the most success with high-stakes testing share several common characteristics. They have maintained bipartisan political support and the backing of a broad coalition of interest groups, including the business community, over a sustained period. High-stakes tests have not only raised standards but have stimulated systemwide reform. Most important, there has been a heavy investment in addressing the academic performance of the weakest students.

Turnaround in Texas

Texas is a dramatic case in point. Once considered one of the nation's educational backwaters, the Texas public school system, according to the *New York Times,* is now viewed by educators as "a model of equity, progress and accountability." The state's education reforms have spanned the administrations of former Democratic governor Ann W. Richards and current Republican governor and presidential hopeful George W. Bush. In a system of 3.7 million students that is half African American and Hispanic, the scores of African-American and Hispanic students on national assessments in reading and mathematics in 1996 and 1998 outranked those of most other states, and scores on state assessments for all students have risen for the fourth straight year.

A unique feature of the Texas system is the Texas Assessment of Academic Skills (TAAS), the state's high-stakes exam program, introduced in 1990. The tests combine clearly stated educational standards with a detailed reporting of results by ethnicity and class. Scores are sorted according to white, African-American, Hispanic, and economically disadvantaged groups. Along with attendance and dropout rates, TAAS scores are used to identify a school as failing if any one of its four demographic cohorts falls below standard. "Disaggregation of scores has focused the schools' attention on kids that were once ignored," according to University of Texas professor Uri Treisman, who is director of the Charles A. Dana Center in Austin. Texas is gradually raising the passing bar to 50 percent for each cohort from the original 20 percent.

Until recently, the high stakes associated with the TAAS have consisted almost entirely of public disclosure of school-by-school test results, a process Gov. Bush calls "shining a spotlight of shame on failure." The ratings, published on the web, identify schools as exemplary, recognized, acceptable, or low-performing and provide strong incentives to improve for adults and students alike. For example, superintendents, principals, and teachers find it hard to get jobs if they come from failing schools. Although low-performing schools are bolstered by additional financial support, they are rarely closed. "There are no great ideas on what to do with really problematical schools," says Treisman.

Elementary and middle-school students are tested in grades three through eight on various combinations of reading, writing, and mathematics, with science and social studies added in the eighth grade. In response to political pressure, Texas will move to end social promotion by 2003. Hoping to avoid widespread retention, the state has instituted the Student Success Initiative, an early-intervention program, starting with the current year's kindergarten class. A skeptic on retention, Treisman cautions that research on the dropout problem indicates that "being overage in your class has the single highest correlation for dropping out and is twice as high as for any other factor, including race." Also, as pressure mounts to pass the TAAS, state officials have become increasingly concerned over outbreaks of alleged cheating.

There is wide agreement that Texas high schools have not shown as much improvement as elementary schools. However, the state plans to beef up the content of the 10th-grade exit exam and move it to the 11th grade and to allow substitution of end-of-course exams in core subjects. The present 10th-grade exam is the subject of a lawsuit by the Mexican-American Legal Defense Fund in the U.S. District Court in San Antonio, which claims the test discriminates against minority students. Gov. Bush counters this claim: "Some say it is a racist test," he told the *New York Times* [recently]. "I strongly say it is racist not to test because by not testing we don't know, and by not knowing we are just moving children through the system." The outcome is sure to have an impact on other states, researchers agree.

Remarkably, the state's educational resurgence has occurred while expenditures remained below the national average: In 1998–99, Texas spent $5,488 per student compared with the national average of $6,407. Striking, too, is the autonomy that Texas gives its principals and teachers as long as test results remain positive. Bilingual education, for example, is a local option. However, scores for Spanish-speaking and special education students must now be included in overall ratings to ensure more accurate results.

Success in Chicago

Just as Texas has drawn raves for educational attainment at the state level, Chicago, with an enrollment of 431,000 students, has become the promised land for city reformers. Mayors, superintendents, and educators have flocked there to study the remarkable turnaround orchestrated by chief executive officer Paul Vallas, formerly budget director under Mayor Richard M. Daley. With no previous experience in education, Vallas has performed what many consider an educational miracle in a school district that U.S. Secretary of Education William J. Bennett in 1987 called "the worst in the country." Vallas achieved credibility largely through the selective but determined application of high-stakes testing. Scores on Chicago's performance benchmark, the Iowa Test of Basic Skills in Reading and Mathematics, have risen for the fourth straight year.

When Vallas took charge in 1995, an earlier reform effort, which stressed decision making by local school councils, had virtually hit bottom. With high truancy, low standards, and rampant grade inflation, Vallas declared, "there was wide agreement that the earlier reform initiative had failed." Vallas exploited public dissatisfaction with the previous reform, while drawing grassroots support from a network of parents, community groups, foundations, and universities to fashion a new strategy.

Fundamental to his success was the solid backing of Mayor Daley and Gery Chico, president of the Chicago School Reform Board (successor to the former elected school board), whose members were all mayoral appointees. Vallas forged a close working relationship with Tom Reece, who heads both the

Chicago Teachers Union and the Illinois Federation of Teachers, and together they have succeeded in avoiding strikes and confrontations by building communication and trust. In addition, he won points with the public for his skills as a financial manager by stamping out waste, ending deficits, and securing state funds for building and renovating schools.

Three years ago, Chicago gained national attention as the first big-city school system to end social promotion. Students who don't meet minimum standards on the Iowa Tests are at risk of retention, but the passing bar was set low at first to avoid massive failure and is only gradually being raised.

Chicago's promotion gates kick in for students in grades three, six, and eight. For those who fail, the city's mandatory Summer Bridge Program, staffed with experienced teachers, provides a scripted curriculum from the central administration with hour-by-hour guidelines. University of Chicago professor Melissa Roderick, a member of the Consortium on Chicago School Research, believes the program goads parents, students, and teachers to work harder to avoid retention. "Students love Summer Bridge," says Roderick, because they know it helps them. Of the estimated 25,000 students who attended summer school last year, two-thirds moved to the next grade. Chicagoans call the policy "retention plus" because it comes front-loaded with ample resources for intervention and remediation. "Retention is a last resort," Vallas maintains.

Chicago also provides tutoring during school, and in an after-school Lighthouse Program (with supper included), for students who fail. Cozette Buckney, the system's chief education officer, shares the prevailing view of education experts that students should not merely repeat the same curriculum once they are held back. "You must teach them differently, use different materials—give them a different experience," she says.

Finally, if students have not passed the eighth-grade test by age 15, they move to "academic prep centers" that offer small transitional classes and intensive test preparation, where expenditures per pupil are one-and-a-half times those for high schools. Most students move on to high school after one year, although some teachers believe the centers accentuate problems of self-esteem and increase the tendency to drop out.

So dazzling is Chicago's success in the lower grades that outside observers have hardly noticed that real achievement stops at the high school door. "In the high schools, we have been at a loss," Buckney admits. Standards remain low, and there is widespread disengagement of students, a weak curriculum, and meager support services. Half of the city's ninth-graders fail two or more courses.

The Chicago Academic Standards Exams (CASE), which are end-of-semester high school tests in core subjects, are currently being upgraded. Teachers now receive detailed content guides from the administration but complain about the rigidity that the guides impose on their teaching. Although most teachers allow the exams to count for only 15 percent of the semester grade, a biology teacher contends that "the tests shape what I teach, what order I teach in, and how long I spend on each subject."

High school teachers have been more resistant to control from the central office than elementary school teachers, according to Vallas. "They view themselves as college professors—they're more set in their ways," he complains. Last year George Schmidt, an activist teacher, published parts of the CASE tests in protest, and students at top-rated Whitney Young High School boycotted the tests. Vallas dismisses such opposition, saying, "There is enough to be irritating but not enough to delay reform."

Recent efforts to close down and reconstitute Chicago's worst high schools have proved unsuccessful, and discharging low-performing administrators and teachers has been difficult. "The burden of proof [on the school administration] in removing failing teachers is pretty strong," Vallas admits.

Vallas is seeking to garner support for Chicago's high-stakes tests by allowing waivers and retesting. He is also identifying at-risk students early and conducting special programs for pregnant teens and teen mothers. "Good attendance, behavior, and grades" can help students get promoted, he says. The time will come, he predicts, when tests will become a diminishing factor in promotion decisions.

Disappointment in New York

Chicago's success in strengthening standards and ending social promotion in the early grades contrasts sharply with New York City's recent dismal experience with high-stakes testing. New York's gigantic scale—it is the nation's largest school system with 1.1 million students—and the fractured relationship between the schools chancellor and the mayor have vastly complicated attempts to impose high stakes on state and city tests. Unlike Chicago, where Paul Vallas and Mayor Daley work in blissful harmony, New York City's Schools Chancellor Rudy Crew has recently been at loggerheads with Mayor Rudolph W. Giuliani.

High-stakes testing [has been brought] to the boiling point. After months of cramming and intense pressure on students, teachers, and parents, the news came in May [1999] that 67 percent of New York City students had failed the state's new and more demanding fourth-grade language arts test. The test was given over three days and included passages to be read for comprehension and answered in essay form. Stunned by the low test scores, the mayor proposed the removal of principals from the bottom third of all city elementary schools and called for a major management shake-up. State Education Commissioner Richard P. Mills recommended summer school for all students who failed the test.

Then came the disappointing results on year-end city tests, administered and graded by CTB/McGraw-Hill, which showed only 44.6 percent of students reading at grade level, a five-point decline from the previous year. Mathematics scores were even lower, falling 10 percent. After this second dose of bad news, the mayor prescribed even stronger medicine. Impressed by Chicago's example, he called for abolishing the semi-independent board of education and placing the schools under his own control.

After constant badgering from the mayor, Crew responded in mid-June with a hastily arranged mandatory summer-school program starting in July for 37,000 third-, sixth-, and eighth-graders who had scored at or below the 15th percentile on the city's standardized reading test and the 10th percentile on the mathematics test, both taken in the spring. Students failing the tests a second time would be held back.

The summer-school program was plagued with problems. For six weeks the schools were forced to cope with thousands of youngsters who needed to pass the city tests to avoid retention. Many teachers were handicapped by a lack of student records and by inadequate course materials, and school buildings were stifling from a record-setting heat wave. Although paid at a lower rate than their school-year salaries, many teachers had to buy their own materials and bring fans from home. In some instances, students who were supposed to take only the mathematics test were drilled mainly for the reading test.

Chancellor Crew's pride in announcing that 64 percent of the students passed the tests was soon dampened when scoring errors by CTB/McGraw-Hill revealed that more than 8,600 students were sent to summer school by mistake. Lack of accurate summer-school attendance figures cast further doubt on the number of students who would be retained. The Puerto Rican Legal Defense Fund and Advocates for Children, a nonprofit legal services organization, have threatened court challenges, citing late warning of the new requirement to attend summer school and the use of a single test to determine promotion.

New York City's problems are likely to be exacerbated by Commissioner Mills' determined belief in high-stakes testing as a means of raising standards for the state's high schools. In a program that is unique in the nation, Mills and the State Board of Regents are requiring that by 2003, all students will have to receive a passing grade of at least 65 percent on the state's tough new Regents examinations in five subjects—English, mathematics, science, global studies, and American history—before they can graduate. Currently less than a quarter of New York City students qualify for a Regents diploma.

Turning aside his critics, Mills contended in a [recent] *New York Times* interview that without high standards, "You simply decide in advance that some students don't have access to the good life. They don't have access to jobs, they don't have access to enriched curriculum and everything that goes with it."

Mills understood the need for a structured program of remediation and support for those who fail the Regents tests. To this end, he proposed a $900 million program targeted toward poor districts, but Gov. George E. Pataki's budget came nowhere near to providing that amount.... [S]tate lawmakers—under pressure from parents, teachers, and school administrators who feared widespread failure on the Regents tests—argued for scaling down requirements. In October a consortium of parents and educators at 35 New York City alternative high schools asked legislators to compel the Regents to exempt its students from the new English Regents exams. With public opposition rising, it is doubtful the Regents will have enough public support to sustain such an extensive testing program with such high stakes over the long term.

As the results of [the] more rigorous six-hour, two-day English Regents tests were being released, accusations of deceptive scoring on the essay questions began to surface. According to a Harlem high-school teacher, "I never would have given points in a regular class for the kind of answers we were getting on those essays."

Many teachers had never seen the state's new standards; nor had they been trained to teach courses to the level of the Regents' demands. "No business or military organization would do that kind of campaign without adequate training," Thomas Sobol, former state education commissioner, asserted at a meeting in Purchase, N.Y.... For New York City's students, the stakes are overwhelming and probably unrealistic.

Making High-Stakes Testing Work

High-stakes tests are transforming the education landscape, and lawmakers and educators are learning to navigate in uncharted terrain. Conditions and requirements vary state-by-state, and progress in meeting the new standards requires patience. But some early lessons can be drawn from states and school districts that are beginning to achieve success:

Make sure that learning—not testing—is the goal   "Are we teaching for testing or teaching for knowledge?" a senior administrator asks. Tests can be important in identifying weaknesses. But too much testing in too many subjects overwhelms teachers, drains resources from enriched educational programs, stifles creativity, and increases cheating.

Give disadvantaged students special assistance   High-stakes tests can be a powerful tool for raising standards for at-risk students, but only if resources are reallocated to schools that serve them. And the testing program must be held accountable for ensuring that the tests are reliable, fair, and free of cultural bias.

Set failure rates at a realistic level   Most schools lack the resources and capacity to absorb masses of failing students in after-school and summer-school remediation programs and to conduct programs for students who repeatedly fail. But setting failure rates too low damages credibility in the system's standards. The right balance will vary according to circumstances, but finding it is crucial.

Invest in a wide range of educational reforms—not just tests   Tests don't work in a vacuum but in an environment that supports systemwide reform. Tests should be part of a program that encourages early childhood education; the recruitment, training, and development of capable teachers; smaller class size; and safer buildings.

Make retention a last resort   Most studies show that retention does more harm than good. Frequent failure erodes self-confidence, and students who are retained have a higher probability of dropping out. If retention helps at all, it does so only when students are supported by innovative learning strategies. Decisions to deny promotion should not be based on a single test and should involve the teacher.

Use publicity to force improvement   School rankings draw attention to the weakest schools and can be used to drive decisions regarding school reform, reorganization, or closure. School officials have an obligation to interpret test results to the public consistently and accurately and to be forthright about problems in the system.

Focus on urban high schools   Tests can be effective in raising standards but only if problems of school climate are addressed. Expect high school exit exams to be challenged in the courts by minority groups. Excessive testing narrows curriculum choice, and the need for remediation may lead to de facto tracking and high dropout rates.

Prepare for the long haul   It is the rare state or school district that gets high-stakes testing right the first time. Success takes time and requires experimentation. Be ready to adapt, adjust, and compromise in order to achieve long-term success.

On balance, high-stakes tests that are well-designed and carefully administered appear to be working, at least in the lower grades. But if their benefits are oversold and their dangers ignored, disenchantment could lead to diminished support for public education. If, on the other hand, they call attention to failure and encourage strategies to ensure success, they could stimulate a long-overdue educational renewal for the nation's neediest students.

NO

**Martin G. Brooks and
Jacqueline Grennon Brooks**

The Courage to Be Constructivist

For years, the term *constructivism* appeared only in journals read primarily by philosophers, epistemologists, and psychologists. Nowadays, *constructivism* regularly appears in the teachers' manuals of textbook series, state education department curriculum frameworks, education reform literature, and education journals. Constructivism now has a face and a name in education.

A theory of learning that describes the central role that learners' ever-transforming mental schemes play in their cognitive growth, constructivism powerfully informs educational practice. Education, however, has deep roots in other theories of learning. This history constrains our capacity to embrace the central role of the learner in his or her own education. We must rethink the very foundations of schooling if we are to base our practice on our understandings of learners' needs.

One such foundational notion is that students will learn on demand. This bedrock belief is manifested in the traditional scope and sequence of a typical course of study and, more recently, in the new educational standards and assessments. This approach to schooling is grounded in the conviction that all students can and will learn the same material at the same time. For some students, this approach does indeed lead to the construction of knowledge. For others, however, it does not.

The people working directly with students are the ones who must adapt and adjust lessons on the basis of evolving needs. Constructivist educational practice cannot be realized without the classroom teacher's autonomous, on-going, professional judgment. State education departments could and should support good educational practice. But too often they do not.

Their major flaw is their focus on high-stakes accountability systems and the ramifications of that focus on teachers and students. Rather than set standards for professional practice and the development of local capacity to enhance student learning, many state education departments have placed even greater weight on the same managerial equation that has failed repeatedly in the past: State Standards = State Tests; State Test Results = Student Achievement; Student Achievement = Rewards and Punishments.

We are not suggesting that educators should not be held accountable for their students' learning. We believe that they should. Unfortunately, we are not holding our profession accountable for learning, only for achievement on high-stakes tests. As we have learned from years of National Assessment of Educational Progress research, equating lasting student learning with test results is folly.

The Emerging Research from Standards-Driven States

In recent years, many states have initiated comprehensive educational reform efforts. The systemic thinking that frames most standards-based reform efforts is delectably logical: Develop high standards for all students; align curriculum and instruction to these standards; construct assessments to measure whether all students are meeting the standards; equate test results with student learning; and reward schools whose students score well on the assessments and sanction schools whose students don't.

Predictably, this simple and linear approach to educational reform is sinking under the weight of its own flaws. It is too similar to earlier reform approaches, and it misses the point. Educational improvement is not accomplished through administrative or legislative mandate. It is accomplished through attention to the complicated, idiosyncratic, often paradoxical, and difficult to measure nature of learning.

A useful body of research is emerging from the states. With minor variations, the research indicates the following:

- Test scores are generally low on the first assessment relating to new standards. Virginia is an extreme example of this phenomenon: More than 95 percent of schools failed the state's first test. In New York, more than 50 percent of the state's 4th graders were deemed at risk of not graduating in 2007 after taking that state's new English language arts test in 1999.
- Failure, or the fear of failure, breeds success on subsequent tests. After the first administration of most state assessments, schools' scores rise because educators align curriculum closely with the assessments, and they focus classroom instruction directly on test-taking strategies.
- To increase the percentages of students passing the state assessments—and to keep schools off the states' lists of failing schools—local district spending on student remediation, student test-taking skills, and faculty preparation for the new assessments increases.
- Despite rising test scores in subsequent years, there is little or no evidence of increased student learning. A recent study by Kentucky's Office of Educational Accountability (Hambleton et al., 1995) suggests that test-score gains in that state are a function of students' increasing skills as test takers rather than evidence of increased learning.

When Tests Constrict Learning

Learning is a complex process through which learners constantly change their internally constructed understandings of how their worlds function. New information either transforms their current beliefs—or doesn't. The efficacy of the learning environment is a function of many complex factors, including curriculum, instructional methodology, student motivation, and student developmental readiness. Trying to capture this complexity on paper-and-pencil assessments severely limits knowledge and expression.

Inevitably, schools reduce the curriculum to only that which is covered on tests, and this constriction limits student learning. So, too, does the undeviating, one-size-fits-all approach to teaching and assessment in many states that have crowned accountability king. Requiring all students to take the same courses and pass the same tests may hold political capital for legislators and state-level educational policymakers, but it contravenes what years of painstaking research tells us about student learning. In discussing the inordinate amount of time and energy devoted to preparing students to take and pass high-stakes tests, Angaran (1999) writes

> Ironically, all this activity prepares them for hours of passivity. This extended amount of seat time flies in the face of what we know about how children learn. Unfortunately, it does not seem to matter. It is, after all, the Information Age. The quest for more information drives us forward. (P. 72)

We are not saying that student success on state assessments and classroom practices designed to foster understanding are inherently contradictory. Teaching in ways that nurture students' quests to resolve cognitive conflict and conquer academic challenges fosters the creative problem solving that most states seek. However, classroom practices designed to prepare students for tests clearly do not foster deep learning that students apply to new situations. Instead, these practices train students to mimic learning on tests.

Many school districts question the philosophical underpinnings of the dominant test-teach-test model of education and are searching for broader ways for students to demonstrate their knowledge. However, the accountability component of the standards movement has caused many districts to abandon performance-based assessment practices and refocus instead on preparing students for paper-and-pencil tests. The consequences for districts and their students are too great if they don't.

Constructivism in the Classroom

Learners control their learning. This simple truth lies at the heart of the constructivist approach to education.

As educators, we develop classroom practices and negotiate the curriculum to enhance the likelihood of student learning. But controlling what students learn is virtually impossible. The search for meaning takes a different route for each student. Even when educators structure classroom lessons and curriculums to ensure that all students learn the same concepts at the same time, each student still constructs his or her own unique meaning through his or her own cognitive processes. In other words, as educators we have great control over what we teach, but far less control over what students learn.

Shifting our priorities from ensuring that all students learn the same concepts to ensuring that we carefully analyze students' understandings to customize our teaching approaches is an essential step in educational reform that results in increased learning. Again, we must set standards for our own professional practice and free students from the anti-intellectual training that occurs under the banner of test preparation.

The search for understanding motivates students to learn. When students want to know more about an idea, a topic, or an entire discipline, they put more cognitive energy into classroom investigations and discussions and study more on their own. We have identified five central tenets of constructivism (Grennon Brooks & Brooks, 1993).

- First, constructivist teachers seek and value students' points of view. Knowing what students think about concepts helps teachers formulate classroom lessons and differentiate instruction on the basis of students' needs and interests.
- Second, constructivist teachers structure lessons to challenge students' suppositions. All students, whether they are 6 or 16 or 60, come to the classroom with life experiences that shape their views about how their worlds work. When educators permit students to construct knowledge that challenges their current suppositions, learning occurs. Only through asking students what they think they know and why they think they know it are we and they able to confront their suppositions.
- Third, constructivist teachers recognize that students must attach relevance to the curriculum. As students see relevance in their daily activities, their interest in learning grows.
- Fourth, constructivist teachers structure lessons around big ideas, not small bits of information. Exposing students to wholes first helps them determine the relevant parts as they refine their understandings of the wholes.
- Finally, constructivist teachers assess student learning in the context of daily classroom investigations, not as separate events. Students demonstrate their knowledge every day in a variety of ways. Defining understanding as only that which is capable of being measured by paper-and-pencil assessments administered under strict security perpetuates false and counterproductive myths about academia, intelligence, creativity, accountability, and knowledge.

Opportunities for Constructing Meaning

Recently, we visited a classroom in which a teacher asked 7th graders to reflect on a poem. The teacher began the lesson by asking the students to interpret the first two lines. One student volunteered that the lines evoked an image of a dream. "No," he was told, "that's not what the author meant." Another student said that the poem reminded her of a voyage at sea. The teacher reminded the student that she was supposed to be thinking about the first two lines of the poem, not the whole poem, and then told her that the poem was not about the sea. Looking out at the class, the teacher asked, "Anyone else?" No other student raised a hand.

In another classroom, a teacher asked 9th graders to ponder the effect of temperature on muscle movement. Students had ice, buckets of water, gauges for measuring finger-grip strength, and other items to help them consider the relationship. The teacher asked a few framing questions, stated rules for handling materials safely, and then gave the students time to design their experiments. He posed different questions to different groups of students, depending on their activities and the conclusions that they seemed to be drawing. He continually asked students to elaborate or posed contradictions to their responses, even when they were correct.

As the end of the period neared, the students shared initial findings about their investigations and offered working hypotheses about the relationship between muscle movement and temperature. Several students asked to return later that day to continue working on their experiments.

Let's consider these two lessons. In one case, the lesson was not conducive to students' constructing deeper meaning. In the other case, it was. The 7th grade teacher communicated to her students that there is one interpretation of the poem's meaning, that she knew it, and that only that interpretation was an acceptable response. The students' primary quest, then, was to figure out what the teacher thought of the poem.

The teacher spoke to her students in respectful tones, acknowledging each one by name and encouraging their responses. However, she politely and calmly rejected their ideas when they failed to conform to her views. She rejected one student's response as a misinterpretation. She dismissed another student's response because of a procedural error: The response focused on the whole poem, not on just the designated two lines.

After the teacher told these two students that they were wrong, none of the other students volunteered interpretations, even though the teacher encouraged more responses. The teacher then proceeded with the lesson by telling the students what the poet really meant. Because only two students offered comments during the lesson, the teacher told us that a separate test would inform her whether the other students understood the poem.

In the second lesson, the teacher withheld his thoughts intentionally to challenge students to develop their own hypotheses. Even when students' initial responses were correct, the teacher challenged their thinking, causing many students to question the correctness of their initial responses and to investigate the issue more deeply.

Very few students had awakened that morning thinking about the relationship between muscle movement and temperature. But, as the teacher helped students focus their emerging, somewhat disjointed musings into a structured investigation, their engagement grew. The teacher provoked the students to search for relevance in a relationship they hadn't yet considered by framing the investigation around one big concept, providing appropriate materials and general questions, and helping the students think through their own questions. Moreover, the teacher sought and valued his students' points of view and used their comments to assess their learning. No separate testing event was required.

What Constructivism Is and Isn't

As constructivism has gained support as an educational approach, two main criticisms have emerged. One critique of constructivism is that it is overly permissive. This critique suggests that constructivist teachers often abandon their curriculums to pursue the whims of their students. If, for example, most of the students in the aforementioned 9th grade science class wished to discuss the relationship between physical exercise and muscle movement rather than pursue the planned lesson, so be it. In math and science, critics are particularly concerned that teachers jettison basic information to permit students to think in overly broad mathematical and scientific terms.

The other critique of constructivist approaches to education is that they lack rigor. The concern here is that teachers cast aside the information, facts, and basic skills embedded in the curriculum—and necessary to pass high-stakes tests—in the pursuit of more capricious ideas. Critics would be concerned that in the 7th grade English lesson described previously, the importance of having students understand the one true main idea of the poem would fall prey to a discussion of their individual interpretations.

Both of these critiques are silly caricatures of what an evolving body of research tells us about learning. Battista (1999), speaking specifically of mathematics education, writes,

> Many... conceive of constructivism as a pedagogical stance that entails a type of non-rigorous, intellectual anarchy that lets students pursue whatever interests them and invent and use any mathematical methods they wish, whether those methods are correct or not. Others take constructivism to be synonymous with "discovery learning" from the era of "new math," and still others see it as a way of teaching that focuses on using manipulatives or cooperative learning. None of these conceptions is correct. (P. 429)

Organizing a constructivist classroom is difficult work for the teacher and requires the rigorous intellectual commitment and perseverance of students. Constructivist teachers recognize that students bring their prior experiences with them to each school activity and that it is crucial to connect lessons to their students' experiential repertoires. Initial relevance and interest are largely a function of the learner's experiences, not of the teacher's planning. Therefore, it is educationally counterproductive to ignore students' suppositions and points of view. The 7th grade English lesson is largely nonintellectual. The 9th grade science lesson, modeled on how scientists make state-of-the-art science advancements, is much more intellectually rigorous.

Moreover, constructivist teachers keep relevant facts, information, and skills at the forefront of their lesson planning. They usually do this within the context of discussions about bigger ideas. For example, the dates, battles, and names associated with the U.S. Civil War have much more meaning for students when introduced within larger investigations of slavery, territorial expansion, and economics than when presented for memorization without a larger context.

State and local curriculums address *what* students learn. Constructivism, as an approach to education, addresses *how* students learn. The constructivist teacher, in mediating students' learning, blends the *what* with the *how*. As a 3rd grader in another classroom we visited wrote to his teacher, "You are like the North Star for the class. You don't tell us where to go, but you help us find our way." Constructivist classrooms demand far more from teachers and students than lockstep obeisance to prepackaged lessons.

The Effects of High-Stakes Accountability

As we stated earlier, the standards movement has a grand flaw at the nexus of standards, accountability, and instructional practice. Instructional practices designed to help students construct meaning are being crowded out of the curriculum by practices designed to prepare students to score well on state assessments. The push for accountability is eclipsing the intent of standards and sound educational practice.

Let's look at the effects of high-stakes accountability systems. Originally, many states identified higher-order thinking as a goal of reform and promoted constructivist teaching practices to achieve this goal. In most states, however, policymakers dropped this goal or subsumed it into other goals because it was deemed too difficult to assess and quantify. Rich evidence relating to higher-order thinking is available daily in classrooms, but this evidence is not necessarily translatable to paper-and-pencil assessments. High-stakes accountability systems, therefore, tend to warp the original visions of reform.

Education is a holistic endeavor. Students' learning encompasses emerging understandings about themselves, their relationships, and their relative places in the world. In addition to academic achievement, students develop these understandings through nonacademic aspects of schooling, such as clubs, sports, community service, music, arts, and theater. However, only that which is academic and easily measurable gets assessed, and only that which is assessed is subject to rewards and punishments. Jones and Whitford (1997) point out that Kentucky's original educational renewal initiative included student self-sufficiency and responsible group membership as goals, but these goals were dropped because they were deemed too difficult to assess and not sufficiently academic.

Schools operating in high-stakes accountability systems typically move attention away from principles of learning, student-centered curriculum, and constructivist teaching practices. They focus instead on obtaining higher test scores, despite research showing that higher test scores are not necessarily indicative of increased student learning.

Historically, many educators have considered multiple-choice tests to be the most valid and reliable form of assessment—and also the narrowest form of assessment. Therefore, despite the initial commitment of many states to performance assessment, which was to have been the cornerstone of state assessment efforts aligned with broader curriculum and constructivist instructional practices, multiple-choice questions have instead remained the coin of the realm. As Jones and Whitford (1997) write about Kentucky,

> The logic is clear. The more open and performance based an assessment is, the more variety in the responses; the more variety in the responses, the more judgment is needed in scoring; the more judgment in scoring, the lower the reliability. . . . At this point, multiple-choice items have been reintroduced, performance events discontinued. (P. 278)

Ironically, as state departments of education and local newspapers hold schools increasingly accountable for their test results, local school officials press state education departments for greater guidance about material to be included on the states' tests. This phenomenon emboldens state education departments to take an even greater role in curriculum development, as well as in other decisions typically handled at the local level, such as granting high school diplomas, determining professional development requirements for teachers, making special education placements, and intervening academically for at-risk students. According to Jones and Whitford (1997),

> [In Kentucky] there has been a rebound effect. Pressure generated by the state test for high stakes accountability has led school-based educators to pressure the state to be more explicit about content that will be tested. This in turn constrains local school decision making about curriculum. This dialectical process works to increase the state control of local curriculum. (P. 278)

Toward Educational Reform

Serious educational reform targets cognitive changes in students' thinking. Perceived educational reform targets numerical changes in students' test scores. Our obsession with the perception of reform, what Ohanian (1999) calls "the mirage theory of education," is undermining the possibility of serious reform.

History tells us that it is likely that students' scores on state assessments will rise steadily over the next decade and that meaningful indexes of student learning generally will remain flat. It is also likely that teachers, especially those teaching in the grades in which high-stakes assessments are administered, will continue to narrow their curriculum to match what is covered on the assessments and to use instructional practices designed to place testing information directly in their students' heads.

We counsel advocacy for children. And vision. And courage.

Focus on student learning. When we design instructional practices to help students construct knowledge, students learn. This is our calling as educators.

Keep the curriculum conceptual. Narrowing curriculum to match what is covered on state assessments results in an overemphasis on the rote memorization of discrete bits of information and pushes aside big ideas and intellectual curiosity. Keep essential principles and recurring concepts at the center.

Assess student learning within the context of daily instruction. Use students' daily work, points of view, suppositions, projects, and demonstrations to assess what they know and don't know, and use these assessments to guide teaching.

Initiate discussions among administrators, teachers, parents, school boards, and students about the relationship among the state's standards, the state's assessments, and your district's mission. Ask questions about what the assessments actually assess, the instructional practices advocated by your district, and the ways to teach a conceptual curriculum while preparing students for the assessments. These are discussions worth having.

Understand the purposes of accountability. Who wants it, and why? Who is being held accountable, and for what? How are data being used or misused? What are the consequences of accountability for all students, especially for specific groups, such as special education students and English language learners?

Students must be permitted the freedom to think, to question, to reflect, and to interact with ideas, objects, and others—in other words, to construct meaning. In school, being wrong has always carried negative consequences for students. Sadly, in this climate of increasing accountability, being wrong carries even more severe consequences. But being wrong is often the first step on the path to greater understanding.

We observed a 5th grade teacher return a test from the previous day. Question 3 was, "There are 7 blue chips and 3 green chips in a bag. If you place your hand in the bag and pull out 1 chip, what is the probability that you will get a green chip?" One student wrote,"You probably won't get one." She was "right" —and also "wrong." She received no credit for the question.

References

Angaran, J. (1999, March). Reflection in an age of assessment. *Educational Leadership, 56*, 71–72.

Battista, M. T. (1999, February). The mathematical miseducation of America's youth: Ignoring research and scientific study in education. *Phi Delta Kappan, 80*(6), 424–433.

Grennon Brooks, J., & Brooks, M. G. (1993). *In search of understanding: The case for constructivist classrooms.* Alexandria, VA: ASCD.

Hambleton, R., Jaeger, R. M., Koretz, D., Linn, R. L., Millman, J., & Phillips, S. E. (1995). *Review of the measurement quality of the Kentucky instructional results information system 1991–1994.* (Report prepared for the Kentucky General Assembly.) Frankfort, KY: Office of Educational Accountability.

Jones, K., & Whitford, B. L. (1997, December). Kentucky's conflicting reform principles: High stakes accountability and student performance assessment. *Phi Delta Kappan, 78*(4), 276–281.

Ohanian, S. (1999). *One size fits few.* Portsmouth, NH: Heinemann.

POSTSCRIPT

Do High-Stakes Assessments Improve Learning?

Whether standardized tests are a crucial tool in improving overall student performance or whether they rob teachers of the autonomy and creativity needed for lasting improvement of learning is among the most hotly debated topics on the current scene. Is Jerry Jesness correct in condemning "floating" standards that shield the status quo and guarantee the reign of mediocrity, or is Susan Ohanian right in demolishing high-stakes testing in her book *One Size Fits Few: The Folly of Educational Standards* (1999)?

Here are some further sources to tilt your thinking one way or the other: Mary E. Diez, "Assessment As a Lever in Education Reform," *National Forum* (Winter 1997); Elliot W. Eisner, "Standards for American Schools: Help or Hindrance?" *Phi Delta Kappan* (June 1995); Jack Kaufhold, "What's Wrong With Teaching for the Test?" *The School Administrator* (December 1998); Donald C. Orlich, "Education Reform and Limits to Student Achievement," *Phi Delta Kappan* (February 2000); David Campbell, "Authentic Assessment and Authentic Standards," *Phi Delta Kappan* (January 2000); Donna Harrington-Lueker, "The Uneasy Coexistence of High Stakes and Developmental Practice," *The School Administrator* (January 2000); Frederick M. Hess and Frederick Brigham, "None of the Above," *American School Board Journal* (January 2000); and Jeff Berger, "Does Top-Down, Standards-Based Reform Work?" *NASSP Bulletin* (January 2000).

Although most of the focus is now on state mandates, proposals for national testing are still under consideration. Long a practice in many foreign countries, high-stakes national examinations in valued subject matter areas are an explosive topic in the United States. A sampling of opinion can be found in "Yes to National Tests," by Diane Ravitch, *Forbes* (May 5, 1997); "Getting Testy," *The New Republic* (September 29, 1997); and "National Tests Are Unnecessary and Harmful," by Monty Neill, *Educational Leadership* (March 1998).

Multiple articles on the standards and testing movement can be located in the May 1999 issue of *Phi Delta Kappan,* the Winter 1999 issue of *Kappa Delta Pi Record,* and the February 2000 issue of *Educational Leadership.*

ISSUE 10

Have Public Schools Failed Society?

YES: William J. Bennett et al., from "A Nation Still at Risk," *Policy Review* (July/August 1998)

NO: Forrest J. Troy, from "The Myth of Our Failed Education System," *The School Administrator* (September 1998)

ISSUE SUMMARY

YES: Former secretary of education William J. Bennett and 36 other leaders and scholars examine the state of public schooling on the 15th anniversary of the publication of the U.S. Department of Education report *A Nation at Risk* and issue a new manifesto for needed reforms.

NO: Veteran newspaper editor Forrest J. (Frosty) Troy counteracts the continued criticism of the public schools with a point-by-point presentation of facts.

T he movement to set national goals and standards, initiated by governors and reinforced by both the Bush and Clinton administrations, reflects a widespread concern about the quality of American public education in general and the wide disparity in quality from state to state and community to community. In November 1996 a "report card" on the "Goals 2000" campaign—a plan in which educational goals to be accomplished nationally by the year 2000 were set—was released by a bipartisan federal panel. The report indicates that progress has been limited and that many states are having difficulty achieving some of the key goals of the effort. The report states that after six years of work the "overall national performance is virtually static."

A significant segment of the educational and political community has expressed disdain over the prospect of internal reform of the public schools. It is the contention of these critics that the "education establishment"—the U.S. Department of Education, the National Education Association (NEA), the American Federation of Teachers (AFT), and the teacher-training institutions—is either unwilling or incapable of improving on the status quo. Critics such as William J. Bennett, E. D. Hirsch, Jr., Chester E. Finn, Jr., Charles J. Sykes, and Cal Thomas contend that young Americans are not learning enough for their own or their nation's good, that international comparisons rank U.S. academic performance from the middle to the bottom year after year, and that many employers say that they cannot find people who have the necessary skills, knowledge, attitudes, and habits to do the work.

Finn, in "What to Do About Education," *Commentary* (October 1994), charges that the education profession is awash in bad ideas, holding to precepts such as these: There is really not much wrong with the public schools; whatever may be wrong is the fault of the larger society; competition is harmful; a child's sense of "self-esteem" counts more than what he knows; what children should learn depends on their race and ethnicity; students should never be grouped according to their ability or prior achievement; only graduates of teacher-training programs should be permitted in the classroom; and none but products of administrator-training programs should be allowed to lead schools. Hirsch, in *The Schools We Need and Why We Don't Have Them* (1996), charges "educationists" with disdaining alternatives to current practices. "Why," he asks, "do educators persist in advocating the very antifact, anti-rote-learning, antiverbal practices that have led to poor results?" He contends that would-be reformers who are not members of the educational community—parents, politicians, and business leaders—have become used to defeat.

There is evidence, however, that American public education has improved in recent decades and continues to do so. Some researchers have sounded hopeful notes and have discounted the naysayers. Stout defenses of the quality of the public schools can be found in Gerald W. Bracey's annual reports in *Phi Delta Kappan,* the U.S. Department of Education's *The Condition of Education* reports, and *The Manufactured Crisis: Myths, Fraud, and the Attack on America's Public Schools* by David C. Berliner and Bruce J. Biddle (1995). Two provocative articles on the topic are "Ten Years of Silver Bullets: Dissenting Thoughts on Education Reform," by Wade A. Carpenter, *Phi Delta Kappan* (January 2000) and "The Deep Structure of Schooling," by Barbara Benham Tye, *The Clearing House* (July/August 1998).

But there are those who say that only choice-driven competition will bring about substantial and lasting improvement. Some public school systems have initiated internal choice, and some have allowed the formation of charter schools, which are essentially independent public schools. Other communities have extended the concept into the realm of privatization and vouchers for use in private schools.

In the following selections, William J. Bennett and his associates lament the persistence of mediocre performance by America's schools and chart two strategies: (1) standards, assessments, and accountability, and (2) pluralism, competition, and choice. Journalist Forrest J. Troy pulls no punches in attacking the attackers of public schooling, but he also gives some advice to public school leaders.

William J. Bennett et al.

 **YES**

A Nation Still at Risk

Fifteen years ago, the National Commission on Excellence in Education declared the United States a nation at risk. That distinguished citizens' panel admonished the American people that "the educational foundations of our society are presently being eroded by a rising tide of mediocrity that threatens our very future as a Nation and a people." This stark warning was heard across the land.

A decade and a half later, the risk posed by inadequate education has changed. Our nation today does not face imminent danger of economic decline or technological inferiority. Much about America is flourishing, at least for now, at least for a lot of people. Yet the state of our children's education is still far, very far, from what it ought to be. Unfortunately, the economic boom times have made many Americans indifferent to poor educational achievement. Too many express indifference, apathy, a shrug of the shoulders. Despite continuing indicators of inadequacy, and the risk that this poses to our future well-being, much of the public shrugs and says, "Whatever."

The data are compelling. We learned in February that American 12th-graders scored near the bottom on the recent Third International Math and Science Study (TIMSS): U.S. students placed 19th out of 21 developed nations in math and 16th out of 21 in science. Our advanced students did even worse, scoring dead last in physics. This evidence suggests that, compared to the rest of the industrialized world, our students lag seriously in critical subjects vital to our future. That's a national shame.

Today's high-school seniors had not even started school when the Excellence Commission's report was released. A whole generation of young Americans has passed through the education system in the years since. But many have passed through without learning what is needed. Since 1983, more than 10 million Americans have reached the 12th grade without having learned to read at a basic level. More than 20 million have reached their senior year unable to do basic math. Almost 25 million have reached 12th grade not knowing the essentials of U.S. history. And those are the young people who complete their senior year. In the same period, more than 6 million Americans dropped out of high school altogether. The numbers are even bleaker in minority communities. In 1996, 13 percent of all blacks aged 16 to 24 were not in school and did not hold a diploma. Seventeen percent of first-generation Hispanics had dropped out of high school, including a tragic 44 percent of Hispanic immigrants in this age group. This is another lost generation. For them the risk is grave indeed.

To be sure, there have been gains during the past 15 years, many of them inspired by the Excellence Commission's clarion call. Dropout rates declined and college attendance rose. More high-school students are enrolling in more challenging academic courses. With more students taking more courses and staying in school longer, it is indeed puzzling that student achievement has remained largely flat and that enrollment in remedial college courses has risen to unprecedented levels.

The Risk Today

Contrary to what so many seem to think, this is no time for complacency. The risk posed to tomorrow's well-being by the sea of educational mediocrity that still engulfs us is acute. Large numbers of students remain at risk. Intellectually and morally, America's educational system is failing far too many people.

Academically, we fall off a cliff somewhere in the middle and upper grades. Internationally, U.S. youngsters hold their own at the elementary level but falter in the middle years and drop far behind in high school. We seem to be the only country in the world whose children fall farther behind the longer they stay in school. That is true of our advanced students and our so-called good schools, as well as those in the middle. Remediation is rampant in college, with some 30 percent of entering freshmen (including more than half at the sprawling California State University system) in need of remedial courses in reading, writing, and mathematics after arriving on campus. Employers report difficulty finding people to hire who have the skills, knowledge, habits, and attitudes they require for technologically sophisticated positions. Silicon Valley entrepreneurs press for higher immigration levels so they can recruit the qualified personnel they need. Though the pay they offer is excellent, the supply of competent U.S.-educated workers is too meager to fill the available jobs.

In the midst of our flourishing economy, we are re-creating a dual school system, separate and unequal, almost half a century after government-sanctioned segregation was declared unconstitutional. We face a widening and unacceptable chasm between good schools and bad, between those youngsters who get an adequate education and those who emerge from school barely able to read and write. Poor and minority children, by and large, go to worse schools, have less expected of them, are taught by less knowledgeable teachers, and have the least power to alter bad situations. Yet it's poor children who most need great schools.

If we continue to sustain this chasm between the educational haves and have-nots, our nation will face cultural, moral, and civic peril. During the past 30 years, we have witnessed a cheapening and coarsening of many facets of our lives. We see it, among other places, in the squalid fare on television and in the movies. Obviously the schools are not primarily responsible for this degradation of culture. But we should be able to rely on our schools to counter the worst aspects of popular culture, to fortify students with standards, judgment, and character. Trashy American culture has spread worldwide; educational mediocrity has not. Other nations seem better equipped to resist the Hollywood invasion than is the land where Hollywood is located.

Delusion and Indifference

Regrettably, some educators and commentators have responded to the persistence of mediocre performance by engaging in denial, self-delusion, and blame shifting. Instead of acknowledging that there are real and urgent problems, they deny that there are any problems at all. Some have urged complacency, assuring parents in leafy suburbs that their own children are doing fine and urging them to ignore the poor performance of our elite students on international tests. Broad hints are dropped that, if there's a problem, it's confined to other people's children in other communities. Yet when attention is focused on the acute achievement problems of disadvantaged youngsters, many educators seem to think that some boys and girls—especially those from the "other side of the tracks"—just can't be expected to learn much.

Then, of course, there is the fantasy that America's education crisis is a fraud, something invented by enemies of public schools. And there is the worrisome conviction of millions of parents that, whatever may be ailing U.S. education in general, "my kid's school is OK."

Now is no time for complacency. Such illusions and denials endanger the nation's future and the future of today's children. Good education has become absolutely indispensable for economic success, both for individuals and for American society. More so today than in 1983, the young person without a solid education is doomed to a bleak future.

Good education is the great equalizer of American society. Horace Mann termed it the "balance wheel of the social machinery," and that is even more valid now. As we become more of a meritocracy the quality of one's education matters more. That creates both unprecedented opportunities for those who once would have found the door barred—and huge new hurdles for those burdened by inferior education.

America today faces a profound test of its commitment to equal educational opportunity. This is a test of whether we truly intend to educate all our children or merely keep everyone in school for a certain number of years; of whether we will settle for low levels of performance by most youngsters and excellence only from an elite few. Perhaps America can continue to prosper economically so long as only some of its citizens are well educated. But can we be sure of that? Should we settle for so little? What about the wasted human potential and blighted lives of those left behind?

Our nation's democratic institutions and founding principles assume that we are a people capable of deliberating together. We must decide whether we really care about the debilitating effects of mediocre schooling on the quality of our politics, our popular culture, our economy and our communities, as dumbing-down infiltrates every aspect of society. Are we to be the land of Jefferson and Lincoln or the land of Beavis and Butthead?

The Real Issue Is Power

The Excellence Commission had the right diagnosis but was vague—and perhaps a bit naïve—as to the cure. The commissioners trusted that good advice would be followed, that the system would somehow fix itself, and that top-down reforms would suffice. They spoke of "reforming our educational system in fundamental ways." But they did not offer a strategy of political or structural change to turn these reforms into reality. They underestimated, too, the resilience of the status quo and the strength of the interests wedded to it. As former commissioner (and Minnesota governor) Albert Quie says, "At that time I had no idea that the system was so reluctant to change."

The problem was not that the Excellence Commission had to content itself with words. (Those are the only tools at our disposal, too.) In fact, its stirring prose performed an important service. No, the problem was that the commission took the old ground rules for granted. In urging the education system to do more and better, it assumed that the system had the capacity and the will to change.

Alas, this was not true. Power over our education system has been increasingly concentrated in the hands of a few who don't really want things to change, not substantially, not in ways that would really matter. The education system's power brokers responded to the commission, but only a little. The commission asked for a yard, and the "stakeholders" gave an inch. Hence much of *A Nation at Risk*'s wise counsel went unheeded, and its sense of urgency has ebbed.

Today we understand that vast institutions don't change just because they should—especially when they enjoy monopolies. They change only when they must, only when their survival demands it. In other parts of American life, stodgy, self-interested monopolies are not tolerated. They have been busted up and alternatives created as we have realized that large bureaucratic structures are inherently inefficient and unproductive. The private sector figured this out decades ago. The countries of the former Soviet empire are grasping it. Even our federal government is trying to "reinvent" itself around principles of competition and choice. President Clinton has declared that "the era of Big Government is over." It should now be clear to all that the era of the Big Government monopoly in public education needs to end as well.

The fortunate among us continue to thrive within and around the existing education system, having learned how to use it, to bend its rules, and to sidestep its limitations. The well-to-do and powerful know how to coexist with the system, even to exploit it for the benefit of their children. They supplement it. They move in search of the best it has to offer. They pay for alternatives.

But millions of Americans—mainly the children of the poor and minorities —don't enjoy those options. They are stuck with what "the system" dishes out to them, and all too often they are stuck with the least qualified teachers, the most rigid bureaucratic structures, the fewest choices and the shoddiest quality. Those parents who yearn for something better for their children lack the power to make it happen. They lack the power to shape their own lives and those of their children.

Here is a question for our times: Why aren't we as outraged about this denial of Americans' educational rights as we once were about outright racial segregation?

The Next Civil Rights Frontier

Equal educational opportunity is the next great civil rights issue. We refer to the true equality of opportunity that results from providing every child with a first-rate primary and secondary education, and to the development of human potential that comes from meeting intellectual, social, and spiritual challenges. The educational gaps between advantaged and disadvantaged students are huge, handicapping poor children in their pursuit of higher education, good jobs, and a better life.

In today's schools, far too many disadvantaged and minority students are not being challenged. Far too many are left to fend for themselves when they need instruction and direction from highly qualified teachers. Far too many are passed from grade to grade, left to sink or swim. Far too many are advanced without even learning to read, though proven methods of teaching reading are now well-known. They are given shoddy imitations of real academic content, today's equivalent of Jim Crow math and back-of-the-bus science. When so little is expected and so little is done, such children are victims of failed public policy.

John Gardner asked in 1967 whether Americans "can be equal and excellent" at the same time. Three decades later, we have failed to answer that question with a "yes." We have some excellent schools—we obviously know how to create them—and yet we offer an excellent education only to some children. And that bleak truth is joined to another: Only some families have the power to shape their children's education.

This brings us to a fundamental if perhaps unpleasant reality: As a general rule, only those children whose parents have power end up with an excellent education.

The National Commission on Excellence in Education believed that this reality could be altered by asking the system to change. Today we know better. It can only be altered by shifting power away from the system. That is why education has become a civil rights issue. A "right," after all, is not something you beg the system for. If the system gets to decide whether you will receive it or not, it's not a right. It's only a right when it belongs to you and you have the power to exercise it as you see fit—when you are your own power broker.

Inside the Classroom

Fortunately, we know what works when it comes to good education. We know how to teach children to read. We know what a well-trained teacher does. We know how an outstanding principal leads. We know how to run outstanding schools. We have plenty of examples, including schools that succeed with extremely disadvantaged youngsters.

Immanuel Kant said, "The actual proves the possible." If it can happen in five schools, it can happen in five thousand. This truly is not rocket science. Nor is it a mystery. What is mysterious is why we continue to do what doesn't work. Why we continue to do palpable harm to our children.

Let us be clear: All schools should not be identical. There are healthy disagreements and legitimate differences on priorities. Some teachers like multi-age grouping. Others prefer traditional age-grades. Some parents want their children to sit quietly in rows while others want them to engage in hands-on "experiential learning." So be it. Ours is a big, diverse country. But with all its diversity, we should agree at least to do no harm, to recognize that some practices have been validated while others have not. People's tastes in houses vary, too, yet all residences must comply with the fire code. While differing in design and size and amenities, all provide shelter, warmth, and protection. In other words, all provide the basics.

Guiding Principles

A.   Public education—that is, the public's responsibility for the education of the rising generation—is one of the great strengths of American democracy. Note, however, that public education may be delivered and managed in a variety of ways. We do not equate public education with a standardized and hierarchical government bureaucracy, heavy on the regulation of inputs and processes and staffed exclusively by government employees. Today's public school, properly construed, is any school that is open to the public, paid for by the public, and accountable to public authorities for its results.

B.   The central issues today have to do with excellence for all our children, with high standards for all teachers and schools, with options for all families and educators, and with the effectiveness of the system as a whole. What should disturb us most about the latest international results is not that other countries' best students outstrip our best; it is that other countries have done far better at producing both excellence and equity than has the United States.

C.   A vast transfer of power is needed from producers to consumers. When it comes to education reform, the formulation of the Port Huron Statement (1962) was apt: "Power to the people." There must be an end to paternalism, the one-size-fits-all structure, and the condescending, government-knows-best attitude. Every family must have the opportunity to choose where its children go to school.

D.   To exercise their power wisely and make good decisions on behalf of their children, education's consumers must be well-informed about school quality, teacher qualifications, and much else, including, above all, the performance of their own children vis-à-vis high standards of academic achievement.

Strategies for Change

We urge two main renewal strategies, working in tandem:

I. Standards, Assessments and Accountability

Every student, school, and district must be expected to meet high standards of learning. Parents must be fully informed about the progress of their child and their child's school. District and state officials must reward success and have the capacity—and the obligation—to intervene in cases of failure.

II. Pluralism, Competition and Choice

We must be as open to alternatives in the delivery of education as we are firm about the knowledge and skills being delivered. Families and communities have different tastes and priorities, and educators have different strengths and passions. It is madness to continue acting as if one school model fits every situation and it is a sin to make a child attend a bad school if there's a better one across the street.

10 Breakthrough Changes for the 21st Century

1.   America needs solid national academic standards and (voluntary) standards-based assessments, shielded from government control, and independent of partisan politics, interest groups, and fads. (A strengthened National Assessment Governing Board would be the best way to accomplish this.) These should accompany and complement states' own challenging standards and tough accountability systems.

2.   In a free society, people must have the power to shape the decisions that affect their lives and the lives of their children. No decision is more important than where and how one is educated. **At minimum, every American child must have the right to attend the (redefined) public school of his choice.** Abolish school assignments based on home addresses. And let the public dollars to which they are entitled follow individual children to the schools they select. Most signers of this manifesto also believe strongly that this range of choices —especially for poor families—should include private and parochial schools as well as public schools of every description. But even those not ready to take that step—or awaiting a clearer resolution of its constitutionality—are united in their conviction that the present authoritarian system—we choose our words carefully—must go.

3.   **Every state needs a strong charter-school law,** the kind that confers true freedom and flexibility on individual schools, that provides every charter school with adequate resources, and that holds it strictly accountable for its results.

4.   More school choice must be accompanied by more choices worth making. **America needs to enlarge its supply of excellent schools.** One way to do

that is to welcome many more players into public education. Charter schools are not the whole story. We should also harness the ingenuity of private enterprise, of community organizations, of "private practice" teachers and other such education providers. Schools must be free to contract with such providers for services.

5. **Schools must not harm their pupils.** They must eschew classroom methods that have been proven not to work. They must not force children into programs that their parents do not want. (Many parents, for example, have serious misgivings about bilingual education as commonly practiced.)

6. **Every child has the right to be taught by teachers who know their subjects well.** It is educational malpractice that a third of high-school math teachers and two-fifths of science teachers neither majored nor minored in these subjects while in college. Nobody should be employed anywhere as a teacher who does not first pass a rigorous test of subject-matter knowledge and who cannot demonstrate their prowess in conveying what they know to children.

7. **One good way to boost the number of knowledgeable teachers is to throw open the classroom door to men and women who are well educated but have not gone through programs of "teacher education."** A NASA scientist, IBM statistician or former state governor may not be traditionally "certified" to teach and yet may have a great deal to offer students. A retired military officer may make a gem of a middle-school principal. Today, Albert Einstein would not be able to teach physics in America's public-school classrooms. That is ridiculous. Alternative certification in all its variety should be welcomed, and for schools that are truly held accountable for results, certification should be abolished altogether. Colleges of education must lose their monopoly and compete in the marketplace; if what they offer is valuable, they will thrive.

8. **High pay for great educators—and no pay for incompetents.** It is said that teaching in and leading schools doesn't pay enough to attract a sufficient number of well-educated and enterprising people into these vital roles. We agree. But the solution isn't across-the-board raises. The solution is sharply higher salaries for great educators—and no jobs at all for those who cannot do their jobs well. Why should the principal of a failing school retain a paycheck? Why shouldn't the head of a great school be generously rewarded? Why should salaries be divorced from evidence of effectiveness (including evidence that one's students are actually learning what one is teaching them)? Why should anyone be guaranteed permanent employment without regard to his or her performance? How can we expect school principals to be held accountable for results if they cannot decide whom to employ in their schools or how much to pay them?

9. **The classroom must be a sanctuary for serious teaching and learning of essential academic skills and knowledge.** That means all available resources —time, people, money—must be focused on what happens in that classroom.

More of the education dollar should find its way into the classroom. Distractions and diversions must cease. Desirable-but-secondary missions must be relegated to other times and places. Impediments to order and discipline must be erased. And the plagues and temptations of modern life must be kept far from the classroom door. Nothing must be allowed to interfere with the ability of a knowledgeable teacher to impart solid content to youngsters who are ready and willing to learn it.

10.   **Parents, parents, parents... and other caring adults.** It is a fact that great schools can work miracles with children from miserable homes and awful neighborhoods. But it is also a fact that attentive parents (and extended families, friends, et cetera) are an irreplaceable asset. If they read and talk to their children and help them with their homework, schools are far better able to do their part. If good character is taught at home (and in religious institutions), the schools can concentrate on what they do best: conveying academic knowledge and skills.

Hope for the Next American Century

Good things are already happening here and there. Most of the reforms on our list can be seen operating someplace in America today. Charter schools are proliferating. Privately managed public schools have long waiting lists. Choices are spreading. Standards are being written and rewritten. The changes we advocate are beginning, and we expect them to spread because they make sense and serve children well. But they are still exceptions, fleas on the elephant's back. The elephant still has most of the power. And that, above all, is what must change during the next 15 years in ways that were unimaginable during the past 15. We must never again assume that the education system will respond to good advice. It will change only when power relationships change, particularly when all parents gain the power to decide where their children go to school.

Such changes are wrenching. No monopoly welcomes competition. No stodgy enterprise begs to be reformed. Resistance must be expected. Some pain must be tolerated. Consider the plight of Detroit's automakers in the 1980s. At about the same time the Excellence Commission was urging major changes on U.S. schools, the worldwide auto market was forcing them upon America's Big Three car manufacturers. Customers didn't want to buy expensive, gas-guzzling vehicles with doors that didn't fit. So they turned to reliable, inexpensive Asian and European imports. Detroit suffered mightily from the competition. Then it made the changes that it needed to make. Some of them were painful indeed. They entailed radical changes in job expectations, huge reductions in middle management, and fundamental shifts in manufacturing processes and corporate cultures. The auto industry would not have chosen to take this path, but it was compelled to change or disappear.

Still, resistance to structural changes and power shifts in education must be expected. Every recommendation we have made will be fought by the current system, whose spokesmen will claim that every suggested reform constitutes an

Table 1

Signatories of *A Nation Still at Risk*

Jeanne Allen	**Howard Fuller**	**Will Marshall***
President Center for Education Reform	Director Institute for the Transformation of Learning, Marquette University	President Progressive Policy Institute
Leslye Arsht	**Carol Gambill**	**Deborah McGriff**
Co-Founder Standards Work	Math Teacher Sewickley, Penn.	Senior Vice President The Edison Project
William J. Bennett	**Mike Gambill**	**Michael Moe**
Co-Director Empower America	Business Leader Sewickley, Penn.	Senior Managing Director Montgomery Securities
Randy Bos	**P. R. Gross**	**Paul Peterson**
District Superintendent Waterloo, New York	Biologist Falmouth, Mass.	Professor of Government Harvard University
Stacey Boyd	**Scott Hamilton**	**Susan Pimentel**
Founding Director, Academy of the Pacific Rim Charter Boston, Mass.	Assoc. Commissioner of Education Massachusetts	Co-Founder Standards Work
Frank Brogan	**Eugene Hickok**	**Albert Quie**
State Commissioner of Education, Florida	Secretary of Education Pennsylvania	Former Governor of Minnesota Member Natl. Comm. On Excellence in Educ.
John Burkett	**E.D. Hirsch**	**Diane Ravitch**
Former Statistical Analyst Office of Educational Research and Improvement, U.S. Dept. of Ed.	Professor of English University of Virginia	Senior Fellow Brookings Institution
Murray Dickman	**William J. Hume**	**Nina Shokraii**
President Pennsylvania Manufacturers' Assn.	Chairman Center for Education Reform	Education Policy Analyst The Heritage Foundation
Dennis Doyle	**Raymond Jackson**	**Jay Sommer**
Senior Fellow Hudson Institute	President ATOP Academies Phoenix, Ariz.	Former Teacher of the Year Member Natl. Comm. on Excellence in Educ.
Dwight Evans	**Lisa Graham Keegan**	**Leah Vukmir**
Member Pa. House of Representatives	State Superintendent of Schools Arizona	Director Parents Raising Educational Standards in Schools
Willard Fair	**Yvonne Larsen**	**Herbert J. Walberg**
President The Urban League of Greater Miami	Board President California State Board of Education Vice-chairman Natl. Comm. on Excellence in Educ.	Research Professor of Education University of Illinois at Chicago
Chester E. Finn Jr.	**Thaddeus S. Lott**	
President, Thomas B. Fordham Foundation	Senior Project Manager Acres Homes Charter Schools Houston, Texas	
Rev. Floyd Flake	**Robert Luddy**	
Pastor Allen A.M.E. Cathedral and School Queens, N.Y.	CEO Captive Aire Systems	

*Mr. Marshall dissents from that portion of recommendation #2 that would have public dollars flow to private and parochial schools on the same basis.

attack on public education. They will be wrong. What truly threatens public education is clinging to an ineffective status quo. What will save it are educators, parents, and other citizens who insist on reinvigorating and reinventing it.

The stakes could not be higher. What is at stake is America's ability to provide all its daughters and sons with necessary skills and knowledge, with environments for learning that are safe for children and teachers, with schools in which every teacher is excellent and learning is central. What is at stake is parents' confidence that their children's future will be bright thanks to the excellent education they are getting; taxpayers' confidence that the money they are spending on public education is well spent; employers' confidence that the typical graduate of the typical U.S. high school will be ready for the workplace; and our citizens' confidence that American education is among the best in the world.

But even more is at stake than our future prosperity. Despite this country's mostly admirable utilitarianism when it comes to education, good education is not just about readiness for the practical challenges of life. It is also about liberty and the pursuit of happiness. It is about preparation for moral, ethical, and civic challenges, for participation in a vibrant culture, for informed engagement in one's community, and for a richer quality of life for oneself and one's family. Test scores are important. But so, too, are standards and excellence in our society. The decisions we make about education are really decisions about the kind of country we want to be; the sort of society in which we want to raise our children; the future we want them to have; and even—and perhaps especially—about the content of their character and the architecture of their souls. In the last decade of this American Century, we must not be content with anything less than the best for all our children.

NO

Forrest J. Troy

The Myth of Our Failed Education System

On a return to earth, Dante almost certainly would establish a new rung in hell for those attempting to obliterate public education. It is the most lied-about, misreported story in America. Newsweekly magazines, mindless editorial pages, television newscasts, talk radio and televangelists malign public education with a ferocity usually reserved for serial killers.

Why? What is it about this 200-year-old institution that makes it a lightning rod? Is it the tool of gluttonous unions as depicted by Rush Limbaugh? Is public schooling the "place of darkness" that Jerry Falwell has termed it? Is it the total academic failure painted by two ex-secretaries of education, Republicans Lamar Alexander and William Bennett?

Name one other institution that flings open itself to all comers—a perfect microcosm of our nation. Every autumn the miracle of America takes place when the doors of those 87,000 schools are thrown open, welcoming the genius and slow learner, rich and poor, average and developmentally disabled. Among them are the loved and unloved, the washed and unwashed.

Those who savage the public schools tear at the heart of this country. Everything America is or ever hopes to be depends upon what happens to those 46.3 million students in public school classrooms.

Myths Versus Facts

I unashamedly speak for public education—warts and all—and have done so for 30 years, delivering more than 2,800 speeches. My remarks are not Pollyannish. Public education has serious problems in the inner cities, and I don't ignore that. I'm not in the self-esteem business.

I've spent 40 years as an award-winning journalist, including a Pulitzer Prize nomination, dealing with hard facts and how those facts are interpreted. But outside of the major cities and rural pockets of poverty, America has a superbly successful public school system—certainly among the best in the world.

Myth: Teachers teach only nine months so why do they bellyache about low salaries?

From Forrest J. Troy, "The Myth of Our Failed Education System," *The School Administrator* (September 1998). Copyright © 1998 by *The School Administrator*. Reprinted by permission.

Fact: Repeated studies show this isn't true. If you count hours worked, the average teacher does in nine months what it takes regular 40-hour workers to do in 11.5 months.

Myth: American students score less well than kids in almost every other country.

Fact: This is the biggest canard of them all. America's smart kids are as smart or smarter than those in any other country. Test scores have recovered after a huge dip due to integration of public education. Separate was never equal.

Myth: Twenty-five per cent of students drop out, evidence of how ineffective public schools are.

Fact: More horse hockey. The dropout rate last year was 11 percent. Add to that a record-high graduation rate and a whopping 450,000 GEDs issued last year and America is among the best educated nations in the world.

Myth: We have students graduating from public schools who can't even read their diplomas.

Fact: You bet! They are among the nearly six million children in special education—most will never read well but they're getting their chance based on whatever gifts they bring to school. It's the best unreported story in America.

Myth: Unions are running the public schools.

Fact: Don't extrapolate to more than 14,400 school districts the mindless contracts (and overpaid janitors) in cities such as Cleveland, New York City or Chicago.

Myth: The PTA is a tool of teacher unions.

Fact: This had to be dreamed up by someone who never has been to a PTA meeting. I ought to know. I am not only a PTA veteran, but I hold the National PTA's Distinguished Service to Children Award.

Myth: Teachers are recruited from the dregs of college graduates.

Fact: Nearly half of the three million teachers in public schools have master's degrees. The political climate is so hateful toward public schools, a third quit within 10 years. Who can blame them? The committed stick, and most perform magnificently.

Myth: Public educators are afraid of competition. That's why they oppose charter schools and vouchers.

Fact: Only a nitwit public educator would favor vouchers, which suck funds from public school systems. Voucher is another way of spelling "segregation" —this time along class lines. Even the charter school movement is hardly the howling success predicted. Been to Arizona? Checked Michigan test scores?

Myth: Kids can't read today because schools don't exclusively use phonics.

Fact: America's 4th-grade readers just outperformed every country in the world except Finland, according to the National Assessment of Educational Progress. Phonics isn't the only way to learn to read. As any good reading teacher knows, this skill often requires a blend of whole language instruction with phonics.

Myth: Look how few American kids make it through college.

Fact: America is second only to Japan in the college graduation rate (by two percentage points). America exceeds every country in the world in graduate-level completion.

Myth: Entering test scores prove public schools don't adequately prepare students for college.

Fact: Any senior can take the SAT or the ACT. As many as 17 percent of those taking the SAT never had earned above a C in their classes. The College Board, which owns the SAT, decries constant misuse of test data by critics with an anti-public education agenda. The SAT score on reasoning just hit a 25-year high. Three out of four test takers this year scored higher than the national average. The ACT is at a five-year high. (My dream is to someday give the ACT exam to members of Congress!)

Myth: Today's students need to take the rigorous courses provided in the good old days.

Fact: I wish somebody who could talk slow enough would explain it to the likes of Rush Limbaugh, William F. Buckley or G. Gordon Liddy that there is a report entitled "The Condition of Education 1995" with 60 indicators related to preschool, elementary, secondary and postsecondary education. It revealed stunning improvement in public education. Between 1985–1995, the percentage of high school graduates taking core courses increased 47 percent. Critics who think schools are soft ought to check today's math, science and social studies texts. They make yesterday's stuff look like kindergarten.

Myth: Public schools locked God out of the classroom.

Fact: The U.S. Supreme Court banned sectarian prayer. Schools that have ignored that opinion have lost every single court case. Student prayer is not illegal —it happens every time there's a final exam.

Myth: Teachers are secular humanists.

Fact: Oh really? Public educators lead all other professions and occupations in teaching Sunday school, according to a survey published in *Parade* magazine.

Myth: Public schools don't teach values.

Fact: Define values. Nearly a third of students receive their only hot meal of the day in public schools. For thousands, the only hug they get is in public school. Teachers spend large sums of personal funds (average $400 last year) for things like workbooks and supplies. Thousands of teachers sponsor everything from drama to chess clubs on their own time, often without reimbursement.

Myth: The National Education Association and the American Federation of Teachers seek only higher salaries for less work.

Fact: The NEA and AFT spend huge sums of money on grants, scholarships and programs to support reform efforts and quality schooling initiatives. I have searched in vain for a list of positive programs financed by the critics.

Myth: School boards have outlived their usefulness. Parents ought to run the schools.

Fact: More than 77,000 school board members are parents and community leaders. Few are reimbursed for their time and selfless efforts.

Myth: There would be more money for schools were it not for overpaid administrators.

Fact: School administrators make a fraction of what they would earn running the same payroll and plant operation in the private sector.

Myth: We don't need school boards—they just get in the way.

Fact: Examples of waste, graft, corruption and illegalities already are emanating from charter schools, which have no comparable boards. School boards are designed to provide accountability, and they do. Check the voucher disaster in Cleveland.

Myth: Catholic schools do a better job with less money.

Fact: The average Catholic per-pupil cost of $3,200 compares with the $5,884 in public schools, but that's where the comparison ends. Public schools are required to provide regular education, vocational education, special education, counseling, dropout prevention, alternative education, attendance control, bilingual education, compensatory education, after-school athletics, regular student transportation, student activities, health and psychological programs, food services, security and violence prevention and much better employee benefits—such as a living wage and retirement programs.

Whom to Believe?

Who are you going to believe, the critics or the consumers? The annual Gallup education poll showed again that 65 percent of the parents who send 52 million children to public schools award those schools honors grades. But only 20 percent of those who have no connection with the schools grant them honors. They get their information from the popular media—the sorriest possible source. (A new Public Agenda poll reveals a 71 percent approval rating of public schools by patrons.)

Chester Finn, a former assistant secretary of education in charge of anti-public school propaganda, has the gall to write that parents should not believe what they personally experience. In other words, they are too dumb to know what a good school is. His motive? Finn is heavily invested in commercial privatization of public schools, writing the curriculum for the Edison Project, a privatization initiative. (To its shame, *Education Week* publishes him regularly without letting readers know of his financial connections.)

Why are public schools in the crosshairs when 90 percent of them are as good as any in the world? One reason is that major news media outlets are in the cities with the majority of failed schools. The blather from network news is almost always negative. Too many viewers with no firsthand knowledge extrapolate those conditions to all public schools. Add to this a heavy dose of racism, religious right fervor and nonstop right-wing slander on talk radio. Stir in 60 percent of adults with no connection with schools today in an environment of declining social and political cohesion, and you have a recipe for disaster.

Who Answers the Bell?

It's tough to be a teacher today. Every possible societal malfunction affects the classroom—drugs, alcohol, divorce, gangs and poverty.

According to the U.S. Department of Education, 46 million students attend 87,125 schools in 14,471 districts. Of that total, nearly six million have disabilities. They are educated at an average cost of $9,900, nearly twice the average spent on other students. More than 6.2 million are limited in their English proficiency with two million speaking no English. Two million are latchkey children. They go home to an empty house.

Nearly two million are abused and neglected. An estimated million kids suffer from the effects of lead poisoning, a leading cause of slow learning. More than 500,000 come from foster and institutional care. Thirty-thousand are products of fetal alcohol syndrome. Nearly 400,000 entering students are crack babies and children of other hard-core drug users.

More than half a million are homeless, coming from no permanent address. One in five students lives with a mother who did not finish high school. One in five kids under 18 (14.4 million) comes from abject poverty—with half showing up at public school hungry. More than half of poor children are white and live in rural and suburban areas.

Today's student body represents a challenge undreamed of by previous generations of educators.

Morale Busters

It's not unusual for an educator to wake up to a bashing on the "Today Show," to read another attack editorial in the morning newspaper, then hear motormouth Rush Limbaugh on the drive home trashing public schools. I have encountered thousands of angry and bewildered educators who want to fight back but don't know how.

The newsweeklies glory in spurious stories. Yet when good news is available, little is reported. When the International Math Olympiad was won by an all-public school cast, *Time* used a paragraph and didn't print the students' names.

Bob Dole described public education as an abject failure in a kickoff speech for his failed presidential campaign at a Milwaukee Catholic school.

("If education were a war, you'd be losing it. If it were a business, you would be driving it into bankruptcy. If it were a patient, it would be dying," he said.)

And who would consider Rush Limbaugh an education expert? He barely graduated from high school and was flunking out when he quit Southwestern Missouri State University. Yet *Family Circle* magazine invited him to produce a full page on how bad the public schools are! Grandma Troy was right—the higher a monkey climbs, the more you see of his ass. Limbaugh's ambition is to die in his own arms.

Religious Right Assault

The assault from radio and television evangelists is the hardest for educators to swallow. Pat Robertson's 700 Club is a nonstop critic, claiming that public schools are teaching a religion, or what he and others have dubbed secular humanism. What Robertson is really after is taxpayer-supported vouchers for Christian and parochial schools and home-schooled students. After he bowed out of his race for president, Robertson said he had it wrong—the way to take over the country was to start with school boards and legislative offices. On that score he's right.

Among this aggregation are TV's ubiquitous D. James Kennedy, the Old-Time Gospel Hour's Jerry Falwell, Focus on the Family's James Dobson, Jimmy Swaggart and several dozen radio and TV clones. They have favorite targets in the public schools: sex education ("Honey, they found you on a stump in the forest!"), school-to-work programs (send every kid to college, able or not) and multiculturalism (if you are not a white fundamentalist, your forefathers didn't exist).

They rage endlessly against condoms in the schools, yet fewer than two percent of schools even make condoms available. The Catholic hierarchy's chronic assaults are designed to pick up federal aid to religious schools via vouchers.

Critics include Phyllis Schlafly, who never spent a day of her life in a public school, yet she produces Eagle Forum reports stating that public education "is a form of child abuse." *Forbes* magazine relentlessly publishes ignorant stories designed for only one purpose—elimination of union affiliation for public educators. There are good unions and bad unions just as there are good magazines and *Forbes*.

Don't be surprised to learn how few educators, especially among three million classroom teachers, possess the ammunition necessary to refute the critics. Teaching is essentially a lonely profession—the classroom door closes and the entire day is spent with children, with only a short break for lunch. The evening is spent grading papers and working on lesson plans. Teachers know what's going on in their classroom and their school but few have the foggiest notion about the system of which they are a part.

Selling the Sizzle

The crisis, if there is one, does not reside in the typical U.S. classroom, and it doesn't infect a majority of students. Scientific acumen isn't needed to recognize that the bedrock of successful education is nurturing parents who play with their infants and read to their toddlers, who belong to the PTA and volunteer in the classroom; who send disciplined children to school. These are the same parents who support school bond issues, vote in school board elections and see education as an investment, not an expense.

If I could go one-on-one with every school administrator in America, my message would be simple: The failure isn't in the product but in the marketing. Or, as they say on Madison Avenue, "You don't sell the steak, you sell the sizzle." Public education's public relations are woefully inadequate. Here's how to merchandise the product:

- No. 1: Never let a newsletter or any other correspondence out of any school that doesn't contain at least one or more positive strokes—latest test scores, individual student and/or educator achievements, etc. (My facts have shown up in hundreds of school bulletins.)
- No. 2: A speaker's bureau is a must for civic clubs, chambers of commerce, etc. Civic organizations are the heartbeat of any community and they love to see and hear kids.
- No. 3: Create a committee on correspondence. Don't give the local news media, the critical letter writers or anyone else a free shot. Fight back with facts. Challenge the mistaken, the misinformed and the outright prevaricator while acknowledging honest criticism.

My grandmother was full of aphorisms. Here's my favorite:

> *Heretic, rebel, thing of doubt,*
> *He drew a circle that shut me out.*
> *But wit and I had the will to win*
> *We drew a larger circle that took him in.*

Ladies and gentlemen, start your drawings.

POSTSCRIPT

Have Public Schools Failed Society?

Failure or success? Research results present a mixed message and an unclear verdict. But regardless of the current evaluation, it is clear that reform is a continuing need in any social institution, especially in an institution that touches so many lives and has a direct impact on society and its economy. The questions for reformers are What most needs fixing? and How can the fixing be done best, and by whom?

Identification of reform targets are set forth in *Dumbing Down Our Kids: Why American Children Feel Good About Themselves But Can't Read, Write, or Add* by Charles J. Sykes (1995); *Poisoned Apple: The Bell-Curve Crisis and How Our Schools Create Mediocrity and Failure* by Betty Wallace and William Graves (1995); *The Things That Matter Most* by Cal Thomas (1994), particularly chapter 8, "The Promise of Progressive Education"; and *Beyond the Classroom: Why School Reform Has Failed and What Parents Need to Do* by Laurence Steinberg (1995).

Many constructive reform ideas may be found in *Horace's Hope* by Theodore R. Sizer (1996), in which the author discusses the many lessons he has learned from his work with reform-minded schools during the past decade; "Shifting the Target of Educational Reform," by William E. Klingele, *Educational Horizons* (Summer 1994); Deborah Meier's "How Our Schools Could Be," *Phi Delta Kappan* (January 1995); Benjamin R. Barber's "America Skips School: Why We Talk So Much About Education and Do So Little," *Harper's* (November 1993); "What General Motors Can Teach U.S. Schools About the Proper Role of Markets in Education Reform," by Richard J. Murnane and Frank Levy, *Phi Delta Kappan* (October 1996); and "A Light Feeling of Chaos': Educational Reform and Policy in the United States," by Karen Seashore Louis, *Daedalus* (Fall 1998).

Multiple articles may be found in the May 1996 issue of *The School Administrator* and the April 1999 issue of *NASSP Bulletin*. The February 17, 1997, issue of *The Nation* offers the symposium "Saving Public Education: Progressive Educators Explain What It Will Take to Get Beyond the Gimmicks." Also recommended are Stanley Pogrow's "Reforming the Wannabe Reformers: Why Education Reforms Almost Always End Up Making Things Worse," *Phi Delta Kappan* (June 1996); "Whose Schools? And What Should We Do With Them?" by John F. Covaleskie, *Educational Theory* (Fall 1997); and "The Public School As Wasteland," by Lawrence Baines, Chris Muire, and Gregory Stanley, *Contemporary Education* (Winter 1999).

On the Internet ...

School Choice

School choice links and resources are provided at this site.

http://www.conservative-digest.com/schools/schools.htm

The Center for Education Reform

Here the center provides information on charter schools, academic standards, and other topics.

http://edreform.com/pubs/charti.htm

Inclusion in Education: A Choice for Your Child

This is a discussion of inclusion from the Center on Human Policy, Syracuse University.

http://soeweb.syr.edu/thechp/incdoc2b.htm

Africana.com

This site offers articles, news, and links on Afrocentrism and related topics.

http://www.africana.com/tt_001.htm

National Association for Bilingual Education

This association is exclusively concerned with the education of language-minority students in American schools.

http://www.nabe.org

Partnerships Against Violence Network

This site is a virtual library of information about violence and at-risk youth.

http://www.pavnet.org

Urban Education Web

This site offers manuals, articles, annotated bibliographies, and conference announcements in urban education.

http://eric-web.tc.columbia.edu

From Now On: The Educational Technology Journal

This site examines issues in integrating technology into the public schools.

http://www.fno.org

PART 3

Current Specific Issues

*T*his section presents specific questions currently being probed and debated by educators, policymakers, scholars, and parents. In most cases these issues are grounded in the more basic questions explored in Parts 1 and 2.

- Are Vouchers an Appropriate Choice Mechanism?

- Can Charter Schools Revitalize Public Education?

- Have Public Schools Adequately Accommodated Religion?

- Is Full Inclusion of Disabled Students Desirable?

- Do Black Students Need an Afrocentric Curriculum?

- Should Bilingual Education Programs Be Abandoned?

- Does School Violence Warrant a Zero-Tolerance Policy?

- Can Self-Governing Schools Rescue Urban Education?

- Should Technology Lead the Quest for Better Schools?

- Is Mandatory Community Service Desirable and Legal?

- Do Teachers' Unions Have a Positive Influence on Reform?

ISSUE 11

Are Vouchers an Appropriate Choice Mechanism?

YES: Kevin Walthers, from "Saying Yes to Vouchers: Perception, Choice, and the Educational Response," *NASSP Bulletin* (September 1995)

NO: John F. Lewis, from "Saying No to Vouchers: What Is the Price of Democracy?" *NASSP Bulletin* (September 1995)

ISSUE SUMMARY

YES: Teacher Kevin Walthers portrays the voucher movement as a means for strengthening professionalism and raising academic standards.

NO: Attorney John F. Lewis argues that vouchers and the school choice ideology do not deal with the problems facing the public schools.

One of the more heated educational debates in recent years has been the one concerned with finding ways to provide parents and learners with a greater range of choices in schooling. Some people see the public school system as a monolithic structure that runs roughshod over individual inclinations and imposes a rigid social philosophy on its constituents. Others feel that the reduced quality of public education, particularly in large urban areas, demands that parents be given support in their quest for better learning environments. Still others agree with sociologist James S. Coleman's contention that "the greater the constraints imposed on school attendance—short of dictating place of residence and prohibiting attendance at private schools—the greater the educational gap between those who have the money to escape the constraints and those who do not."

Measures that emphasize freedom of choice abound and are often connected with desegregation and school reform goals. Some jurisdictions have developed a system of magnet schools to serve the dual purposes of equality and quality; some districts now allow parents to send their children to any public school under their control (given logistical constraints); and a few urban districts (notably Milwaukee, Wisconsin, and Cleveland, Ohio) are experimenting with funding plans to allow private school alternatives.

Two of the much-discussed ideas for providing funding for private school alternatives are tuition tax credits and voucher plans. The first, provided by the federal or state government, would expand the number of families able to send their children to the school of their choice by refunding part of the tuition cost. Voucher plans, first suggested in 1955 by conservative economist Milton Friedman, are designed to return tax monies to parents of school-aged children for tuition use in a variety of authorized public and private educational settings. Opponents of either approach take the position that such moves will turn the public schools into an enclave of the poor and will lead to further racial, socioeconomic class, and religious isolation. The question of church-state separation looms large in the minds of those who oppose these measures.

In his 1995 book *Dumbing Down Our Kids,* Charles J. Sykes raises a crucial point. He states, "The first step of meaningful reform is to recognize that saving our children is not the same as saving the public school system. That means changing our definition of 'public' education by seeing it as a commitment to provide all children with a quality education rather than as the perpetuation of a specific system of funding and bureaucratic organization." Voucher advocates build on this basic shift in the treatment of the concept "public," holding that something valued as a benefit to the public in general or some segment of the public does not have to be provided by a government-run facility. An existing example would be Catholic, Jewish, or Adventist hospitals, which are open to the public and are partially funded by public tax monies.

In a *Washington Post* opinion piece titled "Public Schools: Make Them Private" (February 19, 1995), Milton Friedman put forth the idea that "the most feasible way to bring about a gradual yet substantial transfer from government to private enterprise is to enact in each state a voucher system that enables parents to choose freely the schools their children attend." Other experts feel that such notions demolish the traditional democratic ideal of public schooling and run counter to prevailing interpretations of constitutional legality.

Gregory Shafer, in "The Myth of Competition and the Case Against School 'Choice,'" *The Humanist* (March/April 1999), says that "at the heart of the call for competition is an undying belief that the educational establishment has become bloated, lazy, and unresponsive to the parents who represent their constituency." He also contends that "one of the most disquieting and bizarre aspects of the school competition idea is its unabashed and monolithic adoration of business as a metaphor for success."

In the following selections, Kevin Walthers examines the voucher issue from the point of view of a teacher who wants to restore confidence in American education by objectively examining its ills and opening the institution to unbridled choice. John F. Lewis denies the value of choice and its voucher mechanism and wonders why we are wasting time, money, and effort on what he considers a "dead end on a wrong-way street."

Kevin Walthers

 **YES**

Saying Yes to Vouchers: Perception, Choice, and the Educational Response

In many ways, perception is reality. The 1992 presidential election turned on voter perceptions regarding the state of the U.S. economy. The public believed that an economic malaise gripped the nation, dismissing George Bush's claims that there were no economic problems. That the economy grew in 1992 (albeit at a slower pace than in previous years) was immaterial. Bush failed to properly gauge voter perception, and lost the election.

Public educators now face the same situation George Bush faced: The people perceive that public education is not fulfilling its mission and they are demanding change. Educators and education associations continue to ignore this prevailing negative perspective, claiming that virtually all criticism is motivated by political opportunism or personal vendettas.

What Is the Public Perception?

Unfortunately, the criticisms leveled at public education contain more than a kernel of truth. It is time to analyze the public perception, determine the facts and fallacies of that perception, and initiate a debate that will focus on improving education.

Critics of public education abound. Adults bemoan the lax standards of modern schools, industry leaders complain that students lack basic work skills, college professors decry the lack of logical reasoning in student writing, parents cry out for more and better programs, and taxpayers reject increased funding for schools that are retreating academically while expanding fiscally.

With all this criticism, it seems logical that educators would defend themselves by offering evidence that schools are not failing the public trust. Instead, an amazing set of paradoxes exists in the area of educational criticism.

Schools teach higher order thinking skills, yet fail to perform unbiased self-evaluations. Educators support debate and speech activities designed to develop student abilities to reason and respond to information, yet recoil in dismay if someone claims there are serious problems in education. "Even though educators consider themselves to be 'thinking people,' there is a remarkable absence of substantive arguments in their response to critics. These responses include evading the specifics of the criticism and arbitrarily attributing Utopian beliefs to critics" (Sowell, 1993, p. 249).

Educators must take an objective look at the charges against them without resorting to partisanship and name calling. Refuting false accusations is a simple task. More difficult and more important is creating a remedy for the true problems, even if that means entirely revamping the U.S. education system.

To accomplish this, educators must evaluate the three main areas of education that receive a majority of the criticism: lack of professional standards among educators; lack of appropriate academic standards for students; and the alienation of parents and taxpayers from the educational process.

Barriers to Professionalism

Teaching as a profession is a widely debated concept. Many believe teachers lack the critical attributes necessary to claim the title of professional. "Hallmarks of a profession include mastery of a body of knowledge and skills that lay people do not possess, autonomy in practice, and autonomy in setting standards for the field" (Wise and Leibbrand, 1993, p. 135).

These are the steps to building a profession: Upon mastering a particular body of knowledge, a group may begin to practice unfettered by government regulations, obtaining the authority to establish standards for others to enter the profession. Medical doctors are the ultimate example of an autonomous profession. Doctors are required to complete a rigorous preprofessional curriculum as undergraduates, make an acceptable score on a difficult exam for entrance to medical school, graduate from an accredited medical school, pass another difficult professional exam, and complete an accredited residency (Sykes, 1989).

Not all professions require a structure this rigid, but lawyers, pharmacists, architects, and engineers have established standards that exclude the unqualified, restrict the underqualified, and raise the standard of the profession. The impetus for professionalism in the field of teaching must come from internal sources, as there is no external agency that can bestow such a title on any endeavor.

The National Commission on Excellence in Education (1983) addressed the needs of education in *A Nation at Risk*. The commission offered several recommendations regarding teachers designed "to make teaching a more rewarding and respected profession" (National Commission on Excellence in Education [NCEE], 1983, p. 30). The commission stated that education colleges should require prospective teachers to meet high academic standards and that salaries should be market-sensitive and performance based. These are basic elements of professionalism, yet educational leaders have erected barriers to keep these elements out of the educational process.

The NCEE realized that a need existed for better qualified students to enter the field of education. Historically, students enrolled in colleges of education consistently scored below the national average on standardized tests such as the ACT, SAT, and GRE (Sowell, 1993). The brightest students entering universities were choosing not to enroll in colleges of education, depriving schools of a resource considered very valuable in the private sector: bright, young, educated talent. The NCEE recommended awarding grants and loans to attract outstanding students to the teaching profession (particularly in areas of critical shortage such as science and mathematics), as well as developing strategies such as an 11-month contract that would make teaching more attractive financially (NCEE, 1983).

Enhancing the financial aspect of teaching is a key to building professionalism. One characteristic that all professionals share is the right to negotiate contracts on their own behalf, based on their worth to the employer. Friedman notes that "[p]oor teachers are grossly overpaid and good teachers grossly underpaid" (1982, p. 94). The problem with teacher salaries, the economist/author claims, is not that they are too low but that they are too rigid (Friedman, 1982).

If they are to be considered professionals, teachers should be compensated based not only on their value to the school but also on their value to others who seek to employ them. A lack of market incentives for salaries and the penalizing effect of the certification system lead to critical shortages in education. For example, highly qualified scientists, mathematicians, and language specialists are lured away from teaching because of financial disincentives to enter the classroom, and prevented from entering the educational field by legal barriers requiring a teaching certificate. The teaching certificate is designed to ensure that all teachers meet professional standards, but it is rarely more than a "union card":

> Certification raises problems not just because it fails to screen out the mediocre and the bad. It also raises problems because it sets up formidable barriers to entry that keep many excellent prospects out of the job pool. People who are well educated, bright, enthusiastic, creative, and good with children cannot simply pursue a latent interest in education by simply giving it a try. Nor can talented people already working in other lines of endeavor shift into teaching, or perhaps move in and out of it, as they might in other jobs. Instead, potential teachers are asked by the state to foreclose other options, make a substantial investment of time and resources, and jump through formal hoops. Our society is full of people who could make excellent teachers, but burdensome certification requirements are the best way to ensure that most of them never teach (Chubb and Moe, 1990, p. 196).

Academic Standards

While some question the professionalism of educators, others fear a lack of appropriate academic standards for students. Adults remember "how tough it was when I was in school," but growing evidence supports the public's position that school, while getting easier, ignores the increasing knowledge base needed to compete in a high tech marketplace. Parents and taxpayers see falling test scores, inclusion, affective learning, self-esteem training, and values clarification lessons as proof that schools are not teaching as much material as they used to. Furthermore, they believe the material being taught is not as difficult as it should be.

'Sex education' courses and textbooks, for example, seldom involve a mere conveying of biological or medical information. Far more often, the primary thrust is toward re-shaping of attitudes, not only toward sex, but also toward parents, toward society, and toward life. The same pattern is found in many other programs claiming to be about drug prevention, smoking prevention, and many other worthy purposes (Sowell, 1993, p. 35).

Parents and taxpayers demand that "basic skills" regain the attention of educators. They wonder how a person who lacks the skill to complete an employment application managed to graduate from a public high school. This is a strong perception in the community, one educators would be unwise to dismiss as "hate-mongering from the radical right."

The lack of academic standards in the public school is profound. According to the U.S. Census Bureau, in 1930: "... most of the 1 million white illiterates and 2 million black illiterates were people over the age of 50 who had never been to school. By 1990, 30 to 35 million (American) citizens could not read. Most are people under 50 who have been to school for at least eight years" (Wood, 1992, p. 51).

Educators often dismiss this evidence as anecdotal and isolated, but the news, and the public mind set, is filled with studies showing drops in skills in all academic areas. Until educators meet the challenge, the public will not have faith in the abilities of the public education system.

Alienation

A correlating factor to watered-down curricula is the feeling of alienation held by many taxpayers and parents. Educators cry out for parent and community involvement, then complain when these forces initiate change in school policy. Educators, when asked to identify their "customers," often respond that students or their parents are their clients. One overlooked public school client, however, is the taxpayer. Citizen funding of the educational process creates "a stable and democratic society (that) is impossible without a minimum degree of literacy and knowledge on the part of most citizens" (Friedman, 1982, p. 86). In refusing to acknowledge the role of the community in education, schools are alienating the portion of the population that pays the bills. Therefore, "citizens everywhere, whether or not they have children in school and whether or not they live in the local school district or even the state, have a legitimate hand in governing each and every local school" (Chubb and Moe, 1990, p. 30).

Parents, of course, possess a natural right to be involved directly in the education of their children. The Family Educational Rights and Privacy Act of 1974 arms parents with the legal means to force educators to divulge information regarding course content, among other things. Even without federal law, parents have direct local access to principals, teachers, administrators, and even school board members. This close tie to the schools does not mean, however, that parents should have any more influence on school policy than any other tax-paying member of the community (Chubb and Moe, 1990). The community establishes the schools and sets policies in accordance with the public good, not the individual preference.

A Workable Solution

The public is growing increasingly dissatisfied with public education. This is in no small way due to damaging media coverage that focuses on the negative aspect of events. It is more newsworthy when a gun is fired in a school building (which happens so infrequently as to be statistically insignificant) than it is when thousands of students successfully complete high school and receive scholarships to major universities—which happens in virtually every district every year.

The media are not the sole cause of dissatisfaction, however, when it comes to the public attitude toward public education. Educators must find a way to convince parents that schooling is a professional endeavor. It is unlikely, however, that continuation of the current system will force a change in U.S. attitudes. Our industry thrives because of its competitive nature, and an infusion of capitalism into education would be a fitting remedy for the ailment of complacency in the classroom.

Nobel Prize-winning economist Milton Friedman developed a plan that, though a radical departure from the status quo, would empower parents as well as quality educators. "Free market vouchers" embody the application of Friedman's plan for what Zerchykov (1987) calls "unregulated vouchers." If Friedman did not coin the term vouchers as it relates to school choice, he certainly may be credited with the universal acceptance of the term as it relates to educational policy.

Vouchers, according to Friedman, would provide a mechanism for equalizing educational opportunities: "Governments could require a minimum level of schooling financed by giving parents vouchers redeemable for a specified maximum sum per child per year if spent on approved educational services" (Friedman, 1982, p. 87).

He begins his argument by noting that while it is a responsibility of the government to provide funding for education (which promotes the common welfare), the government is not required to administer education. This could be done much more efficiently in the private sector, with only minimal regulations that would concern health and safety issues (Friedman, 1982). He does not advocate the abolition of the modern public school, but challenges them to compete for students with private and parochial schools.

Thomas Ascik, executive director of the Clearinghouse on Educational Choice, agrees that free market vouchers give parents the liberty to raise their children as they see fit: "Child rearing is the whole and schooling is only a part. Parents have the authority over the whole and, therefore, they should have the ultimate authority over the part" (Ascik, 1986, p. 109).

Ascik and Friedman also claim that free market vouchers will be a greater benefit to the poor than to the wealthy. Friedman explains that a parent in a low income job can save money and buy the same car that the wealthy drive. In like manner, the parent can work an extra job to send his child to private school so that he can get an education on a par with that of a child in a public school in a wealthy neighborhood. A voucher would enable the family to send the child to a better school and devote economic resources to other aspects of making a better life such as home ownership or providing for otherwise unaffordable extracurricular activities.

Opponents of the free market voucher plan call this plan "welfare for the rich," asserting that private schools would merely raise the cost of tuition by the amount of the voucher, keeping the school as unreachable for the poor as it was before. They also claim that the poorest segments of our society are the least educated, so they would not know how to find the best school for their child. Ascik confronts the latter problem by comparing school funding to the food stamp program:

> Annually, governments invest as much in health as in education. Nutrition is a big part of health. Using the same rationale used to justify the status quo in public education, we may wonder why the government should not fund grocery stores directly rather than deliver food stamps to individuals (Ascik, 1986, p. 111).

In response to the first objection, the market theory used by Friedman to advocate free market vouchers holds that if private schools raise their tuition by the amount of the voucher, someone will fill the gap in the market and provide an alternative of equal quality for a lower price. This basic principal of economic efficiency will bring down the tuition price of the other schools as well, creating more educational opportunities for those on the lower end of the economic scale.

Why Should Educators Support Choice?

Educators claim to support choice. They point to alternative schools, open enrollment policies, magnet programs, and GED classes as evidence. When students are restricted to choosing from the programs offered by a single entity (usually the local school district), the promise of choice remains unfulfilled. By implementing a true choice plan, educators would elevate the stature of their field, allow for specialized, relevant academic standards, and intimately involve parents in the education of their children.

Unfortunately, teacher associations and unions adamantly oppose any form of choice that would allow students to attend nonpublic schools. Unions cite student welfare as the reason for their opposition to choice, but self-serving political motives are the driving force against any plan that undermines the power of the unions, especially the National Education Association.

The NEA claims to be interested in student success, yet opposes allowing students to leave the monopolistic school district in search of better schools. Association president Keith Geiger asserted that "the solution to the funding and social inequities that condemn children in inner cities and other impoverished areas to inferior schools is not to encourage the flight of the most promising students" (Dunne, 1991, p. 14).

Geiger fails (or refuses) to see that all students would have access to better schools, not just the top prospects. There is a strong inverse link between economic disadvantage and educational achievement. For this reason, federal block grant funds are distributed based on the income level of the students attending a particular school or district. Wealthy districts get little while poor districts receive a substantial supplement.

This would continue under a voucher plan by giving financial incentives to schools that educate children from economically depressed areas. By increasing the financial value of the child's education, inner-city children would become highly desirable members of the student body (Rinehart and Jackson, 1991). Choice plans in Cambridge, Mass., have increased overall student achievement while closing the educational gap between white and black students. East Harlem, N.Y., has seen a five-fold increase in the rate of students reading at or above grade level since initiating a school choice plan (Nathan, 1990). One study of interdistrict choice plans shows that parents want better schools for their children, even if it means taking the student to a school in another district:

> It would be a mistake to dismiss interdistrict school choice as a phenomenon driven by family convenience. Enrollment patterns in districts where significant numbers of transfers occurred (20 students or more from one community to another) show a strong and unmistakable trend. Families enrolled their children in districts that had higher median family incomes and better educated adult populations than their home communities. They also went to districts that had better standardized test scores at the high school level, lower out-of-school suspension rates, lower dropout rates, and higher per-pupil funding (Fossey, 1994).

The plan that Geiger assails as damaging to the minority student has in fact, proved to work just as Milton Friedman said it would more than 30 years ago, even though the programs are limited in scope. Lower-income parents in Massachusetts choice districts are empowered to seek out an education for their children that is equal to that of families with higher income while the taxpayers are blessed with a young population that will have increased earning power due to an improving educational system.

Even if free market vouchers are not the best option, those who oppose choice refuse to engage in thoughtful debate. Many advocates of choice are intelligent, prominent, and eloquent. They count among their ranks politicians, professors, journalists, and at least one Nobel Laureate. Hurling invective at a group with these credentials, as the education associations continue to do, only strengthens the choice position.

The arguments presented by voucher supporters are solid, gaining widespread acceptance from lawmakers in both major parties. Educators must look at the issue impartially, realizing that the best way to educate children may not be through a government-run monopoly. If educators are to be considered professionals, they must allow for dissent, innovation, and input from the community. Arrogantly claiming to be the sole possessors of educational knowledge and demanding ever-growing infusions of tax money to support public schools is no longer politically viable.

Conclusion

Vouchers hold the promise of elevating teaching to professional status, raising levels of student achievement, and restoring the confidence of the tax paying public. If teachers do not embrace this idea, they should at least develop thoughtful arguments that show why the plan is unworkable. Until educators and their associations agrees that dissent is not only acceptable but encouraged, the public will continue to perceive education as just another in a long list of non-performing, over-bureaucratized, autocratic government programs that usurp individual liberty.

References

Ascik, T. In *Content, Character, and Choice in Schooling*. Washington, D.C.: National Council on Educational Research, 1986.

Chubb, J., and Moe, T. *Politics, Markets, and America's Schools*. Washington, D.C.: The Brookings Institution, 1990.

Dunne, D. *School Choice: Pros, Cons, and Concerns*. Washington, D.C.: ASPIRA Issue Brief, 1991.

Fossey, R. "Open Enrollment in Massachusetts: Why Families Choose." *Educational Evaluation and Policy Analysis* 3(1994): 320–34.

Friedman, M. *Capitalism and Freedom*. Chicago, Ill.: University of Chicago Press, 1982.

——. *Public School Choice: Current Issues/Future Prospects*. Lancaster, Pa.: Technomic, 1990.

Nathan, J. "Progress, Problems, and Prospects of State Education Plans." In *Choice in Education: Potential and Problems*, edited by W. Boyd and H. Walberg. Berkeley, Calif.: McCutchan, 1990.

National Commission on Excellence in Education. *A Nation at Risk*. Washington, D.C.: U.S. Department of Education, 1983.

Rinehart, J., and Jackson, L., Jr. *American Education and the Dynamics of Choice*. New York: Praeger, 1991.

Sowell, T. *Inside American Education: The Decline, the Deception, the Dogmas*. New York: The Free Press, 1993.

Sykes, G. "Teaching and Professionalism: A Cautionary Perspective." In *Crisis in Teaching: Perspectives on Current Reforms*, edited by L. Weis, P. Altbach, G. Kelly, H. Petrie, and S. Slaughter. Albany, N.Y.: State University of New York, 1989.

Wise, A., and Leibbrand, J. "Accreditation and the Profession of Teaching." *Phi Delta Kappan* 2(1993): 135.

Wood, R. "That's Right—They're Wrong." *National Review* 18(1992): 50–53.

Zerchykov, R. *Parent Choice: A Digest of Research*. Boston, Mass.: Institute for Responsive Education, 1987.

John F. Lewis

 **NO**

Saying No to Vouchers: What Is the Price of Democracy?

The year 1995 began with at least 14 state legislatures exploring "school choice" as the answer to the ills facing public education. This surge of activity belies the fact that the idea has been sputtering around since the early 1960s when economist Milton Friedman argued that public schools should not be a government monopoly, and conceived a "voucher" equal to a certain number of public dollars.[1] The voucher would be given to parents who in turn could deliver it as an equivalent to dollars to any school, public or independent, of the parents' choice.

Those who believe in the applicability of market economics to public education believe that parents will use their vouchers to choose the "best" schools —whatever that means. It follows that schools not chosen will either improve to meet the competition or go out of existence.

Since Professor Friedman's suggestion, "school choice" has been heralded as the answer to all kinds of problems facing education. That the idea finds nourishment in this country is not at all surprising, for the soul of "school choice"—allowing parents to use public school funds to enroll their children in any independent school they choose—seems the essence of democracy.[2] Who in a democracy can argue with freedom of choice?

In point of fact, "school choice" is a strategy that does not deal with the problems facing our schools, but in fact runs from them.

The Myth of Choice

Underlying the idea of "school choice" is the fundamental, all-American belief in rugged competition. Simplistically, the argument runs, "If we give parents a choice, they will pick the best. Schools not chosen will improve or get out of education. Those chosen will grow. Ultimately, choice will bring out the best." Note, however, that it is not the actual consumer who makes the choice. Rather it is the consumer once-removed, the child's parent or guardian, who chooses on behalf of the student. This fact may have a significant if not controlling impact on why the choice is made.

This kind of marketplace "choice" is what undergirds the private sector. There, the motivator is dollars. The profit motive, Adam Smith long ago pointed out, will produce the best product.[3] Why? Because the only way you can make money is to produce something others choose to buy. More than that, if people have a choice, they will buy the best. So, if you want to make money, produce the best.

But money is not the primary motivator in education. Motivations come in soft packages: Self-satisfaction? Seeing your students succeed? Intellectual stimulation? Indeed, a principal motivation that undergirds "choice" is fear, the threat of losing students. And students may be lost whether or not you are delivering the "best" educational product you can deliver.

What, then, makes us believe that an economic model rooted in Adam Smith's assumptions and called "choice" will improve education?

Of course the inner cities' social problems are horrendous. Dropout rates exceed a third of the class. Scholastic Aptitude Test scores are widely reported to have dropped. We are repeatedly told graduates are unable to add and subtract.[4] Crime is up and on the rise. So is drug use. So also is teen pregnancy.[5]

Because these problems undeniably feed upon themselves and have an impact on one another, does that make the school the source of the problems? Do schools cause cycles of poverty and despair? Is it the fault of schools that crime and drugs and pregnancy are on the rise? Will going to an independent school solve the problem? These are problems *in* the schools but not *with* the schools. *In* the schools means problems in our society—in our cities—in our suburbs—in our families that are brought into the schools. These are not problems amenable to a "school" solution modeled after classic economic theory. The schools are the community operating tables upon which our deeper sicknesses are displayed.

What, in short, makes anyone believe choice will make the slightest difference in the product we turn out? What makes us think it will reduce crime? Slow down drugs? Stop teen pregnancy? Answer? It will not.

Improving Education

In the past several years, we have explored every conceivable approach to improving education: new curricula, scholarships, vocational supplements, magnets, fast tracks, slow tracks, team teaching, school-within-a-school, and every variation of all the above and more. Nothing has worked to our satisfaction.

Who said schools worked in the 1970s when sex and race discrimination, desegregation, due process, and classroom prayer dominated the Supreme Court agenda? Who said public education worked in the 1960s when desegregation, free speech, armbands, and long hair were the battle cry? Or in the 1950s when we were riding an after-war boom and jobs were plentiful? Who said it worked in the 1940s during World War II? Who paid any attention during the Great Depression of the 1930s when no one had jobs?

The social problems of poverty, crime, drugs, pregnancy, and race relations have grown exponentially during that time. But surely not because of the education being delivered.

In fact, on a number of key international measures U.S. schools do quite well. According to the National Center for Education Statistics, the great majority of U.S. students finished at or near the top of the most recent international comparison of the 19 developed nations in mathematics. Mathematics is, of course, a subject in which our national performance is reported as dismal. Top finishers:

1. Asian students (in the U.S.)—287
2. Taiwan—285
3. Korea—283
4. Advantaged urban students (in the U.S.)—283
5. White students (in the U.S.)—277
6. Hungary—277.[6]

Finally, the United States in 1994 had a 4.5 percent economic growth rate, a gain of three million jobs, and an inflation rate reminiscent of the 1960s. We are the envy of the industrialized world.

The amount the average U.S. worker can produce, already the highest in the world, is growing faster than in other wealthy countries, including Japan. The United States has become the world's low-cost provider of many sophisticated products and services, from plastics to software to financial services.[7]

In July 1992, the International Association for the Evaluation of Educational Achievement (IAEEA) released a report comparing reading skills of 200,000 students in 31 countries. The study found U.S. 9-year-olds reading better than anyone in the world except Finnish 9-year-olds. Using a scale identical to that of the SAT (a mean of 500 and a standard deviation of 100), U.S. 9-year-olds averaged 547, while the Finns came in at 569. Our 14-year-olds finished ninth, with an average score of 535. Interestingly, the U.S. 14-year-olds actually scored almost as close to first place as did the 9-year-olds.[8]

In December 1994, Rand published a monograph, "Student Achievement and the Changing American Family," which throws into substantial question the statistics relied on by so many who would have us believe public education is in free fall. Rand acknowledges SAT scores have dropped significantly since 1970, but points out that the SAT is a totally inappropriate measure. It is not designed to compare student performance over time because it is taken only once or twice and even then not by a statistically representative sample. Moreover, it is taken by a different mix of students each year and even then only by students who intend to go on to college.

A far more reliable measurement of student performance is the National Assessment of Educational Progress (NAEP). Why? Because NAEP is designed to, and does, measure student achievement over time with a standardized test of students at ages 9, 13, and 17. Scores from this test show 13-year-olds' mathematics achievement has, in fact, improved by 6 percent during the 20-year period, and that of 17-year-olds by 4 percent; something is working. Reading scores are also improving with the most dramatic gain being shown by black students (19 percent) and Hispanic students (11 percent.)[9]

Ah, but these achievements don't address the dropouts, the crime, the drugs, pregnancies, the decline in moral values. There is no question these are conditions that need to be corrected. But how?

Opting Out of Democracy

"Choice" is currently a popular answer. It is in the jumbled tradition of so many quick-fix answers—with a dangerous twist: It undermines the very democratic value system it celebrates.

For example, it troubles "choice" advocates that the Supreme Court will not permit the simplest prayer to start the day. This concern is quickly linked to the requirement that students, all students, must by law go to school. And they must go with everyone else regardless of religious persuasion—or lack thereof—with derelicts, with drug addicts, and with immoral mothers and fathers.

It bothers choice advocates that a youngster carrying a gun or drugs is entitled to due process. How can it be a democracy with metal detectors and safety guards? First it surprises, then it angers them that administrators must spend precious hours conducting due process hearings for each student before disciplining the student with a three-day suspension.[10]

It angers them that the school board must do everything in public—that's right, nothing, not even private discussions, can be done in private. They do not understand the significance of public records that are there for all to examine. They are exasperated by Sunshine Laws that require everything in the open.

It frustrates them that students who have had nothing to eat can act up and disrupt a classroom, or that a youngster who needs a urinary catheter can interrupt the normal course of the day and take the teacher from the classroom.

And what is this business about free speech and wearing buttons, and armbands and long hair? "Where is the discipline?" "Why don't you just sit the kid down?" "You mean if you touch him he gets a due process hearing?"

It infuriates the advocates of choice that public schools in most states must by law deal with unions. (It infuriates me, too.) They do not understand that this democracy they wish to brag about to the rest of the world comes with a price—a steep price, and problems—lots of problems. Living together under majority rule, running a public school is not easy.

Consider the fact that a teacher with 10 years' experience and a master's degree in a *public school* will earn twice as much as his or her counterpart in an *independent* school. Moreover, the benefits package in a public school simply has no parallel in private sector education. You bet there are savings. And guess what? An independent school principal simply reassigns a teacher to another class, or directs the teacher to coach soccer. The public school principal has to sit down and *bargain,* and nothing happens unless the union says "O.K." Worse, because of democratically adopted legislation, the termination of an incompetent or inefficient public school teacher costs lots of money and countless administrative hours. And if you do the sensible and courageous thing and spend the money, the public climbs all over you for fiscal irresponsibility. So, no one terminates anyone.

None of this happens in independent schools.

But you know what? As [Walt Kelly's cartoon character] Pogo used to say, "We have met the enemy and he is us." The Constitution and the rule of law are what this country is all about. We put them there. That's what democracy means. That's precisely what our Constitution says.

I do not quarrel with concerns about lack of prayer and rock-hard values in our public schools. I do say the way to address them in this country is not by running to an independent school and asking me to pay. It is by confronting them head-on. This is the heart of the debate. It is not an answer to say that one is entitled in a democracy to choose one's school even if it is independent. I reply "But why should I pay for your independent school?"

It is no answer to our public school problems to set up a dual system and watch as one set of youngsters receives an education unfettered by the bad part of what a democracy means, while others—usually impoverished—must go to schools where the rules of democracy do apply and must, by law, be applied. This is no choice as I understand choice. Capitalistic choice is predicated on an even playing field. If you have problems and you want to change them, you are treated the same as everyone else. Because of laws democracy has thrust upon them, public schools cannot change most of the very reasons that underlie decisions by choice advocates to find fault with them.

Even while opting out of many of democracy's restrictions, independent schools already receive substantial public support. As one compares the efficiencies of public versus independent schools, one often meets the argument that independent school budgets are markedly less.

They are less, first, because teacher compensation (salary and benefits) is dramatically less; second, because the enormous cost of operating under the Constitution and the unfunded mandates of Congress requires public schools to spend more; and third, because the general everyday operating costs are less simply because the clientele wants to be there.

In making the comparisons the pro-choice advocates often forget to add the per-pupil cost of transportation and auxiliary services provided to independent schoolers by the public schools. Not only does this mean the independent schools do not pay the cost, it also means the public schools do pay the cost. In Ohio, that number a year ago was approximately $800 per pupil.

How about auxiliary services? Again in Ohio, a large and representative state, costs grew from $13.26 per pupil in 1967–68 to $338 per pupil in 1992–93. Total cost over those 25 years grew from $5 million to $76 million.[11] In short, at a time when public schools are blamed for costing more, they are subsidizing independent schools.

We Have Tested "Choice"

Bear in mind that a number of U.S. communities already have some experience with a variety of "choice" models. The jury is still out on the very *raison d'être* of school choice advocates: that given a "choice," parents will pursue educational quality. The early data do not support this claim.

Two years ago, emulating Minnesota's much-heralded public school open enrollment law, Ohio inaugurated such a program on a voluntary basis. Of 612 districts, 49 participated in the first year, 178 in the second year.

- The principal reason parents gave for selecting another district was *proximity to work*. This is [classical economist] Adam Smith once removed: The parent, not the students attending school, makes the economically-driven decision because of proximity to the parent's work.[12]
- Of the 618 participating students at the beginning of the second year, only 21 listed a greater academic opportunity or a special teacher.[13]
- In Minnesota statewide open enrollment is mandatory. *Only* one-half of 1 percent (1 of every 1,000 students) took advantage of the opportunity to make a "choice" and geography was again the driving factor.[14]
- The Arizona Department of Education repeatedly determined that only one-third of parents made "choice" decisions for academic reasons.[15]
- The Carnegie Foundation's *School Choice: A Special Report* declares: "Many parents who do decide to send their children to another school appear to do so for non-academic reasons."[16]
- The same report notes only one-third of Iowa parents listed "educational benefits" as the most important reason for changing schools. Indeed, Carnegie's own survey found that only 15 percent of parents wishing to send their children to other schools cite "academic quality" as the reason.[17]

Even where educational quality is cited as a reason in choosing a different inner-city school, it would be no surprise to learn that at least one "quality" of which parents were speaking was the quality of fear from crime or the related quality of discipline.

I would argue that crime and discipline must be confronted head-on. It is no answer to seek freedom from crime by taking public money to supplement private dollars in private education. So also, public money ought not be spent to accommodate proximity to work. Essentially what choice advocates are doing is opting out of the laws, regulations, and restrictions imposed on public education, or they are taking advantage of "choice" options for reasons other than academic excellence.

Vouchers Don't Work

Let us forget for the moment *why* the choice is made. Is it worthwhile? After all the hoopla, with all the claims that the private sector does it better, do we have any voucher experience showing the impact on students who have opted for a private education?

Of the few experiments, the one most talked about, perhaps because it has been around the longest, is the non-religious Milwaukee Parental Choice Program. Twelve private schools—one of which went bankrupt in its first year—participate. By law, no more than 1,500 students may participate. (There are 45 million elementary and secondary public school students in the United

States.)[18] They must come from families whose incomes are no greater than 1.75 times the federal poverty rate. At present, 830 participate. They are selected at random.[19]

In the Milwaukee program, according to the latest report, parents of the participating students are much more involved in their children's schooling than are their public-side counterparts. They have fewer children per family and are better educated, with higher educational expectations and a greater likelihood to work on homework with their children. According to Professor John Witte of the University of Wisconsin, despite this trend in parental involvement, the children showed no significant improvement in attendance.[20] As important, there has been no significant improvement in test scores in reading or math in the first three years.[21]

The Real Choice

There is still another reason choice won't work. A professor of educational leadership at Stanford, Edward Bridge, found that a quarter of low-income parents in a district allowing choice were totally unaware of any schooling alternatives[22]. Nor should this be a surprise: In the inner city, where poverty reigns, the illustrations are legion of youngsters who do not have mentors. There are few, if any, role models who even know about primary and secondary school much less who can show the youngsters why they should go to school in the first place. No one they know completed school. No one they know got a job because of completing school. Indeed, the few successful ones moved out, mentors departing just when they are of value.

As to those whose parents are literate, motivated, driven by high expectations, and who make a carefully reasoned choice to select an independent school, their departure drains the very stuff, the backbone needed to make public schools work. By definition they will, or should, take advantage of such an opportunity. Why, if they have the option, shouldn't they take the easier road? Why should they stay and fight to make this country understand the problem is democracy itself? That's an impossible mission. Yet, when these parents leave, they leave behind an ever-present and growing underclass. The nation is truly at risk if, in the name of democracy, or "choice," it blames the public schools for their inability to deal with the problem.

One cannot argue that the independent school, unfettered by any of the rules and laws that control public schools, backed by literate parents who are determined to see their children succeed and funded with public dollars, ought to succeed.

If they do not succeed, these parents and their new schools are not confronted by tenure. They can, at the blink of an eye, terminate the teachers who are at fault. If that is not enough, they are not hobbled by mandatory education requirements.[23] Perhaps most significant of all, they can remove the troublesome students, or the students who are not interested or won't learn, and return them—where? To the public school, which must take them.

In the final analysis, why are we wasting time, money, and effort heading toward a dead end on a wrong-way street? I quote from a passage written at a different time:

> All children, like all men, rise easily to the common level. There the mass stop; strong minds only ascend higher. But raise the standard, and, by a spontaneous movement, the mass will rise again and reach it. Hence the *removal* of the most forward scholars from the schools is not a small misfortune.... All this inevitably depresses and degrades the public school... until the public school is left to the management of those who have not the desire nor the power to improve....[24]

Horace Mann wrote this in 1830.

> Choice is not a new idea. Leaving aside questions of whether many students will switch schools, whether those that do will switch for convenience or curriculum, and whether their new schools can sustain themselves ultimately, the newness is in who pays for it.
>
> As a nation, we are rightly absorbed with improving education. We cannot do it by isolating its problems, and pretending to leave those problems behind to be dealt with by those least able to solve them.
>
> The problems of our public schools lie deep in the American experience—poverty, racism, decades of public apathy, drugs, and the growing inability of the family, the church, and the neighborhood to nurture many of our children. These problems—and not the attractively sounding 'solution' of private school choice—need to be addressed.[25]

Choosing to put our shoulders to the harness—to turn and address the problems head-on, not run from them—that is the choice we must make.

Notes

1. Milton Friedman, *Capitalism and Freedom,* 1st ed. (Chicago, Ill.: University of Chicago Press, 1962).
2. The author does not take issue with offering "choice" between public schools, or even within a single public school district.
3. Adam Smith, *The Wealth of Nations* (Edwin Cannan ed., Modern Library, 1937) (1776).
4. Louis V. Gerstner, Jr., et al., *Reinventing Education* (New York: Dutton Books, 1994).
5. Davis and McCaul, *The Emerging Crisis: Current and Projected Status of Children in the United States* (University of Maine, 1991).
6. Gerald W. Bracey, "The Fourth Bracey Report on the Condition of Public Education," *Phi Delta Kappan,* October 1994.
7. Sylvia Nassar, "The American Economy: Back on Top," *New York Times,* February 27, 1994, Sec. 3, p. 1.
8. Gerald W. Bracey, "The Fourth Bracey Report on the Condition of Public Education," *Phi Delta Kappan,* October 1994.
9. Rand, 1994, pp. 16–23.
10. Goss v. Lopez. 419 US 565 (1975).
11. Source: Ohio Department of Education, Department of School Finance.

12. Susan Urahn, *Open Enrollment Study: Student and District Participation,* 1989–90 (St. Paul Minn.: House Research Office, Minnesota House of Representatives, 1990).

13. *Id.*

14. *Id.*

15. School Choice: A Special Report (Princeton, N.J.: Carnegie Foundation for the Advancement of Teaching, 1992).

16. *Id.*

17. *Id.*

18. U.S. Bureau of the Census, *Statistical Abstract of the United States: 1994,* 114th ed. (Washington, D.C.: U.S. Government Printing Office, 1994).

19. John F. Witte, et al., *Third-Year Report, Milwaukee Parental Choice Program,* University of Wisconsin-Madison, December 1993.

20. *Id.*

21. *Id.*

22. Jack McKay, "School Choice May Cheat Students of Democratic Ideals," *School Administrator,* December 1992.

23. Some argue persuasively that if public money is channeled into independent education, it will only be a matter of time before the education requirements, laws, regulations and collective bargaining are imposed on independent schools.

24. Lawrence A. Cremin, *The Republic and the School,* pp. 111–12, 1957.

25. Robert W. Carr, "A Responsibility to Speak Out Against Choice," *School Administrator,* October 1992.

POSTSCRIPT

Are Vouchers an Appropriate Choice Mechanism?

V oucher plans have been challenged on the grounds of unconstitutionality (if sectarian schools are included) and as a threat to the public schools as democratic institutions. A number of serious legal and political questions have been raised during the discussion of this innovation, including the following:

- Do voucher programs "skim the cream" from the public school population?
- Does confining choice to the public sector shield government-run schools from authentic competition?
- Will unlimited school choice lead to the further balkanization of America?
- Is the Supreme Court's "child benefit" theory, used in earlier cases to allow public aid to religious schools, applicable to the argument over vouchers?
- Are the regulations imposed on religious schools that accept vouchers a matter of "excessive entanglement" of government and religion?

An article that deals with these and other basic questions is Manu Bhagavan's "The Discourse of School Choice in the United States," *The Educational Forum* (Summer 1996). Further responses to key questions may be gained by examining "The Choice and Vouchers Debate," by John F. Lewis, *Vital Speeches of the Day* (March 15, 1995); Timothy Lamer, "A Conservative Case Against School Choice," *The Washington Post* (November 6, 1996); and Diane Ravitch, "Somebody's Children," *The Brookings Review* (Fall 1994).

A book by Jerome J. Hanus and Peter W. Cookson, Jr., *Choosing Schools: Vouchers and American Education* (1996), addresses the issues of vouchers. And a flurry of journal articles have added a variety of opinions to the debate, including "The Empty Promise of School Vouchers," by Edd Doerr, *USA Today Magazine* (March 1997); "Vouchers: Wrong Medicine for the Ills of Public Education," by Richard V. Pierard, *Contemporary Education* (Summer 1997); "Vouchers for Religious Schools," by Denis P. Doyle, *The Public Interest* (Spring 1997); "The Voucher Debate," by Judith Brody Saks, *The American School Board Journal* (March 1997); and "Teacher of the Year Gives Vouchers a Failing Grade," by Bob Peterson, *The Progressive* (April 1997).

Multiple articles on school choice may be found in *Education and Urban Society* (February 1995), *The American School Board Journal* (July 1996), *Phi Delta Kappan* (September 1996), *Educational Leadership* (October 1996), and *Phi Delta Kappan* (September 1999).

ISSUE 12

Can Charter Schools Revitalize Public Education?

YES: Chester E. Finn, Jr., et al., from "The New School," *National Review* (September 15, 1997)

NO: Phyllis Vine, from "To Market, To Market...: The School Business Sells Kids Short," *The Nation* (September 8/15, 1997)

ISSUE SUMMARY

YES: Former assistant secretary of education Chester E. Finn, Jr., and his fellow researchers at the Hudson Institute argue that charter schools offer the benefits of both public and private schools and can revitalize urban education.

NO: Historian and journalist Phyllis Vine maintains that charter schools and similar entrepreneurial ventures exemplify the right-wing approach to school reform and inevitably sell children short.

T he public education system as currently structured is archaic." So say Diane Ravitch and Joseph Viteritti in "A New Vision for City Schools," *The Public Interest* (Winter 1996). "Instead of a school system that attempts to impose uniform rules and regulations," they contend, "we need a system that is dynamic, diverse, performance-based, and accountable. The school system that we now have may have been right for the age in which it was created; it is not right for the twenty-first century."

Currently, the hottest idea for providing alternatives to the usual public school offering is the charter school movement. Charter schools, which receive funding from the public school system but operate with a good deal of autonomy regarding staffing, curriculum, and spending, began in Minnesota in 1991 through legislative action prompted by grassroots advocates. Charter schools have gained wide support, all the way up to the White House. In the 1998–1999 school year some 1,700 charter schools served about 350,000 students nationwide. The 2000–2001 year will see about 500 additional charters granted.

The movement has certainly brought variety to the school system menu and has expanded parental choice. Community groups, activists, and entrepreneurs seem to be clamoring for available charters for Core Knowledge schools, Paideia schools, fine arts academies, Afrocentric schools, schools for at-risk students and dropouts, technology schools, character education–based schools, job-training academies, and so on.

The National Commission on Governing America's Schools has recommended that every school become a charter school, which would bring an end to the era of centralized bureaucratic control of public school districts. The Sarasota County School District in Florida has already embarked on a decentralized organizational model offering a "100% School Choice Program" through newly conceived "conversion, deregulated, and commissioned schools."

There are obstacles to success, however, and indeed some have already failed. According to Alex Medler in "Charter Schools Are Here to Stay," *Principal* (March 1997), these obstacles include inadequate capital funding and facilities, cash flow and credit problems, regulations and paperwork, disputes with local school boards, and inadequate planning time. A recently released report by the Hudson Institute, *Charter Schools in Action,* indicates wide success in overcoming such obstacles.

Michael Kelly, in "Dangerous Minds," *The New Republic* (December 30, 1996), argues that in a pluralistic society public money is shared money to be used for shared values. He finds that too many of the charter schools are run by extremists who like the idea of using public money to support their ideological objectives. He cites the failed Marcus Garvey School in Washington, D.C., which spent $372,000 in public funds to bring an Afrocentric curriculum to 62 students. However, he notes that this case has not led to a wave of protests against the concept of charter schools.

In fact, *Washington Post* columnist William Raspberry recently declared that he finds himself slowly morphing into a supporter of charter schools and vouchers. "It isn't because I harbor any illusions that there is something magical about those alternatives," he explains. "It is because I am increasingly doubtful that the public schools can do (or at any rate *will* do) what is necessary to educate poor minority children."

An associated topic is privatization. This either involves turning public school management over to private companies, such as Educational Alternatives, Inc., or cooperating with entrepreneurs who want to develop low-cost private alternatives for students currently enrolled in public schools. The most talked-about of the latter is entrepreneur Chris Whittle's Edison Project, an attempt to build a nationwide network of innovative, for-profit schools.

In the following selections, Chester E. Finn, Jr., and his fellow Hudson Institute researchers make the case that charter schools are the most promising education reform strategy around and predict that they will expand in great numbers over the next decade if the "education establishment" allows them to. Phyllis Vine, appalled by the "market mentality" behind charter schools, vouchers, and for-profit enterprises, contends that the intersection of business and ideology will eviscerate a core American institution—the public school.

Chester E. Finn, Jr., et al.

 **YES**

The New School

The fast-spreading charter-school movement is challenging three hoary axioms about American education: that only private schools can elude bureaucratic micromanagement, that worthwhile school choice can be achieved only through vouchers, and that the left-leaning politics of public education have barred the schoolhouse door against any encroachment by entrepreneurial capitalism.

No, this familiar trio hasn't been vanquished, and this is no time to relax. But all three assumptions are in retreat before what some are calling the "reinvention of public education"—a battery of new sorts of schools and educational practices, among which charter schools are the most significant. Today, some seven hundred of these are in operation, enrolling about 170,000 youngsters. Twenty-nine states have authorized charter schools. In some jurisdictions —notably Arizona, Michigan, California, Colorado, Texas, and Massachusetts— they have become major parts of the education-reform scene. In the District of Columbia, despite a rocky start, the prospect of a dozen charter schools is the brightest spot in a grim picture.

What exactly is a charter school? Visualize a hybrid, a public school with some of the most highly prized features of private schools. As a public institution, it is open to all who wish to attend, paid for with tax dollars, and accountable to state or local authorities for good performance (especially student achievement) and decent behavior (e.g., non-discrimination). It has authority to operate for a specified period—normally five years—and gets its charter renewed only if it delivers good results. In the manner of a private school, however, it is self-governing, free from most regulations, able to hire whomever it likes, in control of its own (secular) curriculum, and attended only by youngsters whose parents choose it.

No such schools existed five years ago. That they enjoy wide bi-partisan support today—President Clinton has called for three thousand of them by decade's end—indicates the appeal of this concept. But opposition is intensifying, too, and there are signs that the charter label is being applied loosely. Indeed, some states that boast of "charter laws" actually enacted such weak measures that the teachers unions are applauding—because any schools created on those terms will lack real independence in vital areas such as personnel.

That's so, for example, with the "charter" laws of Kansas, Georgia, Mississippi, and Rhode Island.

Still, "independent public school of choice" is no longer an oxymoron. Nor is it unique to the United States. Margaret Thatcher's England headed down this path first with "grant-maintained" schools that opt out of their local school bureaucracies and become self-governing, funded by block grants from Whitehall. New Zealand has made all its public schools quasi-independent.

Some U.S. charter schools (especially in California) are former public schools that wrested their freedom from the superintendent's office. Several states permit private schools to convert to charter status, too. But most are start-from-scratch schools, founded by parents, teachers, community organizations, even for-profit firms.

Yes, capitalism is welcome in much of the charter world. Companies that design and manage schools are springing up and either obtaining their own charters or (more commonly) contracting to run schools whose charters are held by parent or community groups. Several small firms are managing two or three charter schools apiece this year, and two nationally known outfits (the Edison Project and Educational Alternatives, Inc.) are responsible for more—a full dozen in Edison's case. Whether they'll yield a profit for their investors remains to be seen—but the schools appear to be educational successes.

Instead of running entire schools, other private firms are taking small bites from the charter apple, furnishing, for example, hot lunches, tutoring, testing, or technology. Some of this is happening in regular public schools, too. Elementary/secondary education is a $300-billion enterprise, and private vendors (school-bus companies, textbook publishers) have marketed their wares to it for decades. What is changing is the willingness of schools to entrust instructional and managerial responsibilities to outside sources.

How significant are the educational choices afforded by charter schools? With the crucial exception of religious choice, they're dazzling. In a town where all the regular schools are "progressive" or "child-centered," a back-to-basics charter school is a treasure for disgruntled families. We've also been in communities whose 1950s-style public schools don't suit 1990s-style yuppie parents. In such situations, a charter school that offers open classrooms, open mixed-ability grouping, and "developmentally appropriate" instruction is a pearl beyond price.

The price, moreover, is zero—at least, for the customers, because charter schools don't charge tuition. For low-income families in particular, the charter option is an extraordinary boon.

That is why, contrary to critics' claims that these schools would skim off already-fortunate kids, we find that 40 per cent of charter-school pupils come from families poor enough to qualify for federal lunch subsidies. Half are minorities (compared with one-third of the kids in conventional public schools). Charters also appear to be enrolling many disabled and non-English-speaking students.

Some families are even leaving private schools for charters—11 per cent of the enrollment in our sample and others (3 per cent) are switching from homeschooling to charters. Another 5 per cent of charter pupils are former dropouts.

As for results, the charter phenomenon is too new for pupil achievement to be fully appraised. But early signs are promising. Test scores in Massachusetts and Arizona, for example, indicate that charter schools are doing better than conventional schools, with similar or tougher kids.

We've spent the past two years studying these schools—visiting sixty of them in fourteen states and interviewing hundreds of their constituents. A few are places we wouldn't send our own kids; one or two were a little weird. But the great majority of these schools are what most families crave: small, safe places with coherent academic missions and high standards, schools led and staffed by people who believe in those missions and care about kids' actually meeting the standards, schools full of students and teachers who want to be there—not least because nobody is obliged to remain.

We also gathered survey data from students, parents, and teachers. The numbers attest to the needs these schools meet and the high levels of satisfaction that they are producing. Consider five bits of evidence:

First, charter students and parents both report clear educational improvement. Among children who performed "poorly" in their previous school (as judged by their parents), for example, nearly half are now doing "excellent" or "above average" work. Students of all races report sizable academic gains.

Second, students and parents *like* their charter schools. Three-fifths of the kids say their teachers are better. Half are more interested in their schoolwork. Three-fifths say the charter school is safer and has better discipline than the school their child would otherwise be attending. Four out of five plan to keep their child in the charter school as long as it's available.

Third, families and teachers are turning to charter schools for educational reasons. When asked why they chose their present school, charter parents' top answers are small size, higher standards, the schools' educational philosophy, greater opportunities for parental involvement, and better teachers. Major factors cited by teachers include school philosophy, class size, the presence of like-minded colleagues, committed parents, and greater teacher authority.

Fourth, satisfaction levels are highest when it comes to educational matters (curriculum, teaching, etc.) and lowest in peripheral areas (food, sports, etc.), indicating that charters are successfully deploying their limited resources on the basics. When we asked students what they like best about their charter school, the most frequent answers were: "good teachers," "they teach it until I learn it," and "they don't let me fall behind." Not a bad pupil's-eye summary of what schools are supposed to do.

Finally, the teachers prize the professional opportunities they find in charter schools. More than 90 per cent are satisfied with their school's educational philosophy, with their fellow teachers, and with their students; over three-quarters are pleased with their school's administrators and the level of teacher decision-making, and they like the challenge of starting a new school. Fewer than 3 per cent would rather teach elsewhere.

Tens of thousands of American families have chosen to avail themselves of these new-style schools. Yet the charter movement has reached a fateful intersection. If it is able to follow one path, thousands of these schools-of-choice will develop, offering true educational alternatives for millions of families. Down the other path lies a future not too different from the present: a handful of schools serving a smallish population of determined parents and students who had fared poorly elsewhere.

The second path, alas, seems the likelier. The foes of charter schools—both teachers unions and their allies in the education establishment—are doing their utmost to block access to the first. In fact, the foes are now almost as wary of charter schools as of vouchers—not least because the charter idea has wider political appeal and is spreading faster.

Statutory caps on the number of charter schools are a favorite weapon of the establishment. In Massachusetts, where the legislature just inched up its 25-school limit, the Commonwealth received 123 proposals over the past three years. In Texas, which recently raised the ceiling from 20 to 100 schools, nearly 300 applications are expected. (The Lone Star State has about 6,300 public and 1,300 private schools.) When New Jersey issued its new charter application package a couple of months ago, over 500 requests for copies arrived within days.

Discriminatory financial arrangements are another weapon. Capital funding for charter schools is almost non-existent today—which is why so many of them operate in shabby, rented quarters. Only a few states grant them per-pupil operating budgets equal to those of conventional schools. Most jurisdictions don't turn on the fiscal spigot until the kids arrive (i.e., no start-up funding). Several permit local school boards to charge fat "overhead" fees. And Washington—despite Mr. Clinton's professed support and the popularity of the charter concept among GOP lawmakers—comes nowhere near assuring these schools the federal aid that their students would get in ordinary public schools.

A third weapon is lingering bureaucratic control of crucial parts of a school's finances or program. Recall that the whole idea of chartering a school is to give it operating freedom in return for results-based accountability—the reverse of traditional school practice, which micromanages the production process while turning a blind eye to the quality of the product. A well-crafted charter program keeps a few essential rules in place (in matters such as health, safety, and civil rights) and checks the backgrounds of would-be charter operators and staff. It sets academic standards for the schools to attain. But that's it. All else hinges on whether a school delivers the results it promises—and can attract and hold customers.

That's how it's supposed to work. But in many jurisdictions the enemies of charter schools have kept reels of additional red tape in place. Most California charters have no real fiscal autonomy. New Jersey's charter law retains a form of teacher tenure. North Carolina won't let charter teachers participate in the state retirement system unless their school is under the thumb of a local board. In

Colorado local boards can maintain constant anxiety by issuing charters that last only a year at a time.

So long as barriers like these remain in place, charter schools will remain a modest educational sideshow rather than a widely accessible alternative.

That's today's battleground, and charter foes have recently enjoyed many victories on it. Enabling bills were killed this year in Washington state, Alabama, Indiana, Missouri, Nevada, Virginia, and Tennessee. Gov. Pataki's once-robust proposal is barely breathing in Albany. The new statutes in Illinois and Pennsylvania are weak. And where charter schools got off to a strong start, their enemies are regrouping. Raising the cap in Massachusetts was a bloody political ordeal—and half the Bay State's new charters will be subordinate to local boards and unions. In Colorado, Gov. Roy Romer recently vetoed a bill to give charter schools a fairer financial shake; although Romer was an early charter booster, Colorado's potent school board and teacher groups finally bent him to their will. (That means just a few dozen charters in a state with 1,400 conventional schools.)

Not all charter opponents are found on the left, however, or in the school establishment. Many conservatives have been skittish about these schools because they are a sub-species of "public" education and susceptible to reversals of fortune at the hands of government.

Obviously, charter schools are not a cure-all for American education. They're not immune to curricular fads, fiscal blunders, and personnel mistakes. (That's why five have closed—or been shut down.) Nevertheless, two years of visits, interviews, and surveys have convinced us that charter schools are easily the most promising education-reform strategy around.

To Market, To Market...

If Wall Street has anything to say about it, the same forces gnawing away at the public stewardship of hospitals, prisons and the Social Security system will take on the $600-billion-a-year education market. Mary Tanner, managing director at Lehman Brothers, which sponsored the first educational investment conference last year, compares it to health care—"a local industry that over time will become a global business." Montgomery Securities' Michael Moe claims that "the timing and entry into the education and training market has never been better."

Moe knows. In twenty-eight states, legislation supports privatization through charter schools and vouchers, or contracting of for-profit management companies. (Charter schools themselves are politically neutral—some founded by activists on the right or left who want greater involvement in their children's education, others merely openings for entrepreneurs.) Despite the preliminary findings of two federal studies that neither privatized education nor charter schools have improved test performance—an ostensible goal of their proponents—and the well-known failures of Educational Alternatives Inc.'s schools in Baltimore and Hartford [see Bruce Shapiro, "Privateers Flunk School," February 19, 1996], the campaign for charter schools continues to snowball. President Clinton has given it a boost by calling for an increase from the current 450–500 charter schools to 3,000 by the turn of the century.

The road to for-profit educational enterprises has been paved by the political and financial support of conservative opponents of public education. From the Hudson Institute and the Heritage Foundation, two of the right-wing think tanks driving privatization, come reports about reinventing education to stem the deterioration of schools and replace the "status-quo unions." They speak of giving parents choice, back-to-basics and performance-driven curriculums, management "design teams" and accountability. There's lots of doom-mongering that harks back to the Reagan era's screed on education, *A Nation at Risk*. The Indiana-based Hudson Institute has grown to national importance through the support of the Olin Foundation and the Lynde and Harry Bradley Foundation [see Vince Stehle, "Righting Philanthropy," June 30]. Along with Heritage, the Hudson Institute has nurtured a battalion of veterans from the Education Department in the Reagan and Bush administrations. In addition

From Phyllis Vine, "To Market, To Market...: The School Business Sells Kids Short," *The Nation* (September 8/15, 1997). Copyright © 1997 by *The Nation*. Reprinted by permission.

to Lamar Alexander, Education Secretary from 1991 to 1993, Hudson funded Chester Finn Jr., who was Assistant Education Secretary from 1985 to 1988 and a founding partner of the Edison Project, the four-year-old for-profit school chain started by Whittle Communications.

Finn and Diane Ravitch (Assistant Education Secretary from 1991 to 1993) founded the Educational Excellence Network, a smaller think tank housed at the Hudson Institute. The network serves as a clearinghouse and resource center for their projects, one of which was The Modern Red Schoolhouse, designed by the New American Schools Development Corporation (N.A.S.D.C.), which was formed during the Bush Administration in 1992 to funnel business dollars to education reform. Alexander placed David Kearns, a former Deputy Education Secretary and Xerox chief, in charge of the N.A.S.D.C.

ᴇᴏ⁓

Kearns well illustrates the intersection of business and ideology. He serves on the board of EduVentures, Michael Sandler's investment banking service for the education industry. Sandler worked for Kearns at the N.A.S.D.C., developing projects that would fulfill Alexander's break-the-mold vision for schools. The N.A.S.D.C. offers design teams to help schools restructure. The Modern Red Schoolhouse is one of the nine prototypes that schools can purchase for curriculum, assessment, professional development and technology "as a learning and instructional management tool." The costs range from $90,000 to $150,000; technology is extra.

Sandler moved on in 1995 to co-found "Education Industry Report," a monthly newsletter that announces mergers and acquisitions, new education markets, changes in charter school legislation and major players in government or business. "E.I.R." also analyzes about thirty publicly traded companies that constitute the "education index." David Kearns and Michael Moe both sit on the board of the newsletter, as does Denis Doyle, who alternates between the Hudson Institute and the Heritage Foundation, writing about vouchers and charter schools. Other prominent players who began in the federal government are the Hudson Institute's Bruce Manno, now doing a study on the Massachusetts charter school experience, and Scott Hamilton, associate commissioner of the Massachusetts Education Department, who oversees the state's charter schools.

ᴇᴏ⁓

The right-wing approach to school reform can be seen in the battle over the management of public education in Wilkinsburg, Pennsylvania, where a divided school board hired the Nashville, Tennessee-based Alternative Public Schools, Inc. (A.P.S.), to manage the Turner Elementary School. Turner is one of three elementary schools in a racially mixed, economically distressed suburb of Pittsburgh. Wilkinsburg's once-stable economy sputtered with the decline of the local steel industry. The town has one of Allegheny County's largest percentages of people living in subsidized public housing, and 78 percent of the students at Turner qualify for means-tested lunch programs. Although only half the community is African-American, almost all of Turner's students are.

A.P.S. was new to education when it won the contract for Turner Elementary. Bill DeLoache and John Eason, its founders, were investment counselors, "citizens with a hobby," DeLoache said, when they bid on the Turner initiative. "We came at it from a businessperson's perspective. Charter laws started passing. The market was opening up." In just three years A.P.S. has moved from being "a couple of guys looking for a school" to a major force in the for-profit education industry. Their first bid, on a school in Tennessee in 1992, was unsuccessful. But it put them in touch with the growing network of educational privatizers who gathered regularly at meetings such as the Edventures Conference in Madison, Wisconsin (not related to Sandler's service), where a request for proposals for Turner was advertised in July 1994.

Since March 1995, when the school board announced the contract, the Pennsylvania State Education Association and the Wilkinsburg Education Association have been in court. The union challenged the board for discharging its responsibility and funneling more than $2.4 million of taxpayer money to a private, out-of-state company. It also sued Pennsylvania's Education Secretary, Eugene Hickok, whose furlough of teachers made way for A.P.S. to bring in nonunion employees. (The court later upheld an arbitrator's recommendation to reinstate them with back pay.) Connected to the Heritage Foundation and a member of the Commonwealth Foundation for Public Policy Alternatives board, Hickok is another link between the political right and the drive to transform public education.

Facing huge legal bills, the school board accepted an offer of free representation from the Landmark Legal Foundation shortly after signing the contract with A.P.S. With strong connections to the Heritage Foundation and a mission to challenge "arbitrary, government-imposed barriers to entrepreneurial opportunity," Landmark has battled for vouchers for religious schools in Wisconsin. Landmark then hired the law firm of Strassburger McKenna Gutnick & Potter, which also represents Richard Mellon Scaife, a major financier of right-wing organizations, including the Heritage Foundation and Landmark itself.

The most recent ruling in this case was handed down in August, when a court ordered A.P.S. to vacate the Turner school at the end of this year. But the case is far from settled and appeals are likely to go on for several years, at least through the remainder of the five-year contract.

A.P.S.'s promise to improve student performance backfired. Some blame the new teachers, others cite the lack of school supplies, still others denounce a principal commuting from Chicago. At the end of the first year test scores tumbled, and disappointed parents pulled their children out of Turner. Among them was Ernest Neal Ramsey, the school-board president who struck the original deal. In last spring's school-board elections, neither Ramsey nor the sitting president, an A.P.S. enthusiast, was returned to office. "The company used us to get what they wanted," says Ramsey's wife, Arnella Ramsey. "It's like buying something in the mail and not knowing what you get until you've got it."

Nowhere does the play between politics, profits and policy appear more power-ful than in Massachusetts. And no single group has been more active promoting charter schools in Massachusetts than the Boston-based Pioneer Institute. Pioneer's role in the charter school movement has been evident from the be-ginning. Former director Steven Wilson is largely regarded as the architect of the 1993 Education Reform Act, which he drafted while serving as a special ad-viser to then-governor William Weld. Current executive director James Peyser was named acting Under Secretary of Education by Weld when the first charter schools opened in 1995. And board member William Edgerly influences state legislation by mobilizing C.E.O.s for the organization Fundamental Change in Education and by taking credit for "a more flexible approach to special edu-cation compliance in charter schools [that] was adopted by the Department of Education."

In 1995 Pioneer raised more than $500,000 for charter schools, and it assists the growth of others by "identifying, recruiting, and assisting poten-tial charter school founders." Pioneer also distributes a how-to manual, *The Massachusetts Charter School Handbook,* and sponsors seminars bringing to-gether entrepreneurs selling curriculum packages, management systems and assessment and evaluation programs. Conservatives want to "outsource" these functions as part of an effort to neutralize "the government monopoly on ed-ucation." In addition to companies, such as A.P.S., that supply these services, they can be obtained from Advantage Schools, the for-profit education com-pany Wilson started after leaving state service. Edgerly is chairman of the board of Advantage.

The impetus behind many Massachusetts charter schools has been to re-structure education by removing accountability from local jurisdiction. Critics of the 1993 Massachusetts law point out that it transfers oversight to the polit-ically appointed state Education Department, which decides who gets charters. And even if for-profit companies do not hold the charter, the holders may then hire a market-driven company, with its "learning system" and accompanying services. Although community-based trustees theoretically manage the school that manages the company, Robert Gaudet, who resigned last spring from the Edison Project's Boston Renaissance Charter School, says that's a charade. Of the twenty-five charter schools that have opened in Massachusetts, seven are managed by out-of-state companies. Two (Boston and Worcester) are run by the New York-based Edison Project. Sabis International, a company headquar-tered in Choueifat, Lebanon, opened two (Springfield and Somerville). And Nashville's A.P.S. started out with one (Chelmsford), but last July picked up con-sulting with two more (Franklin and Lawrence) when it acquired The Modern Red Schoolhouse from the Hudson Institute and the N.A.S.D.C. It is ironic that the same people who complain about the government's imposition of standards and regulations invite corporations with anonymous shareholders and highly paid executives to devise and deliver educational values.

When the Edison Project began to manage the Boston Renaissance Char-ter School two years ago, initial publicity promised maximum class sizes of twenty-one, parental involvement, longer days and more of them. Instead, classes grew to twenty-eight, books and materials arrived late, faculty were replaced in midyear and the principal clashed with parents and staff. Edison also botched the job of providing services for kids with special needs. By the middle of the first year, Boston Renaissance had been reprimanded by the state's Bureau of Special Education Appeals for its neglect of two children with learning disabilities. Although both cases were sealed with nondisclosure clauses, the school agreed to provide the special education services these students need.

Two other complaints have been filed with the civil rights office of the U.S. Education Department, describing patterns of racial discrimination and neglect of special education. Both are under investigation. Parents of one boy with a learning disability described how their kindergartner had been suspended for forty-nine days, sent home at noon instead of 3:30 for five months and physically restrained by holding his hands behind his back until he stopped crying. He was subsequently placed in a public school, where he had perfect attendance and won an award for the student who made the most progress.

Children's advocates claim that charter schools have gone out of their way to develop an inhospitable environment for kids with serious special needs. At Edison's Seven Hills Charter School in Worcester, something called "counseling out" resulted in the return of fifteen students to public schools in their first two weeks. The process was subtle, says Robin Foley, chairwoman of the district's parent advisory council for special education. Parents complained that during counseling Edison's staff asked, "Do you think your child can fit in?" Kate Garnett, Edison's consultant for special education, explains that "we wanted to make clear that parents knew what kind of a situation the families were choosing." Of the ninety-two students who returned to the district schools by year's end, nearly one-quarter needed special education services.

Edison's John Chubb attributes the problems to the start-up phase in which students arrived without sufficient records. Edison underestimated the number of special-education students. Their planning was based on the national average of 9 percent, instead of the state average of 17 percent. But Tim Sindelar, an attorney with the Disability Law Center in Boston, says many cases cannot be attributed to start-up problems, since the schools opened two years ago. In testimony before the U.S. House Committee on Education and the Workforce, Sindelar painted a bleak picture for special education in the Massachusetts charter schools: exclusion of students; extension by several months of the required forty-five-day deadline for developing a student's individualized education plan; failure to inform parents of their rights and the schools' obligations.

The Boston Renaissance Charter School has beefed up its special-education staff for the coming year. But critics still fear that the charter schools are simply selecting the students most likely to succeed in any environment and leaving the others to a system that will be further impoverished. "It's a scary thing," said Fred Birkett, former assistant headmaster of Boston Renaissance.

"Those who are hurt the most in public schools have the most to lose in a reform movement."

❦

The Massachusetts law undermines unions and allows companies to set low salaries and determine qualifications for employment. Districts—i.e., taxpayers —pick up transportation costs for charter school pupils, while companies get bargain rent. Sabis International Schools pays $2,800 a month to rent an entire school.

Sabis's Springfield school was not created from the efforts of dissatisfied parents. It was a pure business deal struck after passage of the 1993 law. Sabis, with fifteen schools in the Middle East, England and Europe, has ambitions to start a chain of charter schools in America. With its cookie-cutter curriculum and packaged testing system, Sabis can profitably surf the back-to-basics reform movement and bask in public subsidies.

Sabis approached Advantage Schools/Pioneer Institute's William Edgerly to help it find a school; Edgerly arranged for a meeting between Sabis's owners and Springfield's mayor, Robert Markel, and superintendent of schools Peter Negroni, both of whom eventually ended up on the board of a newly formed partnership. One week before the deadline for submitting an application for a charter school, Sabis put together a board of trustees during a meeting in Negroni's office. The group then agreed to apply for nonprofit status, assuming it would be granted about the time school opened.

Without so much as a site or school building, or youngsters it intended to serve, Sabis submitted its application for a charter school. And in the absence of an actual facility, the application could only refer to the school as "XX" when it claimed, "The XX school is currently running and can be easily adapted to the SABIS program."

Sabis budgeted hefty profits. The company's standard 6 percent management fee comes off the top. For the first year, this amounted to $150,000. Then it charges an additional fee for using its proprietary computerized program for weekly tests. For this it charged $50,000. And there was a combined fee for marketing and for corporate support from its Minnesota site. This amounted to $30,000. But the profits could rise well beyond $230,000, depending on the number of students enrolled.

Linda Wilson, past president of the Springfield Educational Association, points out that "Springfield tax money will be given to an out-of-state private company to be enjoyed as business profits while more than 23,000 Springfield students do without new materials and supplies." In challenging the Springfield School Committee's decision to give Sabis a building rent-free, she said: "The School Committee will go forward to negotiate the contract with the International School Board of Trustees. But who will they negotiate with? The Mayor, two members of the School Committee, the Superintendent, the President of the company who owns the International School, and the Director General are all members of the Board of Trustees of the Charter School. I can't be the only one to see a conflict of interest here!"

Creaming students most likely to succeed, poor management, unionbusting, conflicts of interest and discrimination against kids who need special education (and sometimes discrimination against kids of color)—all are on display in the for-profit school system. And so is the effort to eviscerate a core American institution that has been a laboratory for citizenship. While right-wing education guru Chester Finn insists that "the market... can rise to the challenge of educating America's young," the record suggests otherwise. "The schools belong to us as communities," says Barbara Miner, editor of *Selling Out Our Schools.* "So why should we allow some private company to come in and make money off of our kids?"

POSTSCRIPT

Can Charter Schools Revitalize Public Education?

Charter schools—are they a source of innovation, inspiration, and revitalization in public education or a drain on human and fiscal resources that will leave regular public schools weaker than ever? The debate has just begun, and preliminary results are just beginning to trickle in. But the air is filled with predictions, opinions, and pontifications.

Alex Molnar offers some scathing commentary on the charter school and privatization movements in his article "Charter Schools: The Smiling Face of Disinvestment," *Educational Leadership* (October 1996) and in his book *Giving Kids the Business: The Commercialization of America's Schools* (1996). A more positive assessment is delivered by Joe Nathan in his book *Charter Schools: Creating Hope and Opportunity for American Schools* (1996) and in his article "Heat and Light in the Charter School Movement," *Phi Delta Kappan* (March 1998). Further positive descriptions are provided in James N. Goenner's "Charter Schools: The Revitalization of Public Education," *Phi Delta Kappan* (September 1996) and James K. Glassman's "Class Acts," *Reason* (April 1998).

Additional sources of ideas include *How to Create Alternative, Magnet, and Charter Schools That Work* by Robert D. Barr and William H. Parrett (1997); "Homegrown," by Nathan Glazer, *The New Republic* (May 12, 1997); "Charter Schools: A Viable Public School Choice Option?" by Terry G. Geske et al., *Economics of Education Review* (February 1997); "A Closer Look at Charters," by Judith Brody Saks, *American School Board Journal* (January 1998); "Healthy Competition," by David Osborne, *The New Republic* (October 4, 1999); "Chinks in the Charter School Armor," by Tom Watkins, *American School Board Journal* (December 1999); and Seymour Sarason's *Charter Schools: Another Flawed Educational Reform* (1998).

Discussions of the privatization subtopic can be found in Denis P. Doyle's "The Role of Private Sector Management in Public Education" and Paul D. Houston's "Making Watches or Making Music," *Phi Delta Kappan* (October 1994); "Contracting for Educational Services," by Priscilla L. Feir, *School Business Affairs* (January 1996); and "Lessons Learned: The Edison Project Founder's Musings on American Schooling," by Christopher Whittle, *The School Administrator* (January 1997).

A few more articles worthy of note are "No Magic Bullet," *The American Teacher* (December 1997); "How to Revive America's Public Schools," *The World & I* (September 1997); and "School Reform—Charter Schools," *Harvard Law Review* (May 1997). Multiple articles may be found in *The School Administrator* (August 1999) and *Education and Urban Society* (August 1999).

ISSUE 13

Have Public Schools Adequately Accommodated Religion?

YES: Edd Doerr, from "Religion and Public Education," *Phi Delta Kappan* (November 1998)

NO: Warren A. Nord, from "The Relevance of Religion to the Curriculum," *The School Administrator* (January 1999)

ISSUE SUMMARY

YES: Edd Doerr, executive director of Americans for Religious Liberty, asserts that a fair balance between free exercise rights and the obligation of neutrality has been achieved in the public schools.

NO: Warren A. Nord, a professor of the philosophy of religion, contends that the schools are still too secular and that a place in the curriculum must be found for religion.

The religious grounding of early schooling in America certainly cannot be denied, nor can the history of religious influences on the conduct of governmental functions. For example, U.S. Supreme Court decisions in the early decades of the twentieth century allowed certain cooperative practices between public school systems and community religious groups. However, it must also be recognized that many students, parents, and taxpayer organizations were distressed by some of these accommodating policies. Legal action taken by or on the behalf of some of the offended parties led to Supreme Court restrictions on prayer and Bible reading in the public schools in the 1960s. Particularly notable were the decisions in *Engel v. Vitale* (1962), *Murray v. Curlett* (1963), and *School District of Abington Township v. Schempp* (1963). These decisions curtailed the use of public school time and facilities for ceremonial and devotional religious purposes, but they did not outlaw the discussion of religion or the use of religious materials in appropriate academic contexts.

During the 1970s and 1980s religious activists, led by the Reverend Jerry Falwell's Moral Majority, campaigned against what they perceived to be the tyranny of a public education establishment dominated by the philosophy of secular humanism. Efforts were made to include creationism in the science curriculum as an antidote to the theory of evolution and to legalize voluntary organized prayer in the public schools. Despite these efforts, the courts have generally disallowed the teaching of "creation science," have vetoed organized moments of "silent meditation," and have declared unconstitutional the practice of including prayers in graduation ceremonies. Religious groups gained at least one major victory in the 1980s with the passage of the Equal Access Act, federal legislation that guarantees access to public school facilities for students wishing to engage in religious activities during nonschool hours. The legislation, which has been challenged in some localities, has been upheld by the U.S. Supreme Court.

And the battles continue. Recently, Kansans attempted to remove the theory of evolution from the science curriculum, Texans have pressed for approval of student-led invocations at high school football games, Virginians have tested a new version of daily "meditation moments," and several states have allowed the posting of the Ten Commandments in public schools. In the wake of the Columbine High School massacre and mounting evidence of "moral decay" among American youth, the pressure for further accommodation of religion seems to be growing. In December 1999 President Bill Clinton issued new guidelines promoting stronger partnerships between religious institutions and public schools in local communities, particularly in the areas of school safety, discipline, and literacy. Some national groups, such as Americans United for Separation of Church and State and People for the American Way, raised questions about the vagueness of these guidelines and the absence of clear limits on the extent of involvement. Another type of accommodation involves the providing or lending of secular learning materials and computer equipment to religious schools. A *Washington Post* editorial, "Church-State Muddle" (December 6, 1999), poses this dilemma: To disallow such aid programs discriminates against schools because of their religious affiliations, but to uphold these programs validates public support for religious institutions.

Some sources that examine the current status of this ongoing struggle include Perry Glanzer, "Religion in Public Schools: In Search of Fairness," *Phi Delta Kappan* (November 1998); Oliver S. Thomas, "Legal Leeway on Church-State in School," *The School Administrator* (January 1999); Gilbert T. Sewall, "Religion Comes to School," and Thomas Lickona, "Religion and Character Education," both in *Phi Delta Kappan* (September 1999); and Charles C. Haynes, "Seeking Common Ground," *American School Board Journal* (February 2000).

In the first of the following selections, Edd Doerr reviews what is permitted and what is forbidden on the basis of some 50 years of Supreme Court rulings and expresses belief that accommodation has gone as far as it can. Warren A. Nord, in the second selction, asserts that the study of religious thought and influence has been marginalized in the curriculum and that public school students are systematically taught to think about the world in secular ways only.

Edd Doerr

 **YES**

Religion and Public Education

O n 4 June 1998, the U.S. House of Representatives voted 224 to 203 for the so-called Religious Freedom Amendment, sponsored by Rep. Ernest Istook (R-Okla.) and more than 150 co-sponsors.[1] The measure fell well short of the two-thirds majority required to pass a constitutional amendment. In fact, the 52.4% vote dropped well below the 59.7% garnered on a similar proposal in 1971, the last time a school prayer amendment reached the House floor. The amendment's defeat is especially significant because it had strong backing from the House majority leadership and was the culmination of a massive four-year campaign led by televangelist Pat Robertson's Christian Coalition.

The Istook Amendment aroused strong opposition from education organizations, mainstream religious groups, and civil liberties organizations because it would have embroiled school districts and communities in prolonged, bitter, divisive conflicts over religious activities in the classroom or at graduations, athletic events, school assemblies, and other gatherings. In addition, the amendment's clause against "deny[ing] equal access to a benefit on account of religion" would have cleared the way for massive tax support of sectarian schools and other institutions. Opponents of the amendment correctly worried that it would weaken or wreck the First Amendment, taking the first major bite out of the Bill of Rights since its ratification in 1791.

Two weeks before the vote on the amendment, the U.S. Commission on Civil Rights held the first of three projected hearings on "Schools and Religion." Most of the 16 experts who spoke at the hearing (including this writer, I must disclose) agreed that the relevant Supreme Court rulings and other developments have pretty much brought public education into line with the religious neutrality required by the First Amendment and the increasingly pluralistic nature of our society. A fair balance has been established between the free exercise rights of students and the constitutional obligation of neutrality.

The speakers attributed the current reasonably satisfactory situation to 50 years of appropriate Supreme Court rulings plus two specific developments: passage by Congress in 1984 of the Equal Access Law, which allows student-initiated religious groups or other groups not related to the curriculum to meet, without school sponsorship, during noninstructional time; and the U.S. Department of Education's issuance in August 1995 of guidelines on "Religious Expression in Public Schools."

A minority of speakers at the heating cited anecdotes about alleged violations of students' religious freedom. These turned out to be either exaggerations or cases of mistakes by teachers or administrators that were easily remedied by a phone call or letter. The occasional violations of student rights, like "man bites dog" stories, are few and far between and certainly do not point to any need to amend the Constitution.

Julie Underwood, general counsel designate for the National School Boards Association (NSBA), told the hearing that inquiries to the NSBA about what is or is not permitted in public schools declined almost to the vanishing point once the "Religious Expression in Public Schools" guidelines were published.

The guidelines grew out of a document titled "Religion in the Public Schools: A Joint Statement of Current Law," issued in April 1995 by a broad coalition of 36 religious and civil liberties groups.[2] The statement declared that the Constitution "permits much private religious activity in and around the public schools and does not turn the schools into religion-free zones." The statement went on to detail what is and is not permissible in the schools.

On 12 July 1995, President Clinton discussed these issues in a major address at—appropriately—James Madison High School in northern Virginia and announced that he was directing the secretary of education, in consultation with the attorney general, to issue advisory guidelines to every public school district in the country. This was done in August.

In his weekly radio address of 30 May 1998, anticipating the June 4 House debate and vote on the Istook Amendment, the President again addressed the issue and announced that the guidelines, updated slightly, were being reissued and sent to every district. This effort undoubtedly helped to sway the House vote.

The guidelines, based on 50 years of court rulings (from the 1948 *McCollum* decision to the present), on common sense, and on a healthy respect for American religious diversity, have proved useful to school boards, administrators, teachers, students, parents, and religious leaders. Following is a brief summary.

Permitted

"Purely private religious speech by students"; nondisruptive individual or group prayer, grace before meals, religious literature reading; student speech about religion or anything else, including that intended to persuade, so long as it stops short of harassment; private baccalaureate services; teaching *about* religion; inclusion by students of religious matter in written or oral assignments where not inappropriate; student distribution of religious literature on the same terms as other material not related to school curricula or activities; some degree of right to excusal from lessons objectionable on religious or conscientious grounds, subject to applicable state laws; off-campus released time or dismissed time for religious instruction; teaching civic values; student-initiated "Equal Access" religious groups of secondary students during noninstructional time.

Prohibited

School endorsement of any religious activity or doctrine; coerced participation in religious activity; engaging in or leading student religious activity by teachers, coaches, or officials acting as advisors to student groups; allowing harassment of or religious imposition on "captive audiences"; observing holidays as religious events or promoting such observance; imposing restrictions on religious expression more stringent than those on nonreligious expression; allowing religious instruction by outsiders on school premises during the school day.

Required

"Official neutrality regarding religious activity."

In reissuing the guidelines, Secretary Riley urged school districts to use them or to develop their own, preferably in cooperation with parents, teachers, and the "broader community." He recommended that principals, administrators, teachers, schools of education, prospective teachers, parents, and students all become familiar with them.

As President Clinton declared in his May 30 address, "Since we've issued these guidelines, appropriate religious activity has flourished in our schools, and there has apparently been a substantial decline in the contentious argument and litigation that has accompanied this issue for too long."

As good and useful as the guidelines are, there remain three areas in which problems continue: proselytizing by adults in public schools, music programs that fall short of the desired neutrality, and teaching appropriately about religion.

There are conservative evangelists, such as Jerry Johnston and the Rev. Jerry Falwell, who have described public schools as "mission fields." In communities from coast to coast, proselytizers from well-financed national organizations, such as Campus Crusade and Young Life, and volunteer "youth pastors" from local congregations have operated in public schools for years. They use a variety of techniques: presenting assembly programs featuring "role model" athletes, getting permission from school officials to contact students one-on-one in cafeterias and hallways, volunteering as unpaid teaching aides, and using substance abuse lectures or assemblies to gain access to students. It is not uncommon for these activities to have the tacit approval of local school authorities. Needless to say, these operations tend to take place more often in smaller, more religiously homogeneous communities than in larger, more pluralistic ones.

Religious music in the public school curriculum, in student concerts and theatrical productions, and at graduation ceremonies has long been a thorny issue. As Secretary Riley's 1995 and 1998 guidelines and court rulings have made clear, schools may offer instruction about religion, but they must remain religiously neutral and may not formally celebrate religious special days. What then about religious music, which looms large in the history of music?

As a vocal and instrumental musician in high school and college and as an amateur adult musician in both secular and religious musical groups, I feel qualified to address this issue. There should be no objection to the inclusion of religious music in the academic study of music and in vocal and instrumental performances, as long as the pieces are selected primarily for their musical or historical value, as long as the program is not predominantly religious, and as long as the principal purpose and effect of the inclusion is secular. Thus there should be no objection to inclusion in a school production of religious music by Bach or Aaron Copland's arrangements of such 19th-century songs as "Simple Gifts" or "Let Us Gather by the River." What constitutes "musical or historical value" is, of course, a matter of judgment and controversy among musicians and scholars, so there can be no simple formula for resolving all conflicts.

Certain activities should clearly be prohibited. Public school choral or instrumental ensembles should not be used to provide music for church services or celebrations, though a school ensemble might perform a secular music program in a church or synagogue as part of that congregation's series of secular concerts open to the public and not held in conjunction with a worship service. Sectarian hymns should not be included in graduation ceremonies; a Utah case dealing with that subject has been turned down for Supreme Court review. Students enrolled in music programs for credit should not be compelled to participate in performances that are not primarily religiously neutral.

As for teaching *about* religion, while one can agree with the Supreme Court that public schools may, and perhaps should, alleviate ignorance in this area in a fair, balanced, objective, neutral, academic way, getting from theory to practice is far from easy. The difficulties should be obvious. Teachers are very seldom adequately trained to teach about religion. There are no really suitable textbooks on the market. Educators and experts on religion are nowhere near agreement on precisely what ought to be taught, how much should be taught and at what grade levels, and whether such material should be integrated into social studies classes, when appropriate, or offered in separate courses, possibly electives. And those who complain most about the relative absence of religion from the curriculum seem to be less interested in neutral academic study than in narrower sectarian teaching.

Textbooks and schools tend to slight religion not out of hostility toward religion but because of low demand, lack of time (if you add something to the curriculum, what do you take out to make room for it?), lack of suitable materials, and fear of giving offense or generating unpleasant controversy.

The following questions hint at the complexity of the subject. Should teaching about religion deal only with the bright side of it and not with the dark side (religious wars, controversies, bigotry, persecutions, and so on)? Should instruction deal only with religions within the U.S., or should it include religions throughout the world? Should it be critical or uncritical? Should all religious traditions be covered or only some? Should the teaching deal only with sacred books—and, if so, which ones and which translations? How should change and development in all religions be dealt with?

To be more specific, should we teach only about the Pilgrims and the first Thanksgiving, or also about the Salem witch trials and the execution of Quakers? Should schools mention only the Protestant settlers in British North America or also deal with French Catholic missionaries in Canada, Michigan, and Indiana and with the Spanish Catholics and secret Jews in our Southwest? Should we mention that Martin Luther King was a Baptist minister but ignore the large number of clergy who defended slavery and then segregation on Biblical grounds?

Should teaching about religion cover such topics as the evolution of Christianity and its divisions, the Crusades, the Inquisition, the religious wars after the Reformation, the long history of anti-Semitism and other forms of murderous bigotry, the role of religion in social and international tensions (as in Ireland, in the former Yugoslavia, and in India and Pakistan), the development in the U.S. of religious liberty and church/state separation, denominations and religions founded in the U.S., controversies over women's rights and reproductive rights, or newer religious movements?

The probability that attempts to teach about religion will go horribly wrong should caution public schools to make haste very slowly in this area. In my opinion, other curricular inadequacies—less controversial ones, such as those in the fields of science, social studies, foreign languages, and word literature—should be remedied before we tackle the thorniest subject of all.

And let us not forget that the American landscape has no shortage of houses of worship, which generally include religious education as one of their main functions. Nothing prevents these institutions from providing all the teaching about religion they might desire.

The late Supreme Court Justice William Brennan summed up the constitutional ideal rather neatly in his concurring opinion in *Abington Township S.D. v. Schempp,* the 1963 school prayer case: "It is implicit in the history and character of American public education that the public schools serve a uniquely public function: the training of American citizens in an atmosphere free of parochial, divisive, or separatist influence of any sort—an atmosphere in which children may assimilate a heritage common to all American groups and religions. This is a heritage neither theistic nor atheistic, but simply civic and patriotic."

Notes

1. Text of H.J. Res. 78, Rep. Ernest Istook's Religious Freedom Amendment: "To secure the people's right to acknowledge God according to the dictates of conscience: Neither the United States nor any State shall establish any official religion, but the people's right to pray and to recognize their religious beliefs, heritage, or traditions on public property, including schools, shall not be infringed. Neither the United States nor any State shall require any person to join in prayer or other religious activity, prescribe school prayers, discriminate against religion, or deny equal access to a benefit on account of religion."

2. Copies of the statement are available free of charge from Americans for Religious Liberty, P.O. Box 6656, Silver Spring, MD 20916.

NO

Warren A. Nord

The Relevance of Religion to the Curriculum

For some time now, public school administrators have been on the front lines of our culture wars over religion and education—and I expect it would be music to their ears to hear that peace accords have been signed.

Unfortunately, the causes of war are deep-seated. Peace is not around the corner.

At the same time, however, it is also easy to overstate the extent of the hostilities. At least at the national level—but also in many communities across America—a large measure of common ground has been found. The leaders of most major national educational, religious and civil liberties organizations agree about the basic principles that should govern the role of religion and public schools. No doubt we don't agree about everything, but we agree about a lot.

For example, in 1988, a group of 17 major religious and educational organizations—the American Jewish Congress and the Islamic Society of North America, the National Association of Evangelicals and the National Council of Churches, the National Education Association and American Federation of Teachers, the National School Boards Association and AASA among them—endorsed a statement of principles that describes the importance of religion in the public school curriculum.

The statement, in part, says this: "Because religion plays significant roles in history and society, study about religion is essential to understanding both the nation and the world. Omission of facts about religion can give students the false impression that the religious life of humankind is insignificant or unimportant. Failure to understand even the basic symbols, practices and concepts of the various religions makes much of history, literature, art and contemporary life unintelligible."

A Profound Problem

As a result of this (and other "common ground" statements) it is no longer controversial to assert that the study of religion has a legitimate and important place in the public school curriculum.

From Warren A. Nord, "The Relevance of Religion to the Curriculum," *The School Administrator* (January 1999). Copyright © 1999 by *The School Administrator*. Reprinted by permission.

Where in the curriculum? In practice, the study of religion has been relegated almost entirely to history texts and courses, for it is widely assumed that religion is irrelevant to every other subject in the curriculum—that is, to understanding the world here and now.

This is a deeply controversial assumption, however. A profoundly important educational problem lingers here, one that is almost completely ignored by educators.

Let me put it this way. Several ways exist for making sense of the world here and now. Many Americans accept one or another religious interpretation of reality; others accept one or another secular interpretation. We don't agree—and the differences among us often cut deeply.

Yet public schools systematically teach students to think about the world in secular ways only. They don't even bother to inform them about religious alternatives—apart from distant history. That is, public schooling discriminates against religious ways of making sense of the world. This is no minor problem.

An Economic Argument

To get some sense of what's at issue, let's consider economics.

One can think about the economic domain of life in various ways. Scriptural texts in all religious traditions address questions of justice and morality, poverty and wealth, work and stewardship, for example. A vast body of 20th century literature in moral theology deals with economic issues. Indeed, most mainline denominations and ecumenical agencies have official statements on justice and economics. What's common to all of this literature is the claim that the economic domain of life cannot be understood apart from religion.

Needless to say, this claim is not to be found in economics textbooks. Indeed, if we put end to end all the references to religion in the 10 high school economics texts I've reviewed in the past few years, they would add up to about two pages—out of 4,400 pages combined (and all of the references are to premodern times). There is but a single reference to religion—a passing mention in a section on taxation and non-profit organizations—in the 47 pages of the new national content standards in economics. Moreover, the textbooks and the standards say virtually nothing about the problems that are the major concern of theologians—problems relating to poverty, justice, our consumer culture, the Third World, human dignity and the meaningfulness of work.

The problem isn't just that the texts ignore religion and those economic problems of most concern to theologians. A part of the problem is what the texts do teach—that is, neoclassical economic theory. According to the texts, economics is a science, people are essentially self-interested utility-maximizers, the economic realm is one of competition for scarce resources, values are personal preferences and value judgments are matters of cost-benefit analysis. Of course, no religious tradition accepts this understanding of human nature, society, economics and values.

That is, the texts and standards demoralize and secularize economics.

An Appalling Claim

To be sure, they aren't explicitly hostile to religion; rather they ignore it. But in some ways this is worse than explicit hostility, for students remain unaware of the fact that there are tensions and conflicts between their religious traditions and what they are taught about economics.

In fact, the texts and the standards give students no sense that what they are learning is controversial. Indeed, the national economics standards make it a matter of principle that students be kept in the dark about alternatives to neoclassical theory. As the editors put it in their introduction, the standards were developed to convey a single conception of economics, the "majority paradigm" or neoclassical model of economic behavior. For, they argue, to include "strongly held minority views of economic processes [would only risk] confusing and frustrating teachers and students who are then left with the responsibility of sorting the qualifications and alternatives without a sufficient foundation to do so."

This is an appalling statement. It means, in effect, that students should be indoctrinated; they should be given no critical perspective on neoclassical economic theory.

The problem with the economics texts and standards is but one aspect of the much larger problem that cuts across the curriculum, for in every course students are taught to think in secular ways that often (though certainly not always) conflict with religious alternatives. And this is always done uncritically.

Even in history courses, students learn to think about historical meaning and causation in exclusively secular ways in spite of the fact that Judaism, Christianity and Islam all hold that God acts in history, that there is a religious meaning to history. True, they learn a few facts about religion, but they learn to think about history in secular categories.

Nurturing Secularity

Outside of history courses and literature courses that use historical literature, religion is rarely even mentioned, but even on those rare occasions when it is, the intellectual context is secular. As a result, public education nurtures a secular mentality. This marginalizes religion from our cultural and intellectual life and contributes powerfully to the secularization of our culture.

Ignoring religious ways of thinking about the world is a problem for three important reasons.

It is profoundly illiberal.

Here, of course, I'm not using the term "liberal" to refer to the left wing of the Democratic Party. A liberal education is a broad education, one that provides students with the perspective to think critically about the world and their lives. A good liberal education should introduce students—at least older students—

to the major ways humankind has developed for making sense of the world and their lives. Some of those ways of thinking and living are religious and it is illiberal to leave them out of the discussion. Indeed, it may well constitute indoctrination—secular indoctrination.

We indoctrinate students when we uncritically initiate them into one way of thinking and systematically ignore the alternatives. Indeed, if students are to be able to think critically about the secular ways of understanding the world that pervade the curriculum, they must understand something about the religious alternatives.

It is politically unjust.

Public schools must take the public seriously. But religious parents are now, in effect, educationally disenfranchised. Their ways of thinking and living aren't taken seriously.

Consider an analogy. A generation ago textbooks and curricula said virtually nothing about women, blacks and members of minority subcultures. Hardly anyone would now say that that was fair or just. We now—most of us —realize this was a form of discrimination, of educational disenfranchisement. And so it is with religious subcultures (though, ironically, the multicultural movement has been almost entirely silent about religion).

It is unconstitutional.

It is, of course, uncontroversial that it is constitutionally permissible to teach about religion in public schools when done properly. No Supreme Court justice has ever held otherwise. But I want to make a stronger argument.

The court has been clear that public schools must be neutral in matters of religion—in two senses. Schools must be neutral among religions (they can't favor Protestants over Catholics or Christians over Jews), and they must be neutral between religion and nonreligion. Schools can't promote religion. They can't proselytize. They can't conduct religious exercises.

Of course, neutrality is a two-edged sword. Just as schools can't favor religion over nonreligion, neither can they favor nonreligion over religion. As Justice Hugo Black put it in the seminal 1947 *Everson* ruling, "State power is no more to be used so as to handicap religions than it is to favor them."

Similarly, in his majority opinion in *Abington v. Schempp* in 1963, Justice Tom Clark wrote that schools can't favor "those who believe in no religion over those who do believe." And in a concurring opinion, Justice Arthur Goldberg warned that an "untutored devotion to the concept of neutrality [can lead to a] pervasive devotion to the secular and a passive, or even active, hostility to the religious."

Of course this is just what has happened. An untutored, naïve conception of neutrality has led educators to look for a smoking gun, an explicit hostility to religion, when the hostility has been philosophically rather more subtle— though no less substantial for that.

The only way to be neutral when all ground is contested ground is to be fair to the alternatives. That is, given the Supreme Court's longstanding interpretation of the Establishment Clause, public schools must require the study of religion if they require the study of disciplines that cumulatively lead to a pervasive devotion to the secular—as they do.

Classroom Practices

So how can we be fair? What would a good education look like? Here I can only skim the surface—and refer readers to *Taking Religion Seriously Across the Curriculum,* in which Charles Haynes and I chart what needs to be done in some detail.

Obviously a great deal depends on the age of students. In elementary schools students should learn something of the relatively uncontroversial aspects of different religions—their traditions, holidays, symbols and a little about religious histories, for example. As students mature, they should be initiated into that conversation about truth and goodness that constitutes a good liberal education. Here a two-prong approach is required.

First, students should learn something about religious ways of thinking about any subject that is religiously controversial in the relevant courses. So, for example, a biology text should include a chapter in which scientific ways of understanding nature was contrasted with religious alternatives. Students should learn that the relationship of religion and science is controversial, and that while they will learn what most biologists believe to be the truth about nature, not everyone agrees.

Indeed, every text and course should provide students with historical and philosophical perspective on the subject at hand, establishing connections and tensions with other disciplines and domains of the culture, including religion.

This is not a balanced-treatment or equal-time requirement. Biology courses should continue to be biology courses and economics courses should continue to be economics courses. In any case, given their competence and training, biology and economics teachers are not likely to be prepared to deal with a variety of religious ways of approaching their subject. At most, they can provide a minimal fairness.

A robust fairness is possible only if students are required to study religious as well as secular ways of making sense of the world in some depth, in courses devoted to the study of religion.

A good liberal education should require at least one year-long high school course in religious studies (with other courses, I would hope, available as electives). The primary goal of such a course should be to provide students with a sufficiently intensive exposure to religious ways of thinking and living to enable them to actually understand religion (rather than simply know a few facts about religion). It should expose students to scriptural texts, but it also should use more recent primary sources that enable students to understand how contemporary theologians and writers within different traditions think about those subjects in the curriculum—morality, sexuality, history, nature, psychology and the economic world—that they will be taught to interpret in secular categories in their other courses.

Of course, if religion courses are to be offered, there must be teachers competent to teach them. Religious studies must become a certifiable field in public education, and new courses must not be offered or required until competent teachers are available.

Indeed, all teachers must have a much clearer sense of how religion relates to the curriculum and, more particularly, to their respective subjects. Major reforms in teacher education are necessary—as is a new generation of textbooks sensitive to religion.

Some educators will find it unrealistic to expect such reforms. Of course several decades ago textbooks and curricula said little about women and minority cultures. Several decades ago, few universities had departments of religious studies. Now multicultural education is commonplace and most universities have departments of religious studies. Things change.

Stemming an Exodus

No doubt some educators will find these proposals controversial, but they will [be] shortsighted if they do. Leaving religion out of the curriculum is also controversial. Indeed, because public schools don't take religion seriously many religious parents have deserted them and, if the Supreme Court upholds the legality of vouchers, as they may well do, the exodus will be much greater.

In the long run, the least controversial position is the one that takes everyone seriously. If public schools are to survive our culture wars, they must be built on common ground. But there can be no common ground when religious voices are left out of the curricular conversation.

It is religious conservatives, of course, who are most critical of public schooling—and the most likely to leave. But my argument is that public schooling doesn't take any religion seriously. It marginalizes all religion—liberal as well as conservative, Catholic as well as Protestant, Jewish, Muslim and Buddhist as well as Christian. Indeed, it contributes a great deal to the secularization of American culture—and this should concern any religious person.

But, in the end, this shouldn't concern religious people only. Religion should be included in the curriculum for three very powerful secular reasons. The lack of serious study of religion in public education is illiberal, unjust and unconstitutional.

POSTSCRIPT

Have Public Schools Adequately Accommodated Religion?

O f all the groundless, hurtful attacks on public education, none is more painful than the charge that public schools are 'godless institutions of secular humanism.' . . . The public school day may not start with a Hail Mary or an Our Father, a mantra or a blood sacrifice, but public education does more of God's work for children every day than any other institution in America—and that includes the churches." So says journalist Frosty Troy in "Far from 'Godless' Institutions," *The School Administrator* (March 2000).

For more moderate positions on the issue, see Rachael Kessler, "Nourishing Students in Secular Schools," *Educational Leadership* (December 1998/ January 1999) and two articles in the December 1998 *American School Board Journal*, Jerry Cammarata's "We Haven't Got a Prayer" and Benjamin Dowling-Sendor's "Protecting Religious Vitality."

Students wishing to analyze more closely the controversy over teaching the theory of evolution can consult the following: Jonathan Zimmerman, "Creationism's Political Evolution: Relatively Speaking," *The New Republic* (September 6, 1999); John F. Haught, "The Darwinian Struggle," *Commonweal* (September 24, 1999); Stephen Jay Gould, "Dorothy, It's Really Oz," *Time* (August 23, 1999); Patrick Glynn, "Monkeys on Our Backs," *National Review* (September 13, 1999); William A. Hoesch and Steve Edinger, "Is There a Scientific Basis for Creationism?" *CQ Researcher* (August 22, 1997); and Mano Singham, "The Science and Religion Wars," *Phi Delta Kappan* (February 2000).

Perhaps a reasonable summation of the total situation was provided by Charles C. Haynes in the *American School Board Journal* article cited in the issue introduction:

> The vast majority of educators are caring, dedicated professionals who want nothing more than to uphold the rights of all students and to address issues of religion and values with fairness and respect. But their training has left them ill-prepared to tackle religious-liberty questions or to teach substantively about religion in the curriculum, and they don't feel support from school boards and administrators to do so. Many school districts, in fact, have few or no policies concerning religion because school administrators and board members are often reluctant to address the underlying problems before a crisis erupts. Ironically, this avoidance is precisely what causes conflicts and lawsuits—either because religion is being ignored or because it is being improperly promoted by school officials.

ISSUE 14

Is Full Inclusion of Disabled Students Desirable?

YES: Jean B. Arnold and Harold W. Dodge, from "Room for All," *American School Board Journal* (October 1994)

NO: Karen Agne, from "The Dismantling of the Great American Public School," *Educational Horizons* (Spring 1998)

ISSUE SUMMARY

YES: Attorney Jean B. Arnold and school superintendent Harold W. Dodge discuss the federal Individuals with Disabilities Education Act and argue that its implementation can benefit all students.

NO: Assistant professor of education Karen Agne argues that legislation to include students with all sorts of disabilities has had mostly negative effects and contributes to the exodus from public schools.

The Education for All Handicapped Children Act of 1975 (Public Law 94–142), which mandated that schools provide free public education to all students with disabilities, is an excellent example of how federal influence can translate social policy into practical alterations of public school procedures at the local level. With this act, the general social policy of equalizing educational opportunity and the specific social policy of ensuring that young people with various physical, mental, and emotional disabilities are constructively served by tax dollars were brought together in a law designed to provide persons with disabilities the same services and opportunities as nondisabled individuals. Legislation of such delicate matters does not ensure success, however. Although most people applaud the intentions of the act, some people find the expense ill-proportioned, and others feel that the federal mandate is unnecessary and heavy-handed.

Some of the main elements of the 1975 legislation were that all learners between the ages of 3 and 21 with handicaps—defined as students who are hearing impaired, visually impaired, physically disabled, emotionally disturbed, mentally retarded, or who have special learning disabilities—would be provided a free public education, that each of these students would have an individualized education program jointly developed by the school and the parents, that each student would be placed in the least restrictive learning environment appropriate to him or her, and that parents would have approval rights in placement decisions.

The 1990 version of the original law, the Individuals with Disabilities Education Act (IDEA), has spawned an "inclusive schools" movement, whose supporters recommend that *no* students be assigned to special classrooms or segregated wings of public schools. According to advocates of the act, "The inclusion option signifies the end of labeling and separate classes but not the end of necessary supports and services" for all students needing them.

The primary justification for inclusion, or "mainstreaming," has traditionally resided in the belief that disabled children have a right to and can benefit from inclusion in a regular educational environment whenever possible. French sociologist Emile Durkheim felt that attachment and belonging were essential to human development. If this is the case, then integration of young people with disabilities into regular classrooms and into other areas of social intercourse—as opposed to keeping them isolated in special classrooms—would seem to be highly desirable.

Douglas Fuchs and Lynn S. Fuchs, in "Inclusive Schools Movement and the Radicalization of Special Education Reform," *Exceptional Children* (February 1994), pose this question: How likely is the "inclusive schools" movement to bring special education and general education into synergistic alignment? One viewpoint comes from a five-year government study released in 1994, which found that special-needs students who spend all their time in regular classrooms fail more frequently than those who spend only some. This report, along with the American Federation of Teachers' call for an end to the practice of seeking all-day inclusion for every child, no matter how medically fragile or emotionally disturbed, have helped to keep the issue boiling.

Abigail Thernstrom, in "Courting Disaster in the Schools," *The Public Interest* (Summer 1999), contends that the rights of the disabled stipulated under IDEA have made discipline a "nightmare." The 1997 amendments to IDEA, however, expanded the school's alternatives for dealing with disruptive special needs student. Such students can be suspended for 10 days (or more in some cases); can be placed in an alternative setting for up to 45 days, even over a parent's objection; and can be kept out of the regular classroom for an additional 45 days after a special hearing.

In the selections that follow, Jean B. Arnold and Harold W. Dodge direct specific suggestions toward school board policymakers for complying with the requirements and intentions of the current law regarding full inclusion, and they argue that quality inclusion programs and services for students with disabilities will be beneficial to all students. Karen Agne contends that the inclusion of emotionally disturbed and intellectually unfit students in regular classes robs other students of needed attention, robs teachers of their sanity, and does not serve the special needs students effectively.

Jean B. Arnold and Harold W. Dodge  **YES**

Room for All

Few topics ignite more controversy among educators these days than full inclusion of disabled youngsters in regular classrooms. Part of the reason is that many people don't understand—or wrongly understand—what's required under the law.

One of the greatest myths is that full inclusion obligates a public school district to educate *every* student with a disability in a regular classroom for the *entire* school day. Full inclusion doesn't mean that. It means students with disabilities might be placed in a regular education classroom on a full-time basis, but, if appropriate and necessary, they still can be "pulled out" for special instruction or related services.

That is what Congress originally intended in adopting the statutory provision of the Individuals with Disabilities Education Act (IDEA) concerning placement in the "least restrictive environment appropriate." But many educators have been implementing the concept backward.

Here's what we mean: School officials might decide to place Johnny, a 6-year-old Down's syndrome child with an IQ of 45, in a classroom for the trainable mentally retarded as soon as his parents enroll him in school. They might later determine Johnny can be "mainstreamed" with regular education students for art, music, and lunch.

Actually, the way the law reads, Johnny should be placed in a regular classroom first, along with appropriate supplemental aids and services to assist him in that setting. If Johnny isn't benefiting from the education he receives in that setting, then the district should consider more restrictive and segregated options or settings that would enable him to get a good education, but still remain in his regular classroom as much as possible.

In some cases, even this scenario is not appropriate, and the student needs a more segregated environment, but the determination must be made on a case-by-case basis for each child. And it should begin with the idea of placement in a regular classroom and only then move to the more restricted setting—not vice versa.

Placement

For school boards, understanding inclusion—and what's legally required of your schools in educating disabled students—begins with understanding certain key legal concepts surrounding inclusion, as well as the findings in significant court cases.

The first legal concept to be familiar with is *placement*. Simply defined, placement is the setting in which the disabled child receives instruction. It is *not* the curriculum or program provided the student.

Both IDEA and case law indicate that you should heed certain points when deciding a child's placement:

- If possible, you should place a disabled child in a regular education classroom in the public school the child would attend if he or she had no disability. The deciding factor: whether, given the nature or severity of the child's disability, appropriate goals and objectives for the child can be achieved in a regular classroom, with or without the use of supplemental aids and services. The child's individualized education program, or IEP, determines the appropriate goals and objectives for that child.
- If you rule out the regular classroom for a specific child, you must select an alternative placement from a continuum of settings and arrangements (arrayed from least restrictive to most restrictive) maintained by the school system. The continuum might include, for example, resource-room instruction, a self-contained classroom, or even a private placement. You must select the placement in which the appropriate education goals for the child can be achieved with the fewest restrictions possible.
- Even when you rule out primary placement in the regular education environment, the disabled child must be educated with, and allowed to interact with, other children to the maximum extent appropriate to the needs of the disabled child.
- Placement decisions must be made at least annually by a group of people who consider broad-based, documented information about the child. These people must know the child and understand the evaluation data and the placement alternatives. At a minimum, the school representatives on the committee should include an educator who is knowledgeable about the student's disability, the student's teacher, and a special education supervisor.

Least-Restrictive Environment

Another essential item for you and your school board colleagues to understand is *least restrictive environment,* or LRE. According to IDEA, "Each public agency shall insure: (1) That to the maximum extent appropriate, handicapped children, including children in public or private institutions or other care facilities, are educated with children who are not handicapped, and (2) That special classes, separate schooling, or other removal of handicapped children from the regular educational environment occurs only when the nature or severity of the handicap is such that education in regular classes with the use of supplementary aids and services cannot be achieved satisfactorily." (34 C.F.R. 300.550 [b].)

Note that the law doesn't prohibit separate classes and separate schools; it merely requires they be filled on the basis of student need—not administrative convenience.

The leading court case in defining least restrictive environment is *Daniel R.R. v. State Board of Education* (1989). This case established several questions your district can use to decide whether a disabled child can be educated satisfactorily in the regular classroom. Before removing any child from the regular education classroom, your district should weigh its answers to each of these questions:

1. Have you taken steps to accommodate children with disabilities in regular education? IDEA requires school districts to provide supplementary aids and services and to modify the regular education program in an effort to mainstream children with disabilities. Examples of these modifications include shortened assignments, note-taking assistance, visual aids, oral tests, and frequent breaks. The modifications should be geared to each disabled child's individual needs. If you make no effort to accommodate children with disabilities in the regular education classroom, you violate the law.

2. Are your district's efforts to accommodate the child in regular education sufficient or token? A school district's efforts to supplement and modify regular education so disabled children can participate must amount to more than "mere token gestures," according to the ruling in *Daniel R.R.* The IDEA requirement for accommodating disabled children in regular education is broad. But, the ruling says, a school district need not provide "every conceivable supplementary aid or service" to assist disabled children in regular education. Furthermore, regular education instructors are not required to devote all or even most of their time to one disabled child to the detriment of the entire class.

A district also is not required to modify the regular education program beyond recognition. As the court held in *Daniel R.R.*: "[M]ainstreaming would be pointless if we forced instructors to modify the regular education curriculum to the extent that the handicapped child is not required to learn any of the skills normally taught in regular education." Such extensive modifications would result in special education being taught in a regular education classroom.

3. Will the child benefit educationally from regular education? Another factor to consider is whether the child is capable of benefiting from regular education. Central to this question is whether the child can achieve the "essential elements" of the regular education curriculum.

You must consider both the nature and severity of the child's handicap as well as the curriculum and goals of the regular education class in determining educational benefit. However, a disabled child cannot be expected to achieve on a par with children who don't have disabilities before being permitted to attend the regular education classroom. Furthermore, you must remember that academic achievement is not the only purpose of mainstreaming. Allowing the child to be with children who aren't disabled can be beneficial in itself.

4. What will be the child's overall educational experience in the mainstreamed environment? Just because a child can receive only minimal academic benefit from regular education doesn't mean the child automatically should be excluded from regular education. You must consider the child's overall educational experience in the mainstreamed environment, balancing the benefits of regular and special education. Children who can't comprehend many of the essential elements of a lesson might still receive great benefit from their nondisabled peers, who serve as language and behavior models.

On the other hand, some children might become frustrated by their inability to succeed in the regular education classroom. If this frustration outweighs any benefit received from regular education, mainstreaming might prove detrimental to the child. Similarly, other children might need more structure than is available in the regular education setting. Your district must determine whether mainstreaming would be more beneficial or detrimental to the disabled child, considering both academic and social benefit.

5. What effect does the disabled child's presence have on the regular classroom environment? In determining the LRE, consider whether the child's presence in a regular education classroom adversely affects the education other children are receiving. First, determine whether the child engages in disruptive behavior that negatively affects the other children. Second, determine whether the disabled child requires so much of the teacher's attention that the teacher is forced to ignore the other children. If the teacher spends so much time with the disabled child that the rest of the class suffers, then the child should be educated in a special education classroom.

If you determine the child cannot be educated full time in the regular education classroom, you still have a duty to mainstream the child to the maximum extent appropriate. For instance, if regular academic classes are not appropriate for a given disabled child, the district could mainstream the child for nonacademic classes and activities, such as gym, recess, music, art, or lunch.

In short, placement in regular education is not an "all-or-nothing" proposition. Rather, school districts are required to offer a continuum of services for disabled children. A disabled child should be mainstreamed in regular education for as much of the time as is appropriate. Rarely will total exclusion from children without disabilities be deemed appropriate.

Beyond the Legal Requirements

Regardless of what IDEA says, the issue of whether students with disabilities can or should be served in regular education settings will continue to be debated and decided in the legal arena. Even so, the real issues are not legal; they are based in tradition, values, and beliefs. An increased understanding of how inclusion works, when implemented under the law, will help shape those traditions, values, and beliefs and will help school boards like yours design and put into practice high-quality inclusive programs and educational services for their students with disabilities.

Such services, however, can't be mandated or created without the contributions of teachers, administrators, and parents. Your board can try to reduce the number of potential problems or pitfalls by providing technical assistance for teachers and by finding activities that build consensus between staff and parents and provide information and education for everyone. Also, your district can attempt to learn from the successful experiences of other school districts.

A compelling case for inclusion does exist, supported by research, school statistics, and informal observations about inclusive programs presently in place. The biggest benefit will come when disabled students feel they "belong" with the regular-education children, rather than being segregated in separate classes or separate schools. As Sen. Robert T. Stafford, the Republican senator from Vermont and one of the bill's primary sponsors, said on the final days of passage of the Education of All Handicapped Children Act, the precursor of IDEA, these extraordinary children want only to lead ordinary lives.

NO

Karen Agne

The Dismantling of the Great American Public School

Everybody's talking about it. Public education, rarely a topic of discussion unless teachers are on strike or tax referendums proposed, is now under review everywhere people gather. The same concerns are being voiced in the checkout line, the dentist's office, the shopping mall. So prevalent is this topic that it's not necessary to take a formal survey to get the data. Just listen and take notes.

> "We took our kids out of public school and put them in Catholic school, and we're not even Catholic. The teacher was taking half the morning to get around to the 'regular' kids."
>
> "I'm staying home now to teach my kids. They weren't learning anything at school. We have a Home-Schooling Mothers group. Do you want to join?"
>
> "We had to move because that school had no program for our child; he's accelerated."
>
> "I'm not a teacher, but I'm home schooling. I got tired of hearing my child cry and complain every day about going to school. She was bored silly."
>
> "I don't want to be teaching. It's hard work and I'm afraid I might not be doing it right, but at least he gets individual attention now."
>
> "Public schools are just for kids with problems."

What happened? How did it all slip away while we weren't looking? "How could this be happening in this country?" parents want to know. In a word, inclusion happened. What does inclusion mean? Take a look:

A kindergarten teacher attempts to explain directions to the tiny charges seated on the rug before her. But a child with Down syndrome, focused on her own agenda, remains the center of attention as she crawls about pinching the bottoms of each child she reaches.

Ear-piercing screams come from a third-grade classroom where a behaviorally disabled child is expressing her displeasure at not being first to observe the science artifact being passed amongst her classmates. Her exhausted teacher says, "Oh, this happens every day. I have to call for help to watch my class while I take her out." The eight-year-old child refuses to walk and continues her high-pitched screams, punching and kicking at her teacher, as she is carried bodily down the hall. Returning, the teacher offers, "They'll just bring her right back in here and we'll go through this again. This year I just pray to get through each day."

Several children talk or play together in one corner while classmates read or write. "What are they doing?" I ask. "Oh, they don't understand what we're working on," replies the teacher. "I'm told they're supposed to be here. I've tried, but I don't know what to do with them. An aide comes in for half an hour." This scene is repeated throughout the various classrooms of schools in several counties I've observed.

In some elementary schools teachers team up to get through the day. A disruptive, emotionally disturbed child is sent to sit in the other classroom to "calm down," after which time he may return to his assigned classroom. "This helps give the other children a little break from him," the teachers explain.

A special education teacher shares that she is paid to "teach" one student all year. At eleven years of age, this brain-damaged child is confined to a wheelchair. He cannot speak, he must be fed and diapered, and he "has never, in the three years that I've worked with him, ever demonstrated evidence of understanding anything," she explains. But this child is mandated by law to receive regular classroom time. This means that he is wheeled into a classroom each day. Every twenty minutes he begins gasping and must be suctioned to prevent choking. His specially trained teacher says, "I hate having to take him in there. Where's the benefit? He understands nothing. The other kids are frightened by his constant choking, and they can't just ignore the suctioning procedure. I worry about how much of their learning is lost. I worry that he's being used. But if anyone protests, the parents just holler 'Hearing! Hearing!' So there's nothing anyone can do." This single child is granted more than $140,000 per year to meet his special needs.

What I have related here is but a sampling of many such scenarios I have witnessed. How prevalent must this tendency be throughout the country? No one will speak of it, to avoid reproach as cruel, inhuman, or uncaring. The approach described here can hardly be considered advantageous to either the special needs students or their classmates, let alone their teachers. As a result, concerned parents around the country are quietly taking their "unchallenged" children out of our public schools.

While disquieted parents express their disappointment regarding the state of the public school, few ever utter a word suggesting that children with special needs be sent elsewhere, to other rooms or buildings. They lament only that the present approach, with everyone in the same group for academic activities, isn't working for all students; that, indeed, the majority of schoolchildren is falling behind.

Liberty and justice for all, in today's schools, has come to mean that everyone of the same age shall be lumped together in the same classroom, with the same teacher, regardless of a multitude of mental, emotional, and physical needs and requirements.

By analogy, if a horticulturist were to provide the same amount and type of food, water, soil, and light to every one of the hundreds of plants in her care, easily half would not survive. Moreover, it would surely require many years for the same professional to acquire enough varied knowledge and skill to ensure that each plant will survive, much less thrive.

Now, if every ten months each gardener's stock was replaced with a collection of completely new and different plants, only then would his task begin to compare even slightly with that of today's professional teacher. And the hopeful survivor in her care is of significantly deeper complexity; whose survival, yea, whose desired advancement, is of monumental importance in comparison.

Yet regular in-service teachers, already overtaxed and underpaid, are expected to take on even more responsibility and to educate themselves for the expertise necessary to care for these new special needs. Although special education teachers receive years of training and experience designed to prepare them for working with children of diverse learning needs, most regular classroom teachers receive none. Some new in-service recruits may have taken a three-hour course, suggested or required in their preparation. But, as many colleges of education adjust requirements to include a course in special education—a Band-Aid approach to the problem—countless teachers express resentment.

"If I had wanted to teach special education I would have trained for it. I'm not cut out for that. It takes a certain type of person. This isn't fair to me or to the special students assigned to my classroom."

But, wait a minute—if teachers and parents are so opposed to what's happening in public schools, who's responsible for these changes? How did this happen? Who or what, is to blame? And why is nothing being done about it?

How about P.L. 94-142, or IDEA, the well-known mainstreaming law? Heralded by social scientists and inclusion advocates as an educational equalizer, this "one size fits all approach"[1] is anything but equal. It has systematically removed the individual attention required by the most needy few, while simultaneously denying it to the mainstream majority of students. So, why has this faulty approach remained on the education scene? Because it's cheap! Politicians love it. Supporting this movement makes them appear benevolent but allows them to move funding, for which education is in dire need, to more popular, vote-procuring issues. No need to hire the quantity of specialists required to maintain settings in which student-teacher ratios used to be no more than eight to one. No press to provide accelerated programs for gifted students, for we're pretending that all students are gifted these days. No, these requisites no longer mesh with the "one size fits all" plan.

In spite of studies reported by the U.S. Department of Education showing that students with disabilities included in the regular classroom fail more often than do those taught in special settings,[2] proponents continue to press for inclusion. They urge modifying teaching methods and beliefs in ways designed to camouflage the problems and shoehorn all students into one "equal" mold. Some of these changes include the following:

- Knowledge of facts is not important.
- Students needn't know correct grammar, spelling, or punctuation to graduate.
- Memorization, multiple-choice exams, rewards, and competition are all old-fashioned.

- Ability grouping (except for athletics) must be eliminated.
- Honor rolls, advanced or honor classes, valedictorian, and salutatorian recognition must be eliminated.
- Assign group rather than individual grades.
- Use portfolios for "authentic" assessment.
- Raise standards, but don't use tests to detect mastery.
- Cooperative learning should be practiced 80 percent of the time in the classroom.
- Peer tutoring should be encouraged.
- Disruption in classrooms reflects teacher failure.
- Acceleration robs students of "normal" socialization.
- All students are gifted.[3]

A majority of these ideas are being parroted by educationists, 17 percent of whom have never been a classroom teacher and 51 percent of whom have not been a K–12 teacher in more than sixteen years.[4]

A look at our present school system reflects an anti-intellectual society, forged by a misguided, synthetic egalitarianism. The most able students in our society are being taught to devalue their abilities and also themselves. In many cases they are taught little else in today's schools.

Bumper stickers read, "My athlete can beat up your honor student!" Able students purposely underachieve in order to avoid labels like "geek," "nerd," and "dweeb." It's great to be a superior athlete but not even okay to be a superior scholar in an institution established to disseminate learning. Something is wrong with this picture.

A capable student finally drops out of public school, finding no peers, no appropriate programs, and no superintendent who will permit grade acceleration. Cause for great concern? Yes, but when this student can then proceed to pass college entrance exams and be accepted into several college programs without a high school degree, something is definitely amiss in our formula for assessment and decision-making. Clearly, this is not equal educational opportunity, for there is nothing so unequal as equal educational treatment of students with diverse abilities.

When we permit a few educationists to promote the overuse of certain methods as "best for all students"—when in fact these methods (cooperative learning, peer tutoring) obviously exploit the ablest students and systematically prevent their progress—we establish serious consequences in our schools.

But when the Office of Gifted and Talented is eliminated; only two cents of every dollar for K–12 education is allotted to serve our most promising students; honors classes are dismantled; and a state rules that only disabled students may receive funding for special education; our public school system, yea, our society is dangerously compromised.[5]

Until we come to realize that education can never be equal unless each student is allowed and enabled to progress at his own highest rate, our efforts to reform our public school system will continue to fail. In our urgency to reform we seem to have fallen into a common trap produced by myopic vision. We can see only one way—either-or. This eliminates the possibility of a flexible middle, a healthy balance that permits commitment to all needs, however diverse.

For instance, regarding the inclusionists' list, much benefit may be afforded memorization capabilities. The fact that all children cannot commit certain information to memory, however, should not dictate eliminating that challenge for others. Many professions depend on rote memorization capability. Indeed, daily life may be enhanced by one's memorized information, selected thoughts, and ideas. There is a special feeling of security that comes with "owning" information. Students love participation in theatrical production, a wonderful way to practice memorization. The activity of brain calisthenics can be fun and rewarding.

Portfolios are not even a good, let alone "best," form of assessment, as Vermont discovered. Several years after the state adopted portfolio assessment, its schools were able to manage only 33 percent reliability.[6] That's because portfolios by nature are purely subjective, making them seriously unreliable for overall assessment purposes. Additionally, they are extremely time-consuming for students and teachers alike, while requiring enormous storage space, a luxury lacking in most schools.

"Authentic assessment," like "inclusion," sounds nice and appears more benevolent, but its purpose is to resolve one of the major problems of inclusion. Many included students cannot pass basic skills tests. But performance-based assessment methods are impractical for large-scale assessment and are not supported by many educational evaluation experts. Major concerns include the neglected issues of reliability and validity, the lack of consensus of how this form of assessment should be used, its ineffectiveness in complex subject areas, and the fear that reliance on such an approach reduces motivation for capable students. A common conclusion of educational psychometricians is that "authentic assessment is a fad that will be of only historical interest" in years to come.[7]

Multiple choice and standardized exams, on the other hand, although highly reliable and useful for determining mastery of basic skills, are certainly inadequate for measuring all human capabilities, especially those deemed most important, such as creativity and high-level problem solving. Shouldn't these factors serve to inform us that both methods are necessary for the most efficient and effective evaluation?

Cooperative learning, which may promote motivation for some students, enhanced socialization, and just plain fun in the classroom, is essential for many learning projects and endeavors. Although currently touted as some great panacea, it's hardly new. Effective teachers have always relied on student grouping, teams, squads, and the like for selected classroom purposes. Too much reliance on group learning, "discovery" methods, and peer teaching, however, can become counterproductive. Misinformation and unnecessary remediation may rob precious learning time. Teachers need to direct as well as facilitate. Students need individual study and on-task time. Each student must also be encouraged to seek her own directions, interests, and challenge levels.

Clearly, none of the various notions, methods, and ideas on the foregoing list of "inclusion-ordered" approaches is, by itself, effective. Each must be varied with the "old-fashioned" methods to ensure "best for all" learning. There must be a balance to serve students of all types and abilities equally.

Students must have some experience with others of like ability. Identical age grouping assumes that all students of the same age can learn together adequately. Yet one common definition of a gifted student is a comprehension level two chronological years beyond his same-age peers. When a child reads at three, circling alphabet letters in kindergarten is clearly not a challenge. When she relishes multiplication computer games at home, we must be prepared to ask more of her than to count to ten. We dare not pretend that there is no such thing as a gifted student or that all children are gifted.

Learners must also have time for individual study. Assigned seats placed in rows may well signal emphasis on control rather than learning, but occasionally this arrangement is perfect for the discerning teacher's purpose. Successful education for all requires appropriate individual challenge and remediation, as well as caring interaction and socialization among students. Most important of all is the teacher/student relationship, which is diminished when teachers must devote excessive time to many children with multiple needs. With distance-learning access on the rise, the opportunity for one-to-one interaction between each learner and her teacher becomes all the more crucial. A healthy mentoring relationship between the teacher and the student has always been and remains a pivotal factor for education excellence.

Successful schools must be prepared to offer all these approaches in order to serve all learners equally. It is not about either-or. People are not designed for either-or treatment. Incredibly, miraculously varied in their needs and capabilities, they also require an education with techniques and methods that can fulfill these unparalleled individual distinctions.

Such an education requires much support, much expertise, varied and multiple personnel needs, and therefore, enormous monetary backing. How much are our children worth? How much is our future worth? How can a nation that currently enjoys such increased prosperity afford not to invest in its children? There can be no either-or. All children must be served.

It is possible to build a great public school system, great because it offers everything needed for all its students; those who learn less easily, those who excel, and all those in between. But we can never achieve this ideal state until fanatical inclusionists and overzealous egalitarians allow a complete portrayal of our students, including encouraging and enabling the very highest capabilities among us.

In a poignant article, the father of a physically handicapped child afflicted with the rare Cornelia de Lange syndrome pleaded,

> The advocates of full inclusion speak glibly of giving teachers training necessary to cope with the immense variety of challenges which handicapped children bring to the classroom. No amount of training could prepare a regular teacher for Mark. The requisite expertise and commitment are found only among teachers who have chosen to specialize in the handicapped. Special education is by no means the unmitigated disaster its critics charge. The drive to ditch this flawed program in favor of a radical alternative will almost certainly result in just such a disaster. One can only hope that we

will not repeat the pattern of sabotaging our genuine achievements in the pursuit of worthy-sounding but deeply wrongheaded ideas.[8]

Notes

1. Albert Shanker, "Full Inclusion Is Neither Free Nor Appropriate," *Educational Leadership* (December/January 1995).

2. Lynn Schnailberg, "E.D. Report Documents 'Full Inclusion' Trend," *Education Week,* 19 October 1994, 17, 19.

3. Robert Slavin, "Cooperative Learning and the Cooperative School," *Educational Leadership* 45, no. 3 (1987): 7–13; Ellen D. Fiedler, Richard E. Lange, and Susan Winebrenner, *Roeper Review* 16 (1993): 4–7; and John Goodlad and Thomas Lovitt, *Integrating General and Special Education* (New York: Merrill, 1993), 171–201.

4. Public Agenda, a nonpartisan, nonprofit organization, *Different Drummers: How Teachers of Teachers View Public Education,* an opinion poll comparing ideas of the general public, in-service teachers, and teacher educators, (New York: October 1997).

5. Ellen Winner, *Gifted Children: Myths and Realities* (New York: Basic Books, 1996) and Karen Diegmueller, "Gifted Programs Not a Right, Connecticut Court Rules," *Education Week,* 30 March 1994, 8.

6. Koretz et al., *RAND Corporation* (1992) studied the Vermont statewide assessment program. Average reliability coefficients ranged from .33 to .43. If the reliability of test scores is under .50, there is no differentiation in the performance of an individual student from the overall average performance of students. See also James Popham, *Classroom Assessment: What Teachers Need to Know* (Boston: Allyn and Bacon, 1995), 171–173 and Blaine Worthen, Walter Borg, and Karl White, *Measurement and Evaluation in the Schools* (New York: Longman, 1993), 441–442.

7. Thomas Brooks and Sandra Pakes, "Policy, National Testing, and the Psychological Corporation," *Measurement and Evaluation in Counseling and Development* 26 (1993): 54–58; James S. Terwilliger, "Semantics, Psychometrics, and Assessment Reform: A Close Look at 'Authentic' Tests," ERIC Document Reproduction Service #ED397123, 1996; and Louis Janda, *Psychological Testing: Theory and Applications* (Boston: Allyn and Bacon, 1998), 375.

8. Arch Puddington, "Life with Mark," *American Educator* (1996): 36–41.

POSTSCRIPT

Is Full Inclusion of Disabled Students Desirable?

One wit has stated that P.L. 94–142 was really a "full employment act for lawyers." Indeed, there has been much litigation regarding the identification, classification, placement, and specialized treatment of disabled children since the introduction of the 1975 act.

The 1992 ruling in *Greer v. Rome City School District* permitted the parents to place their child, who has Down's syndrome, in a regular classroom with supplementary services. Also, the decision in *Sacramento City Unified School District v. Holland* (1994) allowed a girl with an IQ of 44 to be placed in a regular classroom full time, in accordance with her parents' wishes (the school system had wanted the student to split her time equally between regular and special education classes). These cases demonstrate that although the aspect of the law stipulating parental involvement in the development of individual education programs can invite cooperation, it can also lead to conflict.

Teacher attitude becomes a crucial component in the success or failure of placements of disabled students in regular classrooms. Some articles addressing this and related matters are "Willingness of Regular and Special Educators to Teach Students With Handicaps," by Karen Derk Gans, *Exceptional Children* (October 1987) and Lynn Miller, "The Regular Education Initiative and School Reform: Lessons from the Mainstream," *Remedial and Special Education* (May–June 1990).

An interview with an authority on this issue can be found in "David Hornbeck on the Changing Face of Special Education," *The School Administrator* (February 1992). Also, interesting personal accounts are offered in Pete Idstein, "Swimming Against the Mainstream(ing)," *Phi Delta Kappan* (December 1993) and Tina Vaughn, "Inclusion Can Succeed," *Equity and Excellence in Education* (April 1994).

Other noteworthy articles are "Disruptive Disabled Kids: Inclusion Confusion," by Diane Brockett, *School Board News* (October 1994) and multiple articles in *Theory into Practice* (Winter 1996), *Educational Leadership* (December 1994/January 1995 and February 1996), *Phi Delta Kappan* (December 1995 and October 1996); *Kappa Delta Pi Record* (Winter 1998), and *NASSP Bulletin* (February 2000). Also see Philip Ferguson and Dianne Ferguson, "The Future of Inclusive Educational Practice," *Childhood Education* (Mid-Summer 1998); Susan G. Clark, "The Principal, Discipline, and the IDEA," *NASSP Bulletin* (November 1999); and Jean Mueth Dayton, "Discipline Procedures for Students With Disabilities," *The Clearing House* (January/February 2000).

ISSUE 15

Do Black Students Need an Afrocentric Curriculum?

YES: Molefi Kete Asante, from "The Afrocentric Idea in Education," *Journal of Negro Education* (Spring 1991)

NO: Arthur M. Schlesinger, Jr., from "The Disuniting of America," *American Educator* (Winter 1991)

ISSUE SUMMARY

YES: Black studies professor Molefi Kete Asante puts forth his argument for providing black students with an Afrocentric frame of reference, which he feels would enhance their self-esteem and learning.2

NO: Noted historian Arthur M. Schlesinger, Jr., documents his concerns about the recent spread of Afrocentric programs, the multiculturalization of the curriculum, and the use of history as therapy.

Amore specific manifestation of the argument over multicultural emphases in the curriculum of public schools can be seen in the recent experimentation with Afrocentric frameworks in predominantly black neighborhood schools and in the attempts to create all-black male classes and schools. Although many school districts are revising the curriculum to embrace a more multicultural perspective, some (such as Atlanta, Georgia) are developing and using an African-centered curricular base. Movement in this direction has been inspired, at least in part, by the work of Temple University scholar Molefi Kete Asante, who framed the Afrocentric idea in his 1980 book *Afrocentricity.*

The Afrocentrists feel that the traditional emphasis on white European history and culture and the disregard of African history and culture alienate black schoolchildren, who are unable to feel an attachment to the content being offered. Many who support the Afrocentrists would agree with Asa G. Hilliard III, a professor of educational psychology, who has stated that there is a vast amount of important information about African people that *everyone,* not only black schoolchildren, should be aware of.

In his much-discussed book *The Disuniting of America: Reflections on a Multicultural Society* (1991), historian Arthur M. Schlesinger, Jr., denounces this movement as an extreme example of a "cult of ethnicity." Agreeing with Schlesinger, David Nicholson, in " 'Afrocentrism' and the Tribalization of America: The Misguided Logic of Ethnic Education Schemes," *The Washington Post* (September 23, 1990), argues that "the sweeping call for 'curricula of inclusion' is based on untested, unproven premises. Worse, because it intentionally exaggerates differences, it seems likely to exacerbate racial and ethnic tensions."

To which Kariamu Welsh, a proponent of Asante's position, would reply:

> The eyes of the African-American must be on his own center, one that reflects and resembles him and speaks to him in his own language.... If one understands properly African history, an assumption can never be made that Afrocentricity is a back to 'anything' movement. It is an uncovering of one's true self, it is the pinpointing of one's center, and it is the clarity and focus through which black people must see the world in order to escalate. [From the foreword to Asante's *Afrocentricity*.]

Lending support to Welsh's position, a study by a North Carolina University researcher showed that studying Africa and African American history and culture leads to improved overall academic performance by black students.

A different slant emerges from the insights of Richard Cohen, a *Washington Post* columnist, writing in an October 7, 1990, column:

> Changing the curriculum in school districts where blacks predominate would tend only to put these students further outside the mainstream. They would know what others do not, which is all right. But they would not know what most others do—and that's been the problem in the first place.

A subissue of the basic controversy involves providing not only an Afrocentric curriculum for black students but all-male classes or even all-male schools. Some commentators contend that federal inattention to poor urban families in the 1980s provided the impetus for proposing such classes and schools. As Larry Cuban states in "Desperate Remedies for Desperate Times," *Education Week* (November 20, 1991), "To advocate a single-sex school, an Afrocentric curriculum taught by black male teachers who enforce strict rules is, indeed, a strong response to a desperate situation." The effort attempts to combat the present epidemic of academic failure and male-on-male violence.

Another subissue involves the official recognition of ebonics as a distinct language. Coverage of many aspects of this controversy may be found in *The Real Ebonics Debate: Power, Language, and the Education of African-American Children* edited by Theresa Perry and Lisa Delpit (1998). Other informative works on the issue are Evelyn Dandy's *Black Communication: Breaking Down the Barriers* (1991) and Lisa Delpit's *Other People's Children* (1995).

In the selections that follow, Molefi Kete Asante establishes the necessity of Afrocentric programs, examines theoretical and philosophical underpinnings of his view, and charts a path for implementation at all levels of education. Arthur M. Schlesinger, Jr., questions the basic assumptions from which Asante's argument flows and expresses fears about divisive strategies and historical manipulation.

Molefi Kete Asante  **YES**

The Afrocentric Idea in Education

Introduction

Many of the principles that govern the development of the Afrocentric idea in education were first established by Carter G. Woodson in *The Mis-education of the Negro* (1933). Indeed, Woodson's classic reveals the fundamental problems pertaining to the education of the African person in America. As Woodson contends, African Americans have been educated away from their own culture and traditions and attached to the fringes of European culture; thus dislocated from themselves, Woodson asserts that African Americans often valorize European culture to the detriment of their own heritage (p. 7). Although Woodson does, not advocate rejection of American citizenship or nationality, he believed that assuming African Americans hold the same position as European Americans vis-à-vis the realities of America would lead to the psychological and cultural death of the African American population. Furthermore, if education is ever to be substantive and meaningful within the context of American society, Woodson argues, it must first address the African's historical experiences, both in Africa and America (p. 7). That is why he places on education, and particularly on the traditionally African American colleges, the burden of teaching the African American to be responsive to the long traditions and history of Africa as well as America. Woodson's alert recognition, more than 50 years ago, that something is severely wrong with the way African Americans are educated provides the principal impetus for the Afrocentric approach to American education.

In this article I will examine the nature and scope of this approach, establish its necessity, and suggest ways to develop and disseminate it throughout all levels of education. Two propositions stand in the background of the theoretical and philosophical issues I will present. These ideas represent the core presuppositions on which I have based most of my work in the field of education, and they suggest the direction of my own thinking about what education is capable

of doing to and for an already politically and economically marginalized people
—African Americans:

1. Education is fundamentally a social phenomenon whose ultimate purpose is to socialize the learner; to send a child to school is to prepare
   that child to become part of a social group.
2. Schools are reflective of the societies that develop them (i.e., a White
   supremacist-dominated society will develop a White supremacist educational system).

Definitions

An alternative framework suggests that other definitional assumptions can provide a new paradigm for the examination of education within the American
society. For example, in education, *centricity* refers to a perspective that involves locating students within the context of their own cultural references so
that they can relate socially and psychologically to other cultural perspectives.
Centricity is a concept that can be applied to any culture. The centrist paradigm
is supported by research showing that the most productive method of teaching
any student is to place his or her group within the center of the context of
knowledge (Asante, 1990). For White students in America this is easy because
almost all the experiences discussed in American classrooms are approached
from the standpoint of White perspectives and history. American education,
however, is not centric; it is Eurocentric. Consequently, non-White students are
also made to see themselves and their groups as the "acted upon." Only rarely
do they read or hear of non-White people as active participants in history. This
is as true for a discussion of the American Revolution as it is for a discussion of
Dante's *Inferno;* for instance, most classroom discussions of the European slave
trade concentrate on the activities of Whites rather than on the resistance efforts of Africans. A person educated in a truly centric fashion comes to view all
groups' contributions as significant and useful. Even a White person educated
in such a system does not assume superiority based upon racist notions. Thus,
a truly centric education is different from a Eurocentric, racist (that is, White
supremacist) education.

Afrocentricity is a frame of reference wherein phenomena are viewed from
the perspective of the African person. The Afrocentric approach seeks in every
situation the appropriate centrality of the African person (Asante, 1987). In education this means that teachers provide students the opportunity to study the
world and its people, concepts, and history from an African world view. In most
classrooms, whatever the subject, Whites are located in the center perspective
position. How alien the African American child must feel, how like an outsider!
The little African American child who sits in a classroom and is taught to accept as heroes and heroines individuals who defamed African people is being
actively de-centered, dislocated, and made into a nonperson, one whose aim in
life might be to one day shed that "badge of inferiority": his or her Blackness. In
Afrocentric educational settings, however, teachers do not marginalize African
American children by causing them to question their own self-worth because

their people's story is seldom told. By seeing themselves as the subjects rather than the objects of education—be the discipline biology, medicine, literature, or social studies—African American students come to see themselves not merely as seekers of knowledge but as integral participants in it. Because all content areas are adaptable to an Afrocentric approach, African American students can be made to see themselves as centered in the reality of any discipline.

It must be emphasized that Afrocentricity is *not* a Black version of Eurocentricity (Asante, 1987). Eurocentricity is based on White supremacist notions whose purposes are to protect White privilege and advantage in education, economics, politics, and so forth. Unlike Eurocentricity, Afrocentricity does not condone ethnocentric valorization at the expense of degrading other groups' perspectives. Moreover, Eurocentricity presents the particular historical reality of Europeans as the sum total of the human experience (Asante, 1987). It imposes Eurocentric realities as "universal"; i.e., that which is White is presented as applying to the human condition in general, while that which is non-White is viewed as group-specific and therefore not "human." This explains why some scholars and artists of African descent rush to deny their Blackness; they believe that to exist as a Black person is not to exist as a universal human being. They are the individuals Woodson identified as preferring European art, language, and culture over African art, language, and culture; they believe that anything of European origin is inherently better than anything produced by or issuing from their own people. Naturally, the person of African descent should be centered in his or her historical experiences as an African, but Eurocentric curricula produce such aberrations of perspective among persons of color.

Multiculturalism in education is a nonhierarchical approach that respects and celebrates a variety of cultural perspectives on world phenomena (Asante, 1991). The multicultural approach holds that although European culture is the majority culture in the United States, that is not sufficient reason for it to be imposed on diverse student populations as "universal." Multiculturalists assert that education, to have integrity, must begin with the proposition that all humans have contributed to world development and the flow of knowledge and information, and that most human achievements are the result of mutually interactive, international effort. Without a multicultural education, students remain essentially ignorant of the contributions of a major portion of the world's people. A multicultural education is thus a fundamental necessity for anyone who wishes to achieve competency in almost any subject.

The Afrocentric idea must be the stepping-stone from which the multicultural idea is launched. A truly authentic multicultural education, therefore, must be based upon the Afrocentric initiative. If this step is skipped, multicultural curricula, as they are increasingly being defined by White "resisters" (to be discussed below) will evolve without any substantive infusion of African American content, and the African American child will continue to be lost in the Eurocentric framework of education. In other words, the African American child will neither be confirmed nor affirmed in his or her own cultural information. For the mutual benefit of all Americans, this tragedy, which leads to the psychological and cultural dislocation of African American children, can and should be avoided.

The Revolutionary Challenge

Because it centers African American students inside history, culture, science, and so forth rather than outside these subjects, the Afrocentric idea presents the most revolutionary challenge to the ideology of White supremacy in education during the past decade. No other theoretical position stated by African Americans has ever captured the imagination of such a wide range of scholars and students of history, sociology, communications, anthropology, and psychology. The Afrocentric challenge has been posed in three critical ways:

1. It questions the imposition of the White supremacist view as universal and/or classical (Asante, 1990).
2. It demonstrates the indefensibility of racist theories that assault multiculturalism and pluralism.
3. It projects a humanistic and pluralistic viewpoint by articulating Afrocentricity as a valid, nonhegemonic perspective.

Suppression and Distortion: Symbols of Resistance

The forces of resistance to the Afrocentric, multicultural transformation of the curriculum and teaching practices began to assemble their wagons almost as quickly as word got out about the need for equality in education (Ravitch, 1990). Recently, the renowned historian Arthur Schlesinger and others formed a group called the Committee for the Defense of History. This is a paradoxical development because only lies, untruths, and inaccurate information need defending. In their arguments against the Afrocentric perspective, these proponents of Eurocentrism often clothe their arguments in false categories and fake terms (i.e., "pluralistic" and "particularistic" multiculturalism) (Keto, 1990; Asante, 1991). Besides, as the late African scholar Cheikh Anta Diop (1980) maintained: "African history and Africa need no defense." Afrocentric education is not against history. It is *for* history—correct, accurate history—and if it is against anything, it is against the marginalization of African American, Hispanic American, Asian American, Native American, and other non-White children. The Committee for the Defense of History is nothing more than a futile attempt to buttress the crumbling pillars of a White supremacist system that conceals its true motives behind the cloak of American liberalism. It was created in the same spirit that generated Bloom's *The Closing of the American Mind* (1987) and Hirsch's *Cultural Literacy: What Every American Needs to Know* (1987), both of which were placed at the service of the White hegemony in education, particularly its curricular hegemony. This committee and other evidences of White backlash are a predictable challenge to the contemporary thrust for an Afrocentric, multicultural approach to education.

Naturally, different adherents to a theory will have different views on its meaning. While two discourses presently are circulating about multiculturalism, only one is relevant to the liberation of the minds of African and White people in the United States. That discourse is Afrocentricity: the acceptance of

Africa as central to African people. Yet, rather than getting on board with Afro-centrists to fight against White hegemonic education, some Whites (and some Blacks as well) have opted to plead for a return to the educational plantation. Unfortunately for them, however, those days are gone, and such misinformation can never be packaged as accurate, correct education again.

Ravitch (1990), who argues that there are two kinds of multiculturalism —*pluralist multiculturalism* and *particularist multiculturalism*—is the leader of those professors whom I call "resisters" or opponents to Afrocentricity and multiculturalism. Indeed, Ravitch advances the imaginary divisions in mul-ticultural perspectives to conceal her true identity as a defender of White supremacy. Her tactics are the tactics of those who prefer Africans and other non-Whites to remain on the mental and psychological plantation of West-ern civilization. In their arrogance the resisters accuse Afrocentrists and mul-ticulturalists of creating "fantasy history" and "bizarre theories" of non-White people's contributions to civilization. What they prove, however, is their own ignorance. Additionally, Ravitch and others (Nicholson, 1990) assert that mul-ticulturalism will bring about the "tribalization" of America, but in reality America has always been a nation of ethnic diversity. When one reads their works on multiculturalism, one realizes that they are really advocating the im-position of a White perspective on everybody else's culture. Believing that the Eurocentric position is indisputable, they attempt to resist and impede the pro-gressive transformation of the monoethnic curriculum. Indeed, the closets of bigotry have opened to reveal various attempts by White scholars (joined by some Blacks) to defend White privilege in the curriculum in much the same way as it has been so staunchly defended in the larger society. It was per-haps inevitable that the introduction of the Afrocentric idea would open up the discussion of the American school curriculum in a profound way.

Why has Afrocentricity created so much of a controversy in educational circles? The idea that an African American child is placed in a stronger posi-tion to learn if he or she is centered—that is, if the child sees himself or herself within the content of the curriculum rather than at its margins—is not novel (Asante, 1980). What is revolutionary is the movement from the idea (concep-tual stage) to its implementation in practice, when we begin to teach teachers how to put African American youth at the center of instruction. In effect, stu-dents are shown how to see with new eyes and hear with new ears. African American children learn to interpret and center phenomena in the context of African heritage, while White students are taught to see that their own centers are not threatened by the presence or contributions of African Americans and others.

The Condition of Eurocentric Education

Institutions such as schools are conditioned by the character of the nation in which they are developed. Just as crime and politics are different in different nations, so, too, is education. In the United States a "Whites-only" orientation has predominated in education. This has had a profound impact on the quality of education for children of all races and ethnic groups. The African American child has suffered disproportionately, but White children are also the victims of monoculturally diseased curricula.

The Tragedy of Ignorance

During the past five years many White students and parents have approached me after presentations with tears in their eyes or expressing their anger about the absence of information about African Americans in the schools. A recent comment from a young White man at a major university in the Northeast was especially striking. As he said to me: "My teacher told us that Martin Luther King was a commie and went on with the class." Because this student's teacher made no effort to discuss King's ideas, the student maliciously had been kept ignorant. The vast majority of White Americans are likewise ignorant about the bountiful reservoirs of African and African American history, culture, and contributions. For example, few Americans of any color have heard the names of Cheikh Anta Diop, Anna Julia Cooper, C. L. R. James, or J. A. Rogers. All were historians who contributed greatly to our understanding of the African world. Indeed, very few teachers have ever taken a course in African American Studies; therefore, most are unable to provide systematic information about African Americans.

Afrocentricity and History

Most of America's teaching force are victims of the same system that victimizes today's young. Thus, American children are not taught the names of the African ethnic groups from which the majority of the African American population are derived; few are taught the names of any of the sacred sites in Africa. Few teachers can discuss with their students the significance of the Middle Passage or describe what it meant or means to Africans. Little mention is made in American classrooms of either the brutality of slavery or the ex-slaves' celebration of freedom. American children have little or no understanding of the nature of the capture, transport, and enslavement of Africans. Few have been taught the true horrors of being taken, shipped naked across 25 days of ocean, broken by abuse and indignities of all kinds, and dehumanized into a beast of burden, a thing without a name. If our students only knew the truth, if they were taught the Afrocentric perspective on the Great Enslavement, and if they knew the full story about the events since slavery that have served to constantly dislocate African Americans, their behavior would perhaps be different. Among these events are: the infamous constitutional compromise of 1787, which decreed that African Americans were, by law, the equivalent of but three-fifths of a person (see Franklin, 1974); the 1857 Dred Scott decision in which the Supreme Court avowed that African Americans had no rights Whites were obliged to respect (Howard, 1857); the complete dismissal and nonenforcement of Section 2 of the Fourteenth Amendment to the Constitution (this amendment, passed in 1868, stipulated as one of its provisions a penalty against any state that denied African Americans the right to vote, and called for the reduction of a state's delegates to the House of Representatives in proportion to the number of disenfranchised African American males therein); and the much-mentioned, as-yet-unreceived 40 acres and a mule, reparation for enslavement, promised to each African American family after the Civil War by Union General William T. Sherman and Secretary of War Edwin Stanton (Oubre, 1978, pp. 18–19, 182–183; see also Smith, 1987, pp. 106–107). If the curriculum were enhanced to include readings from the slave narratives; the diaries of slave ship captains; the journals of slaveowners; the abolitionist newspapers; the writings of the freedmen and freedwomen; the accounts of African American civil rights, civic, and social organizations; and numerous others, African American children would be different, White children would be different—indeed, America would be a different nation today.

America's classrooms should resound with the story of the barbaric treatment of the Africans, of how their dignity was stolen and their cultures destroyed. The recorded experiences of escaped slaves provide the substance for such learning units. For example, the narrative of Jacob and Ruth Weldon presents a detailed account of the Middle Passage (Feldstein, 1971). The Weldons noted that Africans, having been captured and brought onto the slave ships, were chained to the deck, made to bend over, and "branded with a red hot iron in the form of letters or signs dipped in an oily preparation and pressed against the naked flesh till it burnt a deep and ineffaceable scar, to show who was the owner" (pp. 33–37). They also recalled that those who screamed were lashed on the face, breast, thighs, and backs with a "cat-o'-nine tails" wielded by White sailors: "Every blow brought the returning lash pieces of grieving flesh" (p. 44). They saw "mothers with babies at their breasts basely branded and lashed, hewed and scarred, till it would seem as if the very heavens must smite the infernal tormentors with the doom they so richly merited" (p. 44). Children and infants were not spared from this terror. The Weldons tell of a nine-month-old baby on board a slave ship being flogged because it would not eat. The ship's captain ordered the child's feet placed in boiling water, which dissolved the skin and nails, then ordered the child whipped again; still the child refused to eat. Eventually the captain killed the baby with his own hands and commanded the child's mother to throw the dead baby overboard. When the mother refused, she, too, was beaten, then forced to the ship's side, where "with her head averted so she might not see it, she dropped the body into the sea" (p. 44). In a similar vein a captain of a ship with 440 Africans on board noted that 132 had to be thrown overboard to save water (Feldstein, 1971, p. 47). As another wrote, the "groans and soffocating [sic] cries for air and water coming from below the deck sickened the soul of humanity" (Feldstein, 1971, p. 44).

Upon landing in America the situation was often worse. The brutality of the slavocracy is unequalled for the psychological and spiritual destruction it wrought upon African Americans. Slave mothers were often forced to leave their children unattended while they worked in the fields. Unable to nurse their children or to properly care for them, they often returned from work at night to find their children dead (Feldstein, 1971, p. 49). The testimony of Henry Bibb also sheds light on the bleakness of the slave experience:

> I was born May 1815, of a slave mother... and was claimed as the property of David White, Esq.... I was flogged up; for where I should have received moral, mental, and religious instructions, I received stripes without number, the object of which was to degrade and keep me in subordination. I can truly say that I drank deeply of the bitter cup of suffering and woe. I have been dragged down to the lowest depths of human degradation and wretchedness, by slaveholders. (Feldstein, 1971, p. 60)

Enslavement was truly a living death. While the ontological onslaught caused some Africans to opt for suicide, the most widespread results were dislocation, disorientation, and misorientation—all of which are the consequences of the African person being actively de-centered. The "Jim Crow" period of second-class citizenship, from 1877 to 1954, saw only slight improvement in the lot of African Americans. This era was characterized by the sharecropper system, disenfranchisement, enforced segregation, internal migration, lynchings, unemployment, poor housing conditions, and separate and unequal educational facilities. Inequitable policies and practices veritably plagued the race.

No wonder many persons of African descent attempt to shed their race and become "raceless." One's basic identity is one's self-identity, which is ultimately one's cultural identity; without a strong cultural identity, one is lost. Black children do not know their people's story and White children do not know the story, but remembrance is a vital requisite for understanding and humility. This is why the Jews have campaigned (and rightly so) to have the story of the European Holocaust taught in schools and colleges. Teaching about such a monstrous human brutality should forever remind the world of the ways in which humans have often violated each other. Teaching about the African Holocaust is just as important for many of the same reasons. Additionally, it underscores the enormity of the effects of physical, psychological, and economic dislocation on the African population in America and throughout the African diaspora. Without an understanding of the historical experiences of African people, American children cannot make any real headway in addressing the problems of the present.

Certainly, if African American children were taught to be fully aware of the struggles of our African forebears they would find a renewed sense of purpose and vision in their own lives. They would cease acting as if they have no past and no future. For instance, if they were taught about the historical relationship of Africans to the cotton industry—how African American men, women, and children were forced to pick cotton from "can't see in the morning 'til can't see at night," until the blood ran from the tips of their fingers where they were pricked by the hard boll; or if they were made to visualize their ancestors in the burning sun, bent double with constant stooping, and dragging rough, heavy croaker sacks behind them—or picture them bringing those sacks trembling to the scale, fearful of a sure flogging if they did not pick enough, perhaps our African American youth would develop a stronger entrepreneurial spirit. If White children were taught the same information rather than that normally fed them about American slavery, they would probably view our society differently and work to transform it into a better place.

Correcting Distorted Information

Hegemonic education can exist only so long as true and accurate information is withheld. Hegemonic Eurocentric education can exist only so long as Whites maintain that Africans and other non-Whites have never contributed to world civilization. It is largely upon such false ideas that invidious distinctions are made. The truth, however, gives one insight into the real reasons behind human actions, whether one chooses to follow the paths of others or not. For example, one cannot remain comfortable teaching that art and philosophy originated in Greece if one learns that the Greeks themselves taught that the study of these subjects originated in Africa, specifically ancient Kemet (Herodotus, 1987). The first philosophers were the Egyptians Kagemni, Khun-anup, Ptahhotep, Kete, and Seti; but Eurocentric education is so disjointed that students have no way of discovering this and other knowledge of the organic relationship of Africa to the rest of human history. Not only did Africa contribute to human history, African civilizations predate all other civilizations. Indeed, the human species originated on the continent of Africa—this is true whether one looks at either archaeological or biological evidence.

Two other notions must be refuted. There are those who say that African American history should begin with the arrival of Africans as slaves in 1619, but it has been shown that Africans visited and inhabited North and South America long before European settlers "discovered" the "New World" (Van Sertima, 1976). Secondly, although America became something of a home for those Africans who survived the horrors of the Middle Passage, their experiences on the slave ships and during slavery resulted in their having an entirely different (and often tainted) perspective about America from that of the Europeans and others who came, for the most part, of their own free will seeking opportunities not available to them in their native lands. Afrocentricity therefore seeks to recognize this divergence in perspective and create centeredness for African American students.

Conclusion

The reigning initiative for total curricular change is the movement that is being proposed and led by Africans, namely, the Afrocentric idea. When I wrote the first book on Afrocentricity (Asante, 1980), now in its fifth printing, I had no idea that in 10 years the idea would both shake up and shape discussions in education, art, fashion, and politics. Since the publication of my subsequent works, *The Afrocentric Idea* (Asante, 1987) and *Kemet, Afrocentricity, and Knowledge* (Asante, 1990), the debate has been joined in earnest. Still, for many White Americans (and some African Americans) the most unsettling aspect of the discussion about Afrocentricity is that its intellectual source lies in the research and writings of African American scholars. Whites are accustomed to being in charge of the major ideas circulating in the American academy. Deconstructionism, Gestalt psychology, Marxism, structuralism, Piagetian theory, and so forth have all been developed, articulated, and elaborated upon at length, generally by White scholars. On the other hand, Afrocentricity is the product of scholars such as Nobles (1986), Hilliard (1978), Karenga (1986), Keto (1990), Richards (1991), and Myèrs (1989). There are also increasing numbers of young, impressively credentialled African American scholars who have begun to write in the Afrocentric vein (Jean, 1991). They, and even some young White scholars, have emerged with ideas about how to change the curriculum Afrocentrically.

Afrocentricity provides all Americans an opportunity to examine the perspective of the African person in this society and the world. The resisters claim that Afrocentricity is anti-White; yet, if Afrocentricity as a theory is against anything it is against racism, ignorance, and monoethnic hegemony in the curriculum. Afrocentricity is not anti-White; it is, however, pro-human. Further, the aim of the Afrocentric curriculum is not to divide America, it is to make America flourish as it ought to flourish. This nation has long been divided with regard to the educational opportunities afforded to children. By virtue of the protection provided by society and reinforced by the Eurocentric curriculum, the White child is already ahead of the African American child by first grade. Our efforts thus must concentrate on giving the African American child greater opportunities for learning at the kindergarten level. However, the kind of assistance the African American child needs is as much cultural as it is academic. If the proper cultural information is provided, the academic performance will surely follow suit.

When it comes to educating African American children, the American educational system does not need a tune-up, it needs an overhaul. Black children have been maligned by this system. Black teachers have been maligned. Black history has been maligned. Africa has been maligned. Nonetheless, two truisms can be stated about education in America. First, some teachers *can and do* effectively teach African American children; secondly, if some teachers can do it, others can, too. We must learn all we can about what makes these teachers' attitudes and approaches successful, and then work diligently to see that their successes are replicated on a broad scale. By raising the same questions that Woodson posed more than 50 years ago, Afrocentric education, along with a significant reorientation of the American educational enterprise, seeks to respond to the African person's psychological and cultural dislocation. By providing philosophical and theoretical guidelines and criteria that are centered in an African perception of reality and by placing the African American child in his or her proper historical context and setting, Afrocentricity may be just the "escape hatch" African Americans so desperately need to facilitate academic success and "steal away" from the cycle of miseducation and dislocation.

References

Asante, M. K. (1980). *Afrocentricity: The theory of social change.* Buffalo, NY: Amulefi.
Asante, M. K. (1987). *The Afrocentric idea.* Philadelphia: Temple University Press.

Asante, M. K. (1990). *Kemet, Afrocentricity, and knowledge.* Trenton, NJ: Africa World Press.

Bloom, A. (1987). *The closing of the American mind.* New York: Simon & Schuster.

Feldstein, S. (1971). *Once a slave: The slave's view of slavery.* New York: William Morrow.

Franklin, J. H. (1974). *From slavery to freedom.* New York: Knopf.

Herodotus. (1987). *The history.* Chicago: University of Illinois Press.

Hilliard, A. G., III. (1978, June 20). *Anatomy and dynamics of oppression.* Speech delivered at the National Conference on Human Relations in Education, Minneapolis, MN.

Hirsch, E. D. (1987). *Cultural literacy: What every American needs to know.* New York: Houghton Mifflin.

Howard, B. C. (1857). *Report of the decision of the Supreme Court of the United States and the opinions of the justices thereof in the case of Dred Scott versus John F. A. Sandford, December term, 1856.* New York: D. Appleton & Co.

Jean, C. (1991). *Beyond the Eurocentric veils.* Amherst, MA: University of Massachusetts Press.

Karenga, M. R. (1986). *Introduction to Black studies.* Los Angeles: University of Sankore Press.

Keto, C. T. (1990). *Africa-centered perspective of history.* Blackwood, NJ: C. A. Associates.

Nicholson, D. (1990, September 23). Afrocentrism and the tribalization of America. *The Washington Post,* p. B-1.

Nobles, W. (1986). *African psychology.* Oakland, CA: Black Family Institute.

Oubre, C. F. (1978). *Forty acres and a mule: The Freedman's Bureau and Black land ownership.* Baton Rouge, LA: Louisiana State University Press.

Ravitch, D. (1990, Summer). Multiculturalism: E pluribus plures. *The American Scholar,* pp. 337–354.

Richards, D. (1991). *Let the circle be unbroken.* Trenton, NJ: Africa World Press.

Smith, J. O. (1987). *The politics of racial inequality: A systematic comparative macro-analysis from the colonial period to 1970.* New York: Greenwood Press.

Van Sertima, I. (1976). *They came before Columbus.* New York: Random House.

Woodson, C. G. (1915). *The education of the Negro prior to 1861: A history of the education of the colored people of the U.S. from the beginning of slavery.* New York: G. P. Putnam's Sons.

Woodson, C. G. (1933). *The Mis-education of the Negro.* Washington, DC: Associated Publishers.

Woodson, C. G. (1936). *African background outlined.* Washington, DC: Association for the Study of Afro-American Life and History.

NO

Arthur M. Schlesinger, Jr.

The Disuniting of America

Most white Americans through most of American history simply considered colored Americans inferior and unassimilable. Not until the 1960s did integration become a widely accepted national objective. Even then, even after legal obstacles to integration fell, social, economic, and psychological obstacles remained. Both black Americans and red Americans have every reason to seek redressing of the historical balance. And indeed the cruelty with which white Americans have dealt with black Americans has been compounded by the callousness with which white historians have dealt with black history.

Even the best historians: Frederick Jackson Turner, dismissing the slavery question as a mere "incident" when American history is "rightly viewed"; Charles and Mary Beard in their famous *The Rise of American Civilization,* describing blacks as passive in slavery and ludicrous in Reconstruction and acknowledging only one black achievement—the invention of ragtime; Samuel Eliot Morison and Henry Steele Commager, writing about childlike and improvident Sambo on the old plantation. One can sympathize with W. E. B. Du Bois's rage after reading white histories of slavery and Reconstruction; he was, he wrote, "literally aghast at what American historians have done to this field ... one of the most stupendous efforts the world ever saw to discredit human beings...."

The job of redressing the balance has been splendidly undertaken in recent years by both white and black historians. Meticulous and convincing scholarship has reversed conventional judgments on slavery, on Reconstruction, on the role of blacks in American life.

But scholarly responsibility was only one factor behind the campaign of historical correction. History remains a weapon. "History's potency is mighty," Herbert Aptheker, the polemical chronicler of slave rebellions, has written. "The oppressed need it for identity and inspiration." (Aptheker, a faithful Stalinist, was an old hand at the manipulation of history.)

For blacks the American dream has been pretty much of a nightmare, and, far more than white ethnics, they are driven by a desperate need to vindicate

From Arthur M. Schlesinger, Jr., "The Disuniting of America," *American Educator* (Winter 1991). Adapted from Arthur M. Schlesinger, Jr., *The Disuniting of America: Reflections on a Multicultural Society* (W. W. Norton, 1992). Copyright © 1992 by Arthur M. Schlesinger, Jr. This book was first published by Whittle Books as part of the Larger Agenda Series. Reprinted by permission of Whittle Communications, L.P.

their own identity. "The academic and social rescue and reconstruction of Black history," as Maulana Karenga put it in his influential *Introduction to Black Studies* ("a landmark in the intellectual history of African Americans," according to Molefi Kete Asante of Temple University), "is . . . [an] indispensable part of the rescue and reconstruction of Black humanity. For history is the substance and mirror of a people's humanity in others' eyes as well as in their own eyes . . . not only what they have done, but also a reflection of who they are, what they can do, and equally important what they can become. . . ."

One can hardly be surprised at the emergence of a there's-always-a-black-man-at-the-bottom-of-it-doing-the-real-work approach to American history. "The extent to which the past of a people is regarded as praiseworthy," the white anthropologist Melville J. Herskovits wrote in his study of the African antecedents of American blacks, "their own self-esteem would be high and the opinion of others will be favorable."

White domination of American schools and colleges, some black academics say, results in Eurocentric, racist, elitist, imperialist indoctrination and in systematic denigration of black values and achievements. "In the public school system," writes Felix Boateng of Eastern Washington University, "the orientation is so Eurocentric that white students take their identity for granted, and African-American students are totally deculturalized"—deculturalization being the "process by which the individual is deprived of his or her culture and then conditioned to other cultural values." "In a sense," says Molefi Kete Asante, the Eurocentric curriculum is "killing our children, killing their minds."

In history, Western-civilization courses are seen as cultural imperialism designed to disparage non-Western traditions and to impress the Western stamp on people of all races. In literature, the "canon," the accepted list of essential books, is seen as an instrumentality of the white power structure. Nowhere can blacks discover adequate reflection or representation of the black self.

Some black educators even argue ultimate biological and mental differences, asserting that black students do not learn the way white students do and that the black mind works in a genetically distinctive way. Black children are said, in the jargon of the educationist, to "process information differently." "There are scientific studies that show, at early ages, the difference between Caucasian infants and African infants," says Clare Jacobs, a teacher in Washington, D.C. "Our African children are very expressive. Every thought we have has an emotional dimension to it, and Western education has historically subordinated the feelings." Charles Willie of Harvard finds several distinct "intelligences" of which the "communication and calculation" valued by whites constitute only two. Other kinds of "intelligence" are singing and dancing, in both of which blacks excel.

Salvation thus lies, the argument goes, in breaking the white, Eurocentric, racist grip on the curriculum and providing education that responds to colored races, colored histories, colored ways of learning and behaving. Europe has reigned long enough; it is the source of most of the evil in the world anyway; and the time is overdue to honor the African contributions to civilization so purposefully suppressed in Eurocentric curricula. Children from nonwhite minorities, so long persuaded of their inferiority by the white hegemons, need the support and inspiration that identification with role models of the same color will give them.

The answer, for some at least, is "Afrocentricity," described by Asante in his book of that title as "the centerpiece of human regeneration." There is, Asante contends, a single "African Cultural System." Wherever people of African descent are, we respond to the same rhythms of the universe, the same cosmological sensibilities.... Our Africanity is our ultimate reality."

⋅⟨◉⟩⋅

The belated recognition of the pluralistic character of American society has had a bracing impact on the teaching and writing of history. Scholars now explore such long-neglected fields as the history of women, of immigration, of blacks, Indians, Hispanics, and other minorities. Voices long silent ring out of the darkness of history.

The result has been a reconstruction of American history, partly on the merits and partly in response to ethnic pressures. In 1987, the two states with both the greatest and the most diversified populations—California and New York—adopted new curricula for grades one to twelve. Both state curricula materially increased the time allotted to non-European cultures.

The New York curriculum went further in minimizing Western traditions. A two-year global-studies course divided the world into seven regions—Africa, South Asia, East Asia, Latin America, the Middle East, Western Europe, and Eastern Europe—with each region given equal time. The history of Western Europe was cut back from a full year to one quarter of the second year. American history was reduced to a section on the Constitution; then a leap across Jefferson, Jackson, the Civil War, and Reconstruction to 1877.

In spite of the multiculturalization of the New York state history curriculum in 1987—a revision approved by such scholars as Eric Foner of Columbia and Christopher Lasch of Rochester—a newly appointed commissioner of education yielded to pressures from minority interests to consider still further revision. In 1989, the Task Force on Minorities: Equity and Excellence (not one historian among its seventeen members) brought in a report that argued: the "systematic bias toward European culture and its derivatives" has "a terribly damaging effect on the psyche of young people of African, Asian, Latino, and Native American descent." The dominance of "the European-American monocultural perspective" explains why "large numbers of children of non-European descent are not doing as well as expected."

Dr. Leonard Jeffries, the task force's consultant on African-American culture and a leading author of the report, discerns "deep-seated pathologies of racial hatred" even in the 1987 curriculum. The consultant on Asian-American culture called for more pictures of Asian-Americans. The consultant on Latino culture found damning evidence of ethnocentric bias in such usages as the "Mexican War" and the "Spanish-American War." The ethnically correct designations should be the "American-Mexican War" and the "Spanish-Cuban-American War." The consultant on Native American culture wanted more space for Indians and for bilingual education in Iroquois.

A new curriculum giving the four other cultures equitable treatment, the report concluded, would provide "children from Native American, Puerto Rican/Latino, Asian-American, and African-American cultures... higher self-esteem and self-respect, while children from European cultures will have a less arrogant perspective."

The report views division into racial groups as the basic analytical framework for an understanding of American history. Its interest in history is not as an intellectual discipline but rather as social and psychological therapy whose primary function is to raise the self-esteem of children from minority groups. Nor does the report regard the Constitution or the American Creed as means of improvement.

Jeffries scorns the Constitution, finding "something vulgar and revolting in glorifying a process that heaped undeserved rewards on a segment of the population while oppressing the majority." The belief in the unifying force of democratic ideals finds no echo in the report. Indeed, the report takes no interest in the problem of holding a diverse republic together. Its impact is rather to sanction and deepen racial tensions.

꧁꧂

The recent spread of Afrocentric programs to public schools represents an extension of the New York task force ideology. These programs are, in most cases, based on a series of "African-American Baseline Essays" conceived by the educational psychologist Asa Hilliard.

Hilliard's narration for the slide show "Free Your Mind, Return to the Source: The African Origin of Civilization" suggests his approach. "Africa," he writes, "is the mother of Western civilization"—an argument turning on the contention that Egypt was a black African country and the real source of the science and philosophy Western historians attribute to Greece. Africans, Hilliard continues, also invented birth control and carbon steel. They brought science, medicine, and the arts to Europe; indeed, many European artists, such as Browning and Beethoven, were, in fact, "Afro-European." They also discovered America long before Columbus, and the original name of the Atlantic Ocean was the Ethiopian Ocean.

Hilliard's African-American Baseline Essays were introduced into the school system of Portland, Oregon, in 1987. They have subsequently been the inspiration for Afrocentric curricula in Milwaukee, Indianapolis, Pittsburgh, Washington, D.C., Richmond, Atlanta, Philadelphia, Detroit, Baltimore, Camden, and other cities and continue at this writing to be urged on school boards and administrators anxious to do the right thing.

John Henrik Clarke's Baseline Essay on Social Studies begins with the proposition that "African scholars are the final authority on Africa." Egypt, he continues, "gave birth to what later became known as Western civilization, long before the greatness of Greece and Rome." "Great civilizations" existed throughout Africa, where "great kings" ruled "in might and wisdom over vast empires." After Egypt declined, magnificent empires arose in West Africa, in

Ghana, Mali, Songhay—all marked by the brilliance and enlightenment of their administrations and the high quality of their libraries and universities.

Other Baseline Essays argue in a similar vein that Africa was the birthplace of science, mathematics, philosophy, medicine, and art and that Europe stole its civilization from Africa and then engaged in "malicious misrepresentation of African society and people . . . to support the enormous profitability of slavery." The coordinator of multicultural/multi-ethnic education in Portland even says that Napoleon deliberately shot off the nose of the Sphinx so that the Sphinx would not be recognized as African.

Like other excluded groups before them, black Americans invoke supposed past glories to compensate for real past and present injustices. Because their exclusion has been more tragic and terrible than that of white immigrants, their quest for self-affirmation is more intense and passionate. In seeking to impose Afrocentric curricula on public schools, for example, they go further than their white predecessors. And belated recognition by white America of the wrongs so viciously inflicted on black Americans has created the phenomenon of white guilt—not a bad thing in many respects, but still a vulnerability that invites cynical exploitation and manipulation.

⟶⟵

I am constrained to feel that the cult of ethnicity in general and the Afrocentric campaign in particular do not bode well either for American education or for the future of the republic. Cultural pluralism is not the issue. Nor is the teaching of Afro-American or African history the issue; of course these are legitimate subjects. The issue is the kind of history that the New York task force, the Portland Baseline essayists, and other Afrocentric ideologues propose for American children. The issue is the teaching of *bad* history under whatever ethnic banner.

One argument for organizing a school curriculum around Africa is that black Africa is the birthplace of science, philosophy, religion, medicine, technology, of the great achievements that have been wrongly ascribed to Western civilization. But is this, in fact, true? Many historians and anthropologists regard Mesopotamia as the cradle of civilization; for a recent discussion, see Charles Keith Maisels' *The Emergence of Civilization.*

The Afrocentrist case rests largely on the proposition that ancient Egypt was essentially a black African country. I am far from being an expert on Egyptian history, but neither, one must add, are the educators and psychologists who push Afrocentrism. A book they often cite is Martin Bernal's *Black Athena,* a vigorous effort by a Cornell professor to document Egyptian influence on ancient Greece. In fact, Bernal makes no very strong claims about Egyptian pigmentation; but, citing Herodotus, he does argue that several Egyptian dynasties "were made up of pharaohs whom one can usefully call black."

Frank M. Snowden Jr., the distinguished black classicist at Howard University and author of *Blacks in Antiquity,* is most doubtful about painting ancient Egypt black. Bernal's assumption that Herodotus meant black in the 20th-century sense is contradicted, Snowden demonstrates, "by Herodotus himself and the copious evidence of other classical authors."

Frank J. Yurco, an Egyptologist at Chicago's Field Museum of Natural History, after examining the evidence derivable from mummies, paintings, statues, and reliefs, concludes in the *Biblical Archaeological Review* that ancient Egyptians, like their modern descendants, varied in color from the light Mediterranean type to the darker brown of upper Egypt to the still darker shade of the Nubians around Aswan. He adds that ancient Egyptians would have found the question meaningless and wonders at our presumption in assigning "our primitive racial labels" to so impressive a culture.

After Egypt, Afrocentrists teach children about the glorious West African emperors, the vast lands they ruled, the civilization they achieved; not, however, about the tyrannous authority they exercised, the ferocity of their wars, the tribal massacres, the squalid lot of the common people, the captives sold into slavery, the complicity with the Atlantic slave trade, the persistence of slavery in Africa after it was abolished in the West. As for tribalism, the word *tribe* hardly occurs in the Afrocentric lexicon; but who can hope to understand African history without understanding it.

The Baseline Essay on science and technology contains biographies of black American scientists, among them Charles R. Drew, who first developed the process for the preservation of blood plasma. In 1950 Drew, grievously injured in an automobile accident in North Carolina, lost quantities of blood. "*Not one* of several nearby white hospitals," according to the Baseline Essay, "would provide the blood transfusions he so desperately [*sic*] needed, and on the way to a hospital that treated Black people, he died." It is a hell of a story —the inventor of blood-plasma storage dead because racist whites denied him his own invention. Only it is not true. According to the biographical entry for Drew written by the eminent black scholar Rayford Logan of Howard for the *Dictionary of American Negro Biography,* "Conflicting versions to the contrary, Drew received prompt medical attention."

Is it really a good idea to teach minority children myths—at least to teach myths as facts?

⋅⟨⊙⟩⋅

The deeper reason for the Afrocentric campaign lies in the theory that the purpose of history in the schools is essentially therapeutic: to build a sense of self-worth among minority children. Eurocentrism, by denying nonwhite children any past in which they can take pride, is held to be the cause of poor academic performance. Race consciousness and group pride are supposed to strengthen a sense of identity and self-respect among nonwhite students.

Why does anyone suppose that pride and inspiration are available only from people of the same ethnicity? Plainly this is not the case. At the age of twelve, Frederick Douglass encountered a book entitled *The Columbian Orator* containing speeches by Burke, Sheridan, Pitt, and Fox. "Every opportunity I got," Douglass later said, "I used to read this book." The orations "gave tongue to interesting thoughts of my own soul, which had frequently flashed through my mind, and died away for want of utterance.... What I got from Sheridan was a bold denunciation of slavery and a powerful vindication of human rights. The reading of these documents enabled me to utter my thoughts." Douglass did not find the fact that the orators were white an insuperable obstacle.

Or hear Ralph Ellison: "In Macon County, Alabama, I read Marx, Freud, T. S. Eliot, Pound, Gertrude Stein, and Hemingway. Books that seldom, if ever, mentioned Negroes were to release me from whatever 'segregated' idea I might have had of my human possibilities." He was freed, Ellison continued, not by the example of Richard Wright and other black writers but by artists who offered a broader sense of life and possibility. "It requires real poverty of the imagination to think that this can come to a Negro only through the example of other Negroes."

Martin Luther King, Jr. did pretty well with Thoreau, Gandhi, and Reinhold Niebuhr as models—and remember, after all, whom King (and his father) were named for. Is Lincoln to be a hero only for those of English ancestry? Jackson only for Scotch-Irish? Douglass only for blacks? Great artists, thinkers, leaders are the possession not just of their own racial clan but of all humanity.

As for self-esteem, is this really the product of ethnic role models and fantasies of a glorious past? Or does it not result from the belief in oneself that springs from achievement, from personal rather than from racial pride?

Columnist William Raspberry notes that Afrocentric education will make black children "less competent in the culture in which they have to compete." After all, what good will it do young black Americans to hear that, because their minds work differently, a first-class education is not for them? Will such training help them to understand democracy better? Help them to fit better into American life?

Will it increase their self-esteem when black children grow up and learn that many of the things the Afrocentrists taught them are not true? Black scholars have tried for years to rescue black history from chauvinistic hyperbole. A. A. Schomburg, the noted archivist of black history, expressed his scorn long ago for those who "glibly tried to prove that half of the world's geniuses have been Negroes and to trace the pedigree of nineteenth-century Americans from the Queen of Sheba."

The dean of black historians in America today is John Hope Franklin. "While a black scholar," Franklin writes, "has a clear responsibility to join in improving the society in which he lives, he must understand the difference between hard-hitting advocacy on the one hand and the highest standards of scholarship on the other."

◆

The use of history as therapy means the corruption of history as history. All major races, cultures, nations have committed crimes, atrocities, horrors at one time or another. Every civilization has skeletons in its closet. Honest history calls for the unexpurgated record. How much would a full account of African despotism, massacre, and slavery increase the self-esteem of black students? Yet what kind of history do you have if you leave out all the bad things?

"Once ethnic pride and self-esteem become the criterion for teaching history," historian Diane Ravitch points out, "certain things cannot be taught." Skeletons must stay in the closet lest outing displease descendants.

No history curriculum in the country is more carefully wrought and better balanced in its cultural pluralism than California's. But hearings before the State Board of Education show what happens when ethnicity is unleashed at the expense of scholarship. At issue were textbooks responsive to the new curriculum. Polish-Americans demanded that any reference to Hitler's Holocaust be accompanied by accounts of equivalent genocide suffered by Polish Christians. Armenian-Americans sought coverage of Turkish massacres; Turkish-Americans objected. Though black historians testified that the treatment of black history was exemplary, Afrocentrists said the schoolbooks would lead to "textbook genocide." Moslems complained that an illustration of an Islamic warrior with a raised scimitar stereotyped Moslems as "terrorists."

"The single theme that persistently ran through the hearings," Ravitch writes, "was that the critics did not want anything taught if it offended members of their group."

In New York the curriculum guide for eleventh-grade American history tells students that there were three "foundations" for the Constitution: the European Enlightenment, the "Haudenosaunee political system," and the antecedent colonial experience. Only the Haudenosaunee political system receives explanatory sub-headings: "a. Influence upon colonial leadership and European intellectuals (Locke, Montesquieu, Voltaire, Rousseau); b. Impact on Albany Plan of Union, Articles of Confederation, and U.S. Constitution."

How many experts on the American Constitution would endorse this stirring tribute to the "Haudenosaunee political system"? How many have heard of that system? Whatever influence the Iroquois confederation may have had on the framers of the Constitution was marginal; on European intellectuals it was marginal to the point of invisibility. No other state curriculum offers this analysis of the making of the Constitution. But then no other state has so effective an Iroquois lobby.

President Franklin Jenifer of Howard University, while saying that "historical black institutions" like his own have a responsibility to teach young people about their particular history and culture, adds, "One has to be very careful when one is talking about public schools.... There should be no creation of nonexistent history."

Let us by all means teach black history, African history, women's history, Hispanic history, Asian history. But let us teach them as history, not as filiopietistic commemoration. When every ethnic and religious group claims a right to approve or veto anything that is taught in public schools, the fatal line is crossed between cultural pluralism and ethnocentrism. An evident casualty is the old idea that whatever our ethnic base, we are all Americans together.

❦

The ethnicity rage in general and Afrocentricity in particular not only divert attention from the real needs but exacerbate the problems. The cult of ethnicity exaggerates differences, intensifies resentments and antagonisms, drives ever deeper the awful wedges between races and nationalities. The end game is self-pity and self-ghettoization. Afrocentricity as expounded by ethnic ideologues implies Europhobia, separatism, emotions of alienation, victimization, paranoia.

If any educational institution should bring people together as individuals in friendly and civil association, it should be the university. But the fragmentation of campuses in recent years into a multitude of ethnic organizations is spectacular—and disconcerting.

Stanford University, writer Dinesh D'Souza reports in his book *Illiberal Education,* has "ethnic theme houses." The University of Pennsylvania gives blacks —6 percent of the enrollment—their own yearbook. Campuses today, according to one University of Pennsylvania professor, have "the cultural diversity of Beirut. There are separate armed camps. The black kids don't mix with the white kids. The Asians are off by themselves. Oppression is the great status symbol."

Oberlin was for a century and a half the model of a racially integrated college. "Increasingly," Jacob Weisberg, an editor at *The New Republic,* reports, "Oberlin students think, act, study, and live apart." Asians live in Asia House, Jews in "J" House, Latinos in Spanish House, blacks in African-Heritage House, foreign students in Third World House. Even the Lesbian, Gay, and Bisexual Union has broken up into racial and gender factions. "The result is separate worlds."

Huddling is an understandable reaction for any minority group faced with new and scary challenges. But institutionalized separatism only crystallizes racial differences and magnifies racial tensions. "Certain activities are labeled white and black," says a black student at Central Michigan University. "If you don't just participate in black activities, you are shunned."

Militants further argue that because only blacks can comprehend the black experience, only blacks should teach black history and literature, as, in the view of some feminists, only women should teach women's history and literature. "True diversity," according to the faculty's Budget Committee at the University of California at Berkeley, requires that courses match the ethnic and gender identities of the professors.

The doctrine that *only* blacks can teach and write black history leads inexorably to the doctrine that blacks can teach and write *only* black history as well as to inescapable corollaries: Chinese must be restricted to Chinese history, women to women's history, and so on. Henry Louis Gates of Duke University criticizes "ghettoized programs where students and members of the faculty sit around and argue about whether a white person can think a black thought?" As for the notion that there is a "mystique" about black studies that requires a person to have black skin in order to pursue them—that, John Hope Franklin observes succinctly, is "voodoo."

The separatist impulse is by no means confined to the black community. Another salient expression is the bilingualism movement. The presumed purpose of bilingualism is transitional: to move non-English-speaking children as quickly as possible from bilingual into all-English classes.

Alas, bilingualism has not worked out as planned: rather the contrary. Testimony is mixed, but indications are that bilingual education retards rather than expedites the movement of Hispanic children into the English-speaking world and that it promotes segregation more than it does integration. Bilingualism "encourages concentrations of Hispanics to stay together and not be integrated," says Alfredo Mathew Jr., a Hispanic civic leader, and it may well foster "a type of apartheid that will generate animosities with others, such as Blacks, in the competition for scarce resources and further alienate the Hispanic from the larger society."

"The era that began with the dream of integration," author Richard Rodriguez has observed, "ended up with scorn for assimilation." The cult of ethnicity has reversed the movement of American history, producing a nation of minorities—or at least of minority spokesmen—less interested in joining with the majority in common endeavor than in declaring their alienation from an oppressive, white, patriarchal, racist, sexist, classist society. The ethnic ideology inculcates the illusion that membership in one or another ethnic group is the basic American experience.

The contemporary sanctification of the group puts the old idea of a coherent society at stake. Multicultural zealots reject as hegemonic the notion of a shared commitment to common ideals. How far the discourse has come from Crevecoeur's "new race," from Tocqueville's civic participation, from Bryce's "amazing solvent," from Myrdal's "American Creed"!

Yet what has held the American people together in the absence of a common ethnic origin has been precisely a common adherence to ideals of democracy and human rights that, too often transgressed in practice, forever goad us to narrow the gap between practice and principle.

America is an experiment in creating a common identity for people of diverse races, religions, languages, cultures. If the republic now turns away from its old goal of "one people," what is its future?—disintegration of the national community, apartheid, Balkanization, tribalization?

POSTSCRIPT

Do Black Students Need an Afrocentric Curriculum?

How can equal educational opportunities be ensured? What are the current realities of the U.S. educational system, and how should inequalities be addressed? Can opportunities for educational success for black schoolchildren be improved by making the changes Asante recommends? Or is there merit to Schlesinger's contention that Afrocentric programs have the potential to teach myths as facts and do not bode well for addressing the problems of race and inequality in the schools or in U.S. society?

For additional insight into the thinking of the opponents presented here, see Asante's "Afrocentric Curriculum," *Educational Leadership* (December 1991) and Schlesinger's "The American Creed: From Dilemma to Decomposition," *New Perspectives Quarterly* (Summer 1991).

Special collections of articles on Afrocentrism may be found in the *Journal of Negro Education* (Summer 1992), *Counseling Psychologist* (April 1989), and *Time* (July 8, 1991). Another good source is the *Journal of Black Studies,* whose December 1990 issue contains two especially interesting pieces: "Afrocentric Cultural Consciousness and African-American Male-Female Relationships," by Yvonne R. Bell et al., and Bayo Oyebade's "African Studies and the Afrocentric Paradigm: A Critique." Also see these probing articles: Midge Decter's "E Pluribus Nihil: Multiculturalism and Black Children," *Commentary* (Fall 1991); Diane Ravitch's "Multiculturalism: E Pluribus Plures," *American Scholar* (Summer 1990); and C. Vann Woodward's "Equal but Separate," *The New Republic* (July 15 and 22, 1991), which reviews Schlesinger's book *The Disuniting of America.*

The Fall 1992 issue of *Western Journal of Black Studies* contains two excellent pieces: Terry Kershaw's "Afrocentrism and the Afrocentric Method" and Norman Harris's "A Philosophical Basis for an Afrocentric Orientation." The Autumn 1992 issue of *Theory into Practice* is devoted to the theme "Literacy and the African-American Learner: The Struggle Between Access and Denial." Three other noteworthy articles are "The Importance of an Afrocentric, Multicultural Curriculum," by Kimberly R. Vann and Jawanza Kunjufu, *Phi Delta Kappan* (February 1993); "Black Curriculum Orientations: A Preliminary Inquiry," by William H. Watkins, *Harvard Educational Review* (Fall 1993); and Gerald Early, "Understanding Afrocentrism," *Civilization* (July/August 1995). A much-discussed refutation of the Afrocentric interpretation of history is *Not Out of Africa* by classics professor Mary Lefkowitz (1996), which Asante critiques in the July–August 1996 issue of *Emerge.*

ISSUE 16

Should Bilingual Education Programs Be Abandoned?

YES: Rosalie Pedalino Porter, from "The Politics of Bilingual Education," *Society* (September/October 1997)

NO: Richard Rothstein, from "Bilingual Education: The Controversy," *Phi Delta Kappan* (May 1998)

ISSUE SUMMARY

YES: Rosalie Pedalino Porter, director of the Research in English Acquisition and Development Institute, offers a close examination of the major research studies and concludes that there is no consistent support for transitional bilingual education programs.

NO: Richard Rothstein, a research associate of the Economic Policy Institute, reviews the history of bilingual education and argues that, although many problems currently exist, there is no compelling reason to abandon these programs.

The issue of accommodating non-English-speaking immigrants by means of a bilingual education program has been controversial since the late 1960s. Events of the past decades have brought about one of the largest influxes of immigrants to the United States in the nation's history. And the disadvantages that non-English-speaking children and their parents experience during the childrens' years of formal schooling has received considerable attention from educators, policymakers, and the popular press.

Efforts to modify this type of social and developmental disadvantage have appeared in the form of bilingual education programs initiated at the local level and supported by federal funding. Approaches implemented include direct academic instruction in the primary language and the provision of language tutors under the English for Speakers of Other Languages (ESOL) program. Research evaluation of these efforts has produced varied results and has given rise to controversy over the efficacy of the programs themselves and the social and political intentions served by them.

A political movement at the national and state levels to establish English as the official language of the United States has gained support in recent years.

Supporters of this movement feel that the bilingual approach will lead to the kind of linguistic division that has torn Canada apart.

Perhaps sharing some of the concerns of the "official English" advocates, increasing numbers of educators seem to be tilting in the direction of the immersion approach. In *Forked Tongue: The Politics of Bilingual Education* (1990), Rosalie Pedalino Porter, a teacher and researcher in the field of bilingual education for over 15 years, issues an indictment of the policies and programs that have been prevalent. One of her central recommendations is that "limited-English children must be placed with specially trained teachers in a program in which these students will be immersed in the English language, in which they have as much contact as possible with English speakers, and in which school subjects, not just social conversations, are the focus of the English-language lessons from kindergarten through twelfth grade."

Amado M. Padilla of Stanford University has examined the rationale behind "official English" and has also reviewed the effectiveness of bilingual education programs (see "English Only vs. Bilingual Education: Ensuring a Language-Competent Society," *Journal of Education,* Spring 1991). Padilla concludes that "the debate about how to assist linguistic minority children should focus on new educational technologies and *not* just on the effectiveness of bilingual education or whether bilingualism detracts from loyalty to this country."

Recent treatments of the problem, prompted by state initiatives and congressional bills, include "English *Über Alles,*" *The Nation* (September 29, 1997); "Ingles, Si," by Jorge Amselle, *National Review* (September 30, 1996); and "Should English Be the Law?" by Robert D. King, *The Atlantic Monthly* (April 1997), in which the author contends that proponents of "official English" are tearing the nation apart.

Linguistics professor Donaldo Macedo, in "English Only: The Tongue-Tying of America," *Journal of Education* (Spring 1991), maintains that the conservative ideology that propels the movement against bilingual education fails to recognize the need to prepare students for the multicultural world of the twenty-first century and relegates the immigrant population to the margins of society.

In the first of the selections that follow, Rosalie Pedalino Porter exposes the political assumptions behind governmental efforts to help non-English-speaking schoolchildren gain language competency. She finds the "politically correct" native-language instruction approach to be mired in a record of poor results. In the second selection, Richard Rothstein looks at the complexities of the problem, cites historal precedents and modern research findings, and makes a plea for removing the debate from the political realm.

Rosalie Pedalino Porter

 **YES**

The Politics of Bilingual Education

In the United States, the efforts being made and the money being invested in the special programs to help immigrant, migrant, and refugee school children who do not speak English when they enter U.S. schools is still largely misguided. The current population of limited-English students is being treated in ways that earlier immigrant groups were not. The politically righteous assumption is that these students cannot learn English quickly and must be taught all their school subjects in their native language for three to seven years while having the English language introduced gradually. Twenty-seven years of classroom experience with this education policy and a growing body of research show no benefits for native-language teaching either in better learning of English or better learning of school subjects. These facts have hardly dented the armor of the true believers in the bilingual education bureaucracy.

Yet some changes and improvements have occurred in this most contentious area of public education. Research reports contribute additional evidence on the poor results of native-language instruction as the superior road to English-language competency for classroom work. But the successful results from programs emphasizing intensive English are beginning to appear, now that some small measure of funding is being allocated to these so-called alternative model programs.

All too often, it remains almost impossible to voice criticism of bilingual education programs without being pilloried as a hater of foreigners and foreign languages and of contributing to the anti-immigrant climate. Another area in which little positive change has occurred in the past few years is in reducing the established power of state education departments to impose education mandates on local school districts. The power of the bilingual education bureaucracy has hardly diminished, even in states like California where the state bilingual education law expired in 1987. However, there are counterforces opposing the seemingly settled idea that native-language programs are the single best solution for limited-English students, and these challenges are growing at the local school level.

Updating the Research

The basic questions posed in the early years of bilingual education still have not found clear-cut answers. Are there measurable benefits for limited-English students when they are taught in their native language for a period of time, both in their learning of the English language for academic achievement and in their mastery of school subjects? Has a clear advantage emerged for a particular pedagogy among the best-known models—transitional bilingual education, English as a Second Language [ESL], structured immersion, two-way, dual immersion, or developmental bilingual programs? There is no more consensus on the answers to these questions than there was five years ago. However, there is growing evidence of an almost total lack of accountability in states that have invested most heavily in bilingual education for the past fifteen or twenty years and have not collected data or evaluated programs to produce answers to the questions raised above. The research that has been published in recent years includes a study by the General Accounting Office, the ALEC [American Legislative Council] Study, a review of the El Paso Bilingual Immersion Project, a longitudinal study of bilingual students in New York, a report of a two-year study of California's bilingual education programs, and a report of a state commission on Massachusetts's bilingual education.

The GAO Study

Every year since the late 1970s, the school enrollment of limited-English students has increased at a faster rate than the rest of the school population, and the costs of special programs nationwide are beginning to be tallied. The U.S. General Accounting Office (GAO) published a study in January 1994 titled *Limited-English Proficiency: A Growing and Costly Educational Challenge Facing Many School Districts* at the request of the Senate Committee on Labor and Human Resources. The GAO study provides an overview of the serious problems confronting U.S. public schools in meeting the needs of limited-English students, new demographics on where these students are concentrated, and a detailed description of five representative school districts with rapidly growing limited-English proficient (LEP) populations.

Briefly, the GAO report highlights these problems in the five districts that are common to all public schools with LEP students:

- Immigrant students are almost 100 percent non-English speaking on arrival in the U.S.
- LEP students arrive at different times during the school year, which causes upheavals in classrooms and educational programs.
- Some high school students have not been schooled in their native lands and lack literacy skills in any language.
- There is a high level of family poverty and transiency and a low level of parental involvement in students' education.
- There is an acute shortage of bilingual teachers and of textbooks and assessment instruments in the native languages.

The information gathered by the GAO study is valuable to educators, researchers, and policy makers. An alarming fact reported in this study is mentioned only in passing and never explained: *Immigrant children account for only 43 percent of the limited-English students in our schools.* Who, then, make up the other 57 percent and why are such large numbers of native-born children classified as limited- or non-English proficient and placed in native-language instruction programs? In a private conversation with one of the GAO regional managers, I was unable to get an explanation for the high percentage of native-born students classified as limited-English. I was told that the GAO had not found an agreed upon definition of what a "limited-English person" is and that they have included in this category children who speak English but who may not read and write it well enough for schoolwork. In that case, there surely are a large number of students who are wrongly enrolled in programs where they are being taught in another language when what they urgently need is remedial help in reading and writing in English. . . .

The ALEC Study

The ALEC Study makes a bold attempt to unravel the mysteries of exactly how many students are served by special programs that aim to remove the language barrier to an equal education, what kinds of programs they are enrolled in, where these students are concentrated—by state—and how much is actually being spent in this special effort. As a former school administrator, I know firsthand that it is quite possible to account for special costs. In the Newton, Massachusetts, public schools annual budget there is an account for bilingual/ ESL programs that covers all the costs incurred for the LEP students: teachers, teacher aides, books, materials, transportation, and administration. One knew what was spent each year, over and above the school costs for general education, and in Newton this averaged about $1,000 per student per year for LEP students. Not all school districts keep such information, and it is not collected consistently by all state education departments because this is not required by the federal government.

Analyzing data from the National Center for Education Statistics, the Office of Bilingual Education and Minority Languages Affairs (OBEMLA), and various other federal and state sources, the ALEC study synthesizes the data to arrive at these conclusions for the 1991–1992 school year:

- On average, all federal funding for education amounts to 6 percent; state and local sources provide roughly 47 percent each.
- Federal funding for bilingual education, $101 million in 1991 and $116 million in 1992, was mostly allocated to native-language instruction programs, giving only 20–30 percent to ESL programs.
- There were 2.3 million limited-English students enrolled in U.S. public schools while only 1.9 million were enrolled in any special language program, leaving 450,000 LEP students without any special language help.

- Of the 1.9 million students in special programs, 60 percent were enrolled in bilingual programs, 22 percent in ESL, and 18 percent in a category labeled "unknown" because states could not describe their special language programs.
- Candidly explaining the difficulties of collecting strictly accurate data, the costs of programs for LEP students are estimated to be $5.5 billion (56 percent) for bilingual programs, $1.9 billion (20 percent) for ESL, and $2.4 billion (24 percent) for unknown programs, totaling $9.9 billion for 1991–1992.
- Projecting that increases in enrollments in 1993 would be the same as recent increases, spending on special language programs would amount to $12 billion in 1993.

The ALEC study draws some tenable conclusions from the data summarized above while it admits that the approximate cost figures may be over- and underestimations of what is actually spent. Both federal and state agencies do give preference to native-language instruction programs over ESL in funding decisions by a wide margin, even though "there is no conclusive research that demonstrates the educational superiority of bilingual education over ESL." Even if the ALEC cost estimates were overestimated, this is only one of several recent reports that point out the widespread lack of accountability in bilingual education. Twenty-seven years of heavy investment in mainly bilingual programs has not produced exact data on how much these programs cost or how successful they are in realizing their goals in student achievement....

The El Paso Bilingual Immersion Project

In 1992, the Institute for Research in English Acquisition and Development (READ) published a monograph by Russell Gersten, John Woodward, and Susan Schneider on the final results of the seven-year longitudinal study of the Bilingual Immersion Project; the results were summarized by Gersten and Woodward in *The Elementary School Journal* in 1995. This evaluation clearly demonstrates advantages for the immersion approach over the transitional bilingual education (TBE) model.

- The Iowa Test of Basic Skills (in English) results for grades 4 and 5 do show superior performance in all academic areas for students in the immersion program over students in the transitional bilingual program.
- By grade 6, 99 percent of immersion students were mainstreamed; at end of 7th grade, 35 percent of TBE students are still in the bilingual program.
- Well-designed bilingual immersion leads to more rapid, more successful, and increased integration of Latino students into the mainstream, with no detrimental effects in any area of achievement for students who took part in this program. The increased integration may lead to

a decrease in high school dropout rates among Hispanic students. Subsequent research is needed to explore the possibility of this effect of immersion programs.

- The major strengths of the bilingual immersion program are its use of contemporary thinking on language acquisition and literacy development and its relatively stress-free approach to the rapid learning of English in the primary grades.
- Teacher questionnaires revealed much greater satisfaction with the early, systematic teaching of English in the immersion program than with the slow introduction of English in the bilingual program.
- Student interviews indicated no significant differences in reactions to the two programs. No evidence emerged, from students, parents, or teachers, that native-language teaching produces a higher level of self-esteem or that early immersion in a second language is more stressful, two of the common beliefs promoted by bilingual education advocates.

Research such as that conducted in El Paso is invaluable in the ongoing debate on program effectiveness. Because the comparison was made between two radically different teaching methods in the same school district with the same population of limited-English students, this study provides incontrovertible proof of the benefits to students of early second-language learning. More recently, the New York City public schools published a report that threw a metaphorical bombshell into the bilingual education camp.

The New York Study

Educational Progress of Students in Bilingual and ESL Programs: A Longitudinal Study, 1990–1994, was published in October 1994 by the Board of Education of the City of New York. New York City invested $300 million in 1993 in bilingual programs where the instruction was given in Spanish, Chinese, Haitian Creole, Russian, Korean, Vietnamese, French, Greek, Arabic, and Bengali—an investment that was not only misguided but harmful to the student beneficiaries, as the results of the longitudinal study show.

The New York City study is important because, like the El Paso study, it examines student achievement in basically different programs in large, urban school districts and because it charts student progress over a period of years. The criteria of student success measured included number of years served in a special language program before exiting to a mainstream classroom, reading level in English, and performance in math. The two groups of limited-English students whose achievement was monitored were (1) Spanish speakers and speakers of Haitian Creole who were enrolled in bilingual classrooms where they received mostly native-language instruction in reading, writing, and school subjects, with brief English-language lessons, (2) students from Russian, Korean, and Chinese language backgrounds who were placed in ESL classes where all instruction is provided through a special English-language curriculum. The study included children who entered school in fall 1990: 11,320 entering kindergarten, 2,053 entering 1st grade, 841 entering 2nd grade, 797 entering 3rd grade, 754 entering 6th grade, and 1,366 entering 9th grade.

As any disinterested observer might have anticipated, there is strong evidence showing that the earlier a second language is introduced, the more rapidly it is learned for academic purposes. Surprising? Not at all, but it flies in the face of the received wisdom of Jim Cummins's theories that were developed, after the fact, to justify bilingual education: the facilitation theory and the threshold hypothesis. With appropriate teaching, children can learn a new language quickly and can learn subject matter taught *in* that language. Reading and writing skills can be mastered, and math can be learned successfully in a second language; here are the proofs from thousands of New York City schoolchildren.

The most riveting outcome of this research reported in the New York study is the fact that "at all grade levels, students served in ESL-only programs exited their programs faster than those served in bilingual programs." The three-year exit rates were as follows: For ESL-only programs, the exit rates were 79.3 percent, 67.5 percent, and 32.7 percent for students who entered school in grades kindergarten, 2, and 6, respectively; for bilingual programs, the exit rates were 51.5 percent, 22.1 percent, and 6.9 percent, respectively.

The three-year exit rates for LEP students who entered kindergarten from different language groups, whether they were in ESL or bilingual programs, [were] reported as follows: 91.8 percent for Korean, 87.4 percent for Russian, 82.6 percent for Chinese, 58.7 percent for Haitian Creole, and 50.6 percent for Spanish.

Differences among language groups remained steady even for students entering the New York schools in the higher grades. Critics of the study, including Luis O. Reyes of the New York City School Board, allege that Korean, Russian, and Chinese background students are from middle-class families and that the social class difference invalidates the study. Socioeconomic data is not reported in the study. We do not know how many of the children in any of the language groups are from poor, working-class, or middle-class families, and we should not make unwarranted assumptions. One could hazard a guess that most immigrant, migrant, and refugee children attending the New York City public schools do not come from affluent families. The undeniable facts are that children from Spanish and Haitian Creole speaking families are mostly funneled into bilingual classrooms, and children from other language groups are mostly assigned to ESL classrooms. I firmly believe that the type of schooling these children receive makes a large difference in their ability to achieve at their own personal best. I believe, even more firmly, that Haitian and Latino children would succeed in mastering English-language skills better and faster and, therefore, join their English-speaking peers in mainstream classes much sooner than is now the case *if they were given the same opportunity given to Russian, Korean, and Chinese students.*

Exiting the special program classrooms more expeditiously is not only a cost consideration but a matter of integration and opportunity. Remaining in substantially segregated bilingual classrooms for several years does not equip students to compete in the broader life of the school and community—in fact it has the opposite effect. . . .

The California Study and Others

... New York City's willingness actually to monitor the progress of LEP students and report the results to the public is much to be praised when we survey the lack of accountability in other parts of the country. The State of California, with 1.2 million limited-English students (43 percent of all LEP students in the United States) and a twenty-year history of involvement with bilingual education, commissioned an evaluation of educational programs for these students. *Meeting the Challenge of Language Diversity: An Evaluation of Programs for Pupils with Limited Proficiency in English,* the published report of a two-year study, 1990–1992, shows generally poor results for bilingual education programs in California and essentially evades the legislature's requirement that it provide "information to determine which model for educating LEP pupils is most effective and cost effective."

Major findings of this study are the following:

1. California public schools do not have valid assessments of the performance for students with limited proficiency in English. Therefore, *the state and the public cannot hold schools accountable for LEP students achieving high levels of performance* (emphasis added).
2. Many schools do not reclassify students (that is, move them from the bilingual programs with appropriate skills to work in mainstream classrooms), keeping them in native-language classrooms well beyond the time when they are fluent in English. "It is not surprising that many students may wait years to be formally retested for program exit and that many others may never be reclassified, going on to the middle school still bearing the LEP label."
3. Junior and senior high school LEP students do not have access to core academic subjects through Sheltered English or ESL. Long stays in bilingual programs in elementary schools delay the effective learning of the English-language literacy skills that are so important for secondary school work.

Meeting the Challenge presents a bleak picture of the disappointing results of twenty years of bilingual education in California. When the Chacon-Moscone Bilingual Bicultural Act of 1976 expired in 1987, the California State Department of Education sent notification to each school district that the intent of the act would still be promoted by state regulations, principally, "that the primary goal of all [bilingual] programs is, as effectively and efficiently as possible, to develop in each child fluency in English." *Meeting the Challenge* fails to tell us how or if this goal is being properly met but offers a variety of excuses for not fulfilling its mission. The weaknesses in this giant instructional system for limited-English students—one out of every five students in California —are of huge proportions. The fact that the State Department of Education has allowed school districts to evade their responsibility to assess and report on student progress shows an unconscionable lack of accountability by this powerful bureaucracy. If we cannot hold the schools responsible for program outcomes after twenty years, then perhaps the responsibility for this failure rests squarely on the state agency that has forcefully promoted the bilingual education policy.

California's high school dropout rates reported in June 1995 amounted to a statewide average of 5 percent per year, or a four-year average of 20 percent of students leaving school before graduation. Discouraging as that seems, the dropout rate for Latino students statewide is even higher—28 percent, compared to 10 percent for Asian students and 12 percent for white students. The four-year dropout rate for the Los Angeles Unified School District, the district enrolling the highest percentage of LEP students in the state, is a shocking 43.6 percent.

In 1993 the Los Angeles Unified School District embarked on a plan to improve its bilingual education programs, partly through expanded teacher training in the native languages of the students (actually, in Spanish only). Clearly, the increased emphasis on native-language instruction has not had any positive effect on the dropout rates for LEP students in the Los Angeles schools. The latest Los Angeles figures on dropout rates by ethnic breakdown, as reported by the State Department of Education in October 1994 for the 1993–1994 school year, are 44.4 percent for Hispanic students, *three-fourths of whom are enrolled in bilingual classes in the district....*

Massachusetts Revisited

Ironically, the Commonwealth of Massachusetts, which passed the first state law mandating native-language teaching in 1971, Chapter 71-A, has an even more dismal record than California in the area of public accountability. Efforts to reform the Transitional Bilingual Education law have been successfully resisted, even though there can hardly be one legislator who has any documented proof for the effectiveness of bilingual education in Massachusetts. A state commission was appointed by Governor Weld to survey the status of bilingual education in the state, and in December 1994 it reported this conclusion:

> We do not know, on the basis of measured outcomes, whether TBE programs in Massachusetts produce good results or poor results. There are no comprehensive data that evaluate the performance of TBE pupils compared with pupils from other groups. This specialized program which accounts for 5% of all pupils in Massachusetts public schools and 17% of all pupils in Boston public schools is not held separately accountable for its performance.

Apparently, the commission has recommended that the state department of education develop new guidelines on accountability as soon as suitable tests are developed. As a veteran Massachusetts educator who has seen many a set of "guidelines" arrive with a flourish and disappear without a trace, I reserve judgment on the latest pronouncements.

Massachusetts probably leads the country in zany educational experiments. I reported earlier on the Cape Verdean project to try to encourage the use of a nonstandard dialect as the classroom language of instruction. The Boston public school system, in its infinite wisdom, now maintains a K–12 bilingual program in Kriolu, a dialect of Portuguese spoken in the Cape Verde Islands that has no alphabet, no written language, and no books. Massachusetts is thought to be the only place in the world to have schoolrooms in which Kriolu is the language of instruction, with Kriolu programs in Boston, Brockton, and New Bedford schools. Portuguese is the official language of education in Cape Verde.

Aside from the minor matters of alphabets, a written language, or books, there are these exquisite complications. Cape Verdean students may speak one of many dialects and not understand Kriolu, as explained by a science teacher in the Dearborn School, Boston, who says: "Sometimes a student gets upset because he's not understanding the Fogo dialect so you have to go back and help him in Kriolu or Portuguese." Communication between the schools and Cape Verdean parents is not improved either. Massachusetts law requires that all paperwork be sent to parents in the student's native language. A teacher at the Condon School, Eileen Fonseca, says it frustrates parents to receive a notice written in Kriolu: "When we send home report cards and matriculation papers in Kriolu, parents complain. This is new to them. They have to have it read three times, or they just ask for Portuguese or English, often so it can be read to them by family or friends." One parent made this comment: "They sent me a letter apparently to tell me something. I never understood what it was trying to say. I called to say that if the intent of the letter is to communicate, it would be better in Portuguese."

The Kriolu Caper makes an amusing, now-I've-heard-everything anecdote, but the enormity of such folly in education policy is no laughing matter. This program neither helps students learn the language or acquire the literacy skills necessary for school achievement, nor does it facilitate communication between school and family. What it does do is foster resentment in the Cape Verdean community, which does not feel respected or understood, a situation similar to the misguided attempt to make black English the language of instruction for African-American schoolchildren two decades ago. The Peoples Republic of Massachusetts is in serious need of a reality check.

Let me conclude with the review of a chapter in *The Emperor Has No Clothes: Bilingual Education in Massachusetts* by Christine Rossell and Keith Baker that summarizes the major studies on the effectiveness of bilingual education and analyzes those studies that are methodologically acceptable.

Social science research in education is, at best, an approximation of true scientific research. Schoolchildren cannot be isolated in laboratory test tubes and studied under pristine conditions, controlling for minute variables. In the area of bilingual education research, the quality of the product is generally acknowledged to be especially low. The elements of a scientifically valid evaluation of a special effort must include, at the minimum:

- random assignment of subjects to avoid self-selection bias
- a control group to compare with the group receiving the special program (treatment)
- pretesting to establish that students in different groups are starting with the same traits—i.e., that all are limited or non-English speakers—or statistical adjustments to account for pre-treatment differences
- posttesting to determine the effect of different treatments

- assurance that one group does not receive extra benefits, aside from the difference in treatments, such as after-school programs or a longer school day.

In the area of bilingual education research, there is the added problem that the label is applied to a range of educational varieties, from the classic model, in which native language instruction is given 80–90 percent of the school day, to the other extreme, in which the teacher may use a word or two of another language on occasion. This complicates the work of analyzing the effects of bilingual programs.

Rossell and Baker read over five hundred studies, three hundred of which were program evaluations. The authors found seventy-two methodologically acceptable studies, that is, studies that show the effect of transitional bilingual education on English-language learning, reading, and mathematics, compared to (1) "submersion" or doing nothing, (2) English as a Second Language, (3) structured immersion in English, and (4) maintenance bilingual education. The authors' overall finding, which is of crucial importance as this is the most current, comprehensive analysis of the research, is that *"there is still . . . no consistent research support for transitional bilingual education as a superior instructional practice for improving the English language achievement of limited-English-proficient children"* (emphasis added).

Richard Rothstein

 **NO**

Bilingual Education: The Controversy

Bilingual education, a preferred strategy for the last 20 years, aims to teach academic subjects to immigrant children in their native languages (most often Spanish), while slowly and simultaneously adding English instruction.[1] In theory, the children don't fall behind in other subjects while they are learning English. When they are fluent in English, they can then "transition" to English instruction in academic subjects at the grade level of their peers. Further, the theory goes, teaching immigrants in their native language values their family and community culture and reinforces their sense of self-worth, thus making their academic success more likely.

In contrast, bilingual education's critics tell the following, quite different, story. In the early 20th century, public schools assimilated immigrants to American culture and imparted workplace skills essential for upward mobility. Children were immersed in English instruction and, when forced to "sink or swim," they swam. Today, however, separatist (usually Hispanic) community leaders and their liberal supporters, opposed to assimilation, want Spanish instruction to preserve native culture and traditions. This is especially dangerous because the proximity of Mexico and the possibility of returning home give today's immigrants the option of "keeping a foot in both camps"—an option not available to previous immigrants who were forced to assimilate. Today's attempts to preserve immigrants' native languages and cultures will not only balkanize the American melting pot but hurt the children upon whom bilingual education is imposed because their failure to learn English well will leave them unprepared for the workplace. Bilingual education supporters may claim that it aims to teach English, but high dropout rates for immigrant children and low rates of transition to full English instruction prove that, even if educators' intentions are genuine, the program is a failure.

The English First Foundation, a lobbying group bent on abolishing bilingual education, states that most Americans "have ancestors who learned English the same way: in classrooms where English was the only language used for all learning activities."[2] According to 1996 Republican Presidential nominee Bob Dole, the teaching of English to immigrants is what "we have done ... since our founding to speed the melting of our melting pot.... We must stop the practice of multilingual education as a means of instilling ethnic pride, or as a therapy

From Richard Rothstein, "Bilingual Education: The Controversy," *Phi Delta Kappan* (May 1998). Adapted from *The Way We Were?* (Century Foundation Press, 1998). Copyright © 1998 by Twentieth Century Fund/Century Foundation. Reprinted by permission.

for low self-esteem, or out of elitist guilt over a culture built on the traditions of the West."[3]

Speaker of the House Newt Gingrich chimed in as well:

> If people had wanted to remain immersed in their old culture, they could have done so without coming to America.... Bilingualism keeps people actively tied to their old language and habits and maximizes the cost of the transition to becoming American.... The only viable alternative for the American underclass is American civilization. Without English as a common language, there is no such civilization.[4]

This viewpoint has commonsense appeal, but it has little foundation in reality.

Bilingual Education: The History

Despite proximity to their homeland, Mexican Americans are no more likely to reverse migrate than were Europeans in the early 20th century. One-third of the immigrants who came here between 1908 and 1924 eventually abandoned America and returned home.[5]

What's more, the immigrants who remained did not succeed in school by learning English. During the last great wave of immigration, from 1880 to 1915, very few Americans succeeded in school, immigrants least of all. By 1930, it was still the case that half of all American 14- to 17-year-olds either didn't make it to high school or dropped out before graduating. The median number of school years completed was 10.

Far from succeeding by immersing themselves in English, immigrant groups did much worse than the native-born, and some immigrant groups did much worse than others. The poorest performers were Italians. According to a 1911 federal immigration commission report, in Boston, Chicago, and New York 80% of native white children in the seventh grade stayed in school another year, but only 58% of Southern Italian children, 62% of Polish children, and 74% of Russian Jewish children did so. Of those who made it to eighth grade, 58% of the native whites went on to high school, but only 23% of the Southern Italians did so. In New York, 54% of native-born eighth-graders made it to ninth grade, but only 34% of foreign-born eighth-graders did so.[6]

A later study showed that the lack of success of immigrants relative to the native-born continued into high school. In 1931, only 11% of the Italian students who entered high school graduated (compared to an estimated graduation rate of over 40% for all students). This was a much bigger native/immigrant gap than we have today.

While we have no achievement tests from that earlier period by which to evaluate relative student performance, I.Q. tests were administered frequently. Test after test in the 1920s found that Italian immigrant students had an average I.Q. of about 85, compared to an average for native-born students of about 102. The poor academic achievement of these Italian Americans led to high rates of "retardation"—that is, being held back and not promoted (this was the origin of the pejorative use of the term "retarded").

A survey of New York City's retarded students (liberally defined so that a child had to be 9 years old to be considered retarded in the first grade, 10 years old in the second grade, and so on), found that 19% of native-born students were retarded in 1908, compared to 36% of Italian students. The federal immigration commission found that the retardation rate of children of non-English-speaking immigrants was about 60% higher than that of children of immigrants from English-speaking countries.[7] The challenge of educating Italian immigrant children was so severe that New York established its first special education classes to confront it. A 1921 survey disclosed that half of all (what we now call) "learning disabled" special education children in New York schools had Italian-born fathers.[8]

As these data show—and as is the case today—some groups did better than others, both for cultural reasons and because of the influence of other socio-economic factors on student achievement. If Italian children did worse, Eastern European Jewish children did better. This is not surprising in light of what we now know about the powerful influence of background characteristics on academic success. In 1910, 32% of Southern Italian adult males in American cities were unskilled manual laborers, but only one-half of 1% of Russian Jewish males were unskilled. Thirty-four percent of the Jews were merchants, while only 13% of the Italians were. In New York City, the average annual income of a Russian Jewish head-of-household in 1910 was $813; a Southern Italian head-of-household averaged $688.[9]

But even with these relative economic advantages, the notion that Jewish immigrant children assimilated through sink-or-swim English-only education is a nostalgic and dangerous myth. In 1910, there were 191,000 Jewish children in the New York City schools; only 6,000 were in high school, and the overwhelming majority of these students dropped out before graduating. As the Jewish writer Irving Howe put it, after reviewing New York school documents describing the difficulties of "Americanizing" immigrant children from 1910 to 1914, "To read the reports of the school superintendents is to grow impatient with later sentimentalists who would have us suppose that all or most Jewish children burned with zeal for the life of the mind."[10] There may have been relatively more such students among the Jewish immigrants than in other immigrant communities, Howe noted, but they were still a minority.

Immersing immigrants in an English-language school program has been effective—usually by the third generation. On the whole, immigrant children spoke their native language; members of the second generation (immigrants' native-born children) were bilingual, but not sufficiently fluent in English to excel in school; members of the third generation were fluent in English and began to acquire college educations. For some groups (e.g., Greek Americans), the pattern more often took four generations; for others (e.g., Eastern European Jews), many in the second generation may have entered college.

This history is not a mere curiosity, because those who advocate against bilingual education today often claim that we know how to educate immigrant children because we've done it before. However, if we've never successfully educated the first or even second generation of children from peasant or unskilled immigrant families, we are dealing with an unprecedented task, and history can't guide us.

To understand the uniqueness of our current challenge, compare the enormous—by contemporary standards—dropout rate of New York City Jewish students in 1910 with that of Mexican students in the Los Angeles school district today. Like New York in 1910, Los Angeles now is burdened with a rising tide of immigrants. In 1996, there were 103,000 Hispanic students in grades 9–12 in Los Angeles (out of the city's total K–12 Hispanic population of 390,000). Hispanic high school students were about 26% of the total Hispanic student population in Los Angeles in 1996,[11] compared to 3% for Jews in New York in 1910 (only 6,000 high school students out of 191,000 total Jewish enrollment). In Los Angeles today, 74% of Mexican-born youths between the ages of 15 and 17 are still in high school; 88% of Hispanic youths from other countries are still in attendance.[12] More than 70% of Hispanic immigrants who came to the United States prior to their sophomore year actually complete high school (compared to a 94% high school completion rate for whites and a 92% rate for blacks).[13] English immersion programs for Jews early in this century (and certainly similar programs for Italians) cannot teach us anything that would help improve on today's immigrant achievement or school completion, much of which may be attributable to bilingual education programs, even if imperfectly administered.

If the notion is misleading that English immersion led previous generations of immigrants to academic success, so too is the claim that bilingual education repudiates the assimilationist approach of previous immigrants. In reality, today's Hispanics are not the first to seek bicultural assimilation. Some 19th- and early 20th-century European immigrants also fought for and won the right to bilingual education in the public schools.[14] Native-language instruction was absent from 1920 until the mid-1960s only because a fierce anti-German (and then anti-immigrant) reaction after World War I succeeded in banishing it from American classrooms. Even foreign-language instruction for native-born students was banned in most places. If Chicago's Bismarck Hotel found it necessary to rename itself the "Mark Twain," it should not be surprising that bilingual education programs were also abolished.

Before World War I, immigrant groups often pressed public schools to teach children in their native language. The success of these groups depended more on whether adult immigrant activists had political power than on a pedagogical consensus. The immigrants' objective, as it is today, was to preserve a fragment of ethnic identity in children for whom the pull of American culture seemed dangerously irresistible. In this, they were supported by many influential educators. William Harris, the school superintendent in St. Louis and later U.S. commissioner of education, argued for bilingual education in the 1870s, stating that "national memories and aspirations, family traditions, customs and habits, moral and religious observances cannot be suddenly removed or changed without disastrously weakening the personality." Harris established the first "kindergarten" in America, taught solely in German, to give immigrant students a head start in the St. Louis schools.[15]

Nineteenth-century immigrant parents were often split over the desirability of bilingual education, as immigrant parents are split today. Many recognized that children were more likely to succeed ff schools' use of the native language validated the culture of the home. But others felt that their children's education would be furthered if they learned in English only.

The first bilingual public school in New York City was established in 1837 to prepare German-speaking children for eventual participation in regular English schools. The initial rule was that children could remain in German-language instruction only for 12 months, after which they would transfer to a regular school. But the German teacher resisted this rule, believing that, before transferring, the children needed more than the limited English fluency they had acquired after a year of German instruction. The record is unclear about how often the rule was stretched.

Many immigrant children, not just Germans, did not attend school at all if they could not have classes in their native language. In his 1840 address to the New York legislature, Gov. William Seward (later Lincoln's secretary of state) explained that the importance of attracting immigrants to school—and of keeping them there—motivated his advocacy of expanded native-language instruction: "I do not hesitate to recommend the establishment of schools in which [immigrant children] may be instructed by teachers speaking the same language with themselves." Only by so doing, Gov. Seward insisted, could we "qualify . . . [them] for the high responsibilities of citizenship."

Buoyed by Seward's endorsement, Italian parents in New York City demanded a native-language school as well, and in 1843 the Public School Society established a committee to determine whether one should be established. The committee recommended against an Italian-language school, claiming the Italian community was itself divided. "Information has been obtained," the committee stated, "that the more intelligent class of Italians do not desire such a school, and that, like most [but not, apparently, all] of the better class of Germans, they would prefer that those of their countrymen who come here with good intentions should be Americanized as speedily as possible."[16]

Bilingual education, though sometimes controversial, was found nationwide. In Pennsylvania, German Lutheran churches established parochial schools when public schools would not teach in German; in 1838, Pennsylvania law converted these German schools to public schools. Then, in 1852, a state public school regulation specified that "if any considerable number of Germans desire to have their children instructed in their own language, their wishes should be gratified."[17]

In 1866, succumbing to pressure from politically powerful German immigrants, the Chicago Board of Education decided to establish a German-language school in each area of the city where 150 parents asked for it. By 1892 the board had hired 242 German-language teachers to teach 35,000 German-speaking children, one-fourth of Chicago's total public school enrollment. In 1870, a public school established in Denver, Colorado, was taught entirely in German. An 1872 Oregon law permitted German-language public schools to be established in Portland whenever 100 voters petitioned for such a school. Maryland, Iowa, Indiana, Kentucky, Ohio, and Minnesota also had bilingual education laws, either statewide or applying only to cities with large immigrant populations. In Nebraska, enabling legislation for bilingual education was enacted for the benefit of German immigrant children as late as 1913.[18]

There was considerable variation in how these programs arranged what we now call the "transition" to English. In St. Louis, Harris' system introduced English gradually, beginning in the first grade. The 1888 report of the Missouri supervisor of public instruction stated that "in some districts the schools are taught in German for a certain number of months and then in English, while in others German is used part of the day and English the rest. Some of the teachers are barely able to speak the English language." Ohio's 1870 rules provided that the lower grades in German-language public schools should be bilingual (half the instructional time in grades 1 through 4 could be in German), but in grades 5 through 8 native-language instruction had to be reduced to one hour a day. Baltimore permitted public schools in the upper grades to teach art and music in German only, but geography, history, and science had to be taught in both English and German. In some midwestern communities, there was resistance to any English instruction: an 1846 Wisconsin law insisted that public schools in Milwaukee must at least teach English (as a foreign language) as one academic subject.[19]

While Germans were most effective in demanding public support for native-language instruction, others were also successful. In Texas in the late 19th century, there were seven Czech-language schools supported by the state school fund. In California, a desire by the majority to segregate Chinese children seemed to play more of a role than demands by the Chinese community for separate education. San Francisco established a Chinese-language school in 1885; the city later established segregated Indian, Mongolian, and Japanese schools.[20]

San Francisco's German, Italian, and French immigrants, on the other hand, were taught in their native languages in regular public schools. Here, bilingual education was a strategy designed to lure immigrant children into public schools from parochial schools where they learned no English at all. According to San Francisco's school superintendent in 1871, only if offered native-language instruction could immigrant children be brought into public schools, where, "under the care of American teachers," they could be "molded in the true form of American citizenship."[21]

Support for bilingual education was rarely unanimous or consistent. In San Francisco, the election of an "anti-immigrant" Republican school board majority in 1873 led to the abolition of schools in which French and German had been the primary languages of instruction and to the firing of all French- and German-speaking teachers. After protests by the immigrant community, bilingual schools were reestablished in 1874. In 1877, the California legislature enacted a prohibition of bilingual education, but the governor declined to sign it. William Harris' bilingual system in St. Louis was dismantled in 1888, after redistricting split the German vote and the Irish won a school board majority.[22]

In 1889, Republican Gov. William Hoard of Wisconsin sponsored legislation to ban primary-language instruction in public and private schools, claiming the support of German immigrant parents. The *Milwaukee Sentinel* published a front-page story about "a German in Sheboygan County... who sent his children away to school in order that they might learn English." The father, reported the *Sentinel*, complained that "in the public schools of the town, German teachers, who... did not know English... had been employed..., [and] he felt it essential to the welfare of his children, who expected to remain citizens of this country, to know English."[23]

But both the newspaper and Wisconsin's Republican politicians had misjudged the immigrants' sentiments. In response to the anti-bilingual law, enraged German Americans (who had previously supported Republican candidates) mobilized to turn the statehouse over to Democrats and to convert the state's 7-to-2 Republican majority in Congress to a Democratic majority of 8-to-1. The Democrats promptly repealed the anti-bilingual education law.

An almost identical series of events took place in Illinois, where formerly Republican German American voters mobilized in both East St. Louis and Chicago to elect a liberal Democrat, Peter Altgeld, governor in 1890, largely because of his bilingual school language policy. These upheavals in two previously safe Republican states played an important role in the election of Democrat Grover Cleveland as President in 1892. Nonetheless, the controversy continued, and in 1893 the *Chicago Tribune* began a new campaign against German-language instruction. In a compromise later that year, German instruction was abolished in the primary grades but retained in the upper grades, while Chicago's mayor promised German Americans a veto over future school board appointments to ensure that erosion of primary-language instruction would not continue.[24]

But these controversies ended with World War I. Six months after the armistice, the Ohio legislature, spurred by Gov. James Cox, who was to be the Democratic Presidential candidate in 1920, banned all German from the state's elementary schools. The language posed "a distinct menace to Americanism," Cox insisted. The *New York Times* editorialized in 1919 that, although some parents "want German to be taught [because it] pleases their pride..., it does not do their children any good." Within the following year, 15 states in which native-language instruction had flourished adopted laws requiring that all teaching be in English. By 1923, 35 states had done so.[25] Only when Nebraska went so far as to ban native-language instruction in parochial as well as public schools did the Supreme Court, in 1923, strike down an English-only law.[26]

During the next 30 years, bilingual instruction had its ups and downs, even where English was not the native language. In 1950, Louisiana first required English, not French, to be the language of public school instruction. In the Southwest, where teaching in Spanish had long been common, the practice continued in some places and was abolished in others. Tucson established a bilingual teaching program in 1923, and Burbank established one in 1931. New Mexico operated bilingual schools throughout most of the 20th century, up until the 1950s. The state even required the teaching of Spanish to English-speaking children in elementary school. But in 1918, Texas made teaching in Spanish a crime, and, while the law was not consistently enforced (especially along the Mexican border), as recently as 1973 a Texas teacher was indicted for not teaching history in English.[27] In the same year, Texas reversed itself and adopted bilingual education as its strategy.

When bilingual education began to reemerge in the 1970s—spurred by a Supreme Court finding that schools without special provisions for educating language-minority children were not providing equal education—the nation's memory of these precedents had been erased. Today many Americans blithely repeat the myth that, until the recent emergence of separatist minority activists and their liberal supporters, the nation had always immersed its immigrant children in nothing but English and this method had proved its effectiveness.

Bilingual Education: Mixed Evidence

This mixed history, however, does not prove that bilingual education is effective, any more so than English immersion or intense English-language instruction. To an unbiased layperson, the arguments of both advocates and opponents of bilingual education seem to make sense. On the one hand, it's reasonable to insist that children who don't speak English continue their education in a language they understand in history, literature, math, and science, while they learn English. It's also reasonable to expect, however, that this might make it too tempting to defer English-language instruction. Moreover, the best way to do something difficult—e.g., making the transition to English—is simply to do it without delay. It makes sense to acknowledge that children may adapt better to school if the school's culture is not in conflict with that of the home. But some immigrant parents may be more intent on preserving native culture for their children than are the children themselves.

Modern research findings on bilingual education are mixed. As with all educational research, it is so difficult to control for complex background factors that affect academic outcomes that no single study is ultimately satisfying. Bilingual education advocates point to case studies of primary-language programs in Calexico, California; Rock Point, Arizona; Santa Fe, New Mexico; New Haven, Connecticut; and elsewhere that show that children advance further in both English and other academic subjects when native-language instruction is used and the transition to English is very gradual. Opponents point to case studies in Redwood City and Berkeley, California; in Fairfax, Virginia; and elsewhere that prove that immersion in English or rapid and intensive English instruction is most effective.[28] Overall, the conflicting evidence from these case studies does not suggest that abolition of bilingual education or even the substitution of parental choice for pedagogical expertise in determining whether bilingual approaches should be used would improve things much.

The problem is especially complex because not only economic factors but also generational variation apparently affects the achievement of immigrant youths. In 1936, the principal of a high school in New York City that enrolled large numbers of Italian immigrants wrote:

> The problem of juvenile delinquency... baffles all the forces of organized society.... The highest rate of delinquency is characteristic of immigrant communities.... The delinquent is usually the American-born child of

foreign-born parents, not the immigrant himself. Delinquency, then, is fundamentally a second-generation problem. This intensifies the responsibility of the school.[29]

The same is true today. The challenge now facing immigrant educators is that academic achievement for second-generation Hispanic and Asian children is often below that of children who arrive in the U.S. as immigrants themselves.[30] Many of these children of the second generation seem to speak English, but they are fully fluent in neither English nor their home language. Many of their parents, frustrated that their own ambition has not been transmitted to their children, may become convinced that only English immersion will set their children straight, while others seek bilingual solutions to prevent the corruption of American culture from dampening their children's ambition.

In the absence of persuasive evidence, the issue has become politicized. In a country as large as ours, with as varied experience, there is virtually no limit to the anecdotes and symbols that can be invoked as substitutes for evidence.

Opponents of bilingual education promote Hispanic parents to the media when they claim they want their children to learn English without bilingual support; the clear implication is that only liberal ideologues and separatists support native-language instruction. These claims, like those circulated by the *Milwaukee Sentinel* a century ago, may not reflect the feelings of most parents. And the technology of teaching a new language to immigrant children is complex; both bilingual education advocates and opponents claim their goal is full English literacy as rapidly as possible. But there's no reason to expect that politicized parent groups are the best judges of language acquisition research.

There are also successful adult immigrants who brag of their English fluency, acquired either with or without bilingual education. As always, such anecdotal evidence should be treated with caution. Richard Rodriguez' autobiography, *Hunger of Memory*, describes his successful education in an English-only environment. But Rodriguez, unlike most immigrants, was raised in a predominantly English-speaking neighborhood and was the only Spanish speaker in his class.[31] His experience may be relevant for some immigrants, but not relevant for many others.

Whichever method is, in fact, more effective for most immigrant children, there will be many for whom the other method worked well. It may be the case that immigrant children's social and economic background characteristics should affect the pedagogy chosen. Even if some Russian Jewish immigrants did not require bilingual education to graduate from high school, perhaps Italians would have progressed more rapidly if they'd had access to bilingual instruction. Today, the fact that some (though not all) Asian immigrants seem to progress rapidly in school without native-language support provides no relevant evidence about whether this model can work well for Mexican or Caribbean children, especially those low on the ladder of socioeconomic status and those whose parents have little education. Nor does it tell us much about what the best pedagogy would be for Asians who generally do less well in school, such as Hmong, Laotian, and Cambodian children.[32]

It is certain, however, that the American "melting pot" has never been endangered by pluralist efforts to preserve native languages and cultures.

Bilingual instruction has never interfered with the powerful assimilationist influences that overwhelm all children whose parents migrate here. And this is equally true of Spanish-speaking children today.

After the last 20 years of bilingual education throughout America, Spanish-speaking children continue to assimilate. From 1972 to 1995, despite rapidly accelerating immigration (more Hispanic youths are first-generation immigrants today than 20 years ago), the Hispanic high school completion rate has crept upward (from 66% to 70%). Hispanic high school graduates who enroll in college jumped from 45% to 54% (for non-Hispanic whites, it's now 64%). And the number of Hispanic high school graduates who subsequently complete four years of college jumped from 11% to 16% (for non-Hispanic whites, it's now 34%).[33] A study of the five-county area surrounding Los Angeles, the most immigrant-affected community in the nation, found that from 1980 to 1990, the share of U.S.-born Hispanics in professional occupations grew from 7% to 9%, the share in executive positions grew from 7% to 10%, and the share in other administrative and technical jobs grew from 24% to 26%.[34] Overall, 55% of U.S.-born Hispanics are in occupations for which a good education is a necessity, in an area where bilingual education has been practiced for the last generation.

Perhaps we can do better. Perhaps we would do better with less bilingual education. But perhaps not. All we can say for sure is that the data reveal no apparent crisis, and the system for immigrant education with which we've been muddling through, with all its problems, does not seem to be in a state of collapse.

The best thing that could happen to the bilingual education debate would be to remove it from the political realm. Sound-bite pedagogy is no cure for the complex interaction of social, economic, and instructional factors that determine the outcomes of contemporary American schools.

Notes

1. Technically, "bilingual education" refers to all programs designed to give any support to non-English-speaking children, including programs whose main focus is immersion in English-speaking classrooms. In public debate, however, the term generally refers to only one such program, "transitional bilingual education (TBE)," in which native-language instruction in academic subjects is given to non-English speakers. In this article, I use the term in its nontechnical sense to refer only to "TBE" programs.

2. Web site, English First Foundation: http://englishfirst.org.

3. Mark Pitsch, "Dole Takes Aim at 'Elitist' History Standards," *Education Week*, 13 September 1995, p. 18.

4. Newt Gingrich, *To Renew America* (New York: HarperCollins, 1995), pp. 161–62.

5. Irving Howe, *World of Our Fathers* (New York: Simon and Schuster, 1983), p. 58.

6. Michael R. Olneck and Marvin Lazerson, "The School Achievement of Immigrant Children: 1900–1930," *History of Education Quarterly*, Winter 1974, pp. 453–82, Tables 3, 5, 6.

7. David K. Cohen, "Immigrants and the Schools," *Review of Educational Research*, vol. 40, 1970, pp. 13–27.

8. Seymour B. Sarason and John Doris, *Educational Handicap, Public Policy, and Social History* (New York: Free Press, 1979), pp. 155–56, 340–51.

9. Olneck and Lazerson, Tables 11 and 12.

10. Howe, pp. 277–78.

11. *Fall 1995 Preliminary Ethnic Survey* (Los Angeles: Information Technology Division, Los Angeles Unified School District, Publication No. 124, 1996).

12. Georges Vernez and Allan Abrahamse, *How Immigrants Fare in U.S. Education* (Santa Monica, Calif.: RAND Corporation, 1996), Table 3.2.

13. These figures are not strictly comparable; estimates are based on data in Vernez and Abrahamse, Table 4.2, and in National Center for Education Statistics, *Dropout Rates in the United States: 1995* (Washington, D.C.: Office of Educational Research and Improvement, U.S. Department of Education, NCES 97–473, 1997), Table 9.

14. Native-language instruction in public schools was also common in the Southwest, particularly in Texas, New Mexico, and Arizona, which were formerly part of Mexico and whose native populations, not their immigrants, were originally Spanish-speaking Mexicans. It was also common in Louisiana, where French-language public schools were established well after the Louisiana Purchase to preserve native French culture.

15. Diego Castellanos, *The Best of Two Worlds: Bilingual-Bicultural Education in the United States* (Trenton: New Jersey State Department of Education, CN 500, 1983), pp. 23–25.

16. Sarason and Doris, pp. 180–81, 194.

17. Heinz Kloss, *The American Bilingual Tradition* (Rowley, Mass.: Newbury House, 1977), pp. 149–50.

18. Ibid., pp. 61, 86, 180; Castellanos, p. 19; and Mary J. Herrick, *The Chicago Schools: A Social and Political History* (Beverly Hills, Calif.: Sage, 1971), p. 61.

19. Kloss, pp. 69, 86, 158–59, 190; and Castellanos, pp. 24–25.

20. Kloss, pp. 177–78, 184.

21. Castellanos, p. 23; and Paul E. Peterson, *The Politics of School Reform, 1870–1940* (Chicago: University of Chicago Press, 1985), p. 55.

22. Peterson, pp. 55–56; Castellanos, p. 25; and James Crawford, *Bilingual Education: History, Politics, Theory, and Practice* (Trenton, N.J.: Crane Publishing Company, 1989), p. 22.

23. "The School Question," *Milwaukee Sentinel,* 27 November 1889.

24. Herrick, p. 61; Kloss, p. 89; Peterson, pp. 10, 58; William F. Whyte, "The Bennett Law Campaign in Wisconsin," *Wisconsin Magazine of History,* vol. 10, 1927, pp. 363–90; and Bernard Mehl, "Educational Criticism: Past and Present," *Progressive Education,* March 1953, p. 154.

25. Crawford, pp. 23–24; and David Tyack, "Constructing Difference: Historical Reflections on Schooling and Social Diversity," *Teachers College Record,* Fall 1993, p. 15.

26. *Meyer v. Nebraska,* 262 US 390 (1923).

27. Castellanos, pp. 43, 49; Crawford, p. 26; and idem, *Hold Your Tongue* (Reading, Mass.: Addison-Wesley, 1992), p. 72.

28. See, for example, Rudolph Troike, "Research Evidence for the Effectiveness of Bilingual Education," *NABE Journal,* vol. 3, 1978, pp. 13–24; *The Bilingual Education Handbook: Designing Instruction for LEP Students* (Sacramento: California Department of Education, 1990), p. 13; Iris Rotberg, "Some Legal and Research Considerations in Establishing Federal Bilingual Policy in Bilingual Education," *Harvard Educational Review,* May 1982, pp. 158–59; and Rosalie Pedalino Porter,

Forked Tongue: The Politics of Bilingual Education (New York: Basic Books, 1990) p. 141.

29. Leonard Covello, "A High School and Its Immigrant Community—A Challenge and an Opportunity," *Journal of Educational Sociology,* February 1936, p. 334.

30. Ruben G. Rumbaut, "The New Californians: Research Findings on the Educational Progress of Immigrant Children," in idem and Wayne Cornelius, eds., *California's Immigrant Children: Theory, Research, and Implications for Educational Policy* (San Diego: Center for U.S.-Mexican Studies, University of California, 1995).

31. For a discussion of Rodriguez as prototype, see Stephen D. Krashen, *Under Attack: The Case Against Bilingual Education* (Culver City, Calif.: Language Education Associates, 1996), p. 19.

32. Rumbaut, Table 2.6.

33. *Dropout Rates in the United States: 1995,* Table A–37; and National Center for Education Statistics, *The Condition of Education 1997* (Washington, D.C.: U.S. Department of Education, NCES 97–388, 1997), Indicators 8, 22.

34. Gregory Rodriguez, *The Emerging Latino Middle Class* (Malibu, Calif.: Pepperdine University Institute for Public Policy, 1996), Figure 22.

POSTSCRIPT

Should Bilingual Education Programs Be Abandoned?

Research comparing the effectiveness of the several approaches to helping linguistically disadvantaged students remains inconclusive. At the same time, the effort is clouded by the political agendas of those who champion first-language instruction and those who insist on some version of the immersion strategy. Politics and emotional commitments aside, what must be placed first on the agenda are the needs of the students and the value of native language in a child's progress through school.

Some books to note are Jane Miller's *Many Voices: Bilingualism, Culture and Education* (1983), which includes a research review; Kenji Hakuta's *Mirror of Language: The Debate on Bilingualism* (1986); *Bilingual Education: A Sourcebook* by Alba N. Ambert and Sarah E. Melendez (1985); and *Sink or Swim: The Politics of Bilingual Education* by Colman B. Stein, Jr. (1986). Thomas Weyr's book *Hispanic U.S.A.: Breaking the Melting Pot* (1988) presents a detailed plan of action in light of the prediction that "by the year 2000 as many people in the U.S. will be speaking Spanish as they will English."

A number of pertinent articles may be found in the March 1989 issue of *The American School Board Journal,* the March 1988 issue of *The English Journal,* and the Summer 1988 issue of *Equity and Excellence.* Some especially provocative articles are "Bilingual Education: A Barrier to Achievement," by Nicholas Sanchez, *Bilingual Education* (December 1987); " 'Official English': Fear or Foresight?" by Nancy Bane, *America* (December 17, 1988); and "The Language of Power," by Yolanda T. DeMola, *America* (April 22, 1989).

More recent articles include Charles L. Glenn's "Educating the Children of Immigrants," *Phi Delta Kappan* (January 1992); David Corson's "Bilingual Ed Policy and Social Justice," *Journal of Education Policy* (January–March 1992); and Mary McGroarty's "The Societal Context of Bilingual Education," *Educational Researcher* (March 1992). The Fall 1993 *Peabody Journal of Education* features a number of articles devoted to the theme "Trends in Bilingual Education at the Secondary School Level." More recent articles include David Hill's "English Spoken Here," *Teacher Magazine* (January 1998); Jerry Cammarata's "Tongue-Tied," *American School Board Journal* (June 1997); and Glenn Garvin's "Loco, Completamente Loco," *Reason* (January 1998). Donaldo Macedo offers a wide-ranging critique of current educational practices in "Literacy for Stupidification: The Pedagogy of Big Lies," *Harvard Educational Review* (Summer 1993). Also see his book *Literacies of Power: What Americans Are Not Allowed to Know* (1994).

Of especial note are "Americanization and the Schools," by E. D. Hirsch, Jr., *The Clearing House* (January/February 1999) and Lynn W. Zimmerman's "Bilingual Education As a Manifestation of an Ethic of Caring" and Gail L. Thompson's "The Real Deal on Bilingual Education," both in *Educational Horizons* (Winter 2000).

ISSUE 17

Does School Violence Warrant a Zero-Tolerance Policy?

YES: Albert Shanker, from "Restoring the Connection Between Behavior and Consequences," *Vital Speeches of the Day* (May 15, 1995)

NO: Pedro A. Noguera, from "The Critical State of Violence Prevention," *The School Administrator* (February 1996)

ISSUE SUMMARY

YES: Albert Shanker, president of the American Federation of Teachers (AFT), advocates a "get tough" policy for dealing with violent and disruptive students in order to send a clear message that all students are responsible for their own behavior.

NO: Professor of education Pedro A. Noguera maintains that the AFT's zero-tolerance stance and other "armed camp" attitudes fail to deal with the heart of the problem and do not build an atmosphere of trust.

Beyond basic classroom discipline and general civility lies the more serious realm of violence in schools: unpredictable acts of violence against students and teachers and what Jackson Toby refers to as everyday school violence fueled by a disorderly educational and social atmosphere. Toby, in "Everyday School Violence: How Disorder Fuels It," *American Educator* (Winter 1993/1994), states, "The concept of 'school disorder' suggests that schools, like families, also vary in their cohesiveness and effectiveness. What school disorder means in concrete terms is that one or both of two departures from normality exists: A significant proportion of students do not seem to recognize the legitimacy of the rules governing the school's operation and therefore violate them frequently; and/or a significant proportion of students defy the authority of teachers and other staff members charged with enforcing the rules." Toby and other experts feel that teachers lost much of their authority, especially in inner-city high schools, during the 1960s and 1970s when school systems stopped standing behind teachers' disciplinary actions and many teachers became afraid of confronting aggressive student behavior.

A 1978 report to Congress by the National Institute of Education, *Violent Schools—Safe Schools,* documented widespread incidents of theft, assaults, weapon possession, vandalism, rape, and drug use in America's schools. These findings helped lead to the current period of security guards, metal detectors, book bag searches, locker raids, and pursuit of armed teenagers in school halls. "Zero tolerance" has emerged as a rallying cry of the 1990s—zero tolerance for any weapons in school (handguns, semiautomatics, knives, and, in a few cases, fingernail files) and zero tolerance for any drugs in school (crack cocaine, pot, alcohol, and, in some cases, Midol or Tylenol).

These measures have sparked a heated debate over the conflict between students' rights and the need to protect students and professionals from violence. We pride ourselves on being a tolerant society, but it has become obvious that new lines must be drawn. Daniel Patrick Moynihan, senior senator from New York, in "Defining Deviancy Down," *The American Scholar* (Winter 1993), contends that we have become accustomed to alarming levels of criminal and destructive behavior and that the absence of meaningful punishment for those who commit violent acts reinforces the belief that violence is an appropriate way to settle disputes among members of society.

Congressional passage of the Gun-Free Schools Act in 1994 placed an automatic one-year expulsion on weapon-carrying students and demanded referral of offenders to the criminal justice or juvenile delinquency system after due process procedures are carried out. According to Kathleen Vail, in "Ground Zero," *The American School Board Journal* (June 1995), some child advocates, educators, and parents feel that such zero-tolerance policies do not allow enough room for exceptions, especially when young children are involved. There is also a concern that get-tough measures weaken the implementation of conflict-resolution strategies aimed at uncovering deeper explanations of aggressive behavior.

A flurry of articles on school violence has appeared in recent years. Among the best are Jackson Toby's "Getting Serious About School Discipline," *The Public Interest* (Fall 1998); "The Dark Side of Zero Tolerance," by Russ Skiba and Reece Peterson, *Phi Delta Kappan* (January 1999); Abigail Thernstrom's "Courting Disorder in the Schools," *The Public Interest* (Summer 1999); Michael Easterbrook's "Taking Aim at Violence," *Psychology Today* (July/August 1999); "Zero Tolerance for Zero Tolerance," by Richard L. Curwin and Allen N. Mendler, *Phi Delta Kappan* (October 1999); W. Michael Martin's "Does Zero Mean Zero?" *American School Board Journal* (March 2000); and two articles on the controversial practice of profiling potentially violent students in *The School Administrator* (February 2000).

The American Federation of Teachers (AFT) has strongly supported zero-tolerance policies. In the first of the following selections, the late Albert Shanker, former AFT president, makes the case for tough measures to restore safety and confidence in the public schools and thereby stem the exodus of concerned parents. In the second selection, Pedro A. Noguera questions the effectiveness of such measures and offers alternatives that he feels would better address the causes of violence and the social factors that contribute to it.

Albert Shanker

 **YES**

Restoring the Connection Between Behavior and Consequences

Ican't think of a more important topic.... [T]here have been and will be a number of conferences on this issue. I can assure you, all of the other conferences resemble each other, and this one will be very different. It will have a very different point of view.

We have had, over the last decade or more, a national debate on the issue of school quality. And there is a national consensus that we need to do a lot better. We are probably doing better than we used to, but we're not doing as well as other industrial countries. And in order to do well, we are going to have to do some of the things that those other countries are doing, such as develop high standards, assessments related to those standards, and a system of consequences so that teachers and youngsters and parents know that school counts. School makes a difference, whether it's getting a job or getting into a college or getting into a training program.

We're well on the way. It's going to take time, but we're on the way to bringing about the improvement that we need. But you can have a wonderful curriculum and terrific assessments and you can state that there are consequences out there but none of this is going to do much good in terms of providing youngsters with an education if we don't meet certain basic obvious conditions. And those conditions are simply that you have to have schools that are safe and classrooms where there is sufficient order so that the curriculum means something. Without that, all of this stuff is nonsense. You can deliver a terrific curriculum, but if youngsters are throwing things, cursing and yelling and punching each other, then the curriculum doesn't mean anything in that classroom. The agenda is quite different.

And so we have a very interesting phenomenon. We have members of Congress and governors and state legislators talking about choice and vouchers and charter schools, and you know what the big incentive is for those issues. Parents are not really pushing for these things, except in conditions where their children seem to be unsafe or in conditions where they can't learn. And then they say, well, look, if you can't straighten things out here, then give me a chance to take my youngster somewhere else. And so we're about to put in place a ridiculous situation. We're going to create a system of choice and vouchers, so that 98 percent of the kids who behave can go someplace and be safe. And we're going to leave the two percent who are violent and disruptive to take over the schools. Now, isn't it ridiculous to move 98 percent of the kids, when all you have to do is move two or three percent of them and the other 98 percent would be absolutely fine?

Now this is a problem which has a number of aspects and I want to talk about them. First, there is, of course, the problem of extreme danger, where we are dealing with violence or guns or drugs within the school. And, as we look to the schools, what we find is that the schools seem to be unable to handle this. We had headlines here in DC... saying that the mayor and school officials say they don't know what else to do. In other words, they've done everything that they can, and the guns, and the knives, and the drugs are still there. So, it just happens that they have actually said it, but that is, in fact, how many school administrators and school boards across the country behave. They treat violence as a fact of life, that's what society is like, and they just go through a couple of ritual efforts to try to show that they're doing something. But, basically they give up.

What we have is what amounts to a very high level of tolerance of this type of activity. Now, of course, the violence and the guns and the drugs have to be distinguished from another type of activity. This other type isn't deadly in the sense that you are going to read tomorrow morning that some youngster was stabbed or shot. And that's the whole question of just plain out-and-out disruption: the youngster who is constantly yelling, cursing, jumping, fighting, doing all sorts of things, so that most of the time the other students in the class and the teacher is devoted, not to the academic mission of the schools, but to figuring out how to contain this individual. And in this area, we have an even higher tolerance than we do in the area of violence, where occasionally youngsters are suspended or removed for periods of time....

Last year when Congress was debating the Goals 2000 education program, there were an awful lot of people who said, you know, in addition to having different kinds of content standards—what you should learn—and performance standards—how good is good enough—you ought to have opportunity-to-learn standards. It's not fair to hold kids to these standards unless they've had certain advantages. It's not fair, if one kid has had early childhood education and one hasn't, to hold them to the same standard. It's not fair, if at this school they don't have any textbooks or the textbooks are 15 years old, and in that school they have the most modern books. It's not fair, if in this school they've got computers, and in that school kids have never seen a computer.

Well, I submit to you that if you want to talk about opportunity-to-learn standards, there are a lot of kids who've made it without the most up-to-date textbooks. It's better if you have them. There are a lot of kids who've made it without early childhood education. It's a lot better if you've got it, and we're for that. Throughout history, people have learned without computers, but it's better if you've got them. But nobody has ever learned if they were in a classroom with one or two kids who took up 90 percent of the time through disruption, violence, or threats of violence. You deprive children of an opportunity to learn if you do not first provide an orderly situation within the classroom and within the school. That comes ahead of all of these other things.

Now, I said that this conference was going to be different from every conference that I've been to and every conference that I've read about. I have a report here that was sent to me by John Cole [President of the Texas Federation of Teachers], who went to The Scholastic Annual Summit on Youth Violence on October 17 [1994]. I'm not going to read the whole thing, but I'll just read enough that you get the flavor of what these other conferences are like:

> "So start with the concept that the real victims of violence are those unfortunate individuals who have been led into lives of crime by the failure of society to provide them with hope for a meaningful life. Following that logic, one must conclude that society has not done enough for these children and that we must find ways to salvage their lives. Schools must work patiently with these individuals offering them different avenues out of this situation. As an institution charged with responsibility for education, schools must have programs to identify those who are embarking on a life of crime and violence and lift them out of the snares into which they have fallen. Society, meanwhile, should be more forgiving of the sins of these poor creatures, who through no real fault of their own are the victims of racism and economic injustice.

> "Again and again and again, panelists pointed out that the young people we are talking about, to paraphrase Rodney Dangerfield, 'don't get no respect.' The experts assured us that young people take up weapons, commit acts of violence, and abuse drugs because this enables them to obtain respect from their peers. I found myself thinking that we aid and abet this behavior when we bend over backwards to accommodate those young people who have bought into this philosophy. By lavishing attention on them, we may even encourage a spread of that behavior. Many of these programs are well meaning but counterproductive.

> "I don't want to condemn this conference as a waste of time. Obviously, we do need programs to work with these young people, and we should try to salvage as many as we can. However, we must somehow come to grips with the idea that individuals have responsibility for their own actions. If we assume that society is to blame for all of the problems these young people have, may we then assume that society must develop solutions that take care of these young people's problems? We take away from each individual the responsibility for his or her own life. Once the individual assumes that he or she has lost control of his own destiny, that individual has no difficulty in justifying any act because he or she feels no responsibility for the consequences."

Now with that philosophy, the idea is not that we want to be punitive or nasty, but essentially schools must teach not only English and mathematics and reading and writing and history, but also teach that there are ways of behaving in society that are unacceptable. And when we sit back and tolerate certain types of behavior, we are teaching youngsters that certain types of behavior are acceptable, which eventually will end up with their being in jail or in poverty for the rest of their lives. We are not doing our jobs as teachers. And the system is not doing its job, if we send youngsters the message that this is tolerable behavior within society. . . .

All we ask of our schools is that they behave in the same way that a caring and intelligent parent would behave with respect to their own children. I doubt very much, if you had a youngster who was a fire bug or a youngster who used weapons, whether you would say, well, I owe it to this youngster to trust him with my other children to show him that I'm not separating him out or treating him differently. Or I'm going to raise his self-esteem by allowing him to do these things. All of these nutty things that we talk about in school, we would not do. So the starting point of this conference, which is different from all of the others, is that I hope that you people join with me in a sense of outrage that we have a system that is willing to sacrifice the overwhelming majority of children for a handful. And not do any good for that handful either. And we need to start with that outrage, because without that we're not going to change this system.

That outrage is there among parents. That outrage was partly expressed in the recent election as people's anger at the way government was working. Why can't government do things in some sort of common sense way? And this is one of the issues that's out there. Now, what are some of the things that enter into this? Well, part of it is that some people think of schools as sort of custodial institutions. Where are we going to put the kids? Put them here. Or they think the school's job is mostly socialization. Eventually troubled kids will grow up or grow out of this, and they're better off with other youngsters than they are separated. Of course, people who take that point of view are totally ignoring the fact that the central role of schools, the one that we will be held accountable for, is student academic achievement. We know the test scores are bad. And we know that our students are not learning as much as youngsters in other countries. So we can't just say we know we are way behind, but, boy, are we good custodians. Look at how socialized these youngsters are.

People are paying for education and they want youngsters who are going to be able to be employed and get decent jobs. We want youngsters who are going to be as well off or in better shape than we are, just as most of us are with respect to our parents and grandparents. And the academic function is the one that's neglected. The academic function is the one that's destroyed in this notion that our job is mainly custodial.

So our central position is that we have to be tough on these issues, and we have to be tough because basically we are defending the right of children to an education. And those who insist on allowing violence and disruptive behavior in the school are destroying the right to an education for the overwhelming majority of youngsters within our schools.

Two years ago or three years ago, I was in Texas at a convention of the Texas Federation of Teachers. I didn't know this was going to happen, but either just before I got there or while I was there, there was a press conference on a position the convention adopted, and they used the phrase "zero tolerance." They said that with respect to certain types of dangerous activities in schools, there would be zero tolerance. These things are not acceptable and there are going to be consequences. There might be suspension, there might be expulsion, or there might be something else, but nevertheless, consequences will be clear. Well, that got picked up by radio, television, legislators. I was listening to a governor the other night at the National Governors Association, who stood up and came out for zero tolerance. It is a phrase which has caught on and is sweeping the country.

I hope it is one that all of you will bring back to your communities and your states, that there are certain types of activities that we will not tolerate. We will not teach youngsters bad lessons, and we're going to start very early. When a youngster does something that is terribly wrong, and all of the other youngsters are sure that something is going to happen to him because he did something wrong, we had better make sure that we fulfill the expectations of all those other youngsters that something's going to happen. And they're all going to say, "Thank God, I didn't do a terrible thing like that or I would be out there, and something would be happening to me." That is the beginning of a sense of doing something right, as against doing wrong.

And we have to deal with this notion that society is responsible, social conditions are responsible. The AFT does not take second place to anybody in fighting for decent conditions for adults and for youngsters and for minorities and for groups that have been oppressed. We're not in a state of denial; we're not saying that things have been wonderful. But when your kids come home and say "I'm doing these terrible things because of these conditions," if you're a good parent, you'll say, "That's no excuse." You are going to do things right, because you don't want your youngster to end up as a criminal or in some sort of horrible position.…

Now what should schools do? Schools should have codes of conduct. These codes can be developed through collective bargaining or they can be mandated in legislation. I don't think it would be a bad idea to have state legislation that every school system needs to have a code of discipline that is very clear, not a fuzzy sort of thing, something that says these things are not to be done and if this happens, these are the consequences. A very clear connection between behavior and consequences. And it might even say that, if there is a legitimate complaint from a group of parents or a group of teachers or a group of students that clearly shows the school district doesn't have such a code or isn't enforcing it, there would be some sort of financial penalty against the district for failing to provide a decent education by allowing this type of violence and disruption to continue.

Taxpayers are sending money into the district so that the kids can have an education, and if that district then destroys the education by allowing one or two youngsters to wipe out all of the effects that money is supposed to produce, what the hell is the point of sending the money? If you allow these youngsters to so disrupt that education, you might as well save the money. So there's a reason for states to do this. And, by the way, I think that you'll find a receptive audience, because the notion of individuals taking responsibility for their actions is one of the things fueling the political anger in this country—that we have a lot of laws which help people to become irresponsible or encourage them not to take responsibility for their own actions.

Now, enforcement is very important. For every crime, so to speak, there ought to be a punishment. I don't like very much judgment to be used, because once you allow judgment to be used, punishments will be more severe for some kids than for others and you will get unfairness. You will get prejudice. The way to make sure that this is done fairly and is not done in a prejudiced way is to say, look, we don't care if you're white or Hispanic or African-American or whether you're a recent immigrant or this or that, for this infraction, this is what happens. We don't have a different sanction depending upon whether we like you a little more or a little less. That's how fairness would be ensured, and I think it's very important that we insist on that....

One of the big problems is school administrators. School administrators are concerned that, if there are a large number of reports of disruptions and violence in their schools, their reputations will suffer. They like to say they have none of those problems in their schools. Now, how do you prove that you have none of these problems in your school? Very simple. Just tell the teachers that if they report it, it's because they are ineffective teachers. If you tell that to one or two teachers, you will certainly have a school that has very little disruption or violence reported. You may have plenty of disruption and violence. So, in many places we have this gag rule. It's not written, but it's very well understood.

As a teacher, I myself faced this. Each time I reported something like this, I was told that if I knew how to motivate the students properly, this wouldn't happen. It's pretty universal. It wasn't just one district or just my principal. It's almost all of them. Therefore, I think that we ought to seek laws that require a full and honest reporting of incidents of violence and extreme disruption. And that would mean that, if an administrator goes around telling you to shut up or threatening you so that you're not free to report, I think that there ought to be penalties. Unless we know the extent of this problem, we're never going to deal with it adequately.

Of course, parents know what the extent of it is. What is the number one problem? It's the problem of violence and order in the schools. They know it. The second big problem and obstacle we face is, what's going to happen if you put the kid out on the streets? It reminds me of a big campaign in New York City to get crime off the streets, and pretty soon they were very successful. They had lots of policemen on the streets, and they drove the criminals away. The criminals went into the subways. Then they had a campaign about crime in the subways, and they drove them back up into the streets. So the business community, parents, and others will say, you can't just throw a kid out and put them on the streets. That's no good. But you could place some conditions on it. To return to school, students would have to bring with them a parent or some other grown-up or relative responsible for them. There is a list of ways in which we might handle it. But we can't say that we're going to wait until we build new schools, or build new class-rooms, or have new facilities. The first thing you do is separate out the youngster who is a danger to the other youngsters.

Now, let me give an example. And I think it's one that's pretty close. We know that, when we arrest adults who have committed crimes and we jail them, jail will most likely not help those who are jailed. I don't think it does, and I don't think most people do. However, most of us are pretty glad when someone who has committed a pretty bad crime is jailed. Not because it's going to do that person any good, but because that person won't be around to do the same thing for the next ten or fifteen years. And for the separation of youngsters who are destroying the education of others, the justification is the same. I'm not sure that we can devise programs that will reach those youngsters that will help them. We should try. But our first obligation is to never destroy the education of the twenty or twenty-five or thirty because you have an obligation to one. Especially when there's no evidence that you're doing anything for that one by keeping him there.

Now, another big obstacle is legal problems. These are expensive and time-consuming. If a youngster gets a lawyer and goes to court, the principal or some other figure of authority from the school, usually has to go to court. They might sit a whole day and by the end of the first day, they decide not to hear it. And they come a second day, and maybe it's held over again. It might take three or four days for each youngster. So if you've got a decent-sized school, even if you're dealing with only two or three percent of the youngsters, you could spend your full time in court, instead of being in school. Well, I wouldn't want to do that if I were the principal of the school. And then what does the court do when you're all finished? The court says, well, we don't have any better place to put him, so send him right back. So, that's why a lot of teachers wouldn't report it, because nothing happens anyway. You go through all of this, you spend all of that time and money, and when you're all finished, you're right back where you started. So we need to change what happens with respect to the court, and we have two ideas that we're going to explore that have not been done before.

One of the things we need to do is see whether we can get parents, teachers, and even perhaps high school students to intervene in these cases and say, we want to come before the judge to present evidence about what the consequences are for the other children. When you go to court now, you have the lawyer for the board of education, the lawyer for the youngster, and the youngster. And the youngster, well, he's just a kid and his lawyer says, "This poor child has all of these problems," and the judge is looking down at this poor youngster. You know who is not there? The other 25 youngsters to say, this guy beats me up every day. If I do my homework, I get beat up on the way to school because he doesn't want me to do my homework. So instead of first having this one child standing there saying, "Poor me, let me back in school, they have kicked me out, they have done terrible things to me," you also have some of the victims there saying, "Hey, what about us?" You'll get a much fairer consideration if the judge is able to look at both sides, instead of just hearing the bureaucrat from the board of education. None of these board of education lawyers that I've met talk about the other students. They talk about the right of the board of education under the law to do thus, and so what you have is a humane judge who's thinking of the bureaucrat talking about the rights of the board of education as against the child. I think we need to balance that.

Now, there's a second thing we are going to explore. We are all familiar with the fact that most of our labor contracts have a provision for grievance procedures. And part of that grievance procedure is arbitration. Now, you can take an arbitration award to court and try to appeal it, but it's very, very difficult to get a court to overthrow an arbitrator's award. Why? Because the court says, look, you had your day, you went to the arbitrator and you presented all your arguments, the other side presented all their arguments. In order for me to look into that arbitration and turn it over, you're going to have to prove to me that something in this arbitration was so terrible that we have to prove that the arbitrator was absolutely partial or that he broke the law. You've got to prove something outrageous. Otherwise, the judge is going to say, "You've had your day in court."

Now, why can't school districts establish a fair, inexpensive, due-process arbitration procedure for youngsters who are violent or disruptive? So that when the youngster goes to court, they can say, "Hey, we've had this procedure. We've had witnesses on both sides, and here was the determination. And, really, you shouldn't get into this stuff unless you can show that these people are terribly prejudiced or totally incompetent or something else." In other words, we don't have to use the court. We could create a separate school judicial system that had expertise and knowledge about what the impact is on students and teachers and the whole system of these kinds of decisions. Arbitration is a much cheaper, much faster system, especially if you have an expedited arbitration system. There is a system in the American Arbitration Association of expedited arbitration that says how many briefs you're allowed to write and how much time each side can take, and all of that. So we have a legal team and we're going to explore the notion of getting this stuff out of the courts and creating a system that is inexpensive and fair to the youngster and fair to the other youngsters in the school.

Now, let me point out that a lot of the tolerance for bad behavior is about to change, because we are about to have stakes attached to student academic outcomes. In other words, in the near future, we are going to have a situation where, if you don't make it up to this point, then you can't be admitted into college. Or if you don't make it here, then you will not get certified for a certain type of employment. But in Chapter I schools, this is going to start very soon. There is a provision in the new Chapter One, now called Title I, and very soon, if Title I schools do not show a substantial progress for students, the school's going to be punished. And one of the punishments is reconstitution of the school. The school will be closed down, teachers will go elsewhere, students will go elsewhere, and the school will open up with a new student body, slowly rebuild. That's one of the punishments. There are other punishments as well. So if you've got a bunch of these disruptive youngsters that prevent you from teaching and the other students from learning, it won't be like yesterday, where nobody seems to care, the kids are all going to get promoted anyway and they can all go to college, because there are no standards. There are no stakes.

Now, for the first time, there will be stakes. The teachers will know. The parents will know, hey, this school's going to close. I'm going to have to find a way of getting my kid to some other school because of the lack of learning that comes from this disruption. Teachers are going to say, hey, I'm not going to have my job in this school a couple of years from now because they're going to shut it down. I don't know what the rules are, what happens to these teachers, whether other schools have to take them or not. But we are entering a period where there will be consequences and parents and teachers are going to be a lot more concerned about achievement.

Now, one of the other issues that has stood in the way of doing something here is a very difficult one to talk about in our society, and that's the issue of race. And whenever the topic of suspension or expulsion comes up, there's always the question of race. Cincinnati is a good example. The union there negotiated a good discipline code as part of a desegregation suit. And the question was raised, "Well, is there a disparate impact, with more minority kids being suspended than others?" And who are the teachers who are suspending them? Do you have more white teachers suspending African-American kids?

Our position on that is very clear. In any given school, you may have more white kids with infractions or you may have more African-American kids, or you may have more Hispanic kids. We don't know. I don't think anybody knows. But we handle that by saying, "Whatever your crime is and whoever you are, you're going to get exactly the same punishment." If we do that, I'm sure that the number who will be punished will end up being very, very small. Because, as a young kid, if you see that there is a consequence, you will change your behavior....

Now we have another very big problem, and we're going to try to deal with this in legislation. Under legislation that deals with disabled youngsters, we have two different standards. Namely, if a youngster in this class is not disabled and commits an infraction, you can do whatever is in that discipline code for that youngster. But if the youngster is disabled and is in that same class (for instance, the youngster might have a speech defect), you can't suspend that youngster while all of the proceedings are going on because that's a change in placement. It might take you a year-and-a-half in court, and meanwhile that youngster who is engaged in some threatening or dangerous behavior has to stay there. This makes no sense. We have a lot of support in the Congress on this, and we think we have a good chance of changing this....

Well, that's the whole picture. And to return to the theme at the beginning, we have a cry for choice, a cry for vouchers, a cry for charters. It's not really a cry for these things. People really want their own schools, and they want their kids to go to those schools, and they want those schools to be safe and orderly for their youngsters.

It is insane to set up a system where we move 98 percent of our kids away from the two percent who are dangerous, instead of moving the two percent away from the 98 percent who are OK. We need to have discipline codes, we need to have a new legal system, we need to have one standard for all students. We need to have a system where we don't have to wait for a year or a year-and-a-half after a student has perpetrated some terrible and atrocious crime before that student is removed for the safety of the other students. How are we going to do this? We are going to do this, first of all, by talking to our colleagues within the schools. Our polls show that the overwhelming majority accepts these views.

The support of African-American parents for the removal of violent youngsters and disruptive students is higher than any other group within our society. Now very often when youngsters are removed, it's because some parents group or some committee starts shouting and making noise, and the school system can't resist that. Now I think that it's time for us to turn to business groups, it's time for us to turn to parents' groups. When youngsters commit such acts, and when they've had a fair due-process within the system, we need to have a system of public support, just as we have in the community when someone commits a terrible crime. People say, send that person to jail, don't send him back to us. We need to have a lot of decent people within our communities, when you have youngsters who are destroying the education of all the others, who will stand up and say, "Look, we don't want to punish this kid, but for the sake of our children, you're going to have to keep that one away, until that one is ready to come back and live in a decent way in society with all of the other youngsters."

I'm sure that if we take this back to our communities, and if we work on it, the appeal will be obvious. It's common sense. And we will save our schools and we will do something which will give us the basis for providing a decent education for all of our children.

Pedro A. Noguera

NO

The Critical State of Violence Prevention

The problem of violence in schools, like the related problem of violence in society, has become one of the most pressing educational issues in the United States. In many school districts, concerns about violence have surpassed academic achievement as the highest priority for reform and intervention.

Public clamorings over the need for something to be done about school violence has brought the issue to a critical juncture. The threat of violence constitutes a fundamental violation of the social contract between school and community. If effective measures to address the problem are not taken soon, support for public education could be irreparably jeopardized.

Across the country, school districts have adopted various "get tough" measures to address school violence. I believe sound reasons exist to question the effectiveness of these measures and present alternative strategies that have proven successful in reducing the incidence of school violence.

Getting Tough

Not surprisingly, the search for solutions to school violence has generated a package of remedies that closely resemble those used in society to combat the threat of violence and crime.

Some popular measures include the installation of metal detectors at school entrances to prevent students from bringing weapons on to school grounds; the enactment of "zero tolerance" policies (advocated by the American Federation of Teachers and other groups), which require the automatic removal of students (through suspension, expulsion, or transfer) who perpetrate acts of violence; and the use of armed security guards to patrol and monitor student behavior while school is in session.

Accompanying the implementation of such measures has been a tendency of school officials to treat violent incidents, and sometimes non-violent incidents as well, as criminal offenses to be handled by law enforcement officials and the courts, rather than by school personnel. Forced to do something about a growing problem, many politicians and school officials have attempted to quell the tide of violence by converting schools into prison-like facilities.

Yet despite the tough talk and punitive actions, little reason for optimism exists given the track record of these methods and the persistence of violence in schools. For example, despite spending more than $28 million during the 1980s for the installation of metal detectors at public schools in New York City, crime and violence continue to be a major concern. In fact, while teachers and parents are increasingly frustrated about the problem, the mayor and school board were locked last fall in an angry debate over who should bear the blame for the problem. Recently, at a high school in Richmond, Calif., two students were shot at a school despite the presence of metal detectors. In several states, the failure of public schools to curtail violence has been cited as a primary factor influencing public support for school vouchers and school choice proposals.

Misleading Picture

Two main problems exist with "get tough" measures:

- they don't address the causes of school violence, and
- they don't help us understand why schools have become increasingly vulnerable to its occurrence.

As evidence that something is being done about school violence, school officials often point to statistics related to the number of weapons confiscated and the number of students who have been suspended, expelled, or arrested for violent reasons. Such data are used to demonstrate that valiant efforts are being undertaken to reduce the incidence of violence.

The compilation of such data is important because it creates the impression that something is being done even if the problem persists. It also plays an important role in rationalizing the expenditure of resources on school safety—allocations that often result in the elimination of other educational programs and services.

For parents and students who live with the reality of violence and who must contend daily with the threat of physical harm, such data does little to allay fears. When engaging in what were once ordinary activities—such as walking through the halls between classes or playing sports after school—evokes such extreme paranoia as to no longer seem feasible, news that arrests or suspensions have increased provides little reassurance.

Moreover, recognition is growing that many measures used to deter violence have little if any impact on the problem. Suspending students who do not attend school regularly does little to deter poor behavior.

Even at schools where administrators manage to keep the site safe through additional security, victory over violence cannot be declared if kids fight or are attacked on their way to and from school. In such cases, the limited safety provided at the site does little to reduce the fears and anxieties of parents or students.

Quantifying Symbols

Not long ago, I attended a meeting with school officials from an urban district on the West coast. We were reviewing data on the incidence of violence from the past year and discussing what could be done to further reduce violence.

After seeing the disciplinary reports, I jokingly remarked: "Here's some good news, homicides are down 100 percent from last year." To my amazement, an administrator replied: "Yes, the news isn't all bad. Some of our efforts are beginning to pay off."

What surprised me about the comment was his apparent belief that since no murders had occurred at any school in the district at the midpoint of the school year (compared to two during the previous year), there was reason for hope and optimism. I found it hard to believe that district administrators, who generally have little regular contact with school sites, could accept a statistical analysis as evidence that the schools had in fact become safer.

Yet within the context of the fight against violence, symbols such as crime statistics take on great significance, even though they may have little bearing upon the actual occurrence of violence or how safe people feel. Pressed to demonstrate to the public that efforts taken to reduce violence are effective, school districts often pursue one of two strategies: either they present statistics quantifing the results of their efforts, or they go to great lengths to suppress information altogether hoping that the community will perceive no news as good news.

Metal detectors, barbed wire fences, armed guards and police officers, and principals wielding baseball bats as they patrol the halls are all symbols of tough action. However, most students realize that a person who wants to bring a weapon to school can get it into a building without being discovered by a metal detector and that it is highly unlikely that any principal will hit a student with a baseball bat. Still, the symbols persist lest the truth be known that those responsible really don't have a clue about what to do to stem the tide of violence.

Overcoming Fear

To understand why violence has become rampant and how a climate of fear and intimidation has come gradually to be the norm in so many urban schools, we must examine the relationships that are fostered between young people and adults at most schools.

Criminologist Alan Wilson has pointed out that only two ways exist to control behavior and deter crime: (1) by relying on police officers and the courts or (2) by promoting collective morals and sanctions. Any society that comes to rely exclusively on the former to enforce safety is doomed for there will never be enough police officers to go around.

Increasingly, our society, and now our schools, have looked to the police and the courts for answers because we have given up on the possibility that collective morality and sanctions could be effective.

While police officers, security guards, and administrators generally assume primary responsibility for managing and enforcing school discipline, in most cases, teachers make the first referral in the discipline process, and therefore have tremendous influence in determining who receives discipline and why.

In my work with urban schools, the most frequent concern I hear from teachers is that they have trouble disciplining and controlling their students. This problem is particularly true in schools at which the majority of students are black and the majority of teachers are white. Though I don't believe the problem is primarily racial, I do believe racial differences add to the difficulty of dealing with this issue.

Having taught in urban public schools, I am familiar with what classroom teachers are up against. Order and safety are essential requisites to an environment where teaching and learning can occur. However, when I conduct workshops about safety in schools I try to shift the focus of discussion away from discipline to discussion about what teachers know about their students. I do this because I have found that teachers who lack familiarity with their students' lives outside of school are more likely to misunderstand and fear them.

Widening Gulf

The gulf in experience between teacher and student, which is typical in many urban schools, contributes to the problem of violence in schools. Too often, teachers and administrators will fill the knowledge void with stereotypes about their students and the community in which they live. These stereotypes may be based upon what they have read or seen in the news media or what they have picked up indirectly from stories told to them by children.

Lacking another source of information, many teachers begin to fear the children they teach because to some they seem to embody the less-than-civilized images associated with people who reside in the inner city. Fear invariably influences interaction between teachers/administrators and students.

Though it may never be stated, students often can tell when adults fear them, and many will use this to undermine their teachers' authority in the classroom or elsewhere at school.

This is not to say that violence in schools is an imagined problem. However, school violence is a problem exacerbated by fear. A teacher who fears the students that she or he teaches is more likely to resort to discipline when challenged or to ignore the challenge in the hope that she or he will be left alone. Rather than handling a classroom disruption on their own, they are more likely to request assistance from those responsible for handling discipline. They also are less likely to reach out to students in ways that make teaching less impersonal.

Likewise, students who know their teachers fear them are less likely to show respect and more likely to be insolent and insubordinate. When fear is at the center of student-teacher interactions, good teaching becomes almost impossible, and concerns about safety and control take precedence over concerns about teaching and learning.

Alternative Approaches

In critiquing the approaches to discipline that are most widely practiced in the country today, I in no way want to belittle the fact that many classroom teachers and students have become victims of violence and deserve the right to work and attend school in safety. In many schools, violence is real, and the fear that it produces is understandable.

Still, I am struck by the fact that even when I visit schools that have a notorious reputation for the prevalence of violence, I can find at least one classroom where teachers are working effectively with students and where fear is not an obstacle to dialogue and even friendship. While other teachers within the school may be preoccupied with managing the behavior of their students (an endeavor at which they are seldom successful), I have seen the same students enter other classrooms willing to learn and comply with the instructions of their teachers.

Many of these "exceptional" teachers have found ways to cross the borders that separate them from their students. For such teachers, differences based on race, class, or age are unable to prevent them from establishing rapport with their students. Consistently, when I have asked students in interviews what is it that makes a particular teacher special and worthy of respect, the students cite three characteristics these teachers share: firmness, compassion, and an interesting, engaging and challenging style of teaching.

Of course, even a teacher who is perceived as exceptional by students can be a victim of violence because of its increasingly random occurrence. However, such teachers and administrators are less likely to allow fear to paralyze them in their work with students.

The fact that teachers and administrators who possess what the French sociologist Emile Durkheim described as "moral authority" tend to be so few in number compels me to ask why. Are fewer exceptional individuals going into teaching, or is there something about the structure and culture of schools that propagates and reproduces the destructive interpersonal dynamics that are so prevalent?

My experience in schools leads me to believe it is the latter. The vast majority of teachers and administrators whom I meet seem genuinely concerned about their students and sincerely desire to be effective at what they do. Even those who have become cynical and bitter as a result of enduring years of ungratifying work in underfunded public schools generally strike me as people who would prefer more humane interactions with their students.

Social Control

What stands in the way of better relations between teachers and students? And how has it happened that fear and distrust characterize those relations rather than compassion and respect?

My answer to these questions focuses on the legacy of social control that continues to dominate the educational agenda and profoundly influences the structure and culture of schools. So many schools are preoccupied with controlling their students or with ensuring safety that they have lost sight of the fact that schools are supposed to be centers of learning where children receive intellectual and psychological nurturing.

The few safe urban schools I have visited share several characteristics: they are small and attempt to treat students as individuals; they bridge the gap between school and community by involving parents and community residents in the school in a society of mutually supportive relationships; they create a physical environment that is aesthetically pleasant; and they focus less energy on enforcing rules than on developing relationships between adults and students to foster trust and personal accountability.

I have visited urban schools that have found ways to effectively address the problem of violence without relying on coercion or excessive forms of control.

At one middle school in West Oakland, rather than hiring a large man to work as security guard, a grandmother from the surrounding community was hired to monitor students. Instead of using physical intimidation to carry out her duties, this woman greets children with hugs, a smile, and words of encouragement. When some form of punishment is needed, she admonishes the children to behave themselves because she expects better behavior from them. Without relying on force she can break up any fight or handle any disruptive student. She also facilitates dialogue between parents and teachers, often serving as a mediator who helps both parties overcome distrust and resentment to find common ground.

I know of a continuation high school where the principal was able to close the campus at lunch time without installing a fence or some other security apparatus. Concerned that too many students were not returning to campus after lunch, he asked the students for suggestions about what should be done to address the problem.

The students suggested that the school develop a student-managed store and dining area so it no longer would be necessary for them to leave for meals. Without erecting a fence, the school is now officially a closed campus, and at lunch time, students, teachers, and administrators can be seen eating together at the student-operated cafe.

Efforts such as these are effective at addressing the potential for violence because they are based on the assumption that students will respond favorably to humane treatment. When the threat of removal is used as a form of discipline, it is most effective when students genuinely desire to attend school. Public health researchers have called attention to the fact that environmental conditions can either promote or deter violent behavior.

Improving the aesthetic character of schools by including art in the design of schools or making space available within schools for student-run gardens or greenhouses can make schools more pleasant and attractive. Similarly, the divide that separates urban schools from the communities in which schools are located can be overcome by encouraging adults who live within the community to volunteer or, if possible, to be employed as tutors or even teachers, mentors, and coaches.

Undoubtedly, if we can increase the presence of individuals who possess moral authority in the eyes of children, this too will help in reducing the threat of violence at school.

Intrinsic Desires

Ultimately, the promotion of safe schools cannot be separated from the goal of producing schools where children learn. To do so only takes us further down the path of creating prison-like institutions that bring greater control, but do not create an atmosphere of safety and trust.

Those of us who seek to create safe learning environments at our schools must recognize that urban youth today are not passive or compliant and will not be easily controlled. Rather than pursuing that goal we must devise new strategies for providing an education that is perceived as meaningful and relevant and that begins to tap into the intrinsic desire of all individuals to obtain greater personal fulfillment.

Anything short of this will leave us mired in a situation that grows increasingly depressing and dangerous each day.

POSTSCRIPT

Does School Violence Warrant a Zero-Tolerance Policy?

How can the aggressive drive be harnessed so that it provides young people with the energy to live productively in American society rather than being unleashed in the form of violence? This question is posed by Lorraine B. Wallach in "Violence and Agression in Today's Schools" in the Spring 1996 issue of *Educational Horizons*. Wallach contends that "children who accumulate an overload of anger, hate, or jealousy or feel worthless are more likely to be violent, particularly when these feelings are combined with poor inner controls." The building of internal controls and the channeling of normal aggressiveness must begin, of course, in the home and at the presecondary levels of schooling.

To achieve a thorough and balanced approach to the problem of school violence, see *Beyond the Classroom* by Laurence Steinberg (1996); *Violence in Schools: The Enabling Factor* by Carole Remboldt (1995); *Creating Safe Schools* by Marie Hill and Frank Hill (1994); and *Anger Management in Schools: Alternatives to Student Violence* by Jerry Wilde (1995).

Articles of interest include "What to Do About the Children," by William J. Bennett, *Commentary* (March 1995), in which the author discusses the governmental role in dealing with crime, immorality, and uncivilized behavior; "Waging Peace in Our Schools: Beginning With the Children," by Linda Lanteiri, *Phi Delta Kappan* (January 1995); the Carnegie Corporation of New York report *Education for Conflict Resolution,* by David A. Hamburg (1994); and "Ganging Up on Gangs," by Reginald Leon Green and Roger L. Miller, *The American School Board Journal* (September 1996). An excellent array of articles may be found in *The School Administrator* (February 1996); the *NASSP Bulletin* (April 1996); and the *Harvard Educational Review* (Summer 1995), which features Janie V. Ward on cultivating a morality of care, Pedro A. Noguera on violence prevention, and interviews with Noam Chomsky and Peggy Charren. Students who will soon enter the teaching profession may also profit from reading *Safe Schools: A Handbook for Practitioners,* which was released in 1994 by the National Association of Secondary School Principals.

Other recent commentary on the problem may be found in Nancy Day's book *Violence in Schools: Learning in Fear* (1996); Jeanne Wright's "Discipline and Order in the Classroom," *Current* (July–August 1997); and multiple articles in the October 1997 issue of *Educational Leadership,* the Summer 1999 issue of *American Educator,* the February 2000 issue of *The School Administrator,* and the March 2000 issue of *NASSP Bulletin.*

ISSUE 18

Can Self-Governing Schools
Rescue Urban Education?

YES: Deborah Meier, from "Can the Odds Be Changed?" *Phi Delta Kappan* (January 1998)

NO: Emeral A. Crosby, from "Urban Schools: Forced to Fail," *Phi Delta Kappan* (December 1999)

ISSUE SUMMARY

YES: Deborah Meier, a leading urban educator, contends that decaying public schools in large cities can be rejuvenated by the proliferation of self-governing exemplary schools that are given encouragement by the system.

NO: High school principal Emeral A. Crosby, while sharing many of Meier's hopes, maintains that only a powerful political force and a massive infusion of funds can halt the downward spiral of urban school quality.

$\mathbf{I}$n 1991 Jonathan Kozol graphically portrayed the prevailing conditions in inner-city public schools in his book *Savage Inequalities: Children in America's Schools*. The book provided a guided tour of dilapidated buildings, outdated equipment, disheartened teachers, and understimulated students. Kozol's quest for equalization of funding for urban schools began with his 1967 book *Death at an Early Age*, which described the deterioration of poverty-area schools in Boston, Massachusetts.

Has what Gene Maeroff depicted as "Withered Hopes, Stillborn Dreams: The Dismal Panorama of Urban Schools," in *Phi Delta Kappan* (1991), been altered since Kozol made the public more aware of the situation? According to Gary Rosen, in "Are School Vouchers Un-American?" *Commentary* (February 2000),

> By any measure, public education in America's cities is in deep trouble.... On any given day in Cleveland almost one in every six students is likely not to show up. In Washington, D.C. a majority of tenth graders never finish high school. And in Los Angeles school officials recently retreated from a

plan to end the practice of "social promotion," realizing that it would have required holding back for a year more than half of the district's woefully unprepared students.

Gary Rosen advocates following the lead of Milwaukee, Wisconsin, and Cleveland, Ohio, in moving toward voucher plans for poverty-area students, which would allow public funds to be used for private education, sometimes at religious schools. A Florida voucher plan designed for that purpose, however, was recently shelved by court action. Matthew Miller, in "A Bold Experiment to Fix City Schools," *The Atlantic Monthly* (July 1999), states, "A political stand-off has kept vouchers unavailable to nearly 99 percent of urban schoolchildren. Bill Clinton and most leading Democrats oppose them, saying we should fix existing public schools, not drain money from the system." Miller suggests an expanded voucher plan experiment that would provide all poverty-level students with vouchers while simultaneously increasing federal funding for existing inner-city public schools.

Joseph P. Viteritti, in "A Way Out: School Choice and Educational Opportunity," *Brookings Review* (Fall 1999), contends that

> the demand for choice, especially among minorities and the poor, is high. We know this from the size and composition of the waiting lists of applicants who have expressed interest in existing voucher programs, charter schools, and private scholarship initiatives. Even charter schools that do not specifically target poor children tend to attract a disproportionate number of minorities who see them as an escape route from failing schools.

Beyond the voucher and charter school solutions, which are presently limited in scope and often mired in controversy, there are some other rays of hope. Michael Casserly, executive director of Great City Schools, in "Urban Public Schools on the Comeback," *Principal* (January 1999), cites evidence of increased student achievement, lower dropout rates, higher daily attendance, and increased percentages of students taking college entrance exams. The School Reform Demonstration Program has been funded by Congress to develop exemplary schools in order to stimulate reform dissemination. The U.S. Department of Education has released a study entitled *Hope for Urban Education* describing nine poverty-area elementary schools that have fashioned dramatic turnarounds in the past five years. The Success for All program attacks problems involved in the development of literacy. The Children's Scholarship Fund offers some 40,000 scholarships in nearly 50 locales. And Deborah Meier's practical accomplishments in East Harlem continue to inspire other urban educators.

But deep-rooted barriers still exist. The history of political and economic exploitation in inner cities is chronicled by Jean Anyon in *Ghetto Schooling: A Political Economy of Educational Reform* (1997). And Martin Haberman offers a realistic appraisal of the problem in "The Anti-Learning Curriculum of Urban Schools," *Kappa Delta Pi Record* (Spring 1997 and Winter 1999).

In the selections that follow, Meier and Emeral A. Crosby each draw upon their vast experience with urban schools to arrive at somewhat contrary views of what is needed to avert complete disaster.

Deborah Meier  **YES**

Can the Odds Be Changed?

There are numerous stories of schools that have been successful with students who would otherwise count among society's failures. However, such school successes rarely set the stage for Big Reform agendas. These one-of-a-kind schools flicker brightly. A few manage to survive by avoiding the public's attention or by serving powerful constituents; the rest gradually burn out. Can we change that? Can we make the exceptions the norm?

The Search for Silver Bullets

To the vast majority of serious policy makers, the existing exemplary schools offer no important lessons. Most policy makers define *systemic* so that it applies only to the kinds of solutions that can be more or less simultaneously prescribed for all schools, irrespective of particulars. Solutions, in short, that seek to improve schooling by taking away the already too limited formal powers of those closest to the students. Examples range from more prescriptive curricula to new, more centralized testing systems; fiscal rewards and penalties; or changed school governance bodies.

School-level folks are as skeptical about the capacity of any of these top-down recipes to make a significant impact on the minds of teachers or children as policy-level folks are about the idiosyncratic bottom-up ones. Practitioners —in classrooms and central offices—know at heart that "this too shall pass" or can be gotten around or overcome. They wait out the innovators. Policy makers work overtime to come up with ways to circumvent such resistance. The more things change, the more they stay the same.

This is a climate that encourages impatience: enough's enough! If we can't do a better job of marrying top-down and bottom-up reform, we're probably in for big trouble. Giving up on the new thought that all children can learn to use their minds well is hard, especially for those of us who know firsthand that schools as designed are hardly suited to the job and that vastly more children could be well-educated if we came up with a better design. We've "tasted" it. It seems both so near and so far. Perhaps if we posed the problem differently, the oddball schools might offer us systemic answers. The Annenberg Challenge gave a substantial boost to a wave of projects around the country that were, on the one hand, fueled by the growing interest in vouchers and charters but that sought on the other hand a response more compatible with public education and equity concerns. By seeking a solution to the systemic through looking at the particular, different possibilities became thinkable.

Good schools are filled with particulars—including particular human beings. And it is these human beings that lie at their heart, that explain their surprising successes. In fact, it is these particulars that inspire the passions of those involved and draw upon the best in each. Rather than ignore such schools because their solutions lie in unreplicable individuals or circumstances, it's precisely such unreplicability that should be celebrated. Maybe what these "special" schools demonstrate is that *every school must have the power and the responsibility to select and design its own particulars* and thus to surround all young people with powerful adults who are in a position to act on their behalf in open and publicly responsible ways. That may be the "silver bullet."

Will grown-ups all jump at the chance to be such responsible adults? Of course not. Most have never been asked to have their own wonderful ideas, much less to take responsibility for them. Many will be leery because along with the freedom to design their own particulars must come new responsibilities for defending the outcomes. But the resultant practice, responsible citizenship, is not only a good means for running a good school but also the central aim of public schooling. How convenient.

In designing a way to make it easier to invent powerful and responsible schools, we can stack the deck in favor of good schooling, so that great schools are more likely, good schools become ordinary practice, and poor schools are more quickly exposed and dealt with. This effort will require us to learn how to make judgments about schools with standards in mind, but not with a standardized ruler in hand. For too long we've acted as though, in the name of standards, we have to treat students and teachers as interchangeable parts. Nothing could be worse for standards, and nothing would be more unnecessary.

We already know some of the common features of exemplary schools —public or private—that serve ordinary and extraordinary children well. For example:

Smallness.   It helps if schools are of a reasonable size, small enough for faculty members to sit around a table and iron things (such as standards) out, for everyone to be known well by everyone else, and for schools and families to collaborate face-to-face over time. Small enough so that children belong to the same community as the adults in their lives instead of being abandoned in adultless subcultures. Small enough to both feel safe and be safe. Small enough so that phony data can easily be detected by any interested participant. Small enough so that the people most involved can never say they weren't consulted.

Self-governance.   It helps if those most directly involved have sufficient autonomy over critical decisions. Only then will it be fair to hold people accountable for the impact of their decisions. This will entail creating democratic adult communities that have the power to make decisions about staffing, leadership, and the full use of their budget, as well as about the particulars of scheduling, curriculum, pedagogy, and assessment.

Choice. It helps if there are sufficient choices available for parents, students, and teachers so that schools can afford to be different from one another—to have their own definite characters, special emphases, and styles of operating that appeal to some but not all. Responsibility flows more naturally from willing and informed parties. (If schools are small, they can share big old buildings, and choices can be easily available.)

These three qualities—schools that are small enough in size, sufficiently self-governing, and self-chosen—offer a good beginning. They won't in themselves solve anything, although together they could help solve everything.

Two different historic endeavors in New York City—the 22-year experiment with schools of choice in District 4 and the Alternative High School Division's 12-year effort that created dozens of small alternatives, came together in the 1990s to challenge "business as usual." These ventures caught the public's fancy, stimulating a movement on behalf of small schools of choice for all ages and types of students. The genie was out of the bottle and hard to put back. The idea of small alternative schools attracted the attention of families who did not see themselves as "at risk." Word of mouth suggested that students in these schools matched their counterparts academically and surpassed them on many critical dimensions: college attendance, work preparedness, and ability to perform socially valued tasks. They were also achieving improved scores on typical academic assessments. The research community gradually confirmed such impressions. The studies suggest that such schools provide for the possibility of a community powerful enough to be compelling to young people—a club worth joining.

The skeptics say it still can't work en masse. Whether we create another 100 or 200 small schools of choice—some starting from scratch, others carved out of existing schools—they can't be built to last. Everyone agrees that, under present circumstances, such schools have a limited future. The reformers argue, however, that "present circumstances" are not engraved in stone.

Why Exceptions Can't Become the Norm

Without deep-seated changes in the system that surrounds these small schools of choice, history suggests that the critics will be right: most will water down their innovations or give up altogether. As their numbers increase, so, oddly enough, does their vulnerability. This is one case in which there may not be more safety in numbers. For one thing, these maverick schools tax the capacities of the existing institutions—both the formal system and the godfatherly individuals and organizations that spring up to provide nurturance and cover. Second, as their numbers increase, they're more noticeable. This visibility, in turn, creates new demands to bring them into compliance. Their mainstream counterparts ask why the mavericks are allowed to "get away" with this or that. Who do they think they are? Third, as new roadblocks appear, which require new Herculean responses, school folks begin to complain of weariness—the original fire in the belly that fueled the pioneering spirit begins to wane. Doing the new and the old at the same time seems more and more unfair, an imposition rather than an opportunity.

The existing system is simply not designed to support such oddball entities. It believes in its mission of control and orderliness. The people who operate the present system do not see themselves in the business of trying to best match teacher to job, child to school. Nor could they do so if they wanted. Instead, whenever they look at a problem, they've been trained to seek, first and foremost, ways to solve it by rule. If it's not good for everyone, it's not good for anyone. To make exceptions smacks of favoritism and inefficiency. Each exception must thus be defended over and over again. How else can we hold everyone accountable?

The results of such rule-boundedness are well-documented—above all by such thoughtful critics of public education as John Chubb and Terry Moe. (We all know that the expression "to work to the rule" describes a form of job sabotage.) Except for small enclaves within the large institution, in which special constituencies carve out their own intimate subschools (the ones designed for the top students or for the most vulnerable), the school as a whole remains remarkably anonymous and unchangeable, the model of a nonlearning institution. But there is an alternative. It means changing the "circumstances" so that those three magic bullets described earlier—small, self-governing schools of choice—can be in the mainstream, not on the sidelines, of the system.

If nearly all good schools in the private sector share these three characteristics, why can't we offer them publicly for all children? Because, it's said, it's not politically feasible when public monies are at stake. If that's the nub of the argument, then we should either roll over and admit defeat or make it politically feasible. That means inventing a system of accountability for public funds and aiming for educational results that don't require bad educational practice. It's as simple—and every bit as hard—as that.

Changing the Present Circumstances

Small, self-governing schools of choice could be encouraged to flourish, grow like Topsy, spread like weeds, if we built our system *for them,* not them for our system. To create highly personalized schools, however, we have to be willing to shift both our practices and our mindset cautiously and relentlessly over many years. Present practice isn't inevitable. What we have, after all, is a human invention that's only a hundred years old. But just because it's one of those newfangled ideas that doesn't work doesn't mean it will fade away naturally. In fact, it's got a tenacious hold. But our current practice is not the inevitable product of our human nature. In fact, it's peculiarly in conflict with our humanity and with everything we know about rearing the young.

Until the *relationships* between all the people—parents and teachers—responsible for raising our children are changed, changing the parts (curriculum, pedagogy, or assessment) won't matter very much. But it's precisely because, in the long run, these professional "details" matter a great deal that we need to create a system of schooling that allows us to spend our time and energy honing them, close to home. As Theodore Sizer wisely said when Central Park East Secondary School was started, "Keep it simple, so that you can focus on what will always remain complex the mind of each individual learner and the subject matter we're trying to help her master." Schools have been doing the reverse for far too long.

We shouldn't declare all schools independent tomorrow. We shouldn't remove all rules and regulations by fiat. We shouldn't even downsize all schools by fiat. Until we have more parents clamoring for change, more teachers with the skill and confidence to try out new approaches, and more living examples of schools that are both independent and accountable, we need to keep our ambitions in check. We're aiming at a change that sticks, not another fad.

On the immediate agenda, for example, is creating a series of large-scale pilot "laboratories" to see how it might work if we let the existing idiosyncratic schools, with their already eager stalwarts, officially break loose and be different. Add to them all those interested in staffing new schools to replace the worst of our current enterprises. Then we'll need a lean master contract between these schools, the union, the city, and the state—a contract coveting the most basic obligations as well as those unwaivable local, state, and federal rules pertaining to health, safety, and equity. If those on the sidelines can sit back and watch, not rush in, as the pioneers develop their own answers—including mistaken ones—then we'll learn something. The present system of schooling and accountability is chock-full of mistakes, after all, not to mention disasters that are perpetuated year after year. Of course we're accustomed to them, so we barely notice. This time, let's notice the mistakes and the disasters—with equal charity. As a way of noticing, let's honor forms of accountability that support rather than sabotage the very qualities such independence is trying to achieve: accountability through the responsible exercise of collective human judgment.

The "magic" three—smallness, self-governance, and choice—provide some of the necessary basic ingredients for more responsible individual schools and thus for more accountability. Smallness creates self-knowledge, self-governance allows for a range of voices now often missing, and choice permits disgruntled parents and teachers to vote with their feet. But while these three elements appear to undercut some of the pressure for more and more external accountability, there's a strong argument for adding several other ingredients that will support the development of a more responsible community of schools. Not just because it's politically smart—but because without a powerful system of public accountability, good individual schools can too easily become stuck in routines, parochial, smug, and secretive. Even tyrannical. Smallness, for example, makes it harder to hide from the impact of bad leadership as well as good leadership.

There are several forms of public accountability that are not only compatible with but actually supportive of school-based initiatives. One way to improve the odds, compatible with the three magic bullets, is to increase constituents' voices about the work not only of their own schools but also of other people's schools in terms of student outcomes, equity, and fiscal integrity. Experience suggests that networks of schools can offer us an opportunity to have the best of both worlds: individuality and close external accountability. We need ways to hold schools up to a mirror and ask, "Is this what you meant to be doing?" We need to tackle professional myopia and defensiveness. We assume that schoolchildren learn by being exposed to criticism, but we have not transferred that to the way teachers and schools learn. For this to happen, we need to create instruments that are consistent with the very quality that led us to propose small schools in the first place: responsiveness to often nonstandard ways of maintaining high standards. What strong democratic schooling needs are new forms of horizontal accountability focused on the collective work of the school.

The first step involves creating stronger internal accountability systems, such as those pioneered at Central Park East Secondary School, Urban Academy, University Heights, and International High School, which use both peers and external critics—college faculty members, parents, community members, and other high school teachers—to examine their students' work. It's the job of the teachers, for example, to grade their own students and to determine when they meet schoolwide standards—a task too few schools take seriously today. But the teachers, in turn, need to be publicly accountable for such judgments—both to their internal constituents and to the larger public.

At the next step, schools must answer to one another for the quality of their work. Through the creation of networks of sister schools, not uncommon in private schooling, we can learn how to look at one another's work as critical friends. Such networks can also serve to make up for any problems of scale, if schools choose to use them in that way. Schools that provide feedback on the work of sister schools are creating built-in professional development tools, as well as a powerful form of parent and community education. There is nothing better for one's own learning curve than to formally observe and give support to others.

Third, networks need "cooler," noncollegial audiences to answer to. For this we need formal review panels—public auditors—composed of both critical friends and more distanced and skeptical publics, to attest to the credibility of the networks and the work of their schools. It is such bodies that must demand convincing evidence that the network of schools under review is doing its job, is on the right track, and is acting responsibly. Such review panels must ultimately be responsible to the larger, democratically chosen public authorities.

And finally, everyone—teachers, parents, assessors, legislators, and the public—needs a shared body of credible information (actual student work as well as statistical data) as evidence on which to build reflections and judgments. These are the essentials for creating public credibility, but they are also the essentials for producing good schools. The task of these varied groups of observers—the school's immediate community, the networkers, and the external review panels—is not to find the "one right answer" but to push those closest to the action to act with greater enlightenment.

This is no idle dream. In New York City in 1995, with the support of funds from the Annenberg Challenge, nearly 100 small schools broke themselves down into more than 20 such self-chosen networks and began the work of shared support and accountability. More of these schools were in the works within a year. Simultaneously, a system of review panels to accredit such networks and to maintain audits of their work was being developed, as was a system for collecting credible and accessible data. In return, both the union and the city agreed to negotiate new freedoms and greater flexibility. The largest city in the land was on the brink of the biggest experiment on the potential of smallness. But New York City's inability to keep the same chancellor for more than a few years soon put the more risky and experimental aspects of the project on the back burner.

On a smaller scale, also with support from Annenberg, Boston launched a similar approach—called pilot schools—and throughout the country at other Annenberg sites comparable efforts were begun. Not surprisingly, system folks are always tempted by apparently easier solutions that do not change the locus of power and are simpler to implement—at least on paper.

≈◈≈

We periodically imagine that we can avoid the messiness of human judgments and create a foolproof automatic system to make everyone good or smart or intelligent. At least, we pretend to believe it is possible. Then we get upset at the bureaucracy it inevitably spawns. But if juries of our peers will do for deciding life-and-death matters of law, why not juries of our peers to decide life-and-death matters of education? As Winston Churchill once said about democracy itself, nothing could be more flawed—except all the alternatives. Of course, juries need guidelines, a body of precedents, rules of procedure, evidence, and the requirement to reach a publicly shared decision. This will not come easily or overnight, and, like democracy itself, such an approach rests on restoring levels of mutual trust we seem inclined to abandon altogether—to our peril.

The criterion we need to keep at the forefront of our minds is clear: How will this or that policy affect the intelligent and responsible behavior of the people closest to the students (as well as the students themselves)? That's the litmus test. Creating forms of governance and accountability that are mindful first and foremost of their impact on effective relationships between teachers, children, and families will not be an easy task. It may not even show up as a blip on next year's test scores. But shortcuts that bypass such relationships are inefficient.

If we do it right, we might in the process help create responsible and caring communities that are more powerful than those adultless subcultures that dominate far too many of our children's lives and that endanger our larger common community. The problem we face is, after all, more than "academic."

NO

Emeral A. Crosby

Urban Schools: Forced to Fail

Is there anyone who doesn't recall the famous opening sentence of *A Tale of Two Cities*? "It was the best of times, it was the worst of times, it was the age of wisdom, it was the age of foolishness, it was the epoch of belief, it was the epoch of incredulity, it was the season of Light, it was the season of Darkness, it was the spring of hope, it was the winter of despair, we had everything before us, we had nothing before us...."

Such a string of seeming contradictions applies to the late-20th-century world, in which more people have more money than ever before, yet there is more grinding poverty than ever before in isolated rural areas and in the slums of our cities. Affluence exists side by side with deprivation. More young people graduate from high school, yet more young people are classified as dropouts. Good education coexists with miseducation. While there is more security, there is more uncertainty.

For those of us who work in schools, it is also the best of times and the worst of times. Our urban schools, once the pride of our nation, are now a source of controversy and inequity. We have watched with dismay their descent into confusion and failure. Time and space do not permit a thorough discussion of all the factors that bear down on urban schools. However, in this article I will deal with several of the factors that I believe are forcing urban schools to fail.

The Bureaucracy

The decision-making process in urban schools contributes to their failure. But first let me try to define that process broadly. According to many observers, the "decision process" by which both government and private corporations are run in America is a group process. It is not individual ability that determines success in our society; it is the efficient operation of the decision-making process, which is the sum of accumulated information and the skills of a group. The only implication we can safely draw from this fact is that the process has worked for government, private enterprise, education, unions, medicine. No single person or committee can govern these mammoth domains. The "leader" depends on the actions of others, and his actions are dictated to some extent by subordinates who are considered "specialists." This is how a bureaucracy operates.

And that is how things work in America. But making decisions in this way is not always in the best interests of the majority of citizens.

The settling of the American colonies offers an early example of the decision-making process. When the oppression of the controlling powers of 17th-century Europe became too burdensome for the powerless colonists, many fled to the colonial "suburbs"—the new frontiers of America. Flight was their strategy for solving the problems of taxation, inadequate housing, legal injustices, and unemployment.

Flight and the displacement of other people became a pattern in America, but it is a pattern that was determined by the decision of the group. For example, the colonial settlers had to displace the Native Americans in order to establish themselves in new territories. The Native Americans were forced to move on to less desirable areas, to what amounted to ghettos created by the people who displaced them. This policy could be carried out with a clear conscience as long as the Native Americans were considered "different"—barbarians, savages, inferiors, not humans. Of course, no one person made such judgments or decisions. They were made through myriad individual decisions of all members of the group. In this way, everyone and no one was responsible for the outcome.

Such a system continues to operate to this day. The decision-making process is itself an institution, and urban schools are deeply rooted in the decision-making process. To go against it is to be a noncomformist, to act against the group, which amounts to a kind of heresy that can bring misfortune to the offender.

This decision-making process can be described as "bureaucratic." Bureaucracy operates when decisions require that all information be moved upward from one level of specialists to another through a management hierarchy whose multiple levels often distort the nature of the information. Although the bureaucracy is composed of people (aided by computers), it is not controlled by individuals. It is self-generating, self-regulating, and self-perpetuating.

Because the decision-making process is what drives the institution or the organization, the bureaucracy is quite powerful. Because it is an anonymous and faceless collective, it is difficult to control, sidestep, or subvert. Because it seeks to perpetuate itself and its processes, it frequently serves as the brakes that bring innovation and change to a halt.

How does this bear upon the urban schools? They are run by institutional bureaucracies that resist change. Yet the urban schools must change in response to the growing complexities and demands of our society that have made the existing networks and organizational structures obsolete. When the bureaucracy blocks meaningful change, it is inevitable that the urban schools will fail a large number of their clients, the students.

Buildings and Sites

Environment affects learning. We can surely agree on that, but we have yet to measure the magnitude of the role that environment plays in learning—both in aiding it and in hindering it.

While curriculum, school organization, and communication technology undergo significant changes, school buildings themselves are often too old to accommodate to these changes. Many urban schools are well over 50 years old and designed to provide an environment different from what we need today. Often located in the oldest parts of the city, many of these buildings are in violation of modern fire codes and are hazards to safety. The plumbing is obsolete; asbestos insulation poses health problems; lead poisoning from paint and soil has a negative impact on student learning and the brain development of young children. Furthermore, these buildings cannot accommodate the activities, the equipment, and the materials that new programs and modern technology demand.

These old buildings are hard to heat in winter, and they retain heat in the summer. They require constant renovation, but they can never be properly updated to meet the needs of modern students. Even when their condition is not especially dilapidated, their appearance is often oppressive. And research has shown that such oppressive, unattractive surroundings are detrimental to the learning process.

Costly as it is, remodeling offers one solution. But, once again, the process of decision making gets in the way. Of course, flight is still one solution to the problem of these ancient, inadequate structures. Build somewhere else. Build on the periphery of the city or in the suburbs.

When an existing urban school is remodeled or replaced, its architecture often doesn't meet the real needs of the school community. The physical plant often works against successfully housing the thousands of students who attend the urban school. Elementary schools, built for smaller populations, often cram a thousand students into a small building, while large high schools must accommodate up to 3,000 students in a single building. Handling the volume of students entering, passing through the halls, and exiting the building is a tremendous problem. What's more, the lack of a campus means that many interscholastic and intramural activities—such as soccer, softball, and tennis—cannot be offered.

Planners and decision makers do not often consider the importance of environment to the inhabitants of school structures. When it is possible to do significant remodeling and upgrading of an urban school to create a positive educational environment, the needs of the inhabitants of these buildings must be considered. We must ask and answer some basic questions: What should happen in the urban school? How can the environment of an urban school be planned so that desired behaviors and educational goals can be accomplished? Unless sensible and realistic actions result from answering such questions, the physical environment of urban schools becomes just one more factor in the process of failure.

Overload

Most people agree that the central goal of the public schools is to teach students to read, write, and compute. Urban schools today simply have too many other things to accomplish under too many unfavorable conditions. The urban school is no longer merely an academic institution; it is also a social and welfare institution. Among the necessary services it provides are recreation, cultural growth, emotional development, basic health care, food service, voter registration, draft registration, driver education, sex education, employment service, immunization, and the collection of census data. The urban school is, in effect, like a government of a small city. Yet the added responsibilities have come without any administrative or structural change and without the addition of essential personnel. Problems increase, but the means to solve them are not available.

Too much responsibility without the means to carry it out overloads the urban schools. Students come to see their educational experiences in these institutions as if they were looking through the small end of a telescope: their experiences appear artificial, remote, unreal, and irrelevant.

When the system cannot afford to fulfill its responsibilities—already enormous—the solution is often to cut "nonbasic" school programs rather than to reduce the burden of the outer layers of the organization. Because of the power and influence of those people who have positions in the outer organization, the programs cut tend to be the very enrichment programs that children in urban areas need to make use of their basic education. These programs, too important to appear on the list of superfluous classes, include remedial reading, remedial math, guidance counseling, school newspaper, the media center, art, music, and any extracurricular activities that might have survived the last round of cuts. For indifferent students who often come to school unwillingly and reluctantly, these courses—last to be added, first to go—can offer inspiration and a reason to learn.

Unless the organization of education is restructured to handle the additional demands placed on schools, the urban schools will continue to fail large numbers of their clients.

A New Population

"What the best and wisest parent wants for his own child," John Dewey remarked in 1899, "that must the community want for all of its children. Any other idea for our schools is narrow and unlovely; acted upon, it destroys our democracy." Our democracy is in peril because the community is not providing the best education it can for its poor and urban youngsters. Too often minority students and poor students are not provided with the intellectual skills and the academic knowledge needed to earn a decent living and to participate fully in the economic, social, and political life of the community.

Our urban schools were not designed for their present clients. The urban school population changed radically after World War II. Prior to that time, the urban school population included large numbers of white and middle-class students, with even a smattering of the children of the wealthy. Today, this population consists largely of minorities: immigrants, African Americans, and the poor.

In the early 1950s the exodus of the white middle and upper classes from the cities was as dramatic and sudden as the departure of Moses and his people from Egypt. But, once again, this flight was the secondary result of the decision-making process in two areas: the development of the interstate highway system, which made commuting more convenient, and the creation of federal mortgage programs, which financed suburban housing construction. The advertising industry reinforced the desirability of migrating to the suburbs. Automobiles were shown being driven through beautiful suburbs, not through city streets. Children were seen running in from lush green lawns for their Campbell's soup, their Kraft macaroni, or their Cheracol cough syrup. They weren't shown coming in from the city streets where they had been playing basketball so that their mothers could wash their shirts in Tide or give them Kool-Aid from the refrigerator in their middle-class kitchens.

Another development that shifted the demographics was the rapid mechanization of farms, which displaced many rural people and sent them to the cities and their children to urban schools.

The new wave of immigration of the last 25 years from Hispanic countries, from the Middle East, and from Asian countries has washed over the urban schools like a tidal wave, bringing with it additional challenges, this time cultural and linguistic.

As the total population of major cities decreases, the school population decreases as well. But at the same time, the minority population of urban schools increases, and the duties and problems that come with the new population are overwhelming to the institution. There is the need for food and sanitation and for keeping records and storing supplies. There are demands for safety and surveillance, including fire rules and drills and protection against intrusion, robbery, assault, and vandalism. And there are gangs and the problems that come with drugs. Special education is the fastest-growing element in the urban schools. And it is an element for which urban schools are poorly prepared.

Delinquent behavior is too mild a term to describe a problem that can be devastating for urban schools. In the high schools, for example, there is a kind of anarchy or civil war that is more serious than most people outside the schools realize. Students are angry young people, and they question every rule. Students commit acts of defiance that are astonishing in their destructive effect on the population and the institution.

In the face of this multitude of problems, those in authority react with stricter punishments, armed hallway guards, metal detectors, and forms of repression meant to stem the tide. The rules become more mechanical, rigid, and impersonal. The students are known by their I.D. numbers, and the personalities of teachers are effaced by the need to maintain order at great cost to everyone in the school.

I can barely touch on the causes of delinquent behavior in this article. However, as far as the schools are concerned, the following deficiencies are key to delinquent behavior:

- The education being offered is not meaningfully related to the real world—the world of employment and changing social conditions.
- The school does not present itself as a model of the pluralistic society. Students are grouped according to ability, race, and economic class. The school isolates and excludes when inclusion is its reason for being.
- The school often fails to prepare young people for mature life. Students learn through imitation, but they do not have the models of behavior that will benefit them in the future. Consequently, they remain children. Above all, in this bureaucratic institution, students must be allowed to develop personal responsibility and have opportunities for decision making as part of their preparation for adult life.

When school experience is irrelevant to life experience and to employment opportunities, it contributes heavily to dropout rates. When the school organization isolates and excludes according to ability, race, or economic class, it denies young people the opportunity for meaningful interaction with all segments of society. The resulting alienation lies at the heart of delinquency. The system is a machine that is not equal to its task, and it forces the urban schools to fail.

Cost of Security

Imagine the high school as a giant marketplace where consuming and selling occurs every day. In the course of a day, the student purchases food, school supplies, tickets for school events, and items sold for fund-raising. Money is exchanged as a matter of course in a relatively unguarded atmosphere.

Imagine also the young entrepreneur who attends the urban school. What does he see? A free flow of money that is unprotected except by teachers, and those teachers already have more than enough to do. He sees no barriers to taking clothes, shoes, or jackets from his peers. He sees few restraints on the sale of illegal drugs and narcotics. He sees the marketplace, filled with goods for the taking, as a source of income for himself.

Elsewhere—in fact, everywhere else—security measures have been taken to deal with the criminal element that pervades the larger marketplace that we call our society. Security personnel are included in the operating budgets of supermarkets, banks, parking lots, service stations, laundromats, restaurants, and department stores. Security has been a fact of life everywhere except in the marketplace of the school.

When it becomes obvious that the exchange of money demanded protection for the consumer—the high school client, who is still a child and in the care of the adults who staff the school—the first line of defense was the teacher. Put teachers on hall duty. Put teachers in the lunchroom. Then, when they have expended enough psychic energy to exhaust themselves, send them back to the classroom, where they are expected to provide meaningful and challenging instruction in math, science, history, and English.

It never did work, and it isn't working today. It takes away from the teacher preparation time and refueling time. Professionals, who are being paid professional wages, are doing the work of security personnel. In terms of dollars alone, that is an expensive mistake.

Today, even when teachers are used to staff the halls and lunchrooms, at least 10% of every urban school budget is set aside for security-related measures: security personnel, metal detectors, replacement of stolen property. The equivalent of an entire police precinct has been created to serve the security needs of urban schools, and that means more expense for patrol cars, officers, supervisors, and uniforms, as well as coverage for special events and board meetings.

In the last two decades, the decision makers in urban school districts have recognized that the schools need the same level of security as any other agency in the community. After all, aren't our students our most precious commodity? But perhaps that doesn't include urban students, because allocations from the state for education do not allow for security expenses. Therefore, the urban schools have to use some of their classroom allocations for security. It turns out that security eats up from 10% to 12% of their budgets.

What does this mean in terms of dollars? An urban district with a budget of $500 million or more must subtract at least $50 million from its classroom budget, which includes teachers' salaries. In many cases, the costs of security for urban school districts exceed the total budget for many smaller municipalities, and the security force of an urban school often outnumbers the entire police force of small towns.

When we talk about the costs of security in urban schools, we are talking about numbers with a lot of zeroes. And we can't even count all the costs. The hidden expenses of security cannot be calculated. Indeed, it might be too frightening if we examined the costs any further than we have here.

The Professional Staff

Given the new populations in our urban schools, the number of professional staff members is not the result of any general shortage in the supply of teachers. In suburban communities that surround large, urban districts, the ratio of professional personnel to students is higher than in urban districts. Where the need is greatest, the supply is smallest. The higher salaries, better working conditions, and better recruiting methods of the suburban districts are magnets that draw personnel away from the urban districts.

The teacher turnover rate in the urban schools is much higher than in the suburban schools and in other more stable communities. The result is that urban schools, especially those in the inner cities, are often staffed largely by newly hired or uncertified teachers. Teachers who have remained in the urban schools through the traumatic and radical changes of the last three decades are in need of retraining and of rethinking their roles as educators. These teachers, who were trained to teach students from middle-class families and who often come from middle-class families themselves, now find themselves engulfed by minority students, immigrants, and other students from low-income families—students whose values and experiences are very different from their own. Teachers who are unaware of these differences or who are alienated from the norms of their students are often unable to communicate with or understand them. Retraining for these teachers, while essential, is not generally available.

The staffing of urban schools has also been affected by the shift of populations from city to suburbs. Many teachers who have remained in urban schools no longer live in the city where they work but have moved to the suburbs. This is the first step in the disengagement of urban teachers from the urban situation. The teachers withdraw themselves from the community of the students, and the only result can be a growing reluctance to be a part of that community in any way except to earn a paycheck. It is a form of disloyalty to the students. This withdrawal and this disloyalty cannot be cured by a program or a workshop. Yet those are the cures now being offered.

On the other side of the ledger, teachers are forced to fail by the bureaucracy of the decision makers. The loyal teachers experience what can only be called disloyalty on the part of the system, which withdraws from its teachers. The system is reluctant to reward teachers for their devotion to students. The system disengages itself from the classroom, the teacher's workstation, by not providing adequate support in the form of supplies and encouragement. Teachers suffer from a lack of psychic nurturing, and they are virtually alone in the classroom, without adult support.

Indeed, teaching, as it is now practiced in urban schools, is the most isolated of the professions. Some nonurban districts have begun to move toward cooperative teaching, team teaching, and common planning. The professional isolation of the urban teachers must end as well.

One severe ramification of this isolation is that talented teachers do not have the opportunity to pass their talents and expertise on to others. Their skill dies in their classrooms—and, with every teacher retirement, a vacuum is created. Experienced teachers have gotten that way by learning from their mistakes over many years. Sharing the fruits of their experience—the successes and the failures—could help new teachers avoid making the same mistakes. Moreover, it could inspire new teachers to reach the best in themselves. The teacher training institutions have not placed sufficient emphasis on preparing new teachers to work in schools that serve minority students. There are no lucrative college scholarships for prospective teachers, as there are in athletics. Nor are there significant bonuses offered for those who will teach in urban schools. Teacher candidates are not offered courses designed to familiarize them with the history and the culture of their potential students, much less with their learning problems and their psychology. Teachers who are already part of the school organization are generally not provided with inservice training to make them more effective in their classrooms. The current practices of awarding bonuses and scholarships, making personnel assignments, and offering inservice training must be changed.

Every time teachers serve on hall duty or lunchroom duty, their talents are being misused. Teachers could be tutoring students or mentoring other teachers. They could be conferencing, sharing, and doing observations. But urban teachers are denied professional renewal during the course of the school day. The only time they can engage in professional activities is after school—after they have already taught five classes and performed many other mentally and physically exhausting duties. At the end of the day, their minds are not fresh, their energy is low, they are fatigued, and their spirits are depleted. How much professional renewal can we expect? Such abuse of teacher talent is a crime against the profession, but its ultimate victims are the students. When teachers are forced to fail, then the urban schools themselves are forced to fail.

Lack of Political Courage

Revolutions that benefit society rather than destroy the good in it require revolutionary methods and processes. To date, urban school problems have been handled in an ad hoc and inefficient manner. Confusion about goals is matched by lack of commitment to the real cure for educational ills. Indeed, the resistance to change is strong because many people benefit from the status quo in urban education: owners of ghetto housing and small businesses, privileged white workers protected from minority competition, and all those who gain when society's dirty work is done cheaply by others.

But the changes that assault our urban schools are producing a cultural revolution that will spread throughout the entire education community in time. Brought about by vandalism, drug abuse, poverty and unemployment, and changing sexual mores, this revolution could be as significant as any past revolution, whether it be political, religious, military, industrial, or technological. Existing structures are being undermined by immigration, racial integration, freedom schools, court decisions, vouchers and charters, and school takeovers. We have no way of successfully predicting the extent of the changes that the future might bring.

But the current pseudo-revolution that is benefiting no one is called "restructuring the urban school." The social engineers want to rebuild urban education on a shaky foundation; they want to build pyramids on an eroding base of sand. They think, for example, that they can mandate parent involvement with people whose time is totally consumed in a struggle to survive. These social engineers want full participation in the school from parents who lack the means to do what they want to do for their children.

A number of generalizations can be made about minority education in the United States, and they apply in particular to urban schools, where most members of minority groups are educated. First, substantial minority deprivation does exist, along with exploitation and segregation. Second, these types of discrimination are endemic to the form of internal colonialism that has been developed in this country. Third, they continue because important segments of white society profit from such arrangements; therefore, while significant social and educational legislation has been enacted, there is only token enforcement. Fourth, political influence follows economic power, and those with vested interests use their power to resist progressive reforms in education. Indeed, when there is change—either for the sake of appearance or as a result of popular pressure—educational programs are set up in a manner that ensures failure. For example, a special program may be funded for only one year, or an inconsequential appendage may be added to a program. Significant and long-lasting reforms are nearly impossible to bring about because our national priorities are set so as to preclude meaningful change.

There are some things that urban educators never talk about in public. Urban educators are silent when the bureaucracy mandates better student attendance. The problem is bigger than the school, and it is beyond the school's power to solve it. Urban educators know some things about the lives of the people in the communities they serve. They know that the poorest of the poor live farthest from the school. They know that it is dangerous to walk the city streets on dark mornings—or even in broad daylight. They know that an automobile is still a luxury among the very poor. And, in case no one else has noted, urban educators know that city transportation is just not available.

Urban educators shake their heads over the cures proposed for the ills of the public school system: the creation of charter schools or magnet schools or the implementation of vouchers. Tear down the old system and start again—but only in urban areas. Although criticism is leveled against all public schools, the remedies are to be applied only to the *urban* public schools. Suburban school districts have sufficient funds and political support to reach their educational goals. Only an educational heretic would propose the purposeful demolition of an affluent suburban school system. Yet this very demolition is what is being offered as a cure for the ills of urban schools. Only an urban bureaucracy would support such a notion.

By their very nature, institutions resist change. Institutions are power, and power concedes to nothing but greater power. If the urban schools are to offer their population of minority children access to the American dream, a powerful political force must move into the educational arena to represent their cause. The alternative is complete failure and the destruction of urban schools.

For urban schools, it is now "the season of light" and "the season of darkness." We have "everything before us," we have "nothing before us." We are going to succeed, or we will surely fail what rests in our charge—the urban schools and the children who attend them.

POSTSCRIPT

Can Self-Governing Schools Rescue Urban Education?

Rethinking the relationship between private goods and the common good is a first step toward a more adequate response to urban poverty in the United States. So says David Hollenbach in "The Common Good and Urban Poverty," *America* (June 5–12, 1999), and this theme trails through the central issue discussed here and the multiple subissues involved. These subissues include inequities in public school funding, the dropout problem, the racial and ethnic gaps in student achievement, the participation of parents in school improvement, the struggle to attain adequate literacy, the quality of inner-city Catholic schools, and the survival of gifted students in urban public schools.

A wealth of material addresses these many related problems. Particularly recommended recent books are *Fixing Urban Schools* edited by Paul T. Hill and Mary Beth Celio (1998); Gene I. Maeroff's *Altered Destinies: Making Life Better for Schoolchildren in Need* (1998); Joseph P. Viteritti's *Choosing Equality: School Choice, the Constitution, and Civil Society* (1999); and Miles Corwin's *And Still We Rise: The Trials and Triumphs of Twelve Gifted Inner-City High School Students* (2000).

Articles of especial note include Evelyn Hanssen's "A White Teacher Reflects on Institutional Racism," *Phi Delta Kappan* (May 1998); "Lessons Learned," *The New Republic* (October 4, 1999); Bruce R. Joyce's "The Great Literacy Problem and Success for All," *Phi Delta Kappan* (October 1999); Robin Cooper's "Urban School Reform from a Student-of-Color Perspective," *Urban Education* (January 2000); Ronald J. Sider's "Making Schools Work for the Rich and the Poor," *The Christian Century* (August 25, 1999); Richard Nadler's "Low Class: How Progressive Education Hurts the Poor and Minorities," *National Review* (December 21, 1998); "Why Do At-Risk Students Thrive in Catholic Schools?" by Nina H. Shokraii, *USA Today Magazine* (May 1998); and "Dropout Prevention: A Case for Enhanced Early Literacy Efforts," *The Clearing House* (January 1999).

Multiple articles can be found in the November 1998 issue of *Education and Urban Society,* the November/December 1999 issue of *The Clearing House,* and the December 1999 issue of *Phi Delta Kappan.*

ISSUE 19

Should Technology Lead the Quest for Better Schools?

YES: James H. Snider, from "Education Wars: The Battle Over Information-Age Technology," *The Futurist* (May–June 1996)

NO: Neil Postman, from "Virtual Students, Digital Classroom," *The Nation* (October 9, 1995)

ISSUE SUMMARY

YES: James H. Snider, a Northwestern University fellow, analyzes the politics of educational change and details the industrial-age barriers that he feels information-age technologies must overcome in order to implement a vastly improved educational system.

NO: Neil Postman, a professor of media ecology and author of numerous books on education and technology, voices serious concern about the dangers of mindless adherence to technological panaceas.

The schools have not always used or responded to new media constructively, so it is crucial that media experts help teachers, administrators, and curriculum designers carve out appropriate strategies for dealing with new technologies. Some experts—while seeing many exciting possibilities in computer-based instruction, particularly in the realm of individualization and self-pacing —caution that we need far more sophisticated understanding of the processes of learning, human motivation, and factors involved in concentration. Others fear the controlling force of computer programs because it could lead to the diminution of the spontaneity and instinctive responses of the learner. The ultimate effect of the new technology could be a complete transformation of learning and the conception of organized education—but similar predictions were made with the advent of television and even radio.

In 1984 MIT professor Seymour Papert predicted, "There won't be schools in the future; I think that the computer will blow up the school." But Larry Cuban, in "Revolutions That Fizzled," *The Washington Post* (October 27, 1996), warns that the persistent urge to reengineer the schools has continually failed to transform teaching practices. Seymour Papert, writing in the same issue, counters that the computer makes possible John Dewey's depiction of learning through experimentation and exposure to the real world of social experience. Computer enthusiasts Jim Cummins of New York University and Dennis Sayers of the Ontario Institute for Studies in Education, in their 1996 book *Brave New Schools*, urge heavy investment in an Internet-wired nationwide school system.

On the negative side, Richard P. Lookatch, in "The Ill-Considered Dash to Technology," *The School Administrator* (April 1996), warns that "hardware hucksters have found K–12 schools to be open landfills for outdated central processing units, while software pushers find technology-zealous media specialists ideal targets for software, much of which ultimately ends up in a storage cabinet because it is either too frustrating, too complicated, or too poorly correlated to the curriculum." His position is that educational media offer no unique benefits and may well lead to inequity, lower standards, and wasted financial resources.

In "The Emperor's New Computer: A Critical Look at Our Appetite for Computer Technology," *Journal of Teacher Education* (May–June 1996), David Pepi and Geoffrey Schuerman pose several crucial questions, including the following:

- Is technology an effective catalyst for educational reform?
- Are past, current, and anticipated uses of technology consistent with contemporary theories of learning?
- Is using computers synonymous with good teaching?
- Does technology promote critical thinking?
- Does technology build cooperation?
- How much information can we tolerate?

In considering responses to such questions, the authors draw on Neil Postman's 1993 book *Technopoly*, in which "technopoly" is defined as a culture in which all aspects of human life must find meaning in terms of the current technology and in which there is no tolerance of alternative worldviews. It is Postman's opinion that we are moving toward that culture.

Books addressing the issue include Nicholas Negroponte's *Being Digital* (1995); Janet W. Schofield's *Computers and Classroom Culture* (1995); Sherry Turkle's *Life on the Screen: Identity in the Age of the Internet* (1995); Jane M. Healy's *Failure to Connect* (1998); Frederick Bennett's *Computers As Tutors: Solving the Crisis in Education* (1999); and Seymour Papert's *The Connected Family* (1996). In his book Papert states, "Despite frequent predictions that a technological revolution in education is imminent, school remains in essential respects very much what it has always been, and what changes have occurred (for better or for worse) cannot be attributed to technology."

In the opinions that follow, James H. Snider presents an optimistic view of the eventual triumph of information-age technology in the process of education but recognizes that there are political and professional barriers to be overcome. Neil Postman provides some dampening commentary on the "hyperactive fantasies" of the technology "cheerleaders," warning that computer use in education is perhaps a Faustian bargain.

James H. Snider

 **YES**

Education Wars: The Battle Over Information-Age Technology

Most people now recognize that new information technology is radically changing the economics of education. Many also believe that, if only the schools could get the best technology and train teachers how to use it, the wonders of the Information Age will come to K–12 education.

But this belief, held by such prominent individuals as the president of the United States and the U.S. secretary of education, is faulty.

In the shift from Industrial Age to Information Age education, most educators will lose money, status, and power. They cannot be expected to accept this change without a fight. Insofar as public education responds to political and not economic forces, educators have a good chance of preserving, or at least slowing the erosion of, their position.

Until the full dimensions of this problem are understood, the promise of technology in education will never be fulfilled.

The new economics of education include the following trends:

From labor intensive to capital intensive Industrial Age education uses little technology. It is low tech and labor intensive. According to the Educational Research Service, more than 95% of a typical public school's budget goes to teachers; less than 5% goes to instructional capital such as books, software, and computers. Since improved technology tends to drive up productivity, the high proportion of education dollars spent on labor is often used to explain why education has the worst productivity record of any major economic sector in the United States.

Information Age education, in contrast, is capital intensive. Education resources, including individualized instruction, are delivered via the information superhighway, high-definition television, multimedia PCs, and so on.

From local to national Industrial Age education is transportation intensive— the learner must physically travel to the key educational resources. As a result of the high cost of travel, education is geographically bound. Students attend the neighborhood school, not one that is thousands of miles away.

In contrast, Information Age education is communications intensive: The learner can access educational resources produced and distributed anywhere in the world. The traditional textbook with national reach is now joined by the "virtual course," the "virtual classroom," and the "virtual school."

From small-scale to large-scale production Public schools (K–12 level) employ some 6 million individuals, about half of whom are teachers. Tens of thousands of teachers teach similar subjects such as Introductory Spanish, U.S. History and Biology I. At least one highly skilled professional teacher per classroom is considered necessary for adequate instruction.

Information Age education requires far fewer teachers to achieve the same or better results. A few thousand of the best teachers in the United States could replace many of the other 3 million. For example, today's 40,000 Algebra I teachers could be largely displaced by a handful of star teachers working nationally.

From small-scale to large-scale evaluation Industrial Age education requires classroom-by-classroom evaluation. Since each classroom has relatively few students and is a largely private and inaccessible space, comparative course evaluation is an extraordinarily expensive and impractical undertaking.

Information Age education courses may be taken by thousands or even millions of students over many years. This creates a large market for course evaluations; there could be national evaluations for courses, just as there are for cars, mutual funds, and colleges.

From monopoly to competition Industrial Age education is a natural monopoly. Students find it impractical to travel long distances to different schools to take different courses, so students often have a choice of only one course and teacher for a given grade and subject matter.

By eliminating geographic barriers, Information Age education makes it possible for students to choose among many courses and classmates, thus creating natural competition.

In summary, the new education economics suggest a shift in power away from regional educators to national educators and to students. National educators gain power because the key education resources are increasingly being produced and distributed on a national basis. Students gain power because they now have choice; they are less dependent on what their regional (e.g., neighborhood) educator provides. Regional educators lose power because their monopoly over education resources is broken.

The vital question for the future, then, is the extent to which the politics and economics of education are coming into conflict. To the extent that regional educators are successful in using political influence to preserve their power, children and parents will have amateurish, expensive, and unnecessarily restricted education services to choose from.

The Politics of Educational Technology

One of the classic tales of capitalism is the propensity of new technologies to put people out of work. Witness the decline in the agricultural sector from more than 90% of the work force in 1800 to less than 3% today. Or consider the loss of tens of thousands of bank-teller jobs with the introduction of the automatic teller machine over the last few decades.

Public education differs from these other industries in that it primarily responds to political, not economic, forces. Laws, not supply and demand, dictate the working conditions, pay, skills, and education requirements of educators. Just think of the many school districts with 500 to 1,000 applications for a teaching position that nevertheless are unable to fire an incompetent teacher. Previous economic conditions may have been embedded in law, but the political process, often most responsive to entrenched interests, may take decades to catch up with new economic conditions. Accordingly, an extraordinary web of laws has been designed to protect and enhance the monopoly power of regional educators. And these educators have a conflict of interest in implementing Information Age technology.

In the nineteenth century, the Luddites sought to prevent the introduction of new technologies by literally smashing the job-destroying machines. Today, educators can hinder the introduction of new technologies with far more subtle mechanisms, such as:

Public-school unions   Public schools have about 6 million unionized employees, including teachers, administrators, and maintenance workers. These unions are extremely influential in setting local education policy and budgets. Since every dollar spent on capital is a dollar taken away from labor, unions favor more spending on labor. In New York City, out of a total spending of about $8,000 per pupil in 1994, only $44 was budgeted for classroom materials. Much of the money spent on technology in the classroom comes from the federal government, grants from companies in the information industry, PTA fund raising, and special technology bonds. Money subject to union wage demands rarely stays allocated to technology for long.

Unions also oppose efforts to introduce competition among educators by granting parents vouchers to choose their own educator. Unions oppose choice even when parents are restricted to choosing among public schools. The National Education Association has already launched a campaign to restrict technology-based choice in higher education. Across the United States, candidates for political office who support educational choice are consistently and vigorously opposed by the local unions.

Teachers in the classroom   Technology can be a direct threat to the teacher's authority in a classroom. Students can already access long-distance and video-based foreign language instruction superior to that in most U.S. secondary schools. When a mediocre teacher must compete with an outstanding teacher in the same classroom, the mediocre teacher feels threatened. The teacher has little incentive to beg the administration and school board for this type of instructional resource. And if the resource is nevertheless provided, the incentive to use it properly is weak.

An important exception to this argument is that certain applications of computers in the classroom are nonthreatening. These include using technology to teach productivity skills such as keyboarding and using a computer, to mark grades and take attendance, to communicate with peers, and to access impersonal reference works.

Education schools   Education schools in the United States employ close to 18,000 professors and annually enroll hundreds of thousands of students. Almost every professional position in a public school, including superintendent, principal, and classroom teacher, requires a special and expensive license only offered by these schools. Moreover, education schools and educator unions have formed a close alliance. The time-consuming licensing program keeps down the supply of educators and thus bolsters wages. Any time supply decreases, price increases. If education schools act in their self-interest, then they will be a formidable opponent of change.

Other laws and regulations   Thousands of laws, regulations, and contractual agreements serve to preserve the monopoly power of regional educators, including: (1) state licensing laws that prevent people from teaching who haven't spent thousands of dollars and countless hours earning an obsolete education degree; (2) state licensing laws that prevent teachers from teaching across state lines (e.g., via telecommunications) where they don't hold licenses; (3) state licensing laws that prevent people with general management skills, but without extensive training in an education school, from attaining positions such as school superintendent; (4) collective bargaining contracts that dictate working conditions, such as limits on virtual or real class sizes; (5) collective bargaining contracts that require all teachers to be paid the same amount, regardless of the demand and supply for their particular positions and level of job performance; and (6) labor laws that make it hard to replace employees ill-suited to using technology in education.

The Battle to Come

A policy battle between the advocates of Industrial Age and Information Age education is brewing. Here are some of the battle lines likely to arise:

History   Advocates of Industrial Age education will point to the failed promises of educational technology enthusiasts; the well-documented discrepancies between technology hype and reality are an embarrassment.

Advocates of Information Age education will point to the printing press as a technology that fundamentally transformed and improved education. Many technologies (e.g., the airplane, telephone, and fax) take decades to mature and become widely available, but eventually have a major impact. Much of the new educational technology is now at that take-off point.

Equity and public schools Industrial Age advocates will point to the historic role of public schools in providing equal opportunity for all. They will see anything that weakens public schools as fostering inequality.

Information Age advocates see today's public schools as a great bastion of inequity and racism in American society, as a result of an education system that is too geographically based: As long as schools are so heavily based on geography, they will represent the geographic distribution of wealth in America.

Equity and technology Advocates of Industrial Age education will emphasize the tendency of technology to create information haves and have-nots. Technology, they will also claim, replaces labor to cut costs, and so results in impersonal and inferior instruction.

Advocates of Information Age education will again point to the precedent of the printing press and the great democratization of education that followed. Just as the printing press brought high quality and affordable education to the masses, new educational technologies should do the same. By reducing the cost of access to the best instruction in the world, these new technologies, if properly implemented, should decrease the discrepancy between the information haves and have-nots.

Choice and parental competence Industrial Age advocates will argue that education consumers are not competent enough to make decisions and therefore should not be given choice. They will point out how difficult it would be for the average parent to comparison shop for education. Choice will create a hucksterish and highly inefficient education market.

Information Age advocates have more faith in the responsibility and competence of parents. They will argue that new technologies will greatly facilitate comparison shopping for education. The emergence of reliable education assessment systems will mean that educational success will be more closely tied to a student's eventual economic success and that this in turn will lead students and parents to take education more seriously than they do now.

Diversity Industrial Age advocates will compare public and private schools, suggesting that public schools offer more student and intellectual diversity. Information Age advocates will compare geographic to non-geographic schools, arguing that the latter offer far more intellectual and geographic diversity. Looking at the tiny course and teacher offerings of regional schools, as well as their narrow and homogeneous distribution of students, they cannot conceive of how any regional school is intrinsically more diverse.

Educators' motives Advocates of Industrial Age education will argue the dangers of putting for-profit companies in control of education. Such companies will be out for the fast buck, hurting kids and wasting taxpayers' money in the process.

Information Age advocates will point out that schools are not currently run by altruists. Today's educators are not fundamentally different from other human beings. What counts is not the motives of educators, but whether those motives can be harnessed to serve the public interest. If parents are given multiple options and good information on those options, they will not choose exploitive and incompetent educators.

Individualized instruction   Industrial Age advocates will argue that labor-intensive instruction is the same as individualized instruction. Technology in education fosters passive learning, much as television does.

Information Age advocates will counter that one-on-one instruction has been prohibitively expensive for traditional schools. Schools have had to put 20 or more students in a single classroom, often forcing teachers to "teach to the middle." Moreover, the limited choice of teachers, courses, and fellow students means that instruction may not be appropriate to the individual learner's needs. They see labor-intensive public schools as fostering a one-size-fits-all system regardless of a student's individual differences in motivation, knowledge, learning style, and ability.

Socialization   Industrial Age advocates will argue that technology-intensive education is anathema to the development of social skills.

Information Age advocates will maintain that social relations can take place over an interactive, multimedia network just as they can take place in a classroom. Moreover, these are the type of social relations that people will likely have at work in the future. Today's concepts of socialization in the schools reflect an outmoded concept of the world and the workplace, for which schools have traditionally prepared children. Many athletic, cultural, and academic activities will continue to offer opportunities for traditional socialization. But the new balance of social relations, including different modes of interaction and increased contact with people of different ages and locales, will be more reflective of the real world that today's children will live and work in tomorrow.

The New Education Leaders

Although many regional educators are enthusiastic about new educational technology, they are unlikely to lead us into Information Age education because it is not in their self-interest to do so. It is telling that, when technology is introduced into schools, it comes in the guise of resources provided by some outside donor such as a Parent-Teacher Association, telephone company, supermarket coupon program, wealthy individual, or special tax increase.

The people who lead us into Information Age education are likely to be those who benefit from new technologies, not regional educators. These new leaders include parents. According to the Software Publishers Association, American families spent more than $500 million on educational software in 1994, almost double the $277 million spent the previous year. Leading this growth were parents buying computers to provide some degree of "home schooling."

Hard-core home schoolers, despite their reputation for anachronistic values, may be the only ones motivated enough to lead U.S. education into the Information Age. These home schoolers, who seek to completely bypass regional educators, have grown from 10,000 to over 500,000 in the last 20 years. They are already the leading users of educational technology in the United States.

Other parents do not take their children out of public schools but supplement the school curriculum with home education. These parents are also likely to be a constituency for meaningful change in education. In general, new technologies make it easier for ambitious and affluent parents to bypass the public schools. As public school budgets for extracurricular and after-school activities shrink, parents turn to other providers to make up the difference. The dollars spent by these home schoolers on educational technology provide national educators with the research and development funds necessary to develop the next generation of educational technology.

Other advocates for the new technology will likely include such beneficiaries as star administrators and teachers who will have the potential to develop national followings, textbook and software publishers, computer and telecommunications companies, and rural and inner-city homeowners whose property values have been depressed by the comparatively inferior quality of local schools.

Industrial Age educators will fight Information Age education tooth and nail. This opposition will be hard to overcome. However, in the long run they will probably do no more than slow the implementation of an emerging and vastly improved educational system. Not only is the encroachment of information technology into children's lives inevitable, but it is critical to their future —and ours.

NO

Neil Postman

Virtual Students, Digital Classroom

If one has a trusting relationship with one's students (let us say, graduate students), it is not altogether gauche to ask them if they believe in God (with a capital G). I have done this three or four times and most students say they do. Their answer is preliminary to the next question: If someone you love were desperately ill, and you had to choose between praying to God for his or her recovery or administering an antibiotic (as prescribed by a competent physician), which would you choose?

Most say the question is silly since the alternatives are not mutually exclusive. Of course. But suppose they were—which would you choose? God helps those who help themselves, some say in choosing the antibiotic, therefore getting the best of two possible belief systems. But if pushed to the wall (e.g., God does not always help those who help themselves; God helps those who pray and who believe), most choose the antibiotic, after noting that the question is asinine and proves nothing. Of course, the question was not asked, in the first place, to prove anything but to begin a discussion of the nature of belief. And I do not fail to inform the students, by the way, that there has recently emerged evidence of a "scientific" nature that when sick people are prayed for they do better than those who aren't.

As the discussion proceeds, important distinctions are made among the different meanings of "belief," but at some point it becomes far from asinine to speak of the god of Technology—in the sense that people believe technology works, that they rely on it, that it makes promises, that they are bereft when denied access to it, that they are delighted when they are in its presence, that for most people it works in mysterious ways, that they condemn people who speak against it, that they stand in awe of it and that, in the "born again" mode, they will alter their lifestyles, their schedules, their habits and their relationships to accommodate it. If this be not a form of religious belief, what is?

In all strands of American cultural life, you can find so many examples of technological adoration that it is possible to write a book about it. And I would if it had not already been done so well. But nowhere do you find more enthusiasm for the god of Technology than among educators. In fact, there are those, like Lewis Perelman, who argue (for example, in his book, *School's Out*) that modern information technologies have rendered schools entirely irrelevant since there is now much more information available outside the classroom than inside it. This is by no means considered an outlandish idea. Dr. Diane Ravitch, former Assistant Secretary of Education, envisions, with considerable relish, the challenge that technology presents to the tradition that "children (and adults) should be educated in a specific place, for a certain number of hours, and a certain number of days during the week and year." In other words, that children should be educated in school. Imagining the possibilities of an information superhighway offering perhaps a thousand channels, Dr. Ravitch assures us that:

> in this new world of pedagogical plenty, children and adults will be able to dial up a program on their home television to learn whatever they want to know, at their own convenience. If Little Eva cannot sleep, she can learn algebra instead. At her home-learning station, she will tune in to a series of interesting problems that are presented in an interactive medium, much like video games....
>
> Young John may decide that he wants to learn the history of modern Japan, which he can do by dialing up the greatest authorities and teachers on the subject, who will not only use dazzling graphs and illustrations, but will narrate a historical video that excites his curiosity and imagination.

In this vision there is, it seems to me, a confident and typical sense of unreality. Little Eva can't sleep, so she decides to learn a little algebra? Where does Little Eva come from? Mars? If not, it is more likely she will tune in to a good movie. Young John decides that he wants to learn the history of modern Japan? How did young John come to this point? How is it that he never visited a library up to now? Or is it that he, too, couldn't sleep and decided that a little modern Japanese history was just what he needed?

What Ravitch is talking about here is not a new technology but a new species of child, one who, in any case, no one has seen up to now. Of course, new technologies do make new kinds of people, which leads to a second objection to Ravitch's conception of the future. There is a kind of forthright determinism about the imagined world described in it. The technology is here or will be; we must use it because it is there; we will become the kind of people the technology requires us to be, and whether we like it or not, we will remake our institutions to accommodate technology. All of this must happen because it is good for us, but in any case, we have no choice. This point of view is present in very nearly every statement about the future relationship of learning to technology. And, as in Ravitch's scenario, there is always a cheery, gee-whiz tone to the prophecies. Here is one produced by the National Academy of Sciences, written by Hugh McIntosh:

> School for children of the Information Age will be vastly different than it was for Mom and Dad.
>
> Interested in biology? Design your own life forms with computer simulation.
>
> Having trouble with a science project? Teleconference about it with a research scientist.

Bored with the real world? Go into a virtual physics lab and rewrite the laws of gravity.

These are the kinds of hands-on learning experiences schools could be providing right now. The technologies that make them possible are already here, and today's youngsters, regardless of economic status, know how to use them. They spend hours with them every week—not in the classroom, but in their own homes and in video game centers at every shopping mall.

It is always interesting to attend to the examples of learning, and the motivations that ignite them, in the songs of love that technophiles perform for us. It is, for example, not easy to imagine research scientists all over the world teleconferencing with thousands of students who are having difficulty with their science projects. I can't help thinking that most research scientists would put a stop to this rather quickly. But I find it especially revealing that in the scenario above we have an example of a technological solution to a psychological problem that would seem to be exceedingly serious. We are presented with a student who is "bored with the real world." What does it mean to say someone is bored with the real world, especially one so young? Can a journey into virtual reality cure such a problem? And if it can, will our troubled youngster want to return to the real world? Confronted with a student who is bored with the real world, I don't think we can solve the problem so easily by making available a virtual reality physics lab.

The role that new technology should play in schools or anywhere else is something that needs to be discussed without the hyperactive fantasies of cheerleaders. In particular, the computer and its associated technologies are awesome additions to a culture, and are quite capable of altering the psychic, not to mention the sleeping, habits of our young. But like all important technologies of the past, they are Faustian bargains, giving and taking away, sometimes in equal measure, sometimes more in one way than the other. It is strange—indeed, shocking—that with the twenty-first century so close, we can still talk of new technologies as if they were unmixed blessings—gifts, as it were, from the gods. Don't we all know what the combustion engine has done for us and against us? What television is doing for us and against us? At the very least, what we need to discuss about Little Eva, Young John and McIntosh's trio is what they will lose, and what we will lose, if they enter a world in which computer technology is their chief source of motivation, authority and, apparently, psychological sustenance. Will they become, as Joseph Weizenbaum warns, more impressed by calculation than human judgment? Will speed of response become, more than ever, a defining quality of intelligence? If, indeed, the idea of a school will be dramatically altered, what kinds of learning will be neglected, perhaps made impossible? Is virtual reality a new form of therapy? If it is, what are its dangers?

These are serious matters, and they need to be discussed by those who know something about children from the planet Earth, and whose vision of children's needs, and the needs of society, go beyond thinking of school mainly as a place for the convenient distribution of information. Schools are not now and have never been largely about getting information to children. That has been on the schools' agenda, of course, but has always been way down on the list. For technological utopians, the computer vaults information-access to the top. This reshuffling of priorities comes at a most inopportune time. The goal of giving people greater access to more information faster, more conveniently and in more diverse forms was the main technological thrust of the nineteenth century. Some folks haven't noticed it but that problem was largely solved, so that for almost a hundred years there has been more information available to the young outside the school than inside. That fact did not make the schools obsolete, nor does it now make them obsolete. Yes, it is true that Little Eva, the insomniac from Mars, could turn on an algebra lesson, thanks to the computer, in the wee hours of the morning. She could also, if she wished, read a book or magazine, watch television, turn on the radio or listen to music. All of this she could have done before the computer. The computer does not solve any problem she has but does exacerbate one. For Little Eva's problem is not how to get access to a well-structured algebra lesson but what to do with all the information available to her during the day, as well as during sleepless nights. Perhaps this is why she couldn't sleep in the first place. Little Eva, like the rest of us, is overwhelmed by information. She lives in a culture that has 260,000 billboards, 17,000 newspapers, 12,000 periodicals, 27,000 video outlets for renting tapes, 400 million television sets and well over 500 million radios, not including those in automobiles.

There are 40,000 new book titles published every year, and each day 41 million photographs are taken. And thanks to the computer, more than 60 billion pieces of advertising junk come into our mailboxes every year. Everything from telegraphy and photography in the nineteenth century to the silicon chip in the twentieth has amplified the din of information intruding on Little Eva's consciousness. From millions of sources all over the globe, through every possible channel and medium—light waves, air waves, ticker tape, computer banks, telephone wires, television cables, satellites and printing presses—information pours in. Behind it in every imaginable form of storage—on paper, on video, on audiotape, on disks, film and silicon chips—is an even greater volume of information waiting to be retrieved. In the face of this we might ask, What can schools do for Little Eva besides making still more information available? If there is nothing, then new technologies will indeed make schools obsolete. But in fact, there is plenty.

One thing that comes to mind is that schools can provide her with a serious form of technology-education. Something quite different from instruction in using computers to process information, which, it strikes me, is a trivial thing to do, for two reasons. In the first place, approximately 35 million people have already learned how to use computers without the benefit of school instruction. If the schools do nothing, most of the population will know how to use computers in the next ten years, just as most of the population learns how to drive a car without school instruction. In the second place, what we needed to know about cars—as we need to know about computers, television and other important technologies—is not how to use them but how they use *us*. In the case of cars, what we needed to think about in the early twentieth century was not how to drive them but what they would do to our air, our landscape, our social relations, our family life and our cities. Suppose in 1946 we had started to address similar questions about television: What will be its effects on our political institutions, our psychic habits, our children, our religious conceptions, our economy? Would we be better positioned today to control TV's massive assault on American culture? I am talking here about making technology itself an object of inquiry so that Little Eva and Young John are more interested in asking questions about the computer than getting answers from it.

I am not arguing against using computers in school. I am arguing against our sleepwalking attitudes toward it, against allowing it to distract us from important things, against making a god of it. This is what Theodore Roszak warned against in *The Cult of Information:* "Like all cults," he wrote, "this one also has the intention of enlisting mindless allegiance and acquiescence. People who have no clear idea of what they mean by information or why they should want so much of it are nonetheless prepared to believe that we live in an Information Age, which makes every computer around us what the relics of the True Cross were in the Age of Faith: emblems of salvation." To this, I would add the sage observation of Alan Kay of Apple Computer. Kay is widely associated with the invention of the personal computer, and certainly has an interest in schools using them. Nonetheless, he has repeatedly said that any problems the schools cannot solve without computers, they cannot solve with them. What are some of those problems? There is, for example, the traditional task of teaching children how to behave in groups. One might even say that schools have never been essentially about individualized learning. It is true, of course, that groups do not learn, individuals do. But the idea of a school is that individuals must learn in a setting in which individual needs are subordinated to group interests. Unlike other media of mass communication, which celebrate individual response and are experienced in private, the classroom is intended to tame the ego, to connect the individual with others, to demonstrate the value and necessity of group cohesion. At present, most scenarios describing the uses of computers have children solving problems alone; Little Eva, Young John and the others are doing just that. The presence of other children may, indeed, be an annoyance.

⋅⊕⋅

Like the printing press before it, the computer has a powerful bias toward amplifying personal autonomy and individual problem-solving. That is why educators must guard against computer technology's undermining some of the important reasons for having the young assemble (to quote Ravitch) "in a specific place, for a certain number of hours, and a certain number of days during the week and year."

Although Ravitch is not exactly against what she calls "state schools," she imagines them as something of a relic of a pre-technological age. She believes that the new technologies will offer all children equal access to information. Conjuring up a hypothetical Little Mary who is presumably from a poorer home than Little Eva, Ravitch imagines that Mary will have the same opportunities as Eva "to learn any subject, and to learn it from the same master teachers as children in the richest neighborhood." For all of its liberalizing spirit, this scenario makes some important omissions. One is that though new technologies may be a solution to the learning of "subjects," they work against the learning of what are called "social values," including an understanding of democratic processes. If one reads the first chapter of Robert Fulghum's *All I Really Need to Know I Learned in Kindergarten,* one will find an elegant summary of a few things Ravitch's scenario has left out. They include learning the following lessons: Share everything, play fair, don't hit people, put things back where you found them, clean up your own mess, wash your hands before you eat and, of course, flush. The only thing wrong with Fulghum's book is that no one has learned all these things at kindergarten's end. We have ample evidence that it takes many years of teaching these values in school before they have been accepted and internalized. That is why it won't do for children to learn in "settings of their own choosing." That is also why schools require children to be in a certain place at a certain time and to follow certain rules, like raising their hands when they wish to speak, not talking when others are talking, not chewing gum, not leaving until the bell rings, exhibiting patience toward slower learners, etc. This process is called making civilized people. The god of Technology does not appear interested in this function of schools. At least, it does not come up much when technology's virtues are enumerated.

The god of Technology may also have a trick or two up its sleeve about something else. It is often asserted that new technologies will equalize learning opportunities for the rich and poor. It is devoutly to be wished for, but I doubt it will happen. In the first place, it is generally understood by those who have studied the history of technology that technological change always produces winners and losers. There are many reasons for this, among them economic differences. Even in the case of the automobile, which is a commodity most people can buy (although not all), there are wide differences between the rich and poor in the quality of what is available to them. It would be quite astonishing if computer technology equalized all learning opportunities, irrespective of economic differences. One may be delighted that Little Eva's parents could afford the technology and software to make it possible for her to learn algebra at midnight. But Little Mary's parents may not be able to, may not even know such things are available. And if we say that the school could make the technology available to Little Mary (at least during the day), there may be something else Little Mary is lacking.

It turns out, for example, that Little Mary may be having sleepless nights as frequently as Little Eva but not because she wants to get a leg up on her algebra. Maybe because she doesn't know who her father is, or, if she does, where he is. Maybe we can understand why McIntosh's kid is bored with the real world. Or is the child confused about it? Or terrified? Are there educators who seriously believe that these problems can be addressed by new technologies?

I do not say, of course, that schools can solve the problems of poverty, alienation and family disintegration, but schools can *respond* to them. And they can do this because there are people in them, because these people are concerned with more than algebra lessons or modern Japanese history, and because these people can identify not only one's level of competence in math but one's level of rage and confusion and depression. I am talking here about children as they really come to us, not children who are invented to show us how computers may enrich their lives. Of course, I suppose it is possible that there are children who, waking at night, want to study algebra or who are so interested in their world that they yearn to know about Japan. If there be such children, and one hopes there are, they do not require expensive computers to satisfy their hunger for learning. They are on their way, with or without computers. Unless, of course, they do not care about others or have no friends, or little respect for democracy or are filled with suspicion about those who are not like them. When we have machines that know how to do something about these problems, that is the time to rid ourselves of the expensive burden of schools or to reduce the function of teachers to "coaches" in the uses of machines (as Ravitch envisions). Until then, we must be more modest about this god of Technology and certainly not pin our hopes on it.

We must also, I suppose, be empathetic toward those who search with good intentions for technological panaceas. I am a teacher myself and know how hard it is to contribute to the making of a civilized person. Can we blame those who want to find an easy way, through the agency of technology? Perhaps not. After all, it is an old quest. As early as 1918, H.L. Mencken (although completely devoid of empathy) wrote, "There is no sure-cure so idiotic that some superintendent of schools will not swallow it. The aim seems to be to reduce the whole teaching process to a sort of automatic reaction, to discover some master formula that will not only take the place of competence and resourcefulness in the teacher but that will also create an artificial receptivity in the child."

Mencken was not necessarily speaking of technological panaceas but he may well have been. In the early 1920s a teacher wrote the following poem:

> Mr. Edison says
> That the radio will supplant the teacher.
> Already one may learn languages by means of Victrola records.
> The moving picture will visualize
> What the radio fails to get across.
> Teachers will be relegated to the backwoods,
> With fire-horses,
> And long-haired women;
> Or, perhaps shown in museums.
> Education will become a matter
> Of pressing the button.
> Perhaps I can get a position at the switchboard.

I do not go as far back as the radio and Victrola, but I am old enough to remember when 16-millimeter film was to be the sure-cure. Then closed-circuit television. Then 8-millimeter film. Then teacher-proof textbooks. Now computers.

I know a false god when I see one.

POSTSCRIPT

Should Technology Lead the Quest for Better Schools?

A few years ago educational reformer John I. Goodlad declared that "school" should be considered as a concept rather than a place and that this formulation would seem to be an appropriate keynote for education in the twenty-first century. Certainly, advocates of computerization and global networking would be comfortable with the idea.

But as we enter the twenty-first century, and as more school systems are being "wired," questions of initial cost, hardware obsolescence, variable availability, software quality and appropriateness, teacher reluctance, and productive utilization remain to be discussed and resolved.

Help in exploring these and related questions may be found in David Pesanelli's "The Plug-in School: A Learning Environment for the Twenty-First Century," *The Futurist* (September/October 1993); Rick Wilber's "Searching for Terms," *The World & I* (May 1994); Robert J. Simpson's "Education 2000 A.D.: A Peek into the Future," *USA Today Magazine* (January 1992); Gary Kidd's "Using the Internet As a School," *The Educational Forum* (Spring 1996); and "Unfilled Promises," by Jane McDonald, William Lynch, and Greg Kearsley, *The American School Board Journal* (July 1996). The April 1996 issue of *The School Administrator* contains a number of articles on such topics as Internet access and technology's usefulness in the inclusion of disabled students. Other journal issues devoted to the controversy include *Educational Leadership* (November 1997), *Thrust for Educational Leadership* (May 1997), *Contemporary Education* (Winter 1997), *NASSP Bulletin* (November 1997), *Theory into Practice* (Winter 1998), *The School Administrator* (April 1999), *NASSP Bulletin* (May 1999 and September 1999), and *Principal* (January 2000).

Two speeches in *Vital Speeches of the Day* (June 1, 1996) offer some provocative thoughts. In "Reinventing Education: New Classrooms for the Information Age," Richard L. Measelle, of Arthur Andersen and Co., explains that organization's "Schools of the Future" project, citing the following guiding principles: passive learning is passé, teachers must be transformed, self-paced learning should be commonplace, student must learn cooperation, and learners should deal with simulated real-life situations. In "The Shortcomings of the Information Age," Jeff Davidson, founder of the Breathing Space Institute in

Chapel Hill, North Carolina, expresses concern about handling information overload at a time when we have more things competing for our attention than any other generation in history.

Finally, educational psychologist Richard P. Lookatch has argued that multimedia use in school offers students the opportunity to interact with the images behind a glass screen, but the looming danger is that it replaces students' interaction with each other and their environment.

ISSUE 20

Is Mandatory Community Service Desirable and Legal?

YES: Vito Perrone, from "Learning for Life: When Do We Begin?" *Equity and Excellence in Education* (September 1993)

NO: Institute for Justice, from " 'Compulsory Volunteering': Constitutional Challenges to Mandatory Community Service," *Litigation Backgrounder* (1994)

ISSUE SUMMARY

YES: Education professor Vito Perrone makes the case for community service learning as a mechanism for revitalizing schools and building a service ethic in students.

NO: The Institute for Justice, a nonprofit, public-interest law center in Washington, D.C., argues that government-mandated service is unconstitutional and negates the spirit of voluntarism.

In recent years governmental action at the state and national levels has aimed to generate altruism among America's youth through programs of community service. State and local policymakers have added new high school graduation requirements that stipulate the completion of a given number of community service hours. At the federal level, Congress has passed the National and Community Service Trust Act of 1993 (P.L. 103–82), a reauthorization of P.L. 101–610, passed in 1990, and the Domestic Volunteer Service Act. The new legislation, which was strongly promoted by President Bill Clinton, established the Corporation for National and Community Service "to engage Americans of all ages and backgrounds in community-based service" in order to deal with the nation's "education, human, public safety, and environmental needs" while fostering civic responsibility and providing educational opportunity for those who make a substantial contribution to service. Although participation is not compulsory, the federal effort is being driven by the same principles that are animating the more binding state and local programs.

Supporters of state-mandated community service echo the Aristotelian sentiment "We become just by doing just acts." Kathleen Kennedy Townsend, executive director of the Maryland Student Service Alliance, contends that "required service is the best strategy for graduating smart, thoughtful, and committed citizens. Without a requirement whether a student becomes involved in service activities depends on happenstance. With a requirement all young people will learn that they can be effective and powerful, that they can solve problems, and that helping others can be enjoyable." Roland MacNichol, a teacher, contends that service learning is "the right thing to do in helping make our schools thoughtful, caring places with strong belief systems based on service and on young people making a difference."

The movement, however, is not without its detractors. Williamson Evers, for example, argues that students who are not up to grade level in math should not be spending time in a mandatory service program, that a "service learning" program gives teachers a license to instill partisan doctrines, and that the movement is "a chintzy way for politicians to get cheap labor out of young people." Evers further argues that the program's coercion aspect takes the spirit of generosity out of service.

Lawsuits stemming from mandatory service programs have been initiated in a number of localities, including Chapel Hill, North Carolina; Mamaroneck, New York; and Bethlehem, Pennsylvania. The legal challengers have held that mandatory, uncompensated service violates the constitutional prohibition of involuntary servitude and that the policy intrudes improperly on parental responsibility. On October 8, 1996, the U.S. Supreme Court ruled on the Mamaroneck case. Rejecting the "involuntary servitude" argument put forth by the plaintiff, the Court found that the school system's requirement of 40 hours of community service for high school graduation was constitutionally valid.

Harry C. Boyte, director of Project Public Life, argues that community service programs, which are widely touted as the cure for young people's political apathy, in fact teach little about the art of participation in public life. In "What Is Wrong With National Service?" *Social Policy* (Fall 1993), Claudia Horwitz maintains that the federal effort is "sapping the energy of many of our nation's most powerful young leaders" and drawing attention away from the real causes of and possible solutions to very critical problems.

Other views on the issue have been expressed in a variety of articles in the October 1997 *NASSP Bulletin* and the Summer 1997 *Theory into Practice,* as well as in "Learning Through Community Service Is Political," by Bird L. Jones, Robert W. Maloy, and Charlotte M. Steen, *Equity and Excellence in Education* (September 1996) and "Service Learning: Facilitating Learning and Character Development," by Shelly Schaefer Hinck and Mary Ellen Brandell, *NASSP Bulletin* (October 1999).

In the selections that follow, Vito Perrone draws on his own positive experiences in making the case for expanding the various types of community service learning practices that are currently in effect. The Institute for Justice, which has provided legal support for those who have challenged the constitutionality of mandatory service programs, maintains that the decision to serve others is not a choice that should be made by the state.

Vito Perrone  **YES**

Learning for Life: When Do We Begin?

While service learning is currently assuming the role of innovation, seen as a means for enhancing citizenship education and informing reform within schools by encouraging flexibility of schedules and a more active pedagogy, I trust we know that there is a history of consequence. John Dewey, for example, wrote eloquently at an earlier time in this century about the need for education to be seen as active—about doing and acting and being connected to the world. The Dewey School, which existed during the period 1896–1904, had an important outwardness as did many other early 20th century schools that assumed a progressive orientation.

The revival of interest in service learning has many roots—concerns about a growing age stratification, a youth culture that has too few connections to civic life, feelings among youth of having no critical and acknowledged place in the society, disturbing voting patterns in the 18- to 24-year-old population, growing schoolwork transitional difficulties, a deterioration of communities as settings for social growth, an enlarging set of social service needs, increased pessimism about the future, and a belief that schooling is not powerful enough to evoke deep commitments to learning, among others.

The revival of service learning has not, though, been smooth, even as federal legislation and some state actions have given it a big boost. In most settings, service learning is an add-on. It is not a set of activities or orientation integral to the ongoing life of schools. It is often framed as a modest require-ment for graduation with accompanying debates about whether 15 hours, 20 hours, or 40 hours should be the standard. And the issue is in the courts as well. The Bethlehem case—about a 40-hour service requirement over four years —is now in the Court of Appeals in Philadelphia, the challenge being rooted in the 13th Amendment which deals with involuntary servitude.

I have long been attracted to service learning as a means of revitalizing schools and their connections to communities. It is an important way of fully engaging students, of pushing what is done in and around schools toward the *use* of knowledge and not just the *possession* of information. It is also a process directed toward the full integration of all persons, young and old, into the civic and economic aspects of life in their various communities. I invoke this broader view to make sure that we understand clearly the need for service learning to be

From Vito Perrone, "Learning for Life: When Do We Begin?" *Equity and Excellence in Education,* vol. 26, no. 2 (September 1993). Copyright © 1993 by *Equity and Excellence in Education.* Reprinted by permission of Greenwood Publishing Group, Inc., Westport, CT.

more than a single activity. It needs to be more than another course, another requirement or another onetime event. Thinking about many forms of outreach is helpful. Connecting outreach to work, as in cooperative education, which we have long done and are familiar with, is also useful.

CSL [Community Service Learning] Builds Engagement

Currently, children and young people tend to describe their school learning as having very little to do with their lives beyond school. When students speak of the "remoteness" of school, they are really talking about the lack of connection between school and the world outside. They are acknowledging what Alfred North Whitehead noted—that most of what is taught in school is not about life "as it is known in the midst of living it."

Students see homelessness and poverty in the streets around them, they know about immigration as they hear so many languages being spoken. They are aware of racial discord, of community violence, of drugs, of war, of famine and environmental degradation. When schools do not explore such issues deeply, or even ignore them, it reinforces for students that the schools are about something other than the realities of the world. This division is unfortunate.

Further, the content of schools seldom relates to what people in a particular community are worried about or care deeply about. For example, the schools do not often make the local community architecture, its historical and cultural roots, or its economic and political structures a focus of study. The community's storytellers, craftspersons, builders, day-care and health providers are not common visitors. The literature that is read has generally not been selected because it illuminates the life that students see day in and day out outside of the school. Neither is it generally chosen because it helps them assume a larger sense of responsibility for some aspect of the social good or makes it possible for them to engage a non-school mentor more productively or assist a person in need. This disconnectedness trivializes much of what students are asked to learn.

We know all of this intuitively. Indeed, this knowledge causes many in schools to make occasional forays into the community: Students take a walk to the park in relation to a science project; classes go to the local library so that every student will get a library card; teachers invite a couple of persons each year to share some aspect of their experience or host a cultural awareness day related to the special ethnic origins of a dominant community group; or students go sporadically to a senior citizen center or read to children in a lower grade level. These activities tend to be viewed as special events surrounding the *real* work of the school. This is the case even as teachers and their students often view these efforts as the *highlights* of the school year. The real work of school could, of course, be centered a good deal more on aspects of and interaction with the local setting. That could be the principal starting point of learning.

In relation to the aforementioned, I am reminded of the project week organized by a Boston high school a couple of years ago. The week, which involved all the students and teachers, focused on the question: "Is Boston a livable city?" Students conducted a large number of interviews and surveys, visited cultural sites, read city and state crime, health and environmental studies, and the like. They concluded the week with various oral and written reports, what Ted Sizer calls "exhibitions of learning" and many at Harvard call "understanding performances." The intensity *was* very high. It *was*, without question, the highlight of the year, causing many students to ask why this kind of intensive study around authentic issues could not be more the norm, rather than being just an enrichment activity. It seemed to me a reasonable question.

Communities As Classrooms

As I reflect on this kind of outwardness, I am quickly drawn back to Richard Wurman's *Yellow Pages of Learning Resources.* I loved that book when I first read it. It affirmed so much of my outlook about the need to reconceptualize schooling. While many conditions have changed since the book was originally published, the potential for connecting schools with their wider communities remains large. Service learning is, of course, about enlarging those connections.

Wurman provides a number of entry points for using one's city or town as an extended school house. He writes: "Education has been thought of as taking place mainly within the confines of the classroom, and school buildings have been regarded as the citadels of knowledge. However, the most extensive facility imaginable for learning is [beyond the school]" (Wurman, 1972, p. 1). He stresses the need for teachers to become careful observers of their environments, to find in the reality of the world additional learning possibilities. He suggests that "the city is everywhere around us, and it is ripe with learning resources.... But in order to realize the vast learning potential of their resources, we must learn to learn from them... learn not to overlook the obvious, ... hear when we listen, see when we look... realize that good questions are better than brilliant answers."

Any place where something special occurs can be a classroom of consequence. For example, churches, medical facilities, museums, libraries, bakeries, day care settings, senior centers, soup kitchens, social service centers, Ys, city halls, park and recreation facilities, among others, are all possible classrooms of consequence. The people who work in and around these special settings and around the community are teachers as well as workers.

A course I taught several years ago in a secondary school drew heavily on Wurman's understandings of the potential of a community serving as a larger schoolhouse, providing much of the content for an intensive education. Entitled "Growing Up in Grand Forks," its primary purpose, along with enlarging writing and inquiry skills and understandings of how historians and sociologists go about their work, was to enlarge students' consciousness about their own community and their place in it.

As juniors and seniors, most could not, when we began, really describe their community in much detail. They had not observed carefully the special Romanesque architecture of the downtown buildings or taken note of the community's statues or their origins. Most had never been inside the federal court house, the city hall, the Jewish synagogue, the state mill, the downtown art gallery, or the university museum of art, to name only a few sites. They could not identify most of the trees and knew little about city government, tax structures, or the city's development plans. Issues that people cared about—water purity, flood control, recreational uses of the river and its banks, low-income housing policies, the deterioration of the downtown, economic stagnation and tax rates—these were not part of their studies. Few had ever gone to a public hearing about any community issue. Though many were eighteen, they had not really thought much about voting. They knew they could, but most told me they did not really know anything about the issues.

I believe we owe it to our young people to assure that they are deeply involved *with* their communities, that they leave us eager to take an active part in the political and cultural systems that surround them. Enlarging our vision of the school is, therefore, important.

Preparing Productive Citizens

A point of connection in secondary schools that has not been tapped well relates to student work. Close to 70 percent of secondary school students are employed, principally in the burgeoning service sector of the economy. Rather than viewing this work as positive, and as contributing to student responsibility and a sense of usefulness, those in schools speak of it primarily as lessening student commitments to the school's academic and extracurricular programs. They also see it as fostering what they believe to be an unhealthy materialism (Perrone et al., 1981). These perceptions place the work of the school and the work of the larger world in conflict. It denies the possibility that there are connecting points of consequence that actually affect students and their learning.

While I acknowledge that students who work over 20 hours a week tend to suffer academically within the current structure of schools, the work of students and the structure of schools could be thought about more constructively. Many students speak of what they do in their work as "being useful," "being independent" and "responsible." They also tend to enjoy their work. Employers see them as reliable and competent (Perrone et al., 1981). Are such perspectives to be negated? Is there no way to use such awareness?

Why do teachers not have students maintain journals of their work experience? Why not make the kinds of employment students are engaged in the focus of study in courses in health, nutrition, science, economics, mathematics, government, history, and literature? Why do teachers not engage their classrooms in a closer look at the materialist culture which is such a potent force in American society and which also contributes heavily to student employment? Cannot the world that these students have entered into so fully be connected to the ongoing and important work of the schools? While not directly service, it is a starting point for seeing their lives as connected to the world—as tied to the social and economic aspects of their communities. Making such a tie conscious is important.

Those in the schools talk a great deal about preparing their students for social and civic responsibility, but the opportunities to gain experience in these directions are limited, if they exist at all. It is possible for students to complete their schooling and never be involved deeply, in or outside the school, in any service-oriented activity. Too few students are tutoring younger children or classmates, working with the elderly, constructing or maintaining a playground, monitoring a public hearing, completing a community survey, or teaching at a Boy's Club or Y. The absence of connections is notable. In most settings, teaching for social responsibility and active citizenship is merely rhetoric.

Children have a disposition toward outwardness from their very early years. They have a need to learn *about* the world and participate actively in its ongoing life. They have a natural desire to engage others, to be helpful. If this desire to engage others is nurtured in the home and in the schools, such a disposition can develop into a fuller form of social and civic responsibility.

Some of the wonderful remembrances of teens I have talked with are of particular trees they planted as children and which now bring so much pleasure to communities. The trees stand as visible reminders of their earlier service.

The isolation in students' lives between what they do in and outside of schools is being addressed as many schools become centers for community service. Increasing numbers of schools, in fact, have made service an integral part of their curriculum. All schools, though, need to build a service ethic.

Central Park East Secondary School, in New York City, has a school-wide service program that involves all of its students *during* the school day. Approximately one in eight students are involved in a service activity each morning and afternoon, Monday through Thursday. Their placements include such settings as the Museum of the City of New York, the Studio Museum of Harlem, Mount Sinai Medical Center, the Association to Benefit Children, the 92nd Street YMHA, the Jewish Guild for the Blind, the Union Settlement House, the Community Planning Board, the Center for Collaborative Education, Headstart programs, and local elementary schools. Increasingly students are taking roles on school and community decision-making boards.

Efforts are made at Central Park East to integrate the experience students are having in their service placements with their ongoing coursework. This service-academic connection must be an important goal of all service programs. Without it, service is a peripheral activity and the curriculum remains insular. Central Park East is an exceptional school in regard to service. Its example should not be so unique. Every school could do what Central Park East does if it chose to do so.

Enlarging Possibilities

The service I have concentrated on has been beyond the school. The larger, out-of-school community has been my focus in this presentation. Service can also be directed back to the school. It can be aimed at building the community of the school. A social and civic responsibility orientation can certainly be fostered within a school as efforts are made to build its community, to develop more fully its democratic character.

Let me provide one example that has impressed me. Several years ago, at an elementary school in Revere, Massachusetts, the principal of an all-White, fully English-speaking school, learned that a large number of Cambodian children would enter the school that fall. When the 100 Cambodian children arrived, the school was ready. They were greeted with outstretched hands of welcome and friendship.

The principal had earlier decided that it was critical for *everyone* in the school—children, teachers, custodians, secretaries, lunch workers—to know who these Cambodian children were, where they had come from, and why they were coming to Revere. Getting ready for the Cambodian children became the curriculum. It was real and as a result it was vital. Those in the school community learned how to speak to Cambodian children and also gained knowledge about some of their cultural patterns as well as their suffering. As part of their preparation, those in the school learned about prejudice and the harm that prejudice brings to persons who are different. They also learned about how prejudice disrupts communities both in the schools and in the neighborhoods.

Given the heavy flow of immigrant children into the schools, possibly the largest we have had in our history, engaging a school community as was done in the Revere elementary school is exemplary. It addresses an important citizenship responsibility. And, of course, there are many related projects beyond immigration.

My concern has been about enlarging possibilities for students to construct a more productive community-oriented life and helping them to see their learning in more than school terms. That calls for connecting the school and the world beyond the school more directly. It calls for blurring wherever possible the lines which separate them. It calls for providing the ground for a service ethic to be constructed. That is our task. Service Massachusetts needs to be our future.

References

Perrone, V., et al. (1981). *Secondary school students and employment.* Grand Forks, ND: Bureau of Educational Research and Services, University of North Dakota.

Wurman, R. (Ed.). (1972). *Yellow pages of learning resources.* Cambridge: MIT Press.

"Compulsory Volunteering": Constitutional Challenges to Mandatory Community Service

Introduction

Ninth-grader Aric Herndon of Chapel Hill, North Carolina will soon receive his Eagle Scout award. He faithfully serves the Chapel Hill community through his work on Scout-sponsored projects and merit badge requirements.

But Aric may not graduate from high school—not because of any academic failings, but because he does not conform to the Chapel Hill School District's ideal of model citizenship. The community service that Aric performs for the Boy Scouts does not qualify for credit under the school district's new mandatory community service program. In the school district's judgment, since Aric receives an independent "benefit" from his service, such as an award or merit badge, the work does not rise to the level of "true" and selfless community service.

The Chapel Hill School District's twisted logic exemplifies the growing number of public schools around the country that require community service as a condition of graduation. Approximately 21 percent of public schools surveyed impose some type of community service requirement while an additional 10 percent will implement programs in the next year.[1] Like many other mandatory community service plans, the Chapel Hill program requires high school students to "serve" 50 hours in the community as a condition of graduation. The work must be performed after school hours, on weekends, or over summer vacation, and the students cannot receive compensation for their services.

Rye Neck High School in Mamaroneck, New York similarly conditions the receipt of a high school diploma on students performing 40 hours of labor in the community. Daniel Immediato, a student at Rye Neck, currently does not perform community service as defined by the school. Although Daniel does not object to helping others, he instead works as a lifeguard at a public pool and contributes to the modest earnings of the family. Daniel's lifeguarding, while certainly a service to the community, does not count toward the community service requirement since he receives compensation for his work.

Regardless of whether Aric or Daniel's community service qualified for credit, the students and their parents believe that the decision to serve others must come from within, not through government edict. The parents fundamentally object to their sons being forced to participate in a government-created program intended to inculcate a sense of obligation to the community. So they have joined other families in challenging the constitutionality of mandatory community service.

On April 19, 1994, the Institute for Justice will file two lawsuits challenging mandatory community service for public high school students in Chapel Hill and Mamaroneck as a violation of constitutional rights.

The issue of mandatory community service raises important and fundamental questions about the obligations of individuals in a free society to serve others and the role of the government in determining what individuals owe to the "community." The question of whether students can be drafted into a government-mandated community service program goes directly to the heart of the Institute for Justice's commitment to individual liberty and to the principle that voluntarism, not government coercion, is the basis of a free society.

The National Fight Against Mandatory Community Service

Mandatory community service was first challenged in a lawsuit filed in 1990 by the Steirer and Moralis families in Bethlehem, Pennsylvania.[2] Lynn Steirer pioneered the fight against mandatory community service. An avid volunteer and now a senior at Liberty High School in Bethlehem, Lynn compellingly captures the unintended consequences of coerced community service: "People should volunteer because they want to, not because of a government threat. So many kids who do this treat it like a joke; they do the minimum to get the credit."[3]

The lawsuit was unsuccessful in the lower courts and last summer, when the families' resources were exhausted, the Institute for Justice took on their case. The Institute filed a petition for certiorari in the U.S. Supreme Court, which declined to hear the case. This result was not surprising as the Court often lets issues ripen for several years in multiple court cases before addressing them.

The Third Circuit Court of Appeal's ruling in the *Steirer* case emboldened school districts nationwide. More and more school districts now condition the receipt of a high school diploma on students performing community service. And students are not the only targets for the "mandatory volunteering" juggernaut. The Tulsa, Oklahoma school district, citing the *Steirer* opinion as authority, wants to adopt a community service requirement not only for students, but for their parents as well. Under the proposed plan, if the parents do not perform the service, the students do not graduate.

Many community service advocates view mandatory programs as necessary to counter what they perceive as excessive selfishness and materialism in young people today. Recent polls, however, debunk the myth of selfish and lazy youths: a surprising six out of ten 12- to 17-year-olds volunteer their time to others.[4] This outpouring of good will and voluntarism on the part of today's youth counts for naught among community service proponents. Kathleen Kennedy Townsend, one of the most outspoken advocates of the first state-wide service program in Maryland, declared, "You don't choose to do good unless you learn to do good. A lot of people who are forced to do something learn to like it."[5]

In 1993, Maryland imposed the first statewide community service requirement, covering nearly 200,000 public high school students. Much public discussion and debate surrounded the adoption of Maryland's program. Indeed, all but one of Maryland's local school districts adamantly opposed the state-wide program. Because of the outcry by the public and school officials alike, the state board of education granted local schools broad discretion to craft their own programs. As a result, the local school districts in Maryland do not aggressively enforce this new graduation requirement.

Even with local school officials' unenthusiastic acceptance and enforcement of mandatory community service, the Maryland program already exhibits one of the most disturbing aspects of school-sponsored community service: the increasing politicization of programs and service opportunities. The Maryland program teaches that political activism is the highest form of community service.[6] Even the promotional posters for community service produced by the Maryland Department of Education demonstrate the overt emphasis upon political action as a means of solving community problems. One poster depicts a student climbing the mountain of community service. On each layer of the mountain is a type of community service. At the pinnacle of the mountain, above such service as caring for the sick and the aged, rests the form of service Maryland deems most important: lobbying. Another poster shows students in the service program demonstrating outside Maryland's capital for greater public education funding.

Unlike the heated controversy surrounding the Maryland program, the Chapel Hill School District unceremoniously imposed its mandatory community service requirement with little fanfare and seemingly no public discussion. The school district merely notified parents of this great expansion of government power through a letter sent at the beginning of the 1993–94 school year. However, two families in Chapel Hill refused to accept the school district's new intrusion into their lives and have instead joined in a constitutional challenge to mandatory community service.

Several years ago, the Rye Neck School District in Mamaroneck, New York imposed community service after many far wealthier school districts in Westchester County adopted service requirements. Compulsory community service typically exists in public schools with privileged children from wealthy families. Families in Rye Neck, however, have more modest incomes and struggle to provide a good education for their children. Also, many students in Rye Neck, including the Institute's clients, work part-time after school and contribute to the family income. Not surprisingly, these families want their children to concentrate on their studies, rather than be subjected to experiments requiring children to engage in out-of-school activities the authorities deem good for them.

The Institute's new challenges to mandatory community service aim to prevent the dilemma now confronting Bethlehem students Lynn Steirer and David Moralis as their senior year draws to a close. They must either participate in a program that violates their fundamental beliefs about the nature of helping others, or not receive a crucial stepping stone to success in life: a high school diploma. No student should have to face this Hobson's choice in the future.

Litigation Strategy

The Institute challenges the Chapel Hill and Rye Neck coerced service programs under the 13th Amendment's guarantee against involuntary servitude and the Ninth and 14th Amendment rights to parental liberty and due process of law.... While a 13th Amendment claim was raised in the Bethlehem case, a 14th Amendment challenge to mandatory community service has thus far not been presented to a court. With the filing of these lawsuits in the Fourth and Second U.S. Circuit Courts of Appeal, the Institute seeks a "circuit split" among the federal appellate courts, thereby increasing the chances of Supreme Court review.

It is widely known that the 13th Amendment banned the institution of slavery throughout the United States. However, the amendment also prohibits "involuntary servitude," except as punishment for a crime. While slavery involves the ownership and complete control of one individual by another, the U.S. Supreme Court defines involuntary servitude as a "condition of enforced compulsory service of one to another."[7] Mandatory community service programs fit this definition by requiring students to work for others against their will without compensation. The requirement for providing free labor to others, either organizations or individuals, distinguishes service programs from other mandatory school activities, such as gym classes, chemistry labs, and so on.

The Third Circuit Court of Appeals in the *Steirer* case virtually admitted that the program constituted a textbook definition of servitude. However, the court decided to ignore the constitutional text and instead opted for a "contextual" approach to the 13th Amendment. Furthermore, the court held that even if the program was a form of servitude, it was not "involuntary" because students had the "option" of quitting school, going to a private school, or receiving their G.E.D. Logically, this ruling means that the 13th Amendment has no applicability to the public school setting. Under the court's reasoning, public schools could require any type of student labor, from building a new addition to the school to mowing the lawns of school board members, and the students could not raise a claim under the 13th Amendment because they could always leave the public schools. The Institute's new challenges to coerced community service place this unprecedented holding directly at issue.

The 14th Amendment guarantees to parents the right to direct and control the upbringing and education of their children. The U.S. Supreme Court recognized this important right in two landmark U.S. Supreme Court cases: *Meyer v. Nebraska*[8] and *Pierce v. Society of Sisters*.[9] The Court held in those cases that certain "ideas touching the relation of the individual and the state [are] wholly different from those upon which our institutions rest" and do "violence to both the letter and spirit of the Constitution."[10] The decision to help others under our system of law has always been left to the conscience of the individual and to the moral education of children by parents. Programs that require service to others are foreign to the relationship between the individual and the state under the U.S. Constitution and the *Meyer* and *Pierce* cases.

Courts have consistently held that in public schools, mere exposure to ideas or beliefs with which parents disagree does not normally give rise to a constitutional violation.[11] However, when public schools require students to *act* on the basis of those values or beliefs, especially outside of the public school setting, constitutional limits apply. For instance, while public schools can teach the values of thrift and the importance of saving money, could schools require students as a condition of graduation to save a certain percentage of any money they earned? To stress the importance of abstinence to students, could schools require them to sign a pledge stating that they will remain virgins until they graduate? To underscore the importance of participating in our democratic system, could schools condition graduation on proof that students voted in the first election in which they were eligible?

All of the above-described programs would no doubt raise very serious constitutional concerns since in each instance the government intrudes into areas that have always been left to the private domain of individuals and to the relationship between parents and their children. Moreover, mandatory community service programs require students to act in programs that directly clash with their parents' fundamental belief that the decision to help others must be a voluntary one and cannot be imposed by the state.

Under the *Meyer* and *Pierce* cases, intrusion by the government into the relationship between parent and child requires a showing of a compelling state interest. In the mandatory community service context, the government must demonstrate that the programs are justified by such compelling interests. This task will be made difficult for the government by the lack of empirical studies showing mandatory community service programs having any serious educational value, especially when compared to the harm coercive programs do to recognized parental rights. Indeed, a 1991 survey of community service programs concluded that "much of the initiative for school-based service comes from policy makers and politicians—not educators."[12]

The Institute's litigation team in these lawsuits is headed by staff attorney Scott G. Bullock. Local counsel for the challenge in Chapel Hill, North Carolina is Robert H. Edmunds, Jr., former U.S. Attorney for the Middle District of North Carolina, and a partner at the Greensboro law firm of Stern, Graham & Klepfer, L.L.P. Local counsel for the Mamaroneck challenge is Lance Gotko, an attorney in New York.

Conclusion

People across the political spectrum share the desire to build strong and interconnected communities. But the hallmark of community is voluntarism.

Too many people today confuse the ideal of community with what government officials deem the community's interest. In today's highly regulated society, individuals endure many government intrusions into their lives. By filing lawsuits that will have nationwide ramifications, families in Chapel Hill and Mamaroneck draw a line and proclaim that certain decisions, especially the decision to serve others, must be between an individual and his conscience, not the individual and the state. Through this principled stand, the families reinforce institutions that unquestionably build well-functioning communities: true voluntarism and private charitable efforts.

Notes

1. Gordon Cawelti, *High School Restructuring: A National Study,* Educational Research Service, pp. 32–35 (1994).

2. The court opinions are reported in *Steirer v. Bethlehem Area School District,* 987 F.2d 989 (3rd Cir. 1993) and 789 F. Supp. 1337 (E.D. Pa. 1992).

3. Michael Winerip, "Required Volunteerism: School Programs Tested," *The New York Times,* Sept. 23, 1993.

4. "Schools Shouldn't Force Community Service," *USA Today,* Sept. 15, 1993.

5. Aaron Epstein, "Forced Community Service Likened to Slavery," *Phil. Inquirer,* Sept. 3, 1993.

6. For an enlightening article on the workings of the Maryland program, *see* Mark Parenti, "Lobbying School," *Reason,* pp. 56–57 (April 1994).

7. *Hodges v. United States,* 203 U.S. 1, 16 (1906).

8. 262 U.S. 390 (1923).

9. 268 U.S. 510 (1925).

10. *Meyer,* 262 U.S. at 401-02.

11. *See,* for example, *Mozert v. Hawkins County Board of Education,* 827 F.2d 1058 (6th Cir. 1987).

12. Dan Conrad & Diane Hedin, "School-Based Community Service: What We Know From Research and Theory," *Phi Delta Kappan,* p. 744 (June 1991).

POSTSCRIPT

Is Mandatory Community Service
Desirable and Legal?

The Civilian Conservation Corps, the National Youth Conservation Corps, the Peace Corps, Volunteers in Service to America (VISTA), and now Ameri-Corps, an action group sponsored by the new Corporation for National and Community Service, all attest to the success of federal efforts to kindle and reward altruism and idealism. However, the manifestation of this effort at the state and local levels has become far more controversial since "voluntary" service has evolved into "required." In addition to the organizations mentioned above, many advocacy groups support the community service movement, including Youth Service America, the Points of Light Foundation, the National Center for Service Learning in Early Adolescence, and the Community Service Learning Center. But the central questions remain: Can bureaucratically run volunteer programs fulfill their intentions? And can community service be a legal requirement for high school graduation?

Books that address the first of these related questions include Donald J. Eberly, ed., *National Youth Service: A Democratic Institution for the Twenty-First Century* (1990); *National Service: Pro and Con* edited by Williamson M. Evers (1990); *A Call to Civic Service* by Charles C. Moskos (1988); and E. B. Gorham, *National Service, Citizenship, and Political Education* (1992). Theme issues of journals addressing many aspects of the total controversy include *Phi Delta Kappan* (June 1991), *Social Policy* (Fall 1993), *Equity and Excellence in Education* (September 1993), and *Educational Horizons* (Summer 1999).

Some interesting articles, most of them supportive of community service, are "Youth Service: A Profile of Those Who Give More Than They Take," by John Backes, *High School Journal* (April–May 1992); "Making a Difference: Students and Community Service," by Derek Bok and Frank Newman, *Change* (July–August 1992); "School-Based Community Service Programs: An Imperative for Effective Schools," by Harry Silcox, *NASSP Bulletin* (February 1993); Deborah Hirsch, "Politics Through Action: Student Service and Activism in the '90s," *Change* (September–October 1993); and Rogers M. Smith, "American Conceptions of Citizenship and National Service," *The Responsive Community* (Summer 1993).

Somewhat more critical perspectives are offered in Harry C. Boyte, "Community Service and Civic Education," *Phi Delta Kappan* (June 1991); Jonathan Schorr, "Class Action: What Clinton's National Service Program Could Learn from 'Teach America,'" *Phi Delta Kappan* (December 1993); and "National Service and the Ideal of Community: A Commentary on *What You Can Do for Your Country*," *Journal of Education Policy* (May–June 1994).

ISSUE 21

Do Teachers' Unions Have a Positive Influence on Reform?

YES: Bob Chase, from "Do Teachers Unions Have a Positive Influence on the Educational System? Yes," *Insight* (October 21, 1996)

NO: Myron Lieberman, from "Do Teachers Unions Have a Positive Influence on the Educational System? No," *Insight* (October 21, 1996)

ISSUE SUMMARY

YES: Bob Chase, president of the National Education Association, fends off right-wing attacks on the public schools and teachers' unions by citing a record of positive reforms in recent years.

NO: Myron Lieberman, chairman of the Educational Policy Institute, assembles his own data to show that the unions are the major obstacle to school improvement in the United States.

About 85 percent of public school teachers in the United States belong to the National Education Association (NEA) or the AFL-CIO–affiliated American Federation of Teachers (AFT), powerful unions that engage in collective bargaining, lobbying, and political action. While they clearly represent the interests of educational professionals at all levels, the unions have come under increasing scrutiny in recent years regarding their role in influencing the quality of public schooling and the improvement of student academic performance.

The NEA, formed in 1857 as the National Teachers Association, was for many years controlled by school administrators and was disdainful of the union affiliation of the younger AFT. The latter organization, begun in 1916, negotiated detailed contractual agreements with local school boards and was not reluctant to use the threat of strikes to strengthen its position. In recent decades the NEA has adopted union tactics and has built up one of the richest political action committees in the nation, wielding considerable power at the federal level. There has been much talk about the merger of the two unions, but because of substantial differences between the organizations, the rank and file of the NEA rejected a leadership-approved plan to merge at the group's annual convention in July 1998. NEA and AFT officials have announced that they may try to develop a different framework for a merger.

The initial onslaught against teachers' unions was led by William J. Bennett when he was secretary of education in the Reagan administration. Bennett charged that "almost without fail, wherever a worthwhile school proposal or legislative initiative is under consideration, those with a vested interest in the educational status quo will use political muscle to block reform." The late Albert Shanker, for many years the president of the AFT, answered Bennett's criticism by becoming a more vocal advocate of basic school reform, calling for a reconstruction of the profession and a more experimental approach to the improvement of classroom instructional activities.

Shanker's successor, Sandra Feldman, has pledged to accelerate the union's focus on urban schools, particularly removing disruptive students and redesigning programs that do not work. She says that the AFT supports higher standards for discipline, student achievement, and teacher performance. NEA president Bob Chase has recently called for peer review and assistance programs to upgrade teacher quality, stating that "excellent education is the only winning strategy."

But Myron Lieberman, in "Teacher Unions: Two Is Bad Enough, One Is Worse," *The Weekly Standard* (March 16, 1998), states that public sector unions are adamantly opposed to smaller government, lower taxes, and privatization. "Conservatives," he says, "should be working to create alternative representation for teachers, especially if the NEA and AFT eventually merge into one AFL-CIO–affiliated union."

An editorial in *Rethinking Schools* (Summer 1998) contends that both the NEA and the AFT have historically shared two weaknesses: a failure to consistently promote educational equality for all children and an inability to consistently nurture democratic participation among the membership. Regarding this second point, Lieberman has called for a "Teacher Right to Know" law that would help curb some of the worst union abuses that currently prevail. James Bovard, in "Teachers Unions: Are the Schools Run for Them?" *The Freeman* (July 1996), portrays teachers' unions as policy dictators who wield potent political power and who advocate "no-fault" teaching; that is, whatever happens, don't blame the teacher.

The selections that follow pit Chase against Lieberman. Chase argues that teachers' unions protect against efforts to dismantle public education and lobby for increased funding to strengthen the schools. Lieberman asserts that the unions have raised the cost of schooling while lowering the levels of student achievement.

Bob Chase

 **YES**

Unions Lead the Fight for Innovation and Investment in Public Education

 T eachers are hardly strangers to spitballs. But the nasty wad hurled at us by Republican presidential candidate Bob Dole in his speech at the GOP convention marks a new level of escalation. "If education were a war, you [teachers] would be losing it," he said. "If it were a business, you would be driving it into bankruptcy."

Will the spitball stick?

As a junior-high-school teacher for 25 years, I would be obliged to give Dole a failing grade for not doing his homework. (I'd also give him detention for picking fights, but that is a separate issue.) What are the facts about teachers unions and their influence on American education?

If you listen to the relentless drumbeat from critics, you get a pretty frightening picture indeed: America's schools are controlled by the National Education Association, or NEA, whose teacher-members are protected by the Teflon of tenure. These teachers care about paychecks, not children. According to Phyllis Schlafly, director of the pro-life group Eagle Forum, they are following the NEA's wishes "to teach children not to be patriotic" and "to advocate explicit training in incest." What's more, if you believe the latest fund-raising letter signed by Beverly LaHaye of Concerned Women for America, the NEA seeks "to inject rank immorality and godlessness into our nation's classrooms."

Whew! Is there a more telling measure of the shortcomings of American education than that some people actually believe this nonsense?

Are teachers and their unions really the new evil empire? Or are they, as I believe, dedicated men and women who strive mightily to make public education work in an era of stark social and economic challenges?

Ironically, the answer lies partly in the work of William Bennett, one of the campaign advisers who urged Dole to attack the NEA. Several years ago, Bennett published an op-ed in the *Wall Street Journal* titled "Quantifying America's Decline." The article cited an array of truly shocking statistics to document the decay of American society between 1960 and 1992, including: a 419 percent increase in out-of-wedlock births; a quadrupling of the divorce rate; a tripling of the percentage of children living in single-parent homes; an increased average in daily TV viewing from five to seven hours.

Is it possible that these trends, with their profoundly negative consequences for children, also have affected the ability of American kids to learn in school? Indeed, is it possible that the positive gains in student achievement during the last decade—despite the surrounding social decay—are cause for praising teachers rather than demonizing them?

Notwithstanding the media's fixation on underperforming inner-city schools, the last decade has been a time of significant improvements in U.S. public education. In 1983, a mere 13 percent of high-school students completed a core block of rigorous academic course work recommended by the Department of Education; by 1992, 47 percent did—and the percentage is rising steadily. In addition, between 1982 and 1992, the math and science scores of 17-year-olds on the benchmark National Assessment of Education Progress increased by 9 and 11 points, respectively. This roughly is the equivalent of an additional year of learning in high school.

For true believers, the evil influence of teachers unions is an article of faith. But for those who prefer empirical data to hunches, let's look at the record. As it happens, there are 16 states in the United States that do not have collective-bargaining statutes governing public-school employees. In seven of those states, there virtually is no collective bargaining by public-school employees. In short, no teachers unions. It hardly is a coincidence that these seven states—all but one, West Virginia, located in the South—have been notorious for their underfunded education systems and for their low standing in national rankings of student achievement.

In recent years, pro-education Southern governors—including Dick Riley in South Carolina in the 1980s and Zell Miller in Georgia and Jim Hunt in North Carolina in the 1990s—have striven to energize their states' academic performance by, in effect, doing the job that teachers unions perform elsewhere: insisting on decent pay to attract and retain quality teachers, pushing for higher academic standards and prodding state legislatures to boost investments in education.

And what about the superb public-school systems Americans envy in countries such as Germany, France and Japan? You guessed it: They all benefit from strong teachers unions.

Yet, despite this evidence, it would be foolish to claim that teachers unions guarantee educational excellence. To do so would be the flip side of our critics' foolish claim that teachers unions control America's public schools. For the record, the NEA's local affiliates do not certify teachers, hire or fire them, write curricula, determine graduation requirements or set funding levels. What's left to control? In the last analysis, the only thing NEA members control is their individual professional commitment to making public education work for as many children as possible.

Which brings us to the issue of public-school quality. As one might expect, most critics of teachers unions are equally scathing in their denunciation of American public education. Indeed, they have singled out the NEA as a target for abuse precisely because we dare to oppose their efforts to replace public schools with taxpayer-funded private and religious schools.

Critics paint a lurid picture of failing public schools. But the reality is far more complex. Among the 14,626 independent school districts across the nation, there are huge disparities in the quality and rigor of instruction.

The Washington metropolitan area vividly illustrates the extremes. The public-school system in the District of Columbia is grossly mismanaged by a suffocating bureaucracy; it is a disservice to thousands of children and teachers who deserve better. Yet right next door are Montgomery County, Md., Fairfax County, Va., and other suburban jurisdictions whose public-school systems have national reputations for excellence.

What's more, superb public high schools such as Walt Whitman and Bethesda-Chevy Chase in Montgomery County by no means are rare examples. Two years ago, *Money* magazine did a comprehensive survey of public-school systems across the United States and concluded: "About 10 percent of all public schools—or about 2,000 nationwide—are as outstanding academically as the nation's most prestigious and selective private schools."

But aside from the personal initiative of our individual members, how has the NEA as a professional association and union contributed to these successes? Since 1983, we have spent more than $70 million on research and field projects designed to improve teaching and learning. This is not a negligible sum, but it hardly is enough to make a decisive difference.

More significantly, unions are good for education because they give teachers a strong, unified professional voice within their local school systems. Our members and affiliates have fought not just for decent pay and working conditions, but also for issues more directly related to school quality, including smaller class sizes and stricter enforcement of classroom discipline.

A 1988 Rand Corp. study, "Teachers and Educational Reform," found that once teachers unions succeed in obtaining the traditional bread-and-butter items, they advance to larger issues of professionalism and school reform. "In the most innovative school districts," according to Rand, "labor and management have worked collaboratively to restructure teachers' work lives and to enhance their professional responsibilities. In each case, the union has chosen a strategy of active reform leadership."

Beyond the bargaining table, we also campaign in the political arena— on Capitol Hill, in state legislatures and in local communities—for this same agenda of innovation and investment in public education. To take just one recent example, the NEA-affiliated California Teachers Association played the decisive role last spring in passing California's ambitious $177 million program to reduce kindergarten through third-grade class sizes to 20 pupils, down from current class sizes that reach as high as 40.

But recent years have brought a new political challenge: the rise of powerful groups that, for religious and ideological reasons, seek to denigrate, defund and eventually dismantle public education in America. Teachers unions have aggressively and effectively opposed this extreme agenda. Indeed, I believe the single greatest service we render to education today is our fight to preserve public schools as a fundamental institution of American democracy.

Obviously, our differences with those who seek to dismantle public education are irreconcilable. More troubling, to me, are people who share our commitment to strengthening public education but who question whether the NEA's responsibility as a union—specifically, our duty to protect our members —conflicts with its commitment to reform.

These friendly critics fail to see that a new NEA is emerging—an association with a far more sophisticated sense of its members' interest, and self-interest, in school restructuring and renewal. Our younger members, in particular, care principally about what the NEA can do to help enhance their professionalism and to accelerate the pace of change in public education.

Case in point: the NEA's vigorous support of the charter-school movement. In a number of states, charter-school laws have been misused as a vehicle to attack teachers' collective-bargaining rights and to channel public money to schools that remain private in all but name. However, these abuses have not deterred the NEA from embracing the broader promise of charter schools, sponsoring six of them around the country. Indeed, how could we not embrace a movement that invites the bureaucracy to butt out and gives teachers autonomy to create the schools of their dreams?

The NEA's bedrock commitment is to quality public education. This in no way entails a defense of the status quo, especially in school districts that are underperforming. To the contrary, in state after state, it has required the NEA to take the lead in instigating and implementing change.

Ultimately, this is what separates public-school teachers from their critics: Most critics stand on the outside and blow spitballs. Teachers—supported by their unions—stand in the classroom and courageously confront the challenges of public education in the 1990s. The good news is that, in most of America's schools, the teachers are winning.

Unions Deny Choice to Parents and Opportunity to the Nation's Children

Ever since Bob Dole criticized the teachers unions in his acceptance speech at the Republican National Convention, the role of the National Education Association, or NEA, and the American Federation of Teachers, or AFT, has emerged as a campaign and public-policy issue.

Dole said: "I say this not to the teachers, but to their unions: If education were a war, you would be losing it. If it were a business, you would be driving it into bankruptcy. If it were a patient, it would be dying. To the teachers unions I say: When I am president, I will disregard your political power for the sake of the children, the schools and the nation. I plan to enrich your vocabulary with those words you fear—school choice, competition and opportunity scholarships —so that you will join the rest of us in accountability, while others compete with you for the commendable privilege of giving our children a real education."

Was Dole's swing at the NEA and AFT justified? Yes—probably more than Dole himself realized. Take, for example, the union impact on student achievement. When Professor Sam Peltzman of the University of Chicago tried to identify the factors that were responsible for the decline in student achievement from 1960 to 1990, he came up with only two: the shift from local to state funding and the growth of teachers unions. A 1996 study by Caroline Minter Hoxby, published in the *Quarterly Review of Economics,* analyzed the union impact on costs. Hoxby, affiliated with Harvard University and the National Bureau of Economic Research, concluded that unionization has increased costs of public education but not improved outcomes.

How do the NEA and AFT (including their state and local affiliates) raise the costs while lowering the levels of student achievement? Just look at what the NEA and AFT try to achieve in legislation and collective bargaining. A partial list of union objectives includes the following:

- Restrictions on disciplinary action that render it extremely difficult to fire incompetent teachers;

- Elimination of teacher obligations to help pupils before or after regular school hours;
- Abolition of teacher obligations to meet with parents at times the parents can attend such meetings. Despite union rhetoric about the importance of "parental involvement," union-contract proposals render it difficult if not impossible for many parents;
- Requiring that parental complaints be reduced to writing and that teachers be entitled to union representation at meetings to discuss parental complaints. So much for the concept of teacher/parent collegiality;
- Promotions to be based on seniority, thus precluding selection of the most qualified candidates;
- Rigid restrictions on transfers and assignments, depriving school districts of needed flexibility;
- Prohibitions on volunteers, thus minimizing parental participation in their children's education. In the union mind-set, parents who volunteer are taking away paid work from union members.

If your child does not have a qualified mathematics or science teacher, you can thank the NEA and AFT for the salary policies that are to blame. Teachers unions advocate single-salary schedules—paying all teachers the same salary regardless of subject. Under single-salary schedules, teachers are paid solely on the basis of their years of teaching experience and their academic credits. The teachers unions have made sure that teachers' salaries are not based on merit or the type of subjects taught. It is a fact—frequently cited by NEA and AFT officials themselves—that school districts are unable to find and hold qualified mathematics and science teachers.

The obvious solution is to pay mathematics and science teachers more to attract qualified people in these fields. Unfortunately, the unions are opposed to this commonsense solution. They cite the shortage of teachers in mathematics and science as an argument to raise the salaries of *all* teachers, even those in fields where there is a plentiful supply.

Higher-education administrators know it would be practically impossible to operate a university by paying all professors, regardless of subject, the same salary. Universities would be unable to employ qualified medical professors if their salaries were the same as those for English professors. Similarly, people who can teach mathematics and science can earn more in occupations outside of teaching. Thus, when the teachers unions insist that all teachers be paid the same regardless of subject, they help create shortages of qualified teachers of mathematics and science.

Needless to say, the teachers unions claim that their collective goals contribute to academic achievement. Higher salaries are supposed to attract more talented teachers and reduce turnover. Tenured positions for teachers are supposed to protect competent teachers. More preparation time during the regular school day should result in better-prepared teachers. The NEA-PAC even refers to itself as "education's defense fund."

The union's arguments have a superficial plausibility but cannot withstand scrutiny. Take, for example, the union's claim that smaller classes are the key to improving student achievement, since they allow individualized instruction. Actually, class size largely is overrated as a factor in student achievement. In many nations whose students outperform ours, classes are much larger than those in the United States. Of course, smaller classes mean that more teachers are needed, and more teachers mean more union revenues.

The question policymakers should be asking, however, is whether the expenditures required to lower class size are the most productive way to use the money. In many cases, they are not. The funds used to lower class size often could be more productively spent for laboratory equipment or textbooks or supplies. In most situations, reductions in class size benefit the union and teachers much more than they benefit pupils. The same point applies to the other union objectives that allegedly help students.

No matter who is supposed to benefit from a union policy—the poor, the disabled, the preschool child, minorities, whatever—the union proposals always benefit teachers and teachers unions simultaneously. The union litmus test is not whether a policy benefits students; it is whether it benefits teachers or unions. Granted, teachers are not the only group in our society that accords its special interests the highest priority. The teachers unions, however, have been extremely successful in packaging teachers and teachers-union benefits as benefits to pupils or to "education."

"Education's defense fund," it may be argued, is a defense fund for about 6,000 union officers and staff, more than a third of whom I estimate to be earning at least $100,000 a year in salary and benefits. Some citizens wonder whether the union's officers and staff are still in touch with the lifestyle and culture of mainstream Americans when the median household income in 1993 was $31,241. At any rate, we can see why the NEA and AFT are so adamantly opposed to school choice. School choice is not a threat to teachers, but it is to the affluent union bureaucracies; it is much more difficult to organize teachers in private schools, especially denominational schools. Needless to say, the unions say nothing about this in their campaigns against school choice.

What has been the union impact on the cultural and lifestyle problems—teenage pregnancy, drug use, juvenile crime during the last 30 years? It isn't a pretty picture. Naturally every social indicator has been characterized by negative trends. Of course, some of these partly are due to television, divorce rates, the drug trade and a host of other factors. Nonetheless, it is revealing to note which cultural battles the unions decided to fight: abortion on demand, condom availability, domestic partnerships and the legitimacy of all lifestyles—no matter what their long-term consequences. While union leaders argue that schools merely reflect but do not cause family breakdown, NEA and AFT political support goes overwhelmingly to candidates who support agendas that have contributed substantially to it.

For instance, the teachers unions support condom availability in schools, arguing that many students will be sexually active, hence the schools should do everything they can to ensure "safe sex." In fact, teenagers are notoriously ineffective users of contraceptives; providing them with condoms is a sure way of encouraging sexual activities that are virtually certain to culminate in pregnancies or venereal diseases or both.

Meanwhile, in the last decade the teachers unions have painted the religious right as the greatest danger to a democratic society. To hear the unions tell it, the religious right is trying to abolish public education to impose theocratic education upon our young people. In practice, the religious right turns out to be those denominational groups that are fed up with public schools that undermine traditional family values.

And yet, the NEA and AFT attacks on the religious right may spell greater tragedy for American education. In a society increasingly addicted to instant gratification, religion is one of the few institutions that encourages young people to adopt a long-range view and the habits and attitudes that reinforce it. This is why inner-city pupils consistently achieve better in denominational schools than they do in public schools. Denominational schools provide the structure and stability needed by pupils from broken homes and unstable communities. In depriving such children of their best—perhaps their only—opportunity to get the kind of education they need, the NEA and AFT are responsible for an educational as well as a cultural tragedy.

Today, the NEA and AFT have a 25-year track record that was not available in the 1960s, when teacher unionization was emerging on a large scale. Looking at this record, the only conclusion possible is that they are, as Dole asserted, the major obstacle to educational improvement in the United States.

POSTSCRIPT

Do Teachers' Unions Have a Positive Influence on Reform?

The lengthy subtitle of Lieberman's book *The Teachers Unions: How the NEA and AFT Sabotage Reform and Hold Students, Parents, Teachers, and Taxpayers Hostage to Bureaucracy* (1997), certainly reveals his bias and reflects the thinking of many conservatives who fear the unions' political and professional power. Lieberman's view is echoed by Dwight Lee, in "Hypocrisy," *Forbes* (November 4, 1996), who claims that the NEA vehemently opposes reforms such as vouchers, merit-based teacher qualification, and expansion of the school year, and by Caroline Minter Hoxby, in "The Toll of Teachers' Unions: School Productivity," *The Economist* (October 19, 1996), whose research charts the negative impact of unions.

In an address to the National Press Club, published as "The New NEA: Reinventing the Teachers' Unions for a New Era," *Vital Speeches of the Day* (April 1, 1997), Chase stated that industrial-style, adversarial union tactics simply are not suited to the next stage of school reform. He wants to create a union with an entirely new approach to its members, to its critics, and to the colleagues on the other side of the bargaining table. "We cannot go on denying responsibility for school quality.... The new NEA is about action, about putting issues of school quality front and center," he stated.

A subtopic of this issue that has been increasingly discussed of late is the policy of granting tenure to members of the teaching profession. Many are calling for alterations to this time-honored but perhaps outdated practice. Some sources for insights into this topic are "Teacher Dismissal: A Policy Study of the Impact of Tenure," by Bettye MacPhail-Wilcox and Michael E. Ward, *Educational Considerations* (Fall 1995); "Modifying Teacher Tenure to Regain Public Confidence," by Tod Anton, *Thrust for Educational Leadership* (February 1996); and "Time to Get Off the Tenure Track," by Walter Olson, *The New York Times* (July 8, 1997).

Two other subissues currently under discussion involve the national standards board and merit pay. A few sources for these controversies are "Board Games," by Danielle Dunne Wilcox and Chester E. Finn, Jr., *National Review* (August 9, 1999); "Risking Frankness in Education Assessment," by Pamela A. Moss and Aaron Schutz, *Phi Delta Kappan* (May 1999); and "A Case for Merit Pay," by Thomas R. Hoerr, *Phi Delta Kappan* (December 1998).

Students seeking an understanding of the historical growth of unionism among teachers can consult the following books: Edgar B. Wesley, *NEA: The First Hundred Years* (1957); William Edward Eaton, *The American Federation of Teachers* (1982); AFT/NEA, *The Crucial Differences* (1984); S. M. Johnson, *Teacher Unions in Schools* (1984); and Maurice R. Berube, *Teacher Politics: The Influence of Unions* (1988).

Contributors to This Volume

EDITOR

JAMES WM. NOLL has recently retired from his professorial position in the College of Education at the University of Maryland in College Park, Maryland, where he taught philosophy of education and chaired the Social Foundations of Education unit. He has been affiliated with the American Educational Studies Association, the National Society for the Study of Education, the Association for Supervision and Curriculum Development, and the World Future Society. He received a B.A. in English and history from the University of Wisconsin–Milwaukee, an M.S. in educational administration from the University of Wisconsin, and a Ph.D. in philosophy of education from the University of Chicago. His articles have appeared in several education journals, and he is coauthor, with Sam P. Kelly, of *Foundations of Education in America: An Anthology of Major Thought and Significant Actions* (Harper & Row, 1970). He also has served as editor and editorial board member for Dushkin/McGraw-Hill's *Annual Editions: Education* series.

STAFF

Theodore Knight   List Manager
David Brackley   Senior Developmental Editor
Juliana Poggio   Developmental Editor
Rose Gleich   Administrative Assistant
Brenda S. Filley   Director of Production/Design
Juliana Arbo   Typesetting Supervisor
Diane Barker   Proofreader
Richard Tietjen   Publishing Systems Manager
Larry Killian   Copier Coordinator

AUTHORS

MORTIMER J. ADLER, a professor emeritus at the University of Chicago, is director of the Institute for Philosophical Research in Chicago, Illinois, and chairman of the board of editors for *Encyclopaedia Brittanica*. He is also the author of *Intellect: Mind Over Matter* (Collier Macmillan, 1990) and *The Time of Our Lives*, rev. ed. (Fordham University Press, 1996).

KAREN AGNE is an assistant professor of education in the Center for Educational Studies and Services at the State University of New York at Plattsburgh. She is a 20-year veteran of the Illinois public schools, where she served as a specialist in programs for gifted students.

JEAN B. ARNOLD is an attorney with the law firm McGuire, Woods, Battle, and Boothe in Charlottesville, Virginia.

MOLEFI KETE ASANTE is a professor in and chair of the Department of African American Studies at Temple University in Philadelphia, Pennsylvania. A leading proponent of the Afrocentric philosophy, he is the author of 35 books, including *Kemet, Afrocentricity, and Knowledge* (Africa World, 1992) and *Malcolm X As Cultural Hero: And Other Afrocentric Essays* (Africa World, 1993).

WILLIAM J. BENNETT, codirector of Empower America, served as U.S. secretary of education in the Reagan administration. His most recent book is *The Educated Child*, coauthored with Chester E. Finn, Jr., and John T. E. Cribb, Jr. (Free Press, 1999).

JACQUELINE GRENNON BROOKS is an associate professor in the Professional Education Program at the State University of New York at Stony Brook.

MARTIN G. BROOKS is superintendent of the Valley Stream Central High School District in New York.

R. FREEMAN BUTTS is the William F. Russell Professor Emeritus in the Foundations of Education at Columbia University's Teachers College in New York City. His publications include *The Civic Mission in Educational Reform: Perspectives for the Public and the Profession* (Hoover Institute Press, 1989) and *In the First Person Singular: The Foundations of Education* (Caddo Gap Press, 1993).

BOB CHASE is president of the National Education Association, where he served as vice president from 1989 to 1996. He taught social studies at the junior high school level for 25 years.

ROBERT L. CORD is a professor of political science and the University Distinguished Professor at Northeastern University in Boston, Massachusetts. He is the author of several books and articles about the U.S. Constitution, including *Separation of Church and State: Historical Fact and Current Fiction* (Baker Book House, 1988), which has been cited in numerous constitutional law books and in the opinions of U.S. Supreme Court justices for cases involving the church and the state. He received a Ph.D. from the Maxwell Graduate School of Citizenship and Public Affairs at Syracuse University.

EMERAL A. CROSBY is principal of Pershing High School in Detroit, Michigan.

JOHN DEWEY (1859–1952) was a philosopher and a leader in the field of education. He taught on the faculties of the University of Michigan, the University of Chicago, and Columbia University. He emphasized the importance of "learning by doing," and his writings and teachings profoundly affected such diverse fields as philosophy, educational theory, psychology, law, and political science. His many works include *The School and Society* (1899) and *Democracy and Education* (1916).

HAROLD W. DODGE is superintendent of schools in Cumberland County, Virginia.

EDD DOERR is executive director of Americans for Religious Liberty in Silver Spring, Maryland, and a columnist for *The Humanist.*

THOMAS J. FAMULARO is operations manager for Bowne Financial Printers in Secaucus, New Jersey. He is a former English instructor at the City University of New York.

CHESTER E. FINN, JR., is the John M. Olin Fellow at the Hudson Institute. He served as assistant U.S. secretary of education from 1985 to 1988, and he was a member of the National Assessment Governing Board from 1988 to 1996.

JOHN HOLT (1923–1985) was an educator and a critic of public schooling. He authored several influential books on education, including *How Children Fail* (Pittman, 1964) and *Instead of Education: Ways to Help People Do Things Better* (Holt Associates, 1976).

NINA HURWITZ was a high school teacher in Westchester County, New York, for 23 years.

SOL HURWITZ is an education consultant and a freelance writer.

ROBERT M. HUTCHINS (1879–1977) was chancellor of the University of Chicago, cocompiler of Encyclopaedia Britannica, Inc.'s *The Great Books of the Western World,* and director of the Center for the Study of Democratic Institutions. His publications include *The Higher Learning in America* (Yale University Press, 1936) and *University of Utopia* (University of Chicago Press, 1964).

INSTITUTE FOR JUSTICE is a nonprofit public interest law center in Washington, D.C., that seeks to promote a free and responsible society.

ALFIE KOHN writes and lectures widely on education and human behavior. His books include *Punished by Rewards* (Houghton Mifflin, 1993) and *Beyond Discipline: From Compliance to Community* (Association for Supervision and Curriculum Development, 1996).

JOHN F. LEWIS is a managing partner in the Cleveland, Ohio, office of the law firm Squire, Sanders, and Dempsey.

THOMAS LICKONA, a developmental psychologist, is a professor of education at the State University of New York at Cortland and director of the Center for the Fourth and Fifth Rs (Respect and Responsibility). He is a member of the board of directors of the Character Education Partnership, a national coalition working to promote character development in schools and communities. He is the author of *Educating for Character* (Bantam Books, 1991), and he has lectured in Canada, Japan, Switzerland, Ireland, and Latin America on teaching moral values in the school and at home.

MYRON LIEBERMAN is an adjunct scholar in the Social Philosophy Center at Bowling Green State University. He is the author of *Public Education: An Autopsy* (Harvard University Press, 1993) and *Teachers Evaluating Teachers: Peer Review and the New Unionism* (Transaction Publishers, 1998).

HORACE MANN (1796–1859), a lawyer and a politician, served as secretary of the Massachusetts State Board of Education for 12 years. He was instrumental in bringing about publicly supported schools in the United States, and his writings on education can be found in numerous books, including *Lectures on Education* and *A Few Thoughts on the Powers and Duties of Woman: Two Lectures.*

BARRY McGHAN retired in 1995 after serving as a teacher and an administrator in Flint, Michigan, for 33 years. He recently launched the Center for Public School Renewal. His research interests include private/public school comparisons, charter schools, and teacher autonomy.

DEBORAH MEIER is vice-chair of the Coalition of Essential Schools and founder of the Central Park East public elementary and secondary schools in East Harlem. She is the author of *The Power of Their Ideas: Lessons for America from a Small School in Harlem* (Beacon Press, 1996).

SONIA NIETO is a professor of language, literacy, and culture at the University of Massachusetts, Amherst. She is the author of *The Light in Their Eyes: Creating Multicultural Learning Communities* (Teachers College Press, 1999) and *Affirming Diversity: The Sociopolitical Context of Multicultural Education,* 3rd ed. (Longman, 2000).

PEDRO A. NOGUERA is a professor of education at the University of California, Berkeley. He is a former president of the Berkeley School Board.

WARREN A. NORD is director of the Program in the Humanities and Human Values and teaches philosophy of religion at the University of North Carolina, Chapel Hill. He is the author of *Religion and American Education* (University of North Carolina Press, 1995) and coauthor, with Charles Haynes, of *Taking Religion Seriously Across the Curriculum* (Association for Supervision and Curriculum Development, 1998).

VITO PERRONE is chair of the Department of Teaching Curriculum and Learning Environment at Harvard University in Cambridge, Massachusetts, and director of the university's Teacher Education Program. He is also a senior fellow at the Carnegie Foundation for the Advancement of Teaching. His latest book is *Teacher With a Heart* (Teacher's College Press, 1998).

ROSALIE PEDALINO PORTER is chairman of the board and acting director of the Research in English Acquisition and Development (READ) Institute in Amherst, Massachusetts. She served as director of bilingual and English as a Second Language programs in the Newton, Massachusetts, public schools for 10 years, and she has lectured widely on the subject of bilingualism both in the United States and abroad. She is the author of *Forked Tongue: The Politics of Bilingual Education* (Transaction Publishers, 1996).

NEIL POSTMAN, founder of New York University's Program in Media Ecology, is a professor in and chair of the Department of Culture and Communication in the School of Education at New York University in New York City, where he has been teaching since 1962. He is also a member of *The Nation*'s editorial board. He has published 18 books and over 100 articles for the scholarly and popular press on media, culture, and education, one of which, *Amusing Ourselves to Death* (Viking Penguin, 1985), has been translated into eight languages and has sold 200,000 copies worldwide. In 1986 he received the George Orwell Award for Clarity in Language from the National Council of Teachers of English.

RAY C. RIST is evaluation adviser to the Economic Development Institute at the World Bank. His research and writings focus on minority youth and schooling. He has authored and edited many publications, including *Policy Evaluation: Linking Theory to Practice* (Elgar, 1995) and *Carrots, Sticks and Sermons: Policy Instruments and Their Evaluation* (Transaction, 1998), coedited with Marie-Louise Bemelmans-Videc and Evert Vedung.

CARL R. ROGERS (1902–1987), a noted psychologist and educator, taught at the University of Chicago and the University of Wisconsin–Madison. He introduced the client-directed approach to psychotherapy in 1942, stressing the importance of a personal doctor-patient relationship, and he was the first psychologist to record and transcribe therapy sessions verbatim, a practice that is now standard with psychotherapy. His publications include *On Becoming a Person* (Houghton Mifflin, 1972).

RICHARD ROTHSTEIN is a research associate at the Economic Policy Institute in Washington, D.C., and the author of *The Way We Were? Debunking the Myth of America's Declining Schools* (Twentieth Century Fund Press/Priority Press, 1998).

ARTHUR M. SCHLESINGER, JR., is the Albert Schweitzer Professor of the Humanities at the City University of New York and the author of prize-winning books on Presidents Andrew Jackson, Franklin Roosevelt, and John F. Kennedy. His publications include *The Cycles of American History* (Houghton Mifflin, 1986) and *History of American Life* (Simon & Schuster, 1996).

ALBERT SHANKER (1928–1997) was president of the American Federation of Teachers in Washington, D.C., an organization that works with teachers and other educational employees at the state and local levels in organizing, collective bargaining, research, educational issues, and public relations. A leader in the educational reform movement, he is recognized as the first labor leader elected to the National Academy of Education. He was the author of the Sunday *New York Times* column "Where We Stand."

B. F. SKINNER (1904–1990), a noted psychologist and influential exponent of behaviorism, was the holder of the William James Chair in the Department of Psychology at Harvard University in Cambridge, Massachusetts. His major works include *About Behaviorism* (Random House, 1976) and *Reflections on Behaviorism and Society* (Random House, 1978).

JAMES H. SNIDER is a university fellow in the political science department at Northwestern University in Evanston, Illinois. A former school board member, he is coauthor, with Terra Ziporyn, of *Future Shop: How New Technologies Will Change the Way We Shop and What We Buy* (St. Martin's Press, 1992).

FORREST J. (FROSTY) TROY is editor of *The Oklahoma Observer* and the author of many articles on controversial issues in education.

PHYLLIS VINE is a historian and a journalist based in New York who has written extensively about mental health issues. She is the author of *Families in Pain: Children, Siblings, Spouses, and Parents of the Mentally Ill Speak Out* (Pantheon Books, 1982).

KEVIN WALTHERS teaches government at Mesquite High School in Dallas, Texas.

DORIS Y. WILKINSON is a professor of sociology at the University of Kentucky. She is also former president of the Society for the Study of Social Problems, of the District of Columbia Sociological Society, and of the Eastern Sociological Society. She has published extensively in the areas of critical theory and race and ethnic relations, including *Race, Class, and Gender: Common Bonds, Different Voices* (Sage Publications, 1996), coedited with Esther Ngan-ling Chow and Maxine Baca Zinn.

Index